FEB 2009

ALSO BY ALISON WEIR

MISTRESS
OF THE
MONARCHY

BALLANTINE BOOKS

New York

MISTRESS
OF THE
MONARCHY

The Life of Katherine Swynford,
Duchess of Lancaster

ALISON WEIR

Published in the United States by Ballantine Books, an imprint of The Random House
Publishing Group, a division of Random House, Inc., New York.

BALLANTINE and colophon are registered trademarks of Random House, Inc.

Originally published by Jonathan Cape,
a division of Random House Group Limited, London, in 2008.

LIBRARY OF CONGRESS CATALOGING-IN-PUBLICATION DATA
Weir, Alison.
[Katherine Swynford]
Mistress of the monarchy : the life of Katherine Swynford, Duchess of Lancaster / Alison Weir.
p.   cm.
Originally published under title : Katherine Swynford : the story of John of Gaunt
and his scandalous duchess. London : Jonathan Cape, 2008.
Includes bibliographical references and index.
ISBN 978-0-345-45323-5 (hardcover)
1. Katherine, Duchess of Lancaster, 1350?–1403. 2. John, of Gaunt,
Duke of Lancaster, 1340–1399. 3. Nobility—Great Britain—Biography.
4. Great Britain—Court and courtiers—History—To 1500. 5. Nobility—Great Britain—
History—To 1500. 6. Great Britain—History—Edward III, 1327–1377.
7. Great Britain—History—Richard II, 1377–1399. I. Title.

DA247.K38W45   2009
942.03'8092—dc22   [B]   2008044408

Printed in the United States of America on acid-free paper

www.ballantinebooks.com

2   4   6   8   9   7   5   3   1

FIRST U.S. EDITION

Book design by Caroline Cunningham

THIS BOOK IS DEDICATED TO

Bruce and Sandy,

Peter and Karen,

AND

John and Joanna

TO MARK THEIR MARRIAGES.

LIST OF ILLUSTRATIONS

Mary de Bohun: The Bodleian Library, University of Oxford, MS Auct. D.4.4.fol.181v

Katherine's arms as Duchess of Lancaster: www.english.upenn.edu

Pontefract Castle, painting of ca. 1630, Pontefract Museum © Wakefield Museums and Galleries, West Yorkshire/The Bridgeman Art Library

Ely Place in the 16th century, model in the crypt of St Etheldreda's, Ely Place, London. Photo © Jarrold Publishing, by Peter Smith of Newbery Smith Photography

St. Etheldreda's Church, Ely Place © John Crook

Richard II receives his child bride, Isabella of Valois, 1396, British Library Harleian MS. 4380, f.89: The British Library (MS. Harley 4380, f.89)

John Beaufort's arms: www.geocities.com

Cardinal Henry Beaufort's arms: Southwark Diocesan Communications Department

Thomas Beaufort's arms: www.geocities.com

Joan Beaufort's seal, British Library: The British Library (Seal XLVII.64)

John Beaufort and Margaret Holland, from The Beaufort Hours, British Library Royal MS. 2 A.XVIII, f.23v: akg-images/British Library

John Beaufort, tomb effigy in Canterbury Cathedral © Angelo Hornak

Cardinal Beaufort, tomb effigy in Winchester Cathedral © John Crook

Possibly Cardinal Henry Beaufort, oil portrait called "Cardinal Albergati" by Jan Van Eyck, ca. 1430–35, Kunsthistorisches Museum, Vienna: akg-images/Erich Lessing

Joan Beaufort, tomb effigy beside that of her husband, Ralph Neville, 1st Earl of Westmoreland, and his first wife, Staindrop Church, Co. Durham: The Katherine Swynford Society

Joan Beaufort, drawing of the Staindrop effigy, from R. Gough: Sepulchral Monuments in Great Britain, London, 1786–96: The British Library (HLL393.1)

Joan Beaufort and her daughters, from The Neville Book of Hours, ca. 1427, Bibliothèque Nationale, Paris—MS Latin 1158 f.34v: Bibliothèque nationale de France (MS Latin 1158, f.34v)

Thomas Chaucer and Maud Burghersh, brass in Ewelme Church, Oxon. © John Crook

John of Gaunt in later life, miniature from The Golden Book of St. Albans, British Library Cotton MS. Nero D. vii, f.66–7 © British Library, London/© British Library Board. All rights reserved/The Bridgeman Art Library

Every effort has been made to contact copyright holders, but the author and publishers will be pleased to hear from any who have not been traced.

ACKNOWLEDGMENTS

I should like to express my warmest gratitude to various people who have helped with this book. To Anthony Goodman, our finest late medieval historian, for his assistance with references and original documents; I am also indebted to him for his two booklets, *Katherine Swynford* and *Honourable Lady or She-Devil?*, and his magnificent collection of essays on John of Gaunt, which have all proved profoundly useful. To Dr. Nicholas Bennett, Librarian of Lincoln Cathedral Library, and his wife Carol for their kindness in welcoming me to the library, making available various sources, and arranging a visit to the Priory, where Katherine Swynford lived toward the end of her life. To Roger Joy, founder of the Katherine Swynford Society and a walking authority on Katherine, for generously sharing his knowledge with me, and for sending me his unpublished articles. To Patricia McLeod and the staff of Sutton Library for their efforts in tracking down numerous books and articles. To Abigail Bennett of the University of York, for translating into English numerous texts in medieval Latin. To Andrew Barr and his team at the National Trust East Midlands Regional Office. To the staff at Lincoln Central Library for their assistance in locating books.

I am indebted also to the many people who have published information about Katherine on the Internet, foremost among whom is Judy Perry, who has been researching her subject for over twenty-five years.

My gratitude to my editors for commissioning this book is acknowledged separately, in the Introduction, but I should also like to express it here on account of their unflagging enthusiasm, their sensitive insights, and their illuminating input. I wish also to thank my inspirational and ever-supportive agent, Julian Alexander, and all the people at Random House who have helped to create this book.

Lastly, I wish to thank my family and friends, who have all cheerfully put up with me while the book was being written. And to Rankin, my husband—thanks for all the wonderful meals, and just for being there.

CONTENTS

AUTHOR'S NOTE

I have used the form "Katherine" (rather than "Catherine") throughout, as Katherine's name is usually spelled with a K in contemporary sources.

The correct medieval form of her name is "Katherine de Swynford," but I have chosen to refer to her as "Katherine Swynford," as she is traditionally and popularly known. It is worth noting that in *John of Gaunt's Register*, Katherine's name is given as either "Katherine" or "Kateryn(e)." The language of the court and the aristocracy at this time was Norman French, and these spellings indicate that John—and others—probably pronounced her name in the French way as "Katrine."

The modern equivalent of fourteenth-century monetary values has been given in parentheses throughout the book. For currency conversion, I have used an invaluable Internet website, measuringworth.com, produced by Lawrence H. Officer, professor of Economics at the University of Illinois, Chicago, and Samuel H. Williams, professor of Economics, emeritus, of Miami University.

INTRODUCTION

This is a love story, one of the greatest and most remarkable love stories of medieval England. It is the extraordinary tale of an exceptional woman, Katherine Swynford, who became first the mistress and later the wife of John of Gaunt, Duke of Lancaster, one of the outstanding princes of the high Middle Ages.

Katherine Swynford's story first captured my imagination four decades ago, when I read Anya Seton's famous novel about her, *Katherine*. This epic novel made a tremendous impact on me as an adolescent, and still has the power to move me today. And I am not alone, because it has hardly been out of print since its first publication in 1954, and ranked ninety-fifth in the top one hundred favorite books voted for by the public in BBC TV's "The Big Read" in 2003. (Interested readers will find more about this novel in the Appendix.)

It would not be an exaggeration to say that I have wanted to write this book for forty years. But even when I became a published author in the late eighties, no publisher would have contemplated commissioning a biography of this relatively obscure woman. And that remained the situation for many years, until the recent explosion of interest in all things historical, which inspired me to seize the chance to make my longstanding secret dream come true. I am truly indebted to my editors, Will Sulkin, Anthony Whittome, and Susanna Porter, for their support and enthusiasm for this project, and to Elisabeth Dyssegaard, who suggested that I write about Katherine as well as John of Gaunt, the subject I originally proposed.

Katherine Swynford deserves a biography for many reasons. First and foremost, she was romantically linked to John of Gaunt, one of the most charismatic figures of the fourteenth century, and their passionate and ultimately poignant love affair is both astonishing and moving. Katherine was clearly beautiful and desirable, not to say enigmatic and intriguing, and some of her contemporaries regarded her as dangerous also. Her existence was played out against a vivid backdrop of court life at the height of the age of chivalry, and she knew most of the great figures of the epoch. The renowned poet Geoffrey Chaucer, author of *The Canterbury Tales*, was her brother-in-law. She lived through the Hundred Years War, the Black Death, and the Peasants' Revolt, knew passion, loss, adversity, and heartbreak, and survived them all triumphantly. Her story gives us unique insights into the life of a medieval woman.

Yet Katherine was unusual in that she did not conform to many of the conventional norms expected of women in that age, and in several respects her story has relevance for us today. Feminist scholars are now beginning to see her from a new perspective, as a woman who was an important personage in her own right, a woman who—in a male-dominated age—had remarkable opportunities, made her own choices, flouted convention, and took control of her own destiny. Katherine was intelligent, poised, and talented, and fortunate enough to move in circles where these qualities were valued and encouraged in women. Among the choices she faced were ones that would be familiar to women today, although her modern counterparts would not have to endure the moral backlash that at one time rebounded on Katherine and probably wrecked her life. Yet they would identify with her as a woman who coped brilliantly with the sweeping, and sometimes devastating, changes of fortune that befell her.

Above all, Katherine Swynford occupies an unprecedented position in the history of the English monarchy; dynastically, she is an important figure. She was the mother of the Beauforts, and through them the ancestress of the Yorkist kings, the Tudors, the Stuarts, and every other British sovereign since—a prodigious legacy for any woman. Without her, the course of English history would have been very different.

Writing a biography of Katherine Swynford poses its own particular problems, however, for her voice has been silenced forever: No letter survives, no utterance of hers is recorded. None of her movable goods are extant, and we have barely any details of the clothes she wore, so we cannot determine her tastes in art, literature, or dress. Her will is lost, and with it any insights it might give us into her feelings for John of Gaunt, her moral outlook, her family relationships, or her charities. She is one of the most important women in late fourteenth-century England, and yet so much about her is a mystery to us. She is famous but, paradoxically, she is little known.

Furthermore, the contemporary sources to support a biography of Katherine Swynford are meager and fragmentary at best. She rates barely a mention in the chronicles of the period, and such references as there are, usually reflect monastic prejudice against a woman who was regarded as "a she-devil and enchantress." The best evidence for her life lies mainly in the dry entries in John of Gaunt's *Register*, the *Calendar of Patent Rolls*, the *Duchy of Lancaster Records* in the National Archives, and the civic and clerical records of Lincoln, Leicester, and other places. The rest is largely inference. Yet there is a wealth of evidence on which to base those inferences, as will be seen. There is monetary evidence, and archaeological evidence. Much remains of the many castles and manor houses owned by John of Gaunt, in which Katherine would often have resided, not the least of which is his magnificent range and great hall at Kenilworth, which she would have known well. Houses in which she herself lived for long periods—Kettlethorpe Hall in Lincolnshire, and the Chancery and the Priory in the close of Lincoln Cathedral—also survive in part. There is, in addition, much surviving documentation on John of Gaunt's fabulous but long-lost Savoy Palace, so it is possible to place Katherine and her prince in the context of vividly recreated authentic settings.

So although there is a great deal that is not known about Katherine Swynford, and the tantalizing glimpses of her that appear in the sources often raise more questions than they answer, there is enough to justify a long overdue biography. This book therefore represents a quest to discover the truth about this most intriguing of royal ladies. It has led to the most fascinating historical investigation I have ever undertaken, affording unique opportunities for original research, which has encompassed delving into numerous contemporary sources (and in some cases having them retranslated), following up significant clues—sometimes into unexplored territory—examining the remains of the houses in which Katherine lived, interpreting intriguing allusions in stained glass and ancient manuscripts, and studying a wealth of pictorial evidence.

In drawing up a detailed chronological framework for Katherine's life, then piecing together the myriad pieces of information I had gathered and analyzing them within the context of that framework, I was surprised by the interesting revelations that emerged, some of which challenge the received wisdom about my subject, or lend weight to existing theories. Time and again I was surprised at what I have been able to infer from my research. It is, above all, my hope that what will unfold in the pages that follow is a convincing and challenging portrayal of a most fascinating—but elusive—woman.

ALISON WEIR
CARSHALTON, SURREY
APRIL 2007

MISTRESS
OF THE
MONARCHY

Spring 1378

I n March 1378, putting aside "all shame of man and fear of God," John of Gaunt, Duke of Lancaster, the mightiest subject in the realm of England, was to be seen riding around his estates in Leicestershire "with his unspeakable concubine, a certain Katherine Swynford." Not only was the Duke brazenly parading his beautiful mistress for everyone to see, but he was "holding her bridle in public," a gesture that proclaimed to all his possession of her, for it implied that the rider thus led was a captive, in this case one who had surrendered her body, if not her heart. And as if this were not shocking enough, the fact that the Duke was flaunting his mistress "in the presence of his own wife" created a scandal that would soon spread throughout the length and breadth of the kingdom and beyond. Even today, echoes of that furor still reverberate in the pages of history books.

John of Gaunt's conduct in that long distant spring led disapproving contemporaries to conclude that he had "made himself abominable in the eyes of God," and that Katherine Swynford was "a witch and a whore." Thus was born the legend of the "famous adulteress" who occupies a unique place in English history. There can be no doubt that in her own lifetime she was the subject of great scandal and notoriety, for she was closely linked to John of Gaunt for a quarter of a century before they married, and had already known him for many years before he wed the desirable young wife who was so openly insulted on that tour of Leicestershire in 1378. Years later, after John's wife had died and he married Katherine, controversy and criticism surrounded their union, for she was far below him in status, morally unacceptable, and considered highly unsuitable in many respects. But she confounded her critics and gradually came to be tolerated and even respected.

Indeed, all the evidence suggests that Katherine Swynford was no lightly principled whore, which is what hostile chroniclers would have us believe; on the contrary, she was one of the most important female figures of the late fourteenth century, and more likely to have been a woman deserving of our admiration and esteem. Her partner in adultery—later her husband—was the son of King Edward III of England and one of the epoch's most famous and celebrated paragons. From her is descended every English monarch since 1461, and no fewer than five American presidents.

The truth about Katherine Swynford has been obscured by people down the centuries accepting at face value the calumnies that were written about her by a few disapproving contemporaries; and too because nearly every aspect of her story is shrouded in mystery, exaggerated by debate, or simply obliterated by time. Nearly everything about her is controversial. When and where was she born? What did she look like? How many children did she bear? When did she become John of Gaunt's mistress? What influence did she have? And what was the nature of their relationship over the years? Above all, did she really deserve all the moral opprobrium heaped upon her after her lover paraded her in public on that fateful spring day?

We will never know the whole truth about Katherine and John, for only echoes of their voices and their deeds have come down to us, but one thing is certain, and it shines forth from nearly every source: These two were lovers, and their love endured through prosperity and adversity, war and endless separations, time and distance. Love and destiny brought them together, sealing their fate and changing the course of English history itself. So this is, essentially, a love story.

ONE

Panetto's Daughter

Katherine Swynford, that "famous adulteress,"[1] was set on the path to notoriety, fame, and a great love at the tender age of two or thereabouts, when she was placed in the household of Philippa of Hainault, wife to Edward III of England. This would have been around 1352, and Katherine's disposition with the popular and maternal Philippa was almost certainly due to her father, Sir Paon de Roët, having rendered years of faithful service to the Queen and the royal family of Hainault.

Like her benefactress, Katherine was a Hainaulter. She was born Katherine de Roët, her surname variously given as Rouet, Roëlt, or Ruet, and pronounced "Roay." The Roëts were a prominent family in Hainault, then an independent principality located in the western reaches of the Holy Roman Empire, bordering on the kingdom of France and occupying much of what is now Belgium. This fertile and prosperous county stretched from Liège and Brussels in the north to Lille and Valenciennes in the south, and contained other thriving cloth cities: Mons, Charleroi, and Tournai; all of which provided a market for England's raw wool, her chief export. Formed at the time of the division of Charlemagne's empire in the ninth century, Hainault had been an imperial fief since 1071, and in the early fourteenth century it was ruled by the House of Avesnes, which had come to power in 1244.

Katherine possibly had noble or even royal connections through her mother, but claims that she was closely related through her father to the aristocratic lords of Roeulx cannot be substantiated. The Roeulx were a great and powerful Hainaulter family that could trace its descent from the ancient counts of Flanders and Hainault, who were themselves descended from the Emperor Charlemagne, and from England's famous King Alfred. William the Conqueror had married a princess of that house, Matilda of Flanders, and by her was the founder of the ruling dynasties of England, the Norman and Plantagenet kings. Since the twelfth century the lords of Roeulx had prospered mightily.[2] Their landholdings centered mainly on the town of Le Roeulx, which lies eight miles northeast of Mons, but their name is also associated with Roux, forty miles east of Mons, and Fauroeulx, twenty miles to the south.

That Katherine shared a close kinship with the lords of Roeulx is doubtful on heraldic evidence alone—or the lack of it.[3] Her family was relatively humble. The chronicler Jean Froissart, a native of Hainault, who appears to have been quite well informed on Katherine Swynford's background, states that Jean de Roët, who died in 1305 and was the son of one Huon de Roët, was her grandfather. Neither bore a title. Yet it is possible that there was some blood tie with the Roeulx. Paon de Roët, the father of Katherine Swynford, whose name appears in English sources as Payn or Payne,[4] and is pronounced "Pan," was almost certainly baptized Gilles, a name borne by several members of the senior line of the Roeulx, which is one reason some historians have linked him to this branch of the family.[5] Of course, the similarity in surnames suggests a connection—in that period, the spellings of Roeulx and Roët could be, and were, interchangeable—as does the fact that both families are known to have had connections with the area around Mons and Le Roeulx. But discrepancies in arms would appear to indicate that Paon was at best a member of a junior branch of the House of Roeulx; all the same, it is possible that the royal blood of Charlemagne and Alfred the Great did indeed run in Katherine's veins.

The arms of the town of Le Roeulx were a silver lion on a green field holding a wheel in its paw;[6] this is a play on words, for "wheel" in French is *roue*, which is similar to, and symbolic of, Roeulx. It was a theme adopted by Paon's own family: His arms were three plain silver wheels on a field of red;

they were not the spiked-gold Katherine wheels later used by his daughter.[7] On the evidence of heraldic emblems on the vestments given by her to Lincoln Cathedral, Katherine Swynford used not only her familiar device of Katherine wheels, which she adopted after 1396, but also her father's device of three plain silver wheels.[8]

If Jean de Roët was his father, as seems likely, then Gilles alias Paon was born by 1305–06 at the very latest. Thus he did not marry and father children until comparatively late in life. The references in the *Cartulaire des Comtes de Hainaut* to "Gilles de Roët called Paon or Paonnet" imply that the name Paon was almost certainly a nickname, although it was the name by which Gilles became customarily known, and it even appeared on his tomb memorial. In French, *paon* means "peacock," which suggests that Paon was a vain man who liked dressing in brightly colored, fashionable clothes, possibly in order to impress the ladies. However, in the form *pion*, it means "usher,"[9] a term that may be descriptive of Paon's duties at court.[10]

John of Gaunt's epitaph states that Katherine came from "a knightly family," and Paon's knighthood is attested to by several sources,[11] although we do not know when he received the accolade. In 1349 he is even referred to as a lord, and his daughter Elizabeth as "noble,"[12] which reflects his landed status and probably his links to aristocratic blood. This is also evident in his ability to place his children with royalty,[13] which suggests—in the case of his daughters, at least—that there was the prospect of some inheritance that would ensure they made good marriages.[14] We know Paon held land in Hainault, because in 1411 his grandson, Sir Thomas Swynford, Katherine's son, was to pursue his claim to lands he had inherited there from his mother.[15] Paon is unlikely, however, to have owned a large estate and was probably not a wealthy man[16] since he was to rely heavily on royal patronage to provide for his children's future.

Paon had first come to England in December 1327 in the train of Philippa of Hainault, who married the young King Edward III on January 24, 1328, in York Minster. Paon perhaps served as Philippa's usher, and may have been present in that capacity at the royal wedding, which took place in the as yet unroofed minster in the midst of a snowstorm.

After Philippa's nuptial celebrations had ended, nearly all her Hainaulter servants were sent home. Apart from a handful of ladies, only Paon de Roët and Walter de Mauney, her carving squire, are known to have been allowed to remain in her retinue,[17] a mark of signal royal favor, which suggests that Paon was highly regarded by both the young king and queen, and was perhaps a kinsman of Philippa, possibly through their shared ancestry.

That kinship may also have been established, or reinforced, through marriage. No one has as yet successfully identified Katherine's mother, for the name of Paon's wife is not recorded in contemporary documents. The slender evidence we have suggests he perhaps married more than once, that his first marriage took place before ca. 1335, and that his four known children, who were born over a period of about fifteen years or more, may have been two sets of half siblings; in which case Katherine was the child of a second wife, whom he possibly married in the mid-late 1340s. We know he maintained links with Hainault, probably through the good offices of Queen Philippa and other members of her house, so it may be that at least one of his wives was a Hainaulter.[18]

It is also possible that Katherine's mother herself was related to the ruling family of Hainault,[19] and while this theory cannot be proved, it is credible in many respects. If Paon was linked by marriage, as well as by blood, to Queen Philippa, that would further explain his continuing links with the House of Avesnes and the trust in which he and his family were held by the ruling families of England and Hainault. It would explain too why all his children received royal patronage and why Queen Philippa took such an interest in them; and it was possibly one reason why John of Gaunt may have felt it was appropriate to ultimately marry one of them.

But there is unlikely to have been a close blood tie.[20] If Paon's wife was related to the House of Avesnes, it must have been through a junior branch or connection. Had the kinship been closer, we would expect Paon to have enjoyed more prominence in the courts of England and Hainault. There have, of course, been other unsubstantiated theories as to who Katherine's mother could have been,[21] but this is the most convincing.

Whether Paon was related by marriage to Queen Philippa or not, he was evidently held in high regard by her, and he played his part in the early conflicts of the Hundred Years War, which broke out in 1340 after Edward III claimed the throne of France. For a time Paon served Queen Philippa as Master of the House,[22] and in 1332 there is a record of her giving money to "Panetto de Roët de Hanonia";[23] this is the earliest surviving reference to him. His lost epitaph in Old St. Paul's Cathedral describes him as Guienne King of Arms,[24] and it may have been through Philippa's influence that he was appointed to this office in ca. 1334,[25] Guienne being part of the Duchy of Aquitaine and a fief of the English Crown.

By the mid-1340s, Paon was back in Queen Philippa's service as "one of the chevaliers of the noble and good Queen."[26] In 1346 he fought at Crécy under Edward III. That same year, "Sir Panetto de Roët" was present at the siege of Calais, and in August 1347 he was Marshal of the Queen's Household, and one of two of her knights—the other was Sir Walter de Mauney—assigned to conduct to her chamber the six burghers who had given themselves up as hostages after Calais fell to Edward III, and whose lives had been spared thanks to the Queen's intercession.[27]

Philippa, however, never courted criticism by indiscriminately promoting her compatriots, which may explain why Paon, although well thought of and loved by the Queen because he was her countryman,[28] never came to greater prominence at the English court[29] and why he eventually sought preferment elsewhere.

By 1349, the year the Black Death was decimating the population of England and much of Europe, Paon had apparently returned to Hainault. From that year on, there are several references to him in the contemporary *Cartulaire des Comtes de Hainaut*, the official record of service of the counts of Hainault.[30] The first reference concerns a "noble adolescent, Elizabeth de Roët, daughter of my lord Gilles, called Paonnet, de Roët," who, sometime after July 27, 1349, was nominated as a prebendary, or honorary canoness (*chanoinness*),[31] of the chapter of the Abbey of St. Waudru in Mons by Queen Philippa's elder sister, Margaret, sovereign Countess of Hainault and Empress of Germany. The choice of a convent in Mons, so close to the former Roeulx estates, reinforces the theory that Paon was connected to that family and that his lands were located in this area.

Girls were not normally accepted into the novitiate before the age of thirteen, so Elizabeth de Roët, who was described as being "adolescent" at the time of her placement, was probably born around 1335–36 at the latest. St. Waudru was a prestigious and influential abbey, and it was an honor for a girl to be so placed by Countess Margaret; it further demonstrates the close ties between the Roëts and the ruling family of Hainault, and suggests yet again a familial link between them. It was unusual for the eldest girl of a gentle family to enter the cloister, but given the fact that Paon's daughters were both to offer their own daughters as nuns, we might conclude that giving a female child to God was a Roët family custom.

Paon also had a son, Walter de Roët, possibly named after Sir Walter de Mauney,[32] who in 1355–56 was in the service, in turn, of Countess Margaret and her son, Duke Albert, and Edward III's eldest son and heir, Edward of Woodstock, Prince of Wales, popularly known to history as the "Black Prince." As Walter was a Yeoman of the Chamber to the Prince in 1355, and probably fought under his command at Poitiers in 1356, he is likely to have been born no later than 1338–40.

Between 1350 and 1352 there are seven references to Paon in the *Cartulaire des Comtes de Hainaut*. For example, on May 11, 1350, he is recorded as preparing to accompany Countess Margaret's sons—Duke Albert, Duke William, and Duke Otto—on a pilgrimage to the church of St. Martin at Sebourg near Valenciennes to make their devotions at the shrine of the twelfth-century hermit, St. Druon. It was probably in that year that Paon's famous daughter was born.

C L. Kingsford, in his article on Katherine Swynford in the *Dictionary of National Biography*, suggested that she was born in 1350. There is no contemporary record of her date of birth, but since the minimum canonical age at which a girl could be married and have marital intercourse was twelve, and Katherine probably married around 1362–63 and had her first child ca. 1363–64, a date of 1350 is feasible, although she could have been born a little earlier. November 25 is the feast day of St. Katherine, so it is possible that Paon's second daughter was named for the patron saint on whose anniversary she was born, and for whom she was to express great devotion and reverence.

In the Middle Ages, St. Katherine of Alexandria was one of the most popular of female saints. Edward III and Philippa of Hainault had a special devotion to her; their accounts show that Katherine wheels, the symbol of her martydom, adorned counterpanes on the royal beds, jousting apparel, and other garments. Like other English medieval queens, Philippa was patroness of the royal hospital of St. Katherine-by-the-Tower in London, which had recently been rebuilt under her auspices, and with which Katherine Swynford herself would one day be associated.[33]

St. Katherine probably never even existed. There is no record of her in antiquity, and her cult did not emerge until the ninth century. She was said to have been of patrician or even royal birth, beautiful, rich, respected, and learned. Her studies led her to convert to Christianity at a time when Christians were being persecuted in the Roman Empire, and she dared to publicly protest to the Emperor Maxentius (reigned AD 306–312) against the worship of pagan idols and the persecution itself. Maxentius was greatly impressed by her beauty and her courage in adhering to her convictions, and sent fifty of his sages and philosophers to reason with her. When they failed to demolish her arguments, he was so infuriated that he had them all burned alive. He then demanded that Katherine abjure her Christian faith and marry him, but she refused on the grounds that she was a bride of Christ. At this, the emperor's patience with her gave out, and she was beaten, imprisoned, and sentenced to be broken on a spiked wheel that had its two halves rotating in different directions. But just as her agony was about to begin, an angel appeared and smote the wheel with a sword, breaking it into pieces. This miraculous intervention is said to have inspired the mass conversion of two thousand Roman soldiers, whereupon an even more enraged Maxentius had Katherine beheaded. Afterward, other angels appeared and miraculously carried her remains to Mount Sinai, where a Greek Orthodox monastery was built to house her shrine. It should be noted that there are many variations on this fantastical tale.

Throughout the Middle Ages the cult of St. Katherine gained momentum. She was revered for her staunch faith, her courage, and her blessed virginity, and was believed to have under her special protection young maidens, churchmen, philosophers, students, craftsmen, nurses, and the dying. Numerous churches and bells were dedicated to her, and miracle plays were written about her. Her story, and her symbol of a wheel, appeared widely in art, mural paintings, manuscripts, ivory panels, stained glass, embroideries, vestments, and heraldry.[34] And many little girls were named in her honor, in the hope that they would emulate her manifold virtues.

That Katherine was Paon de Roët's daughter is not in doubt. The chronicler Jean Froissart, himself a native of Hainault and a servant of Queen Philippa, may well have met Katherine—he certainly took an interest in her—and he states that she was "the daughter of a knight of Hainault called Sir Paon de Roët, in his day one of the knights of good Queen Philippa of England."

Paon's fourth child, Philippa,[35] was probably so called in honor of the

Queen, who may have been her godmother. It is often claimed that Philippa de Roët was placed in royal service in the household of Elizabeth, Countess of Ulster, by 1356, in which case she would have been born in the early 1340s at the latest. However, as will be proposed below, this claim is probably unfounded.

In 1631, John Weever[36] asserted that Katherine was the oldest of Paon's daughters, but this can hardly be the case, as that would make her at least twenty-eight when she married, middle-aged by medieval standards; but perhaps Weever knew nothing of Elizabeth de Roët and had Katherine's other sister, Philippa, in mind, in which case he was probably correct in saying that Katherine was the elder.

Philippa de Roët was certainly in the Queen's service on September 12, 1366, and was married by then; she was therefore likely to have been born in the early 1350s, and was probably Katherine's younger sister, as Weever implies, rather than the elder of the two, as is usually assumed.[37] Thus, Paon appears to have had two older children, Elizabeth and Walter, born between ca. 1335 and ca. 1340, and two younger daughters, Katherine and Philippa, born around 1350 or later. The long gap between the births of Walter and Katherine suggests that Paon married twice and that each marriage produced two surviving children.

It is sometimes erroneously stated that Katherine Swynford was born in Picardy, France; this error has arisen from some historians confusing Philippa de Roët with a waiting woman of the Queen, Philippa Picard, but they were in fact two different people,[38] so there was no Roët connection with Picardy. Froissart refers to Katherine as a Hainaulter, and in England she was regarded, by virtue of her birth and descent, as a stranger or alien, the chronicler Henry Knighton calling her "a certain foreign woman." We may therefore conclude that she was born in Hainault, probably on her father's lands near Mons. This being the case, the earliest possible date for her birth is 1349.

K atherine was born into a troubled world, and would not long remain in the country of her birth. In 1351, Paon was in the service of Countess Margaret as the Knight Master of her household, in which capacity he seems to have been responsible for enforcing the observance of protocol.[39] But Margaret's position was by no means secure: In 1350, she renounced her claims to Holland, Zeeland, and Friesland in favor of her second son, William, in the hope of retaining Hainault for herself, but in the spring of 1351, William seized control of it. Several attempts at negotiation failed, and all four counties became embroiled in the conflict. When Margaret was forced to flee from Zeeland and take refuge in Hainault, her followers were exiled, their castles destroyed, and their property and offices redistributed. Paon must have been caught up in this political maelstrom, and may temporarily have found himself faced with ruin.

In December 1351, hoping to enlist the support of Edward III, Margaret fled to England with her household, taking Paon with her.[40] Given the uncertainty of any future in Hainault, he is likely to have brought with him his children, Walter, Katherine, and possibly Philippa, and indeed his wife, if she was still alive. Elizabeth, of course, was left behind in her convent; it is doubtful if Katherine ever knew her elder sister.

A settlement was quickly reached between Margaret and her son, whereby Margaret was to keep Hainault, and early in 1352, William came to England to be married to King Edward's cousin, Matilda (or Maud) of Lancaster. In March, when the Hainault royals returned home, Paon was with them,[41] but after August 1352 he disappears from contemporary sources entirely. His date of death is nowhere recorded, and we know only that he was buried in Old St. Paul's Cathedral in London, where a memorial inscription to him was put in place after 1396. In 1631, in his *Ancient Funerary Monuments*, John Weever described Paon's sepulchre, which was "in this cathedral church, and near unto Sir John Beauchamp's tomb, upon a fair marble stone, inlaid all over with brass (of which nothing but the heads of a few brazen nails are at this day visible) and engraven with the representation and coat [of] arms of the party defunct. Thus much of a mangled funeral inscription was of late time perspicuous to be read, as followeth: *Hic jacet Paganus Roët miles Guyenne Rex Armorum Pater Catherine Ducisse Lancastriae.*" (Here lies Paon Roët, soldier, Guienne King of Arms, father of Catherine, Duchess of Lancaster.)

The likelihood is that Katherine herself commissioned this tomb and memorial for her father. Weever's description suggests that the tomb was of great antiquity in 1631, and the use of Katherine's title without anything to qualify it (such as "late Duchess") implies that it was executed in her lifetime, which would date the tomb to the period 1396–1403. The question is, did Paon survive until then? It is just possible, but not at all probable in those days, that he lived well into his nineties, and witnessed Katherine's ultimate triumph. What makes his survival improbable, though, is the complete absence of references to him in contemporary records after 1352, although of course he may have continued to serve Countess Margaret until her death in 1356 and then retired to his modest holdings in Hainault. No Inquisition Postmortem has been found for him,[42] which suggests that he did not die in England. The most likely conclusion is that he died long before 1396, possibly even as early as 1352, but more probably in 1355, as is suggested below; that he was buried either in St. Paul's—which in itself would underline his importance and the honor and esteem in which he had been held by the royal families of England and Hainault—or elsewhere; and that after 1396, Katherine or John of Gaunt perhaps had his remains transferred to St. Paul's, or simply placed a new memorial over his resting place, wanting his memory to be invested with her own greatness.[43]

When Paon left England in 1352, he probably took his teenage son Walter back to Hainault with him and left his tiny daughters in the care of the kindly Queen Philippa. It was then customary for gently born children to be placed in noble households with patrons who could provide an appropriate education and advance their prospects of preferment and an advantageous marriage, but these little girls were mere infants then, both too young to serve the Queen in any way. Paon placing them with her so young suggests that they were already motherless, their mother perhaps having died in childbirth. The likelihood is that Philippa offered or agreed to make them her wards, educate them, and find them husbands, and that a relieved Paon left them with her, secure in the knowledge that the Queen's patronage would be to his daughters' lasting benefit.

This early placement of Katherine de Roët in the Queen's household is corroborated by Froissart's statement that she was continuously brought up from her youth in princely courts, and by a reference in *John of Gaunt's Register* to Katherine's nurse, Agnes Bonsergeant, who doubtless was appointed by the Queen to care for her.

Early in 1355 we find Walter de Roët in the service of Countess Margaret at Mons; by May he was in England, having been appointed a Yeoman of the Chamber to the Black Prince, Queen Philippa's eldest son. We might infer from this that Paon had died early in 1355, and that the countess at once sent Walter to Queen Philippa, who was caring for his sisters and quickly arranged for him to join her son's household. Had the girls' mother still been alive in 1352, they would probably have returned to Hainault with their father, in which case there would have been no reason for Countess Margaret to send all three children to England; she had, after all, placed their elder sister, Elizabeth, in a convent in Mons, and could surely have made provision for the three younger siblings herself. Thus, the evidence suggests that their mother was dead by 1352, and that Katherine and Philippa were placed with the Queen that year and were already in England in 1355, when their father probably died. If so, Katherine would hardly have known her father, still less her mother.

Katherine and Philippa were fortunate indeed to be taken into the care of the motherly Philippa of Hainault, a "full noble and good woman"[44] who had borne twelve children of her own—the youngest, Thomas of Woodstock, had been born as recently as January 1355—and had undertaken the upbringing of several other nobly or royally born children. The Queen was now about forty-four, a tall, plump, kindly lady who was wonderfully generous, wise, "gladsome, humbly pious," and greatly loved and respected.[45] She was interested in education, art, and literature, and her charities were legion. At the same time, she was inordinately fond of rich adornment—"blessed be the memory of King Edward III and Philippa of Hainault, his Queen, who first invented clothes," observed one chronicler caustically—and she maintained a large and very costly household. As a result, her income did not meet the demands made on it, which resulted in complaints in Parliament about her frequently getting into debt, and ultimately obliged the King to amalgamate her establishment with his own. Yet Philippa made a great contribution to the stability and success of the monarchy, with her genius for fostering a degree of family unity and closeness unique in the history of the Plantagenet dynasty. Her large brood all adored her, as did her husband, the King (whose pet name for her was "mine biddiny") and those children fortunate enough to be fostered by her. Jean Froissart, Philippa's countryman, called her "the good Queen, that so many good deeds had done in her time, and so many knights succoured, and ladies and damsels comforted."

Although it was the normal practice for well-born little girls to spend some of their formative years in a convent, where they received an education of sorts and were taught good behavior and household skills,[46] there is no evidence that Katherine was ever in a convent; on the contrary, we have Froissart's evidence that she was continuously brought up from her youth in princely courts—starting, of course, in the Queen's household. The fact that Philippa spoke Dutch as well as French—two languages with which the young Katherine and her sister would surely have been familiar—must initially have been a great help to both girls. Doubtless, Katherine quickly learned to speak Norman French, the official language of the English court, a much corrupted version of the Norman dialect spoken by William the Conqueror and his companions, and somewhat different from the French spoken on the Continent. However, in her own lifetime Katherine would see Norman French overtaken by English as the language of the law courts (1362), Parliament (1363), and fashionable literary circles, although it remained in use by the nobility for letters and everyday converse until well into the first half of the fifteenth century.

Katherine herself must have learned English too; her long tenure as lady of the manor of Kettlethorpe, and the fact that her brother-in-law, Chaucer, wrote his great works in the vernacular, make this more than likely.

In the Queen's Chamber (i.e., her household), Katherine and her sister would not have lacked for company of their own age. The younger princesses—Mary, born in 1344, and Margaret, born in 1346—would have been among their companions. Margaret married in 1359, Mary in 1361, but both sadly died in the winter of 1361–62. The other surviving princes and princesses—Edward, the Black Prince, born 1330; Isabella of Woodstock, born 1332; Lionel of Antwerp, born 1338; John of Gaunt, born 1340; and Edmund of Langley, born 1341—were much older and had long left the nursery. Froissart says that Katherine was "brought up in her youth" with Blanche of Lancaster, a cousin of the King and the future wife of John of Gaunt. Blanche was eight years older than Katherine, and did spend some of her formative years in the care of Queen Philippa;[47] there is later evidence to show that she and Katherine came to be fond of each other. Living in the Queen's household, Katherine would have come to know all the members of the royal family well, including John of Gaunt, who had an affair with Marie de St. Hilaire, one of his mother's ladies, probably in the mid to late 1350s,[48] and later on doubtless came frequently to the Queen's apartments to pay court to Blanche, his future bride.

Katherine grew up to be "a woman of such bringing up and honorable demeanor," and in this the influence of Queen Philippa can easily be detected. Although Katherine was a gentlewoman, she had not been born into the highest echelons of society, but the education she received in the Queen's household formed her into a lady of many accomplishments who was able to mingle seamlessly with the elite of the kingdom. She must have been well-educated and sophisticated; the fact that, at the age of only about twenty-three, she would be appointed governess to John of Gaunt's two eldest daughters, who grew up to be highly cultivated and charming women, testifies to this, as do the intellectual interests of at least two of her own children, Henry and Joan Beaufort. Katherine's upbringing in the Queen's household would have qualified her uniquely for the post of governess.

From an early age, Katherine displayed a certain piety, which was perhaps in part due to Queen Philippa's early training. The Queen was also a practical woman, and it was doubtless from her that Katherine learned the skills of household management that prepared her efficiently to run the knightly estates entrusted to her care, and to understand the functioning of the ducal establishments of John of Gaunt. And she must have learned from Philippa of Hainault the generosity of heart and tactful diplomacy that later enabled her to draw together the diverse strands of what otherwise might have proved a highly dysfunctional family.

Katherine's character and outlook on life would have been shaped by the formative years she spent in the privileged world of the English court. It was a brilliant but itinerant court, and she would find herself moving from place to place, lodging in turn at Windsor Castle, Westminster Palace, Woodstock Palace, Havering-atte-Bower, and a number of other luxurious residences of the King and Queen. The court attracted people of rank, intellect, and sophisticated tastes, and was a center of learning and culture. Its members were wealthy, privileged, and overwhelmingly preoccupied with securing patronage and acquiring of material luxuries. Display was what mattered: They dined in style on rich and novel cuisine, drank to excess, and dressed in extravagantly fashionable and colourful clothes; women's necklines were very low and often left the shoulders and breasts half bared, while young men wore such clinging hose beneath their short jackets (paltocks) that little was left to the imagination. Elaborate headgear, shoes with long pointed toes, trailing sleeves, and belts clasped seductively low on the hips completed these ensembles for both sexes, and a profusion of jewelry was de rigueur. Unsurprisingly, these pampered, gaudily attired courtiers shocked the King's

more sober subjects, not only by their revealing dress but also by their sometimes licentious conduct. All, however, could be redeemed by the exercise of
good manners.

Katherine would have learned early on the strict codes of protocol and
formal courtesy that were observed by royalty and the aristocracy: Froissart
tells us that "she had a perfect knowledge of court etiquette, because she had
been brought up in it continually since her youth." Doubtless she was also
taught something of the accomplishments deemed desirable in a court into
which Queen Philippa had introduced many more women than had graced
it in previous reigns, and hence injected a somewhat civilizing influence on
what was essentially a male-dominated, militaristic society. Katherine would
have learned dancing, embroidery, riding, hunting, hawking, and social
skills. That she was a competent horsewoman is evident from the fact that
she would one day ride beside John of Gaunt through his estates, and later
still kept a dozen of her horses in his stables.[49]

She would have become familiar with the parlor games so beloved of
courtiers, the songs and music performed by the King's musicians, and with
the cult of courtly love, which informed and underpinned sexual relationships within the rarefied world of castle or palace; its idealized code permitted bachelors of usually inferior rank to pay their passionate addresses to
great ladies who were often married and theoretically unattainable. In practice, this code facilitated adulterous relationships. Yet its emphasis on the
lover posing as a devoted servant to his mistress, or wearing her favor at a
tournament, or languishing hopelessly in the face of her disdain, set the tone
for social interaction between men and women, and its influence on sexual
behavior in the western world is still evident today. Needless to say, courtly
love had little to do with the hardheaded medieval approach to marriage,
which among the landed classes was essentially a business contract made for
material, political, or dynastic advantage, gave full control of a wife to her
husband, and took no account of love or personal inclinations.

But it was of love that the courtiers talked, sang, and composed verse—
love and martial exploits. The latter were a favorite topic of discussion in a
court predominantly inhabited by a martial aristocracy and a multitude of
knights. For the ladies, however, love was of paramount interest. Manuscripts of romances and love poems were always in circulation in female circles at court, and Katherine, under the guidance of her royal patroness,
would surely have been taught to read, if not to write, so she could partici-

pate fully in the social milieu of which she was to be a part for so much of her life. Her daughter, Joan Beaufort, and both her future royal charges were literate, as were many of the women in her social circle, so it is inconceivable that Katherine herself was unable to read, if not write.

The game and play of love was all very well, but it would have been drummed into growing girls like Katherine that they must wait to be addressed before speaking, keep their eyes modestly lowered and their hands folded, and avoid being overfamiliar with men if they wanted to avoid scandal. But the court was a licentious place where promiscuity was rampant, since so many young men could not afford to marry, and frank, bawdy tales—such as those of Giovanni Boccaccio and, later, Geoffrey Chaucer—were very popular; Chaucer, in "The Squire's Tale," speaks of the revels, jollity, and "dancings" that provided opportunities for erotic intrigue, "when each person fully experiences the being of another." In such an environment, young people could hardly have grown up ignorant of the facts of life, or its temptations.

The social and moral tone of the English court was set by King Edward III himself, who could be described as the archetypal medieval monarch: chivalrous, warlike, and accomplished in statecraft and diplomacy. Born in 1312, Edward had succeeded to the throne in 1327. His contemporaries admired him immensely: "This King Edward was of infinite goodness and glorious among all the great ones of the world. He was great-hearted, clement and benign, familiar and gentle to all men; affable and gentle in courtesy of speech, and profuse in largesse. His body was comely, and his face like the face of a god. He was liberal in giving and lavish in spending."[50] Like his wife, he dressed lavishly, ever the showman.

By the time Katherine came to court, Edward's subjects "thought that a new sun was rising over England, with peace abounding, the wealth of possessions and the glory of victory."[51] In prosecuting his claim to the French throne, the King had inflicted resounding defeats on England's ancient enemy at Sluys in 1340, Crécy in 1346, and Calais in 1347, and won high renown, a substantial foothold in France, and international prestige for his kingdom. "He was the flower of this world's knighthood, for whom to do battle was to reign, to contend was to triumph," observed the chronicler Henry Knighton admiringly.

Edward had created a lavish and extravagant court that was a center of chivalry and culture. In 1348 he founded the celebrated Order of the Garter in honor of England's patron saint, St. George, and in emulation of King

Arthur and his legendary knights. The annual feast of St. George, celebrated each April at Windsor, was one of the greatest social occasions of the year, ranked with the Easter and Christmas festivities. Edward also established a pattern of court ceremonial that underlined his majesty, proclaimed his magnificence, and provided his courtiers and subjects with an endless procession of fascinating spectacles.

King Edward was devoted to Queen Philippa, and they were to enjoy a long and happy marriage. Yet he was not faithful to her: Indeed, he was often "passionately smitten"[52] with the charms of other ladies, and there was even an unsubstantiated tale that he took what he wanted by force.[53] At the dances, hunts, tournaments, and feasts that were a regular feature of court life, he was often to be found "entertaining ladies." In other respects he was a loving husband, and a good and affectionate father who was clearly indulgent toward his large brood. By marrying his sons to English heiresses, he secured lands and titles for them without impoverishing himself, and in the process identified the interests of the nobility with those of the royal family. The remarkable harmony within that family was due to this careful policy of the King and the warmly unifying influence of the Queen. Thus, Edward III could count on his sons' unquestioning loyalty and support, which was rare in the history of the medieval English monarchy.

K atherine grew up in the rarefied and privileged enclave of the court, but a wider world also played its part in shaping her. She lived in a society that faced similar problems to those we face today, a postimperial world in which people were fast losing faith in an authoritarian government that seemed unable or unwilling to deal effectively with the practical problems it faced, and insisted on pursuing victory at all costs in a war that could never be won. A world suffering from the effects of rampant monetary inflation, a terrible increase in lawlessness, a decline in morality, and the rise of muscular mercantile organizations whose power was equal to that of today's multinational corporations. A world in which people suffered under unjust increases in taxation; in which the rich experienced the breaking up of great estates, and the working classes increasingly flexed their political muscles. A world in which religious fundamentalism was challenged by a society grown disillusioned with organized religion. And a world that, at the same time, witnessed an improvement in standards of living and the unprecedented growth of a consumer culture.

Yet in many other respects Katherine's world would be largely unrecognizable to us today. In the second half of the fourteenth century, England was still essentially a feudal society, with a social hierarchy that represented medieval man's preoccupation with the divinely appointed order of civilization. At the very top of this pyramid was the king; next came his tenants-in-chief, the great barons; then the knightly classes and the gentry—the class to which Katherine belonged; then the freemen and rising merchant classes; and at the very bottom of the pyramid, the villeins or serfs, peasants who were tied to their manors and worked the land for their lords and themselves.

Feudalism had evolved in the Dark Ages in the insecure landscape of western Europe, when territorial borders were constantly changing or under threat, wars were endemic, and kings had to rely on a military aristocracy to supply them with armies, while peasants needed the protection that only an overlord—with his strong castle or fortified manor, and his train of knights—could provide. However, in England, by the thirteenth century, a strong centralized government and increasing material prosperity had led to the growth of towns, trade, and commerce, and a population boom.

All this was to change, however, just before Katherine was born. In 1348–49 the Black Death, a particularly virulent form of bubonic plague, scythed its way across Europe, killing between two-fifths and three-quarters of the population. In his *Decameron* (1358), Giovanni Boccaccio described the dreaded symptoms: "It first betrayed itself by the emergence of certain tumors in the groin or armpits, some of which grew as large as an apple, after which the form of the malady began to change, black spots making their appearance in many cases on the arm or the thigh." Both the tumors and the spots were "infallible tokens of approaching death" that could overtake the victim within hours. The English chronicler Henry Knighton wrote that, spread by rats, "the fearful mortality rolled on, following the course of the sun into every part of the kingdom." Few souls remained untouched by it.

The Black Death left the world a very different place. Its impact was felt in every walk of life. Because it was seen as the judgment of God on a sinful universe, religious hysteria and fanaticism flourished and people began to question the old certainties of the universal faith preached by the Roman Catholic Church. Yet while acts of sacrilege became more commonplace, mysticism—with its emphasis on man's striving to attain unity with God—began to thrive as people sought to find some meaning to the horrific mortality and a deeper understanding of the mysteries of faith. When Margery Kempe—an English mystic who was once the guest of Katherine's daughter, Joan Beaufort—had a vision of the suffering Christ "all rent and torn with scourges, rivers of blood flowing out plenteously from every limb, she fell down and cried, twisting and turning her body amazingly, and could not keep herself from crying because of the fire of love that burned so fervently in her soul with pure pity and compassion."

This obsession with death and suffering revealed itself in literature, poetry, art, and particularly in sculpture, with the appearance of cadaver tombs with an effigy of the deceased in life above, and another depicting his or her rotting corpse below—a grisly reminder of the end of all flesh. This was the cultural atmosphere in which the young Katherine spent her growing years.

Decomposing bodies must have been a common sight during the plague years, for often there was no one left alive to bury the dead. According to the Rochester chronicler William Dene, "the plague carried off so vast a multitude of people that nobody could be found who would bear the corpses to the grave. Men and women carried their dead children and threw them into the common burial pits, the stench from which was so appalling that scarcely anyone dared to walk beside them." Sometimes there was no one to perform the funerary rites, since so many priests had died. Whole villages succumbed to the pestilence, their buildings left to decay and disappear. Law enforcement collapsed and there was a sharp decline in public morality, as many poor mortals—aware that death was stalking them—made the most of the time left to them, committing theft, murder, and fornication unchecked by state or Church.

Never again would the social hierarchy be as stable. In the years following the Black Death, it became clear that feudalism was crumbling. A severe shortage of manpower on the manors and farms meant that the services of the remaining peasants were in high demand by the landed classes, and that they could demand good wages for those services. This sounded the death knell of feudalism, for no man wanted to remain in bond to his lord when he could benefit from the free market the plague had created, and lords found they had little choice but to release their serfs from villeinage and pay for their services, knowing they would otherwise just abscond and sell their labor elsewhere. In England, Parliament intervened to reverse this trend, passing in 1351 the Statute of Laborers, which tried to impose maximum wages and minimum prices. "Many workmen and servants," it complained, "will not serve unless they receive excessive wages, and some are rather will-ing to beg in idleness than labor to get their living." Hence every villein "shall serve the master requiring him or her." But it was too late—the tide of change had turned too far, and the law proved unenforceable. "The world goeth from bad to worse," grumbled the poet John Gower in 1375. "Labor is now at so high a price that he who will order his business aright must pay five or six shillings now for what cost two in former times." The late four-teenth century witnessed the emergence of the hired hand and the yeoman farmer who owned his own land. Of course, this did not happen overnight, but it was prevalent throughout Katherine Swynford's lifetime and beyond.

As capitalism gradually replaced feudalism, trade expanded and the mid-dle classes came to enjoy ever greater prosperity and influence. Katherine's own sister married into a rich merchant family, and that sister's son rose to great political and social prominence, while her granddaughter became a duchess. In Parliament, founded in the thirteenth century in the aftermath of the wars between Crown and barons, the Commons increasingly made their voices heard, much to the dismay of conservative lords like John of Gaunt, who were determined to resist the relentless changes brought about by the new social order.

Katherine lived in an England that was largely rural, with a population of perhaps three million and an economy based on farming, wool, and over-seas trade. It was not an industrial society—that came centuries later—and most people lived in tight communities, in villages or on manors, in crude wattle-and-daub cottages. Katherine herself spent many years as a lady of the manor, responsible for a farming community. Commerce was centered upon the towns, which were far smaller than they are today: London had around 23,000 inhabitants in 1377, although it boasted a hundred churches. Even York, the second most important city and the virtual capital of the North, had a population of only 7,500 at most. Towns were where prosper-ous burgesses lived and guilds of craftsmen controlled trade, but they were often crowded and dirty, with buildings and people crammed into narrow streets with overjutting upper stories, and within walls that prevented ex-pansion. In 1419, City of London authorities ordered that each citizen "shall make clean of filth the front of his house under penalty of half a mark" (£73) and that "no one shall throw dung into the King's highway or before the house of his neighbor." In an age of poor sanitation, in which people relied on horses as the fastest and most efficient form of travel, the nuisance of dung and human waste was an ever-recurring concern.

In the towns, one could find all kinds of commodities on sale in the shops. When the poet John Lydgate walked through London in the early fifteenth century, he was offered "hot peascods [peas in the pod] and sheep's feet, strawberries ripe," spices, pepper, velvet, silk, lawn, mackerel, green rushes to strew on the floor, a hood, "ribs of beef and many a pie," pewter pots, harps, pipes, and plenty of "stolen goods." It was hardly surprising that towns and cities needed to expand, and with the country largely at peace, suburbs were beginning to emerge, as people built houses beyond the safety of the walls, with gardens and orchards. Katherine Swynford had strong links with the important city of Lincoln—population 3,400—and was fortunate enough to rent, at different times, two very imposing houses in its exclusive cathedral close.

Outside the towns and cities, the countryside was quiet and peaceful. The land was mostly fertile, but farming was still based on the three-field system, with crops rotated and one field left fallow each year. Farm animals were regularly slaughtered in the autumn, and their meat salted down or smoked for winter consumption. Any surplus farm produce was sold locally or taken to the markets held regularly, by royal charter, in the cities and towns.

"The riches of England," wrote an Italian traveler in the fifteenth century, "are greater than those of any other country in Europe. This is owing in the first place to the great fertility of the soil, which is such that, with the exception of wine, they import nothing from abroad for their subsistence." Other foreigners waxed lyrical about the beauty of rural England, its lush green pastures, rolling hills, pretty stone or timbered dwellings, towering castles, and moated manor houses. The contents of a well-set-up knightly household—as listed in a will of 1410—might comprise a canopied or "tester" bed, "covers, blankets, linens, coverlets, mattresses, painted cloths, rugs, napkins, towels, washbasins, candelabra of bronze, marble and silver gilt, bronze pots and pans, twelve silver spoons, spits, poles, iron pots, vessels of silver gilt and lead for beer, silver-gilt salt cellars, three iron braziers, trestles and boards for tables." Furniture itself was sparse, and might also have included cupboards, buffets, and stools. Katherine Swynford would have owned such household goods for much of her married life.

England was known as "the ringing isle" because of the constant pealing of bells from numerous parish churches and abbeys. In the cities, the spires of the great cathedrals soared heavenward, drawing the focus of humanity toward God, who was an ever-constant presence in people's lives.

The power and influence of the medieval Church was all-encompassing. Today, in our materialistic and secular society, it is hard for us to comprehend how large a part religion played in the lives of medieval men and women. Religion underpinned all aspects of political life. The sacraments of the Church marked every human rite of passage from birth to death. The rituals of the mass and the divine offices set the timetable for daily life. Holidays were the holy days of the Church, the great feasts of Christmas, Easter, and Pentecost, and numerous saints' or feast days. If people made long journeys—which was not always easy, as the roads were generally poor and often badly maintained—it was usually to go on pilgrimage to the many saints' shrines, such as St. Thomas of Canterbury or Our Lady of Walsingham; a few even got as far as Rome, Compostela, or Jerusalem. "People long to go on pilgrimages, and palmers long to seek the stranger strands of far-off saints, hallowed in sundry lands," Chaucer observed in *The Canterbury Tales*.

A good Christian was expected to go to confession at least three times a year, and would regularly pray to the Virgin Mary or to his or her favorite saints to intercede on his behalf with a stern, loving, but sometimes vengeful deity; people talked about the saints as familiarly as if they were members of their own circle. The Church was also the final arbiter of public morals, and contravening its doctrines or decrees could lead to charges of heresy, which was interpreted as anything that deviated from or challenged the divinely appointed order of Christendom and the tenets of the Roman Church.

Medieval English churches were much more colorful places than they appear today; much of their decoration, stained glass, and statuary was destroyed during the Reformation of the sixteenth century. In Katherine's day, brilliant paintings adorned the walls, ceilings, and pillars in churches, put there to instruct a largely illiterate populace in biblical stories or the lives of the saints; and such visual aids to spiritual understanding were often necessary, since all services were conducted in Latin, the language of the universal Church. Many churches had a doom painting, depicting Christ in majesty judging souls and sending the righteous to Heaven and the sinful to Hell, the latter depicted in stark, gruesome detail in order to bring the wicked to repentance. Besides paintings, there were statues of the saints as aids to devotion, and invariably a rood—a large wooden carving of Christ on the Cross—hung high on a screen at the entrance to the chancel.

Many men and women, including Katherine's sister and daughter, devoted their lives to God. They entered the priesthood, or withdrew from the world into monasteries or convents, where they carried out the *opus Dei*—the work of the Lord—through prayer, manual labor, and the preservation of written knowledge and works of faith, history, and literature in illuminated manuscripts.

The religious houses, of which there were nearly seven hundred in England, also provided practical services for the community at large: They ran schools, hospitals, or infirmaries, and guest houses for travelers. They offered work for laypeople. They succored the aged, the infirm, and the destitute, providing food and shelter for beggars and the homeless. Wealthy people with pious aspirations would endow abbeys and priories with money, annuities, and gifts, or found chantries or colleges of priests, so their souls could be prayed for after death and their passage through Purgatory—that hellish preparation for Heaven in which venial sins were expurgated—could be eased. Katherine Swynford lies today in the chantry chapel founded for the salvation of her soul.

Of course, many of the Church's practices were open to abuse. The sale of indulgences for the forgiveness of sins, the worldly luxury of many clergy and religious houses, the perceived immorality of those in holy orders—all were commonplace during the fourteenth century and the focus of increasing concern on the part of a growing number of radical free-thinkers. The poet William Langland, in *The Vision of Piers Plowman* (ca. 1376) wrote of hermits on their way to Walsingham "with their wenches following after," friars "preaching to the people for what they could get, interpreting the Scriptures to suit themselves and their patrons," doctors of divinity "dressing as handsomely as they please, now that Charity has gone into business," priests who sought to "traffic in masses and chime their voices to the sweet jingling of silver," pardoners "claiming to have power to absolve all the people from vows of every kind," and bishops who shut their ears to what was going on around them. Above all, the "Babylonish captivity" of the Papacy from 1309 at "the sinful city of Avignon," a papacy in thrall to the powerful kings of France, brought the Roman Catholic Church into disrepute throughout Christendom and weakened its moral authority. Not for nothing was John Wycliffe—a courageous and highly controversial priest who spoke out against the corruption in the Church and who enjoyed John of Gaunt's patronage—called "the morning star of the Reformation."

Alongside the Church, the state—in the form of the king, the lords in council, Parliament, and the administration—governed the lives of the population. The king, whose sovereignty had the almost supernatural authority of a crowned priest, was responsible for maintaining the peace of his realm, defending it from invasion, and administering justice to all in the form of good laws.

In the fourteenth century, England was ruled by the Plantagenets, a dynasty of generally vigorous and able monarchs who had kept a largely unbroken grip on their realm since 1154, when the dynamic Henry II succeeded to the throne. The name Plantagenet derives from the nickname given to Henry II's father, Geoffrey, Count of Anjou, who habitually wore a broom flower—*planta genista*—in his hat. The name was not actually used as a royal surname until the fifteenth century.

Henry II had married Eleanor of Aquitaine, the greatest heiress in Europe, and through her acquired the rich Duchy of Aquitaine and the County of Poitou; he already held the Duchy of Normandy, which he had inherited from his great-grandfather, William the Conqueror, who had established his Norman dynasty in England in 1066; and he was Count of Anjou, which he had inherited from his father. Thus, he was master of all the land from the Scottish border to the Pyrenees. But Henry's great empire did not long survive him. The ineptitude of his son, King John, and the aggressive determination of successive French monarchs to gain control of the Plantagenet dominions, resulted in the loss of Normandy and Anjou, and by the fourteenth century England's territory in France consisted of a couple of northern towns and a much reduced Duchy of Aquitaine that centered largely upon Bordeaux, Gascony, and parts of the Dordogne region.

As we will see, it was Edward III, who succeeded to the throne in 1327 and to whose court Katherine came nearly thirty years later, who had the audacity to claim the throne of France itself, which he insisted was his because of his mother, Isabella, the sister of the last surviving kings of the House of Capet. But the French had no desire to see an Englishman on their throne, for England and France had long been traditional enemies, and they chose a member of the royal House of Valois as their monarch. Thus began a war that famously was to last for a hundred years, a war that would have a profound effect not only in western Europe, but also on the life of Katherine Swynford herself.

◆   ◆   ◆

By May 1355, as has been noted, Katherine's brother, Walter de Roët, had joined the Black Prince's household as a yeoman of the Chamber.[54] This was a brilliant opportunity for a young man, as the prince enjoyed an international reputation as a chivalric hero and warrior who was second to none. He was the "comfort of England," the "flower of chivalry of all the world,"[55] and "for as long as he lived and flourished, his good fortune in battle, like that of a second Hector, was feared by all races."[56] Already, at twenty-five, he was a legend.

Born in 1330, the sixteen-year-old Edward of Woodstock had won his spurs in 1346 at the Battle of Crécy, in which he "magnificently performed" astounding feats of arms.[57] He was "fair, lusty and well-formed," brave, intelligent, charismatic, and inspirational. His sixteenth-century nickname—it is not known to have been used earlier—probably derived from the black armor it is said he wore, but it could equally well have described his vicious and much feared temper. He could be—it has to be said—impatient, arrogant, and capable of great cruelty.

The prince's household provided an environment in which any aspiring young man would have been gratified to be placed. He spent lavishly on his residences, notably his palace at Kennington in Surrey, and lived in great splendor and luxury. He loved tournaments, hunting, gambling, and women, and fathered at least four bastards. His admiring contemporaries, whose priorities were those of the fourteenth century and not the twenty-first, regarded him as the epitome of knighthood.

Before May 9, 1355, the Black Prince arranged for two of his retainers—Walter de Roët and Sir Eustace d'Aubrécicourt—to deliver letters to his aunt, Countess Margaret, in Hainault, and to one of her clerks, Stephen Maulyons, provost of the church of Mons. Maulyons owed the prince £40, but Edward ordered him to divide it equally and pay it "as a gift" to Walter and Sir Eustace; £20 was a munificent sum—today it would be worth £7,800—so Walter was clearly highly regarded by his employer. The prince gave Walter forty shillings (about £780) for his traveling expenses on May 10, so either a long trip was anticipated—you could never be sure how long a Channel crossing might take—or Walter was to travel in some comfort. By September he had returned from his mission, for that month he accompanied the Black Prince, now King's Lieutenant in Aquitaine, on a military expedition to the duchy,[58] and he may well have fought under the prince in 1356 when Edward won a great victory over the French at the Battle of Poitiers and captured John II, King of France, himself, thus further enhancing his dazzling reputation. It is possible that Walter was killed at Poitiers, because no more is heard of him. In 1411, Katherine's son, Sir Thomas Swynford, laid claim to lands in Hainault that he had inherited from his mother on her death in 1403; had Walter de Roët been alive in 1403, those lands would have passed to him, not to the heirs of his sisters.[59]

It is often claimed that Philippa de Roët was placed by the Queen in the household of her daughter-in-law, the Countess of Ulster, around August 1355. Elizabeth de Burgh, Countess of Ulster in her own right and a former ward of the Queen, was then twenty-three and had been married to the King's second surviving son, the blond giant Lionel of Antwerp, since 1342, he taking the title Earl of Ulster in her right. There was indeed a girl called Philippa in the countess's service at this time, perhaps engaged to help care for her mistress's first and only child, yet another Philippa, who was born on August 16, 1355, at Eltham Palace in Kent. This girl's name was Philippa Pan.

For a long while historians did entertain doubts as to whether Philippa Pan was Philippa de Roët. These doubts arose from the use of the abbreviated name "Philippa Pan." in the fragmentary accounts that survive for the countess's household.[60] On July 24, 1356, a payment was made for the making of trimmings for the clothes of "Philippa Pan."; the following year the countess paid 2s.6d (£37) "for the fashioning of one tunic" for her, and in December 1357 gave a serving boy 12d (£15) to escort Philippa Pan. from a place called "Pullesdone" to Hatfield in Yorkshire, where Earl Lionel and his wife were to keep Christmas. In April 1358, Countess Elizabeth presented Philippa Pan. with a bodice and some furs to wear at the great feast given to mark St. George's Day. This is the last mention of her in the accounts, which come to an abrupt end in November 1359.

In recent years several historians have subscribed to the theory that Pan. stands for "Philippa, Paon de Roët's daughter," or "Philippa, Panetto's daughter," Panetto being the name by which Paon de Roët was familiarly known at court;[61] this theory seems rather far-fetched and contrived, especially since the Christian names of women in royal households were almost invariably accompanied by their surnames in accounts, registers, and official documents. So the "evidence" connecting Philippa Pan with the Roëts is slender indeed.

Who was she, then? It was at one time thought that Pan was short for *panetaria*, or Mistress of the Pantry, but it was virtually unheard of for such a post to be held by a woman, and there is no other instance of the word *panetaria* being thus abbreviated. Besides, a woman serving as Mistress of the Pantry would never be provided with furs by her mistress.[62]

Pan. is probably an abbreviation for a surname, and the most convincing theory is that this Philippa was the daughter or kinswoman of a London mercer, William de la Panetrie (who died between 1349 and 1367), who lived in Soper Lane at the east end of Cheapside, in the parish of St. Pancras. The Panetries were acquainted with the prosperous Chaucer family, who lived nearby on Thames Street in the Vintry Ward, and who managed to place a son in Countess Elizabeth's household;[63] this son was a highly gifted youth who was not only to become famous in his own right, but would also play an important part in the lives of Philippa de Roët and Katherine Swynford. Geoffrey Chaucer, born probably between 1339 and 1346, is renowned today as one of the greatest English poets who ever lived. Finding Philippa Pan in the same household lends weight to the theory that she was a Panetrie by birth and that she had perhaps obtained her place by recommendation. As for her link with "Pullesdone"—a place that cannot conclusively be identified—she could have been performing an official errand for her mistress, visiting relatives prior to Christmas, or accompanying a family member on business there; London merchants had far-flung interests.

Geoffrey Chaucer was the son of a rich and influential London vintner, and he is first recorded as a page in the household of Countess Elizabeth on April 4, 1357, when she purchased shoes, black and red breeches, and one of those short, revealing jackets called a "paltock" (to which hose and sleeves could be attached) for "Galfridus Chaucer" of London. The following month she gave him two shillings (£30). He is last mentioned in these accounts in December, when he was present at the Christmas gathering at Hatfield and received a grant of 3s.6d (£52) for necessities.

From 1357 to 1359, Chaucer appears to have served Lionel of Antwerp, possibly as a page. In 1359, having received arms and become a squire—he was never knighted—he served in Edward III's army against the French, and was captured at the siege of Rheims. The King himself paid his considerable ransom of £16 (£5,489)—which must demonstrate the high regard in which he was already held by the royal family—and he was freed by October 1360, when he brought a letter to England from Lionel of Antwerp, who was at that time in Calais. Chaucer then disappears from the historical record for six years. There has been much learned speculation about what happened to him during this period: that he was perhaps studying at Oxford (as his son Lewis later did) or Cambridge, or at the Inner Temple, a theory suggested by his signing himself "attorney" in the 1390s—his writings reveal that he had a good knowledge of the law. Chaucer may have transferred to John of Gaunt's household,[64] although there is no record of this, yet he was certainly on familiar terms with John of Gaunt by 1368, and John did later award him a life annuity. Most likely, when Lionel of Antwerp went to Ireland to serve as the King's Lieutenant there in September 1361,[65] taking his wife and daughter with him, Geoffrey Chaucer went with them. Lionel was created Duke of Clarence in 1362. Tragically, Elizabeth de Burgh died in Dublin on December 10, 1363.

Geoffrey Chaucer possibly returned to England in 1364, perhaps as a member of the party escorting little Philippa of Clarence to her grandmother's household, where she would be brought up. On his return he may have begun a period of study at university or the Inns of Court.[66] It is possible too that he was sponsored by a member of the royal family, possibly John of Gaunt, who is known to have maintained several students at Oxford.[67]

So if Philippa de Roët was not the Philippa Pan recorded in the Countess of Ulster's household in 1356–58, where was she? The likeliest place was the Queen's own household, with the probability that she was brought up there with her sister; by 1366, she had been appointed a *damoiselle* of the Queen's Chamber, where her duties would increasingly have involved nursing her ailing mistress: After a riding accident in 1360, in which Queen Philippa possibly suffered internal injuries that were never treated, her health declined and her enforced immobility caused her legs to swell, which her contemporaries diagnosed as "dropsy."

By 1366, Katherine de Roët had left the Queen's household; it may have been as early as 1360 that she was placed by Philippa in the chamber of the latter's daughter-in-law, Blanche, Duchess of Lancaster, Katherine's former playmate, now the wife of John of Gaunt. And within two to three years of joining the duchess's establishment, Katherine was probably married to Sir Hugh Swynford, one of John of Gaunt's knights.

TWO

The Magnificent Lord

During her childhood Katherine had benefited from the tutelage and example of Queen Philippa; now she was to come under the admirable influence of another great lady, the new Duchess of Lancaster, who was about eight years her senior and one of her former companions in the Queen's household.

The exquisite Blanche of Lancaster was the daughter of the King's cousin, the "valiant" and "well-respected" Henry of Grosmont, Duke of Lancaster.[1] While Edward III was the grandson of Edward I, Duke Henry was the grandson of Edward I's younger brother, Edmund Crouchback, who had been created Earl of Lancaster in 1267 and died in 1296. Earl Edmund's eldest son, Thomas, Earl of Lancaster, had been executed for treason in 1322 by Edward II, but his younger brother, blind Henry, was restored to the earldom two years later; Duke Henry was his son. He succeeded his father as Earl of Lancaster in 1345 and was created Duke in 1351, the second man in the realm ever to be raised to ducal rank, the first being the Black Prince, who had been created Duke of Cornwall in 1337.

Henry of Grosmont, who could have doubled for Chaucer's "perfect, gentle knight," was the greatest nobleman in the kingdom. Not only was he Duke of Lancaster, but also Earl of Derby, Earl of Leicester, Earl of Lincoln, and Lord of Beaufort and Nogent in France. Consequently, his landed interests were vast. He was the greatest of the magnates, an experienced and masterly general, and utterly loyal to the King, who thought very highly of him and treated him as a valued friend. The duke was a tall and imposing figure, genial and suave. He liked the fine things in life: good food and wine, luxurious and tasteful surroundings, and the robust charms of common women.[2] Yet he was also temperate, pious, and charitable, the founder of many religious houses, churches, and hospitals.

Henry's duchess was Isabella de Beaumont; sadly, they had no son to succeed to his great inheritance. Instead, there were two daughters, Matilda and Blanche. Matilda of Lancaster was probably born in 1340; after a brief first marriage to Ralph de Stafford, which saw her widowed by the age of ten, she was married in 1352 in the King's Chapel at Westminster to William, Duke of Bavaria,[3] who became Count of Holland in 1354 and Count of Hainault in 1356, on the death of his mother, Countess Margaret; he was the son with whom the countess had been briefly at war prior to this marriage, and it was on his account that she fled to England in 1351, bringing Paon de Roët with her.

After their wedding, Matilda went to Hainault to live with her husband, but in 1357 the insanity that was to render William incapable of ruling became alarmingly evident, and there were unfounded rumors attributing his madness to an attempt to poison him while he was in England. By 1358 he was being kept in confinement at The Hague, and later was moved to the fortress of Quesnoy, where he remained shut up until his death thirty-one years later.[4] There were no children born of his marriage to Matilda.

Blanche of Lancaster, the younger of Duke Henry's daughters, had probably been born on March 25, 1342.[5] She spent some of her formative years at court in the care of Queen Philippa, and came to know the royal family well. As we have seen, Katherine and Philippa de Roët were among her younger companions.

Edward III, needing to provide for his rapidly expanding family, was vigorously pursuing his successful policy of marrying his sons to English heiresses, and thus consolidating his own interests and binding nobles and Crown closer together. Blanche was the greatest unmarried heiress in England, and Edward was determined to marry her to his third surviving son,

John of Gaunt, and secure for John her share of the rich Lancaster patrimony. On June 7, 1358, the King petitioned Pope Innocent VI for a dispensation allowing the young couple to wed—they were within the forbidden degrees of consanguinity—which was granted on January 8, 1359.[6]

It was in honor of the memory of "Blanche the Fair" that Geoffrey Chaucer later wrote his dream poem, *The Boke of the Duchesse*.[7] Allusions in the text make this clear: Chaucer uses the word "Duchess" in the title, and there was only one duchess in England at the time; he makes a play on Blanche's name, calling her "my Lady White," or "good, fair White"; and he refers to "a long castle" (Lancaster), St. John (the duke's name saint), and "a rich mount" (a pun for Richmond, John's earldom). The context of the poem will be discussed in Chapter 4, but it contains a eulogistic description of Blanche, whom Chaucer calls "the flower of English womanhood": "Gay and glad she was, fresh and sportive, sweet, simple [i.e., straightforward] and of humble semblance, the fair lady whom men call Blanche."

Chaucer's description reveals that, like her father, Blanche was intelligent, well-mannered, self-controlled and moderate in behavior, "not too grave and not too gay." Her speech was "low-toned and gentle," friendly and eloquent, and her character "inclined to good." She was no flatterer, but was truthful, "devoid of malice," and never voiced a criticism. Happy and carefree in her demeanor, she was "like a torch so bright that everyone could take its light." Froissart echoes Chaucer's praise of Blanche, calling her "gay, sociable, gentle, of humble semblance," and above all "good."

There is a corbel head said to be Blanche at Edington Priory in Wiltshire, and a statue of a girl holding a pet monkey, whom some have identified as her, on Queen Philippa's tomb in Westminster Abbey; but these are in no sense portraits, nor can we glean any idea of what she looked like from drawings of her tomb effigy, because the effigy depicted is not the original, which was sculpted in the fourteenth century. So it is to Chaucer that we must turn for a detailed description of Blanche. Her hair, he says, was "glittering golden," her eyes "gentle and good, steadfast yet glad, not set too wide." She did not "shyly glance aside," but gazed openly with a "candid mien" that was "free of artfulness" and in no way wanton. Here, one suspects, was a young woman who knew her own worth, for although her look "made men smart" with desire, she affected not to notice: "well she guarded her good name." Her lovely face was "pink and white, fresh, lively-hued, [the] highest example of Nature's work"; her neck was graceful, her shoulders lovely, her breasts rounded, her skin unblemished. She was tall and straight-backed, with "well-broad" hips, and her arms and legs were "well-clothed in flesh," suggesting a degree of plumpness fashionable in the fourteenth century.

It has often been asserted that Chaucer's *The Boke of the Duchesse* is not intended as a realistic portrayal of Blanche; undoubtedly, the poem was conceived as a dream sequence, and it was inspired by several well-known works: those of Ovid and Froissart, the popular medieval romance poem, *Le Roman de la Rose*, and the innovative verse of the avant-garde French writer and composer, Guillaume de Machaut.[8] Yet although Chaucer's laudatory and idealized description of Blanche conforms to the literary conventions of the age, it does convey an impression of a real person. After all, this poem would have been circulated at court and among the duke's circle, so its portrayal of Blanche and her relationship with John of Gaunt would have had to be recognizable and convincing to those who had known her well. And Blanche may well have been lucky enough to have had the kind of looks that were fashionable in that period. Furthermore, Chaucer himself was a member of the royal household when he wrote the poem; he knew John of Gaunt and the rest of the royal family. So what he wrote must to a degree have been drawn from life.

John of Gaunt was probably born in March (certainly by May 28) 1340 at St. Bavon's Abbey in Ghent, Flanders[9]—hence his appellation, "Gaunt" being an English corruption of "Ghent." He was always to demonstrate a sense of affiliation with the country of his birth and with Hainault, his mother's birthplace.[10] This affinity might partly explain why he would be attracted to Katherine Swynford, herself a Hainaulter.

His early years were spent in the care of a nurse, Isolda Newman, under the supervision of his mother, Queen Philippa. The "Lord John" was created Earl of Richmond on November 20, 1342; the King himself solemnly girding the two-year-old child with the sword of his earldom, which had been held by the Dukes of Brittany since the Norman Conquest, and was vacant on account of the death of the last duke, whose infant heir had been passed over.[11] This earldom brought young John an income of 2,000 marks (£303,882) per annum. At the age of three, with his father and his elder brothers, he was accepted into the confraternity of Lincoln Cathedral, thus forging the first of his close links and attachment to Lincoln, its cathedral chapter,[12] and the social orbit of the Swynford family.

John's nurse was pensioned off in February 1346,[13] at which time he would have been assigned a male governor to oversee his education and his training in the knightly arts. We know little about his childhood, but all the evidence suggests that he was fond of his parents—he was especially close to his mother[14]—and his siblings, and grew up in a happy, stable family, which was not always the case where royal princes were concerned.

Above all, John would have grown up to the heady awareness that his father, the King, was winning great victories over the French and international renown, and that his glorious brother, the Black Prince, ten years his senior, had assisted most nobly in achieving those victories. It was an era of growing national confidence and pride, and the young John's world was surely dominated by triumphal heroes.

One man whose influence on him was paramount was Henry, Duke of Lancaster, the man who, next to his father and eldest brother, he seems to have revered most. In Duke Henry he had the example of a great lord who was honorable, trustworthy, and pious, and doubtless the young John thrilled to tales of the duke's youthful crusading adventures and his distinguished victories over the Scots and the French. John seems to have spent his life trying to emulate Henry of Lancaster, from his military successes and diplomatic achievements to his charitable enterprises and elegant mode of living.

On August 29, 1350, when he was only ten years old, John first saw active service in the war with France, when he accompanied his father and the Black Prince on a naval expedition that ended in a dramatic victory over enemy ships off Winchelsea, with the King capturing twenty vessels. John was too young to take part, but Froissart says his father took him along "because he much loved him." And that decision nearly proved fatal, for the ship carrying the King and his sons was rammed by an enemy vessel and began to sink; they were saved only through the courageous intervention of Duke Henry, who brought his ship alongside that of the aggressor, boarded it and heroically rescued them. For John, it was a salutary initiation into the realities of warfare, and another reason for hero worship of the duke.

John was always close to his eldest brother, whom he obviously looked up to and tried—apparently without jealousy—to emulate, and from at least

March 1, 1350, until May 20, 1355, he lived in the Black Prince's household, residing with him mainly at Berkhamsted Castle and the manor of Byfleet in Surrey. The prince acted as a mentor to the boy and supervised his training in arms; according to Froissart, he was "very fond" of John and always referred to him as his "very dear and well-beloved brother."[15]

In July 1355 the fifteen-year-old John received the accolade of knighthood, whose chivalrous tenets he was to follow to the best of his ability all his life. That year, he served on a campaign in France under Duke Henry, and in the winter of 1355–56 was in Scotland with the King, forcing a stand-down by the Scots that became known as "Burnt Candlemas." He was a witness to their surrender of Berwick on January 13, 1356. The young man's qualities evidently impressed the Scots, because in 1357 they proposed naming him as the successor to their childless King David II, a plan that—sadly for John—came to nothing. John was to retain a special understanding and respect for the Scots throughout his career and would achieve significant diplomatic successes with them in future years.

In *The Boke of the Duchesse*, Chaucer, who must have come to know John of Gaunt fairly well, and observed him on many occasions, has him say that from his youth he had "most faithfully paid tribute as a devotee to love, most unrestrainedly, and joyfully become his thrall, with willing body, heart and all," and that he had carried on in this fashion "for ages, many and many a year," with "lightness" and "wayward thoughts." But his only recorded early love affair was with Marie de St. Hilaire (or Hilary), one of his mother's *damoiselles*, who, like Katherine Swynford, came from Hainault.[16] According to Froissart, this youthful indiscretion, which almost certainly occurred when John was in his teens, resulted in the birth of an illegitimate child— the only one, apart from the Beauforts, that John ever acknowledged. Her name was Blanche,[17] and it's likely she was born well before his marriage to Blanche of Lancaster, probably in the later 1350s. Certainly no hostile chronicler mentioned the affair later on, nor attempted to make political capital out of it, which supports the theory that it happened before John came to political prominence.

In 1360, Edward III granted Marie an annuity of £20 (£5,779) per annum,[18] the same amount as that given in 1359–60 to Joan de St. Hilary (who was surely Marie's sister), and in 1367 to Elizabeth Chandos, two of Marie's fellow *damoiselles*. This parity suggests that the annuity, handsome as it was, and more than the other *damoiselles* ever received, was awarded as much for exceptional service to the Queen as to support the mother of the Queen's bastard granddaughter. Marie remained in Philippa's service until 1369, and was still alive in 1399, when she was in receipt of a pension from John of Gaunt "for the good and agreeable service she has rendered for a long time to our honored lady and mother, Philippa, late Queen of England."[19] Thus, in his characteristically honorable fashion, John provided for Marie and—as will be seen—their daughter all their lives.

John of Gaunt would surely have known Blanche of Lancaster well. Their fathers were cousins and staunch friends, and she was a frequent presence in the Queen's household. Given that they were close in age—she was the younger by two years—John and Blanche may have been childhood playmates from infancy.

At Christmas 1357 and New Year 1358, John was a guest of his brother Lionel of Antwerp, Earl of Ulster, and Countess Elizabeth at the Queen's manor of Hatfield, near Doncaster in Yorkshire.[20] Young Geoffrey Chaucer was also present at the gathering, perhaps the occasion at which the talented Chaucer first came to John's notice.

Blanche of Lancaster may also have been present at Hatfield,[21] and if so, John may have taken the opportunity to pay court to her. It was six months later that Edward III applied for a dispensation for the young couple to marry.

Chaucer, in *The Boke of the Duchesse*, recalled John telling him that he was first taken with Blanche's charms after being struck by how vividly she stood out among a group of fair ladies:

> In beauty, courtesy and grace,
> In radiant modesty of face,
> Fine bearing, virtue, every way,
> It was my sweet, her right true self—
> Demeanour steadfast, calm and free,
> And poise imbued with dignity.

He watched her dancing gracefully, singing and laughing, and noticed that her eyes were gracious, her voice "warm with kindliness." To him, she appeared "a treasure house of utter bliss": "that flower of womanhood was life and joy," the chief source of his "well-being." But when he embarked on his "mighty quest" to win her love, he initially met with cool rejection. Blanche "gave no false encouragement; she spurned such petty artifice." Her ardent swain composed songs that, while "not well done," were written "in passion for my heart's delight," but he held back from confessing to her how much pain he was suffering on her account, fearing lest she might take offense at his presumption. Yet in the end, "I had to tell her, or die." Quaking in dread, he declared his love and devotion, swore "to guard her honor evermore," and begged for mercy, not daring to look Blanche in the eye. Afterward, he could not recall exactly what her response had been, but "the gist of it was simply 'No.' "

Thus rejected, John stole away and hid his sorrow for many days. But his desire was such that he determined to persist in his suit, intent on overcoming all resistance, and in the end, after many months, he joyfully won the heart of his lady. "To seal the gift, she gave a ring," which to him was "the utmost precious thing"; he felt as if he had been "from death to life upcast."

All this had little relevance to the realities of royal matchmaking but everything to do with the game of courtly love, and no doubt the young and ardent John of Gaunt took full advantage of the opportunities afforded by that convention, though his was essentially an arranged marriage. From what Chaucer tells us, we may infer that he set himself to win Blanche's heart as well as her hand. For him, she would always be "my lady bright, whom I have loved with all my might."

There is other testimony besides Chaucer's to support the claim that John fell in love with Blanche: His apparent faithfulness to her through all their years of marriage, his inconsolable grief at her passing, his enduring homage to her memory, and his desire to be buried beside her. Of course, that could equally have been inspired by a wish to be laid to rest beside the woman from whom he had derived his title and wealth, and who was the mother of his heir. But taken with all the other evidence, it would appear to have been motivated by deep affection and tender memories too. And given that this was a love match, it is feasible that John's ardor for his lady was well established by the time he spent that Christmas at Hatfield, for Chaucer tells us that Blanche kept him at bay for a year. This combination of true love and political and dynastic desirability was most unusual in that era of arranged marriages—but John of Gaunt was more than once to prove unconventional when it came to love and marriage.

•   •   •

John of Gaunt and Blanche of Lancaster were married on Sunday, May 19, 1359, in a lavish ceremony in the Queen's Chapel at Reading Abbey, one of the foremost Benedictine monasteries in the realm.[22] He was nineteen, she seventeen. Thomas de Chynham, clerk of Queen's Chapel, officiated,[23] and Robert Wyvil, Bishop of Salisbury, pronounced the benediction.[24] John's wedding gift to Blanche was a gold ring with a great diamond set in pearls.[25]

Two weeks of festivities followed the wedding. There were feasts, boat races, and three days of jousting in the meadows on the banks of the Thames. Then the royal family and their guests rode to London, where tournaments were held over a further three days at Smithfield before huge crowds. Here, the King, his four eldest sons, and nineteen of his lords disguised themselves as the Lord Mayor and aldermen of London, acquitted themselves with great honor in the lists, then revealed their true identity, to the lyrical delight of the spectators. Alongside the captive kings of France and Scotland, the Queen was watching, as well as her daughters and her ladies, and it is more than likely that the Roët sisters were present too.

If Chaucer is to be believed, John's love for Blanche deepened after marriage and he was convinced he could not have chosen a better wife, for she was good, loyal, and true, the "queen of all my body." Throughout their marriage, he "belonged to her entire": there is no record of him dishonoring his marriage vows, and no breath of scandal tainted his name, in sharp contrast to the reputation he would gain during his second marriage. Chaucer has John declare:

> "Our joy was ever fresh and new,
> Our hearts were so in harmony
> That neither was ever contrary
> To the other heart when sorrows came."
> In truth, they bore all things the same
> Whatever joy or grief they had.
> Alike, they were both glad or sad;
> "Assured in union we were,
> And thus we lived for many a year,
> So well, I cannot tell you how."

Although Blanche was younger than John and sworn to obedience and subservience to him, Chaucer implies that he always deferred to her. For:

> When I was wrong and she was right,
> Always in generosity
> [She] forgave me most becomingly.
> In every youthful circumstance
> She took me in her governance.
> Always her counsel was so true.

It is worthy of notice that, in his idyllic portrayal of the married love between John and Blanche, Chaucer made a dramatic departure from contemporary literary practice, in which marriage is often seen as sounding the death knell to love, which can only truly flourish in an illicit or courtly context. This striking departure suggests that the conjugal relationship between John and Blanche was unusually close and tender.

It is tempting to speculate on the kind of sexual relationship those two shared. Chaucer makes it clear that Blanche had a degree of worldly knowledge and an understanding of good and evil, but says her self-esteem was such that she would not permit any diminution of respect toward her person. One would imagine that the young John, with his well-bred ideals of love and chivalry, treated his wife with deference, and even reverence, in bed. A later assertion by the chronicler Thomas Walsingham, that John brought prostitutes to share in bedtime romps with his understandably distressed wife, is almost certainly malicious and groundless, and invented purely for the purposes of character assassination.

Devoted as she was, Blanche, unlike the Queen, did not accompany her husband on his frequent expeditions overseas.[26] First, John was usually sent abroad on military campaigns in which there was no place for women; and second, Blanche was frequently pregnant.

The young couple were both pious, and took their spiritual life very seriously. They were joint founder members of St. Mary's College next to St. David's Cathedral in Wales;[27] they petitioned the Pope for the right to choose or change their confessors, for permission for themselves and members of their households to have portable altars, and for "plenary remission [of sins] at the hour of death."[28] Like most aristocratic ladies, Blanche undertook charitable works, and in 1367 successfully pleaded with the King to pardon a condemned murderer.[29]

As we have seen, Blanche won high praise from Chaucer and Froissart, both of whom knew her personally. She could read and write, had literary interests and enjoyed poetry,[30] so she may have been their patron. Thomas Speght, in his 1602 edition of Chaucer's works, claims that one of the poet's earliest poems, "An ABC," was "made, as some say, at the request of Blanche, Duchess of Lancaster, as a prayer for her private use, being a woman in her religion very devout." Speght may have had access to sources that are lost to us, and his claim cannot be proved because there are no perceptible allusions to Blanche in "An ABC."[31]

Blanche conceived her first child by the end of June 1359, and was four months pregnant when her husband left England on October 28 to accompany the King on a new military expedition to France, Edward III being determined to have himself crowned at Rheims. It was on this campaign that Geoffrey Chaucer was captured by the French and had to be ransomed.

Blanche's baby, named Philippa in honor of the Queen (who was probably her godmother), was born on March 31, 1360.[32] Out of "the concern that we feel for her condition," Edward III had arranged for Blanche to stay with the Queen for the last months before her confinement,[33] but her child was actually born at Leicester Castle: On May 21, Philippa paid the expenses of the ceremony to mark her daughter-in-law's "uprising" (or "churching") at Leicester.[34] The midwife in attendance had perhaps been "our well-beloved Elyot, midwife of Leicester," who later attended John's second wife and Katherine Swynford, and was rewarded for her services in both cases.[35]

Blanche had her own household, separate from that of her husband, with her own staff of officers, ladies, and servants. There is no record of Katherine de Roët being in that household before January 24, 1365—when she is referred to as Blanche's *ancille* (maidservant)[36]—but the registers of John of Gaunt for this period have not survived, so it is quite possible that Katherine was serving the countess considerably earlier than that and had been placed by the Queen in Blanche's nursery in 1360 to help care for the new baby, possibly as a rocker, a job often assigned to a young girl of Katherine's age; she was then about ten. Froissart just says that "in her youth, she had been of the household of the Duchess Blanche of Lancaster," but he doesn't specify how old she was at the time.

The female attendants of noblewomen were routinely required to help care for their mistress's offspring, and given Katherine's later appointment as governess, and her evident rapport with the young, it would appear that she had early on gained experience in looking after children and demonstrated a talent for it, thus earning the confidence of her employers. It may be that Katherine's placement with Blanche came about as a result of arrangements made by the Queen when the pregnant Blanche was staying with her, and that Katherine was one of those who traveled with the countess to Leicester.

Leicester Castle, the principal seat of the Earls of Leicester, was to become one of John of Gaunt's favorite residences, probably because of its associations with Duke Henry; John "especially loved to be with his household" here,[37] keeping great state, entertaining lavishly, and hunting in nearby Leicester Forest, where he had a substantial hunting box called— delightfully—Bird's Nest.[38] And he was popular in Leicester, for thanks to his frequent presence in their midst, the townsfolk enjoyed greater prosperity than they had ever known.

Over the years, Katherine would probably stay in Leicester Castle on many occasions. It had been built in 1068–88 and extended in the middle of the twelfth century, when the great aisled hall of stone that John and Katherine knew, with its lofty roof of braced beams, was put up; below, there were cellars or dungeons. Inside the castle was the ancient Saxon church of St. Mary de Castro, rebuilt in the twelfth century by the earls of Leicester; its slender spire was added in the fourteenth century.[39]

In the outer ward of the castle was the Hospital of the Annunciation of the Blessed Virgin, founded by Henry, Earl of Lancaster, in 1331 for the care of the poor and infirm of Leicester. This foundation was extended by his son, Duke Henry, in the 1350s to house a precious relic, a thorn from the Crown of Thorns, and it was at that time the small but "exceeding fair"[40] collegiate church of St. Mary was built beside it, with cloisters and pretty houses for the prebendaries. The whole area of four acres, which was enclosed by the thick castle wall and accessed by a stately triple-arched and vaulted gateway, became known as the *novum opus*, or the new work, which was soon colloquially referred to as the Newarke,[41] a name still in use today.

Whether Katherine was in Blanche's household sooner rather than later, she had again been exceedingly fortunate in being placed with a kind and affectionate mistress. Blanche's many qualities would have made her an easy person to serve, and her piety and literary interests were bound to make some impression upon a young and intelligent girl of Katherine's age. In Blanche, Katherine could profit from the example of a lady who conducted herself with dignity and honor, who was moderate in all her doings, with an effortless grace and serene demeanor, and who expected and received the respect that was her due, not just as a duchess but as a woman. The young and impressionable Katherine would have observed too the great love that lay between the duke and his lady, and perhaps hoped that she herself, in due course, would find such unusual happiness in marriage.

Katherine spent her youth, indeed her life, in the shadow of the Hundred Years War, but in 1360 that war was going well for England. Having failed to assert his claim to the Crown of France, Edward III had resorted to diplomacy, and on May 8 concluded the Treaty of Brétigny, which ceded to him all the lands he had won by conquest as well as an extended Duchy of Aquitaine in full sovereignty. On May 18 the King and his sons returned home to England in triumph, John having the added joy of greeting his new daughter. On May 20, doubtless in recognition of his son's good service in France, the King granted John the honor and castle of Hertford and other property.[42]

Hertford Castle was a residence that suitably befit the exalted estate of the young Earl and Countess of Richmond. Formerly the property of John's grandmother, Isabella of France (the widow of Edward II), who died in 1358, it had been built three centuries before by William the Conqueror on low-lying land on the encircling banks of the River Lea. Successive monarchs embellished the hall, chapel, and royal apartments, but the ancient fortifications had crumbled and were never replaced, because there was no longer any need for them in this more peaceful age. Hertford was also conveniently situated, being within easy riding distance of London and Westminster. John of Gaunt instituted an ongoing program of lavish improvements there, transforming the castle into a virtual palace, and unsurprisingly, it remained one of his favorite residences throughout his life.[43]

John was abroad again, in France with the King, from August to November 1360, and on November 20 received his first summons to Parliament, as Earl of Richmond. This marked his debut in political life.

The year 1361 saw another virulent outbreak of the dreaded Black Death, which claimed no less than a quarter of the already decimated population of England. Its most notable victim was the widely mourned Henry, Duke of Lancaster, who died on March 23 and was buried near the high altar in St. Mary's Church in the Newarke at Leicester, the foundation he himself had handsomely endowed, doubtless intending it to serve as a mausoleum for the House of Lancaster; the church was unfinished at his death, and it was left to John of Gaunt to take Duke Henry's place as its patron and pay for its completion.[44]

Not long afterward, the Duchess of Lancaster also died of plague at Leicester. She too was buried in the Newarke. Losing both her parents at almost the same time must have been a terrible blow to poor Blanche, who was probably pregnant with her second child.

But Duke Henry's death brought about a spectacular change in John of Gaunt's fortunes, for the dead man's great titles and estates were to be divided between his two co-heiresses, whose husbands would inherit them in their right.[45] Not surprisingly, Edward III acted swiftly: Only two days after the Duke expired, in the absence of Matilda of Lancaster, who was in Hainault, John was granted temporary custody of all the duke's lands until a fair division could be made.

Resplendent in "a scarlet robe embroidered with garters of blue taffeta,"[46] John was admitted by the King to the Order of the Garter that April. Edward III had founded this prestigious order of chivalry in 1348, in honor of England's patron saint, St. George, and in emulation of King Arthur's Round Table. Its motto, *Honi soit qui mal y pense* (Evil be to he who evil thinks), is said to have originated when, in the face of much coarse jesting on the part of his courtiers, the King gallantly retrieved the Countess of Salisbury's garter, which had slipped off while she was dancing; the motto was adapted from the words he used to rebuke the onlookers, adding that they would soon see the garter much honored. Membership of the order was limited to the King and twenty-five knights, and admittance to it was one of the highest accolades of chivalry. The Queen herself was an associate member, as a Dame of the Fraternity of the Garter, and one day Katherine Swynford would also be associated with this famous order.

In July 1361 the Lancaster inheritance was apportioned between Matilda and Blanche, by mutual consent.[47] Matilda, who now hastened back to England,[48] succeeded as Countess of Leicester, and Blanche as Countess of Lancaster, Lincoln, and Derby; from henceforth, in right of his wife, John of Gaunt was earl of those counties, and in possession of the vast northern estates that went with these great titles.[49] He also became Lord of Beaufort and Nogent in France, Lord High Steward (or Seneschal) of England (his hereditary right as Earl of Lincoln), and Constable of Chester. Overnight, he had become immensely rich and powerful.

The royal family spent Christmas 1361 at Berkhamsted Castle as guests of the Black Prince and his bride, Joan of Kent, whom he had married in October. The marriage occasioned no little stir within the royal family, because Joan had a scandalous past; Queen Philippa in particular was unhappy about it, although she had attended the wedding. But the Black Prince had been determined to marry Joan.[50] She was "in her time the most beautiful lady in all the realm of England, and the most amorous, famous for the extravagance of her dress," and their precipitate secret wedding suggests that the prince was in love with her—Froissart calls it a love match. As far back as 1348, Edward had given his cousin "Jeanette" a silver beaker; the nickname suggests a long familiarity between them, and of course they would have known each other from childhood. Because of the illicit nature of their marriage—which took place without the King's knowledge, and had to be solemnized a second time after the requisite dispensation was granted—the Pope required the prince and princess to do penance. If it had been unusual for John and Blanche to find love in an arranged union, it was astonishing for the heir to the throne, the most desirable catch in Europe, to marry for love and gain no political or material advantage from it. But despite this, and the misgivings of her in-laws, Joan proved to be a model Princess of Wales, being of a gentle and kindly nature, a peacemaker by inclination, a loyal and loving wife who kept well out of public affairs—and a good friend to John of Gaunt.[51]

It would be the last Christmas the Black Prince was to spend with his family for many years. In July 1362 the King created him Duke of Aquitaine, and he and the princess crossed the sea to take up permanent residence in Bordeaux.

The childless Matilda of Lancaster died unexpectedly in England on April 9, 1362.[52] John of Gaunt had much to gain from her death, for it brought him the other half of the Lancastrian inheritance—his wife Blanche being Matilda's sole heir—and made him the most powerful man in the realm after the King; he would now own about one-third of all England, and enjoy an annual income of approximately £12,803 (£3,442,075), which far exceeded that of any other peer, only a lucky few realizing even £4,000 (£1,075,396).[53]

The acquisition of such wealth—his landed estate was worth £43 billion in today's values—gave rise to the first of the many scurrilous rumors that were to blight John's life. By June 1362, when he and Blanche were touring their new estates and came to Leicester Castle, the "vulgar repute" that Matilda had been poisoned by her brother-in-law was rife.[54] In fact, it appears that the rumors were entirely baseless, and that, like her parents, she had died of plague.[55] But these calumnies never quite went away.

To mark his own fiftieth birthday on November 13, 1362, Edward III formally created John of Gaunt Duke of Lancaster: "and then our lord the King invested his said son John with the sword [and] garbed him with a fur cape and above it a gold circlet"; at the same time, John's brothers Lionel and Edmund, his junior by a year, were created Duke of Clarence and Earl of Cambridge, respectively.[56] From now on John would be known as "Monseigneur de Lancaster."

The Duchy of Lancaster was effectively a state within a state,[57] with lands and property extending mainly across the Midlands, the North, and the Welsh Marches; hundreds of manors, a well-oiled administration, and vast revenues. John was to spend the bulk of his income on maintaining, rebuilding, or remodeling his numerous castles, houses, and estates; keeping his enormous household and retinue; affording the lavish hospitality and gifts expected of a great prince; financing military expeditions and diplomatic trips; and providing for his growing family.

The new duke's establishment now increased in size and splendor to reflect his magnificence. Only the King's was greater. John had his own council, receiver-general, secretariat, and hierarchy of household officers, as well as an army of officials to administer and care for his estates and properties. His household numbered 115 persons, and he maintained the greatest and most powerful noble retinue in the kingdom, "a chivalrous company" of between 160 and 200 men,[58] including between 80 and 125 "highly-regarded knights conspicuous for their courtly and chivalrous skills,"[59] who were required to model themselves on King Arthur's Knights of the Round Table.

They were bound to the duke by indentures, having promised to serve him in times of war and peace in return for more than generous annuities, grants of land, liberal patronage, and the social prestige that came from being allied to so great a magnate. Needless to say, demand for places in the duke's retinue was high. John of Gaunt's retainers and servants sported his livery of white and blue, and the officers of his household wore the famous Lancastrian livery collar of linked S's.

A survey of the ducal warrants shows that John exercised a close degree of personal interest in all aspects of his affairs, and that he was frequently generous, benevolent, and merciful to his bondsmen and tenants, showing himself "in all his actions good and gentle."[60] He ensured that their dwellings were kept in good repair, excused them rents and dues in times of hardship, and willingly permitted them to go on pilgrimage or take holy orders. He distributed £2 (£626) in alms every Friday and Saturday, sent gifts of firewood to the poor lepers of Leicester, and wine to the prisoners in Newgate gaol. He allowed his villeins to perform their service of carrying wood to his castle at Tutbury in summer, to spare them the discomfort of doing it in the winter cold.[61] The chronicler Knighton, who lauded him for his clemency, tells how he refused to hang certain servants who had stolen some of his silver, declaring, "No man should lose his life for my chattels." In the years to come, Katherine Swynford herself would benefit repeatedly from John's open-handedness and consideration.

Thanks to the enormous wealth and power that had come to him through his magnificent marriage, John of Gaunt was for the rest of his life to play a leading role at the center of English—and indeed international—politics. And with the Black Prince in Aquitaine, and Lionel serving as the King's deputy in Ireland, John, at just twenty-two, was now the most important man in England after the monarch himself. Edward III quickly came to rely on him as both a soldier and a diplomat, although it must be said that he was to enjoy considerably more success in the latter capacity. The acquisition of the Lancaster inheritance also gave John the capacity to raise large armies from his estates, and thus play a prominent role in the war with France. At home he was to be active in Parliament and highly influential at court.

It was an honor to serve such a prince, and a signal responsibility to help nurture the ducal children, which is what Katherine de Roët was probably doing at this time. And she would have been kept busy. Around 1362 (or

1364), Blanche bore a son and heir, John, who tragically died young, probably before May 4, 1366, when his mother gave birth to another son who was also named John. The first John was probably still living in 1365, when a second son, Edward, was born; the fact that two of the ducal sons were called John after their father suggests that this was the name of choice for the heir, so we may infer from the use of the name Edward for the second son that the first John still lived when he was born, but that the latter had died by the time the third son was given the same name. This first John was probably the child buried under an arch near the high altar in St. Mary's Church in the Newarke at Leicester.[62] By February 21, 1363, Blanche was also the mother of a second daughter, Elizabeth,[63] having borne three children in fewer than three years.

Like all great medieval households, John of Gaunt's was itinerant, moving around the country to satisfy the demands of politics, estate business, law enforcement, hunting, and the social calendar. The duke himself would ride from house to house, resplendent on his hunting courser, but kept horse-drawn carriages for the use of his wife and children. The whole household went with them, accompanied by a long train of carts, packhorses, and sumpter mules carrying furniture, hangings, household effects, clothing, documents, and the ornaments of the ducal chapel.[64]

Nearly every summer, John made a habit of spending time on his lands in the Midlands and the North. Katherine would soon have become familiar with an array of luxurious Lancastrian residences, including the imposing castles at Kenilworth, Higham Ferrers, Bolingbroke, Tutbury, Knaresborough, and Pontefract—there were more than thirty in all. But for much of the rest of the year, John was at Hertford or in London, and when he was in the capital, he was to be found at his chief residence, the magnificent palace of the Savoy,[65] the pride of his properties and the outward symbol of his greatness. It was here that he entertained visiting royalty and ambassadors, who were invariably suitably impressed by their luxurious surroundings.

The Savoy Palace, that "very fine building on the Thames,"[66] was to figure large in Katherine's life. Standing a mile beyond the western walls of the City of London, among the aristocratic and episcopal mansions that lined the Strand on the Thames side, it occupied a large area that today stretches from Waterloo Bridge to Durham House Street. In those days the Strand was paved as far as the Savoy. The churches of St. Mary-le-Strand and St. Clement Danes stood a little to the northeast, and the convent gardens of Westminster

Abbey (now Covent Garden) were opposite. Further east was the Temple, and beyond it the City of London itself. Immediately to the south of the palace was the London residence of John's "faithful friend," the Bishop of Carlisle; then beyond it, the house of the Bishop of Durham; the cross at Charing, built in memory of Edward I's queen, Eleanor of Castile; the Church of St. Martin-in-the-Fields; and the Hospital of St. Mary of Rouncevalles, which enjoyed John of Gaunt's patronage and stood at the entrance to the present Northumberland Avenue. Beyond it, as the Thames curved south, lay York Place, the town palace of the Archbishops of York, and Westminster, the seat of government, with its imposing royal palace and abbey.

The Savoy Theater (built 1881) and the Savoy Hotel (built 1889) now occupy "the Precinct of the Savoy" in which the palace was sited, and Savoy Street, Savoy Place, Savoy Way, Savoy Steps, Savoy Row, Savoy Court, Savoy Buildings, and Savoy Hill are reminders of it. The Duchy of Lancaster, which is now incorporated in the Crown, still has its offices where the mighty palace once stood, in Lancaster Place by Waterloo Bridge.

Although there had been a mansion on the site as early as 1189, the original Savoy Palace was built by Peter, Count of Savoy, an uncle of Henry III's queen, Eleanor of Provence, in the thirteenth century. In 1245, Peter was granted a parcel of land east of Westminster "in that street called the Strand," and in 1263 raised a palace there. It is his gilded statue that stands above the doorway of the modern Savoy Hotel. In his will he bequeathed this property to the Hospice of St. Bernard, a monastic community in Savoy, from whom Queen Eleanor purchased it for her son, Edmund Crouchback, Earl of Lancaster, in 1284. In the 1350s, at a cost of £35,000 (£13,660,715),[67] his grandson, Henry, Duke of Lancaster, "entirely rebuilt"[68] the Savoy as a sumptuous palace, paying for it out of the profits he had made in the Hundred Years War. In 1357–60, the captive King John II of France enjoyed "a most agreeable" stay at the Savoy, and when he returned to England as a hostage in 1364, he specifically asked to stay there; he died there in April of that year.

The palace was reputed to be the most beautiful and opulent building in England—it was "a marvelous structure unmatched in the kingdom," "the fairest manor in Europe," "unto which there was none in the realm to be compared in beauty, splendor, nobility, and stateliness."[69] It rivaled even the King's great palace at Westminster. It was built on a quadrangular collegiate plan; at its core was a magnificent great hall, which was surrounded by do-

mestic and service ranges erected around courtyards and connected by cloisters and alleyways; the ducal apartments lay behind the great hall, and had
windows facing the river. The whole precinct was surrounded by a fortified
wall, bisected by a massive gateway with a portcullis on the Strand, a smaller
gate next to it for pedestrians, and a river gate at the side. There was a chapel
to the right of the front gateway, a library, a treasure chamber, extensive wine
cellars, accommodation for an army of servants and retainers, stables, orchards, a fish pond, and beautiful rose and vegetable gardens with ornamental rails and flower borders, all sloping down to the Thames; the duke loved
his gardens, and actively involved himself in their planning and maintenance. At the rear of the palace, elegant terraces overlooked the Thames,
which in the fourteenth century was much wider and shallower than it is
today. A low wall ran along the river's edge, and stairs led down to the landing stages, where barges could be moored. With the narrow streets of London so congested, most people preferred to travel by river. John's richly
appointed barges—he bought a new one in 1373—had a master and a crew
of eight oarsmen,[70] and he would use them whenever he wished to visit the
court at Westminster or, later on, the Black Prince at Kennington Palace on
the Surrey shore of the Thames.

John of Gaunt made yet more improvements to the Savoy. He employed
the great master mason, Henry Yevele, whose work can still be seen in Westminster Hall, Westminster Abbey, and Canterbury Cathedral. Yevele was
much in demand, for it was he who refined and improved the new "Perpendicular" style of architecture, with its flattened arches and fan vaulting; he
had worked for the Black Prince at Kennington, and would do so for Edward III and Richard II at Westminster, the Tower of London, Eltham
Palace, Sheen Palace, and Leeds Castle. John of Gaunt also commissioned
Henry Yevele to make improvements to Hertford Castle.

The interiors of the Savoy were sumptuous. The furniture, rich beds,
and headboards—one of which, emblazoned with heraldic shields, was said
to be worth 1,000 marks (£125,221)[71]—French tapestries,[72] silk hangings,
gold and silver plate, stained glass, carpets, cushions, fine napery, and ornaments, all afforded lavish evidence of the duke's immense wealth and superb
taste. His registers record payments for numerous luxury items, including
jeweled goblets, devotional books with gem-encrusted leather bindings, images of the Virgin Mary, sculpted reliefs of the crucifixion, enamels, and rich
silks from Constantinople in the Lancastrian colors of blue and white. The

contents of the palace alone were valued at £10,000 (£3,756,616), and those of the chapel at £500 (£187,831). Nothing survives, but the tapestries must have been similar to those John owned in 1393, which depicted the Frankish King Clovis, Moses confronting Pharaoh, and *The Life of the Lover and the Beloved*. The palace was also the repository for John's priceless treasures, his armor, his furs and cloth of gold, his fabulous collection of jewels and precious stones, and his wardrobe. "No prince in Christendom had a finer wardrobe, and scarcely any could even match it, for there were such quantities of vessels and silver plate that five carts would hardly suffice to carry them."[73] The Savoy also housed the duke's secretariat and many of the written records, deeds, and muniments of his duchy.

Although he had his private apartments, John would have taken his meals in the great hall of his palace, at a table set on the dais or in a window embrasure, accompanied by his *familia*. This word applied not only to his family members, but also to the knights of his retinue, his confessor, and honored guests. The food was prepared by his master cook and an army of helpers, who worked in the various service departments: the kitchen, pantry, buttery, poultry, scullery, and saltery. Dishes served at the ducal table included venison, game, salmon, bream, stockfish, herring, rabbit, poultry, and lampreys. At the great feasts of the year—Christmas, Epiphany, Easter, and Pentecost—the duke's arrival in the hall was heralded by his trumpeters.[74]

There is no way of knowing if the present Savoy Chapel, which is owned by the Queen as Duchess of Lancaster, occupies the site of the original palace chapel, because no plans of the palace survive, and in the early sixteenth century Henry VII "beautifully rebuilt" the Savoy[75] as the Hospital of St. John, for the succor of the poor. This tiny gem of a chapel, which was part of Henry VII's foundation, suffered damage by fire in 1864, and was largely rebuilt in the Perpendicular style the following year by Queen Victoria; since 1937 it has served as the Chapel of the Royal Victorian Order. Interestingly, the Savoy Chapel, like the hospital it served, was originally dedicated to St. John the Baptist, one of John of Gaunt's own name saints.[76]

What was he like, this exalted duke in whose household Katherine lived, and whose amorous interest she would one day ignite? He is known to most people largely through his brief appearance in Shakespeare's *Richard II*, in which "old John of Gaunt, time-honor'd Lancaster" features as a dying elder statesman who makes a famously patriotic speech about the kingdom he has loyally served for many decades:

> This royal throne of kings, this sceptred isle,
> This earth of majesty, this seat of Mars,
> This other Eden, demi-paradise,
> This fortress built by Nature for herself
> Against infection and the hand of war;
> This happy breed of men, this little world,
> This precious stone set in the silver sea . . .
> This blessed plot, this earth, this realm, this England,
> This nurse, this teeming womb of royal kings.

But this is not the sum of the man—far from it, for these sentiments are unlikely to have informed the thinking of the real John of Gaunt, who was a remarkable and complex character, entirely undeserving of the poor reputation cast upon him for centuries by historians and other writers, who mostly followed the calumnies of hostile chroniclers or accepted Sir John Fortescue's fifteenth-century view of John as the oppressive overmighty subject par excellence. For them, he was an unscrupulous and immoral tyrant.[77] It was not until 1904, with the appearance of Sydney Armitage-Smith's monumental biography, that a fairer and more considered view of John of Gaunt emerged.

For better or worse, John of Gaunt made a tremendous impact on the history of England; even today, oral traditions, legends, and folk memories of him still survive throughout the Lancastrian "countries," as his domains were called.[78] His name is writ large in the annals of the age of chivalry. He was the greatest English nobleman of his time.

In appearance, even as a young man, John of Gaunt was commanding. In *The Boke of the Duchesse*, Chaucer gives us a tantalizing glimpse of him at the age of twenty-eight, describing him as "a splendidly looking knight . . . of noble stature" with a "stately manner." Traditionally, it has been asserted that John was unusually tall, because from 1625 it was claimed that a suit of armor measuring six feet eight inches in height, which is still preserved in the Tower of London, had been made for him; in 1699 a visitor to the Tower admired its codpiece, "which was almost as big as a poop-lantern, and better worth a lewd lady's admiration than any piece of antiquity in the Tower";[79] but—sadly for those who relish such "evidence" of the duke's famed virility—it has now been established that this armor dates only from around 1540, was made in Germany, and has nothing to do with John of Gaunt.

The only other surviving description of John is to be found in the Portuguese chronicle written by Fernão Lopes, whose account was based on the recollections of people who had known the duke. According to this he was "a man with his limbs well-built and straight"; spare and lean, "he did not seem to have as much flesh as was required by the height of his body," yet he was vigorous and healthy, as befit a warrior who played a prominent part in no fewer than a dozen military and naval campaigns,[80] and had "high majestic features and piercing eyes." Surviving representations of "this vial full of Edward's sacred blood"[81] depict a hollow-cheeked, bearded man with the angular bone structure and aristocratic aquiline nose of the Plantagenets. In youth, John probably looked young for his years: in 1368, Chaucer thought he was twenty-four, when he was actually twenty-eight, but then he was "not bushy-bearded at this stage."

There are several surviving images that enable us to gain some idea of what John of Gaunt looked like. The earliest known contemporary picture of him was in a mural depicting Edward III, his family, and St. George adoring the Virgin. This once adorned a wall at the eastern end of St. Stephen's Chapel in the Palace of Westminster, and was painted after 1355, since Thomas of Woodstock, the King's youngest son, who was born that year, is included. In no sense were these portraits. Like his father and brothers, John appears in armor, kneeling. Although the faces of each of the eighteen-inch-high figures are all different, John's is a blank, for the paint had perished before the picture was copied.[82] This mural, hidden under paneling for centuries, was discovered in 1800, only to be covered up again almost immediately and then destroyed in the fire that burned down the palace in 1834. It is known only through colored drawings made from tracings in 1800, which were engraved by Richard Smirke for the Society of Antiquaries of London.

John also appeared in armor on his tomb effigy, but the only surviving drawings of his lost tomb depict the effigy that replaced the original in the sixteenth century.[83] His seal as King of Castile and León shows him enthroned, bearded, and wearing a coronet over his chin-length hair. This is a conventional image of a king rather than a portrait.[84]

There is a contemporary colored miniature of John of Gaunt in the Liber

Benefactorum of St. Albans Abbey, which dates from ca. 1380. It shows him at prayer, wearing a long gold and pink robe embroidered in red, with a gold collar, four large buttons down the front, red undersleeves, and red boots; he sports wavy reddish-brown hair—again chin length—crowned by a gold coronet, wears a fashionable forked beard, and has somewhat florid features, the delineation of which suggests that the artist, a lay illuminator named Alan Strayler, knew what his subject looked like. John was about forty at this time.[85]

There are posthumous stained-glass portraits of John of Gaunt in the chapel of All Souls College, Oxford, executed in 1437, and in the St. Cuthbert memorial window in York Minster, which dates from ca. 1440.[86] Parts of the head in the All Souls glass were replaced in the seventeenth century, but in both windows he is portrayed with the same forked beard as in the St. Albans miniature and bears a remarkable resemblance to his father, Edward III, as he appears in the effigy on his tomb in Westminster Abbey. The small statue of John as a weeper on that tomb, which dates from the same period as the St. Albans miniature, also shows him with a forked beard and long gown. The beard would have been kept trimmed by the duke's barber, Godfrey.[87]

A panel portrait in oils of John of Gaunt, wearing armor and helm, in which his finely chiseled facial features bear a striking similarity to those in other representations of him, is in the collection of his descendant, the Duke of Beaufort, at Badminton. Once thought to have been painted from life in 1390, we now know it was executed between 1600 and 1650. It is ascribed to a Dutch artist, Luca Cornelli, of whom nothing more has been discovered; it was once claimed erroneously that he was a court painter to Henry VIII. There is a possibility that this vivid portrait is based on a lost original; interestingly, John is identified by his arms as King of Castile and León, and by the heraldic symbols of those kingdoms—a castle and three lions. As he renounced his claims to Castile and León in 1388, one would expect any later portrait to refer to him simply as Duke of Lancaster, so this portrait might possibly be a copy of one executed from life before 1388. Richard II, in whose reign such an original would have been painted, pioneered the novel art of royal portraiture in England, commissioning, in ca. 1395 or later, the *Wilton Diptych* and the commanding full-length portrait of himself enthroned that is now in Westminster Abbey. There may well have been other portraits of the King that did not survive, so it is not beyond the bounds of belief that an artist working in England under his patronage might also have painted John of Gaunt, the foremost lord in the realm, and that the Cornelli is a copy of that lost original. Alternatively, since the pose is more typical of the seventeenth than the fourteenth century, the artist could have used John's funeral effigy in St. Paul's as a model.

John dressed stylishly and elegantly, even magnificently, but there was an element of well-bred restraint about his clothes, unusual in that age of brash display. "His garments were not full wide," observed Thomas Hoccleve, but they did reflect his elevated status; like most aristocrats of the period, he loved ceremony, ritual, and the outward trappings of rank.

John was reserved and dignified in character, a proud man who was ever conscious of the gravitas of his high estate. According to the laudatory Chandos Herald, he "had many virtues." Courteous and charming, he "spoke well, very measured, temperately and with good judgment, being self-controlled and good-humored."[88] Skilled in logic and rhetoric, he was a powerful orator and accomplished at debating; Froissart calls him "wise and imaginative," and the author of the *Anonimalle Chronicle* describes him arguing his point in Parliament "in good form, as if he was a man of law." Edward III himself paid tribute to the "probity, activity, and excelling wisdom of his dearest son John." A great traditionalist, the duke was conventional in his tastes and outlook, and reactionary in his views. Rarely did he abuse his power. Instead, he was liberal, generous, prudent, thoughtful, and above all possessed of a strong sense of honor and firm principles. He never shirked his obligations or responsibilities, nor failed in his duty. He was applauded for his sense of fair play, and once won golden opinions when he threatened to hang a cheating duelist as a traitor.[89] For him, the laws of chivalry were sacrosanct, and he tried all his life to remain true to his knightly oath while modestly protesting, "I am no great knight myself." Yet, he added, "My greatest delight is hearing of gallant deeds of arms."[90]

The duke did not take kindly to criticism or to being contradicted. When provoked, he was quick to explode with anger or act on impulse, being "jealous of honor, sudden and quick in quarrel." He was capable of using "great harsh words" in Parliament,[91] and could be peremptory when giving orders: "Get this done without any slip-up," he once commanded, or "Make sure this is done in such a manner, understanding that, if it is disrupted, we would not wish to impute the blame to you; and do not neglect this, as you wish to avoid upsetting us."[92] His grand manner often made him appear haughty, autocratic, aloof, and even intimidating, which did not endear him to his envious contemporaries, and alienated a number of his fellow nobles. But he cared little for that—public opinion was rarely of concern to him. Because of his wealth and power, he had no need to court favor or heed resentment.

Chaucer, however, found John to be a "wonder and well-faring knight" who was "so treatable, right wonder skillful, and reasonable" that he put the poet at his ease "and got me acquaint with him."[93]

> How kindly spoke this knight,
> Without false style or sense of rank;
> . . . I felt that he was too frank,
> And found him most approachable,
> And very wise and reasonable.

This suggests that John was more relaxed and outgoing among those he knew well. He could be engagingly self-deprecating, candidly confessing to his own faults, such as having "a head and memory feeble at remembering."[94] And he was willing to be flexible, and to heed advice that ran contrary to his own inclinations.[95]

John was undoubtedly ambitious. His birth, connections, wealth, and landed status made him an important player, not only on the English political stage, but in the arena of European politics, where he was to carve out for himself a major role. Later, ill-informed people in England, misled by his overbearing hauteur and distrustful of his vast power and wealth, would often express suspicion of John's ambition and where it might lead him, but abroad it was a different story, for these very characteristics made him widely admired throughout Europe. The distrust was misplaced, for his loyalty to the Crown and his patriotism were astonishingly unshakable, and for all his life he was a mighty champion and defender of royal authority and prestige. "The King had no more faithful servant than himself, and he would follow wherever he would lead."[96]

John's loyalty and steadfastness extended to his friends and was evident even when such friendships compromised his reputation, as was the case with John Wycliffe. He was true and decent to his family too, and set much store by "the natural ties of kinship." He clearly held his parents and siblings in deep affection and respect; he became a devoted and caring father, and was to prove steadfast in love for many years to two women in turn. He was generous to them and to those close to him: Much of the money in his privy purse was spent on personal gifts carefully chosen by himself.

Although he was not violent by nature—unlike his brother the Black Prince—John was a courageous, dedicated, and energetic soldier. "His campaigns were always physically arduous to himself," wrote Froissart. He was also a competent and prudent commander who was at his best when laying siege to a town. But for various reasons, not all his fault, military success continually eluded him, and he was to prove far more fortunate and productive in the fields of diplomacy and politics than as a military leader, for he possessed "admirable judgment" and "a brilliant mind."[97] Nonetheless, Froissart ranked him with Edward III, the Black Prince, and Duke Henry among the "valiant *chevaliers*" of the age.

"The pious Duke," as the admiring Knighton calls him, was a devout Catholic with orthodox views and as conventional in his observance of religion as he was in all other things. He evinced a deep devotion to his patron saint, St. John the Baptist, as well as St. Cuthbert and the Virgin Mary.[98] A hugely generous benefactor, he endowed monastic houses, collegiate churches, and friaries—the Carmelites were especially favored by him, and he chose all his confessors from their order.[99] He was also a munificent patron of St. Albans Abbey, and in its Liber Benefactorum it is recorded that "this Prince had an extreme love and affection for our monastery and Abbot, and greatly enriched the church with his magnificent and oft-repeated oblations."[100] He sent food and firewood to poor parish priests in his domains, rebuilt their churches and parsonages, and ensured they were kept in repair. However, his concern about abuses within the Church and his resentment of the corrupt power of wealthy ecclesiastics led him to adopt an anticlerical stance that was to prove controversial.

In his leisure hours John loved above all to go hunting; he owned numerous chases, forests, and parks, and took great pains to keep them well maintained, and his itinerary was usually tailored to availing himself of their sport at the appropriate season.[101] He was equally passionate about falconry, and his mews, stocked with costly birds, were renowned throughout Europe.[102]

Where indoor pursuits were concerned, he enjoyed games of dice and, like Blanche, had literary interests. He was indeed an intelligent, cultivated, and accomplished man with refined and sophisticated tastes. In youth, Chaucer tells us, he had studied "science, art, and letters."[103] He shared an interest in astronomy with Chaucer himself and with Joan of Kent, and in 1386, Nicholas of Lynn dedicated his *Kalendarium* to John.[104]

The duke patronized artists, funded poor scholars at the universities, was an active patron of Corpus Christi College, Cambridge, and appointed masters to grammar schools.[105] He loved music and employed talented choristers, musicians, and minstrels in his chapel and household. To judge by their names, his company of minstrels were of Flemish or Hainaulter origin. His musicians played on the pipes, clarions, and "nakers," an early form of kettledrum, with drumsticks of silver.[106] According to Chaucer, John, in his youth, wrote songs that he himself admitted "fell short."[107]

He spoke Norman French on a daily basis, read French with ease, had a good grasp of English—in 1363 he became the first person ever to open Parliament in that language—and must have learned some Flemish from his mother, but he was also apparently well-tutored in Latin, and enjoyed reading the classics as well as contemporary romance literature;[108] we have seen that he kept a library at the Savoy, although there is no surviving record of its contents. He is not known to have directly patronized Chaucer, but would have been familiar with his works—for reasons that will shortly become clear—and Chaucer probably wrote *The Boke of the Duchesse* with him in mind, knowing that John and his circle would appreciate its literary significance and understand its allegorical and mythological allusions. Chaucer later addressed a short poem entitled "Fortune" to "three or two" princes—probably John and his brothers Edmund of Langley and Thomas of Woodstock—in the knowledge that they would know who he was talking about when he referred to Socrates; and it was claimed in the fifteenth century, by the copyist John Shirley, that John himself had commissioned another of Chaucer's poems, "The Complaint of Mars,"[109] although this cannot be substantiated.

It has also been suggested that John commissioned the epic courtly poem *Sir Gawain and the Green Knight*, which was written in York or the northern Midlands, in Lancastrian territory, possibly around 1375, but again there is no proof to support this claim. John could certainly discriminate between good and bad poetry—when a monk, Walter of Peterborough, seeking a reward, dedicated a dreadful piece of doggerel to him in 1367, he pointedly ignored it.[110]

This was the "magnificent lord" whose wife Katherine now served, and whose children she would care for. She must have seen and perhaps conversed with him frequently when he was at home and visiting the duchess's apartments or presiding over meals in the great hall, and doubtless she was as in awe of him as most people were. She was, after all, just a young teenager at the time. She may well have found him attractive and admired him from afar, yet there is nothing to show that she was anything to him at this time. Quite the contrary, for the evidence we have strongly suggests that he had eyes only for his beautiful wife. Katherine could therefore never have dreamed that the duke's fancy would one day fix itself upon her, and anyway, she had other things to occupy her mind, not the least of which was marriage.

THREE

The Trap of Wedding

B y 1363, Katherine de Roët had entered her teens, and her beauty, which would one day be so famous, was becoming evident.

The epitaph on John of Gaunt's tomb in Old St. Paul's Cathedral, which was lost in the Great Fire of 1666, described Katherine as *eximia pulchritudine feminam*—"extraordinarily beautiful and feminine." This epitaph was not contemporary, but placed on the restored sepulchre in the reign of Henry VII, who wanted to restore the good reputation of this rather dubious ancestress. It is unusual to find words of this kind in an epitaph—the emphasis is usually on virtue and good works—but since Henry VII could hardly laud Katherine's virtue, it is possible that he ordered reference to be made to her beauty because it was one of the things people remembered her for, and it may even have been referred to in the original tomb inscription, destroyed well within living memory.

It has long been claimed that there are no adequate surviving pictorial representations of Katherine. The only one we can say for certain is meant to be her is Dugdale's crude seventeenth-century sketch of her lost brass in Lincoln Cathedral, done before the desecrations of the civil war. In no way could this be described as a portrait. It is a formalized line drawing of a woman in a widow's veil and wimple.[1]

Two tiny carved heads in the Pulpitum in Canterbury Cathedral, each no bigger than a walnut and dating from around 1400, have been identified—on questionable grounds—as Katherine Swynford and John of Gaunt.[2] They are said to have closed eyes to indicate that both had passed away, but this may be a fanciful interpretation because pupils were not always incised in facial sculpture of the period. Two of John of Gaunt's sons were later buried in the cathedral, but in both cases sometime after the probable date of these carvings, so no link is feasible. Even if this identification were correct, neither head could be said to be a portrait.[3]

Because we have a good idea of what John of Gaunt looked like, we might search for evidence of physical features perhaps inherited from Katherine in the surviving tomb effigies of three of their children. These may be fairly accurate likenesses, for from the fourteenth century, sculptors attempted to portray their subjects realistically: Effigies of Philippa of Hainault, Edward III (based on his death mask), Richard II, and Anne of Bohemia are good examples. It has been claimed that a portrait of a cardinal by Jan Van Eyck is Katherine's son, Henry Beaufort, and while that attribution cannot be proved, the face is round and fleshy, where John of Gaunt's was long and thin, with aquiline features and a straight nose that were inherited by his daughter Elizabeth and his great-granddaughter Margaret Beaufort, the mother of Henry VII. By contrast, the effigies of Katherine's children all have round or oval faces, which they perhaps inherited from their mother.

Writers and historians have long—and fruitlessly—searched the poems of Chaucer for allusions to his famous sister-in-law, Katherine Swynford. Silva-Vigier, in her biography of John of Gaunt, thought it was not fanciful to suggest that the young Katherine was the model for the beautiful Virginia, the heroine of "The Physician's Tale."

> The maiden was fourteen, on whose array
> Nature had spent her care with such delight.
> For, just as she can paint a lily white,
> Redden a rose and teach it to unfurl
> Her petals, so she touched this noble girl
> Ere she was born; her limbs so lissom she

Had touched with colours where they ought to be;
Phoebus her mass of tresses with a gleam
Had dyed in burnish from his golden stream;
And if her beauty was beyond compare,
Her virtue was a thousand times more rare.

Sadly, there is nothing in these lines specifically to link them to Katherine. By the time they were written, her affair with John of Gaunt was notorious, and her reputation such that Chaucer could hardly have gotten away with that last line. Nor does the poem tell us much about Virginia except that she was beautiful and golden-haired, attributes that several young girls Chaucer knew probably had.

Yet Katherine too may have been golden-haired, and we may indeed possess something approaching a likeness of her. An early fifteenth-century illuminated frontispiece to a manuscript of Chaucer's *Troilus and Criseyde*[4] shows the poet reciting his work to the court of Richard II. The identity of the courtiers ranged about him has been the subject of much learned discussion: One of the figures is clearly supposed to be King Richard (with the face rubbed out), his first queen, Anne of Bohemia, is said to be next to him, wearing a pink gown; one of the five well-dressed men in the foreground is probably John of Gaunt; and a lady in a blue gown trimmed with ermine, kneeling in the front, has been tentatively identified as Joan of Kent, the King's mother.[5] It has also been suggested that the lady seated next to her, attired in a flowing blue gown called a "houppelande"—which has long hanging sleeves, a wide stand-up collar lined with white fabric, and a gold girdle clasped beneath the breasts—is Katherine.[6] She has a round face, fashionably high forehead, and blond plaits coiled high above each temple and roped around the crown of her head.

There are problems with this theory. Chaucer probably wrote *Troilus and Criseyde* between 1385 and 1388, by which time Joan of Kent was dead. Even so, the manuscript was not produced until early in the fifteenth century, and so would likely depict courtiers who were prominent toward the close of Richard II's reign. The lady in pink next to the faceless man identified— probably correctly—as Richard may actually be his child-queen, Isabella of Valois; it was common for children to be represented as adults in an age that did not fully understand realism or perspective. Almost certainly John of Gaunt is one of the five well-dressed men, probably the dignified bearded man in striking red robes standing to the left. At the end of Richard's reign, Katherine was his duchess, and as such the second lady in the land; thus the prominent female figure in the ermine and gold trimmed tight-fitting blue gown, whose dress clearly marks her as being a royal lady of some importance, must be her. The fair girl in blue to the left, hitherto tentatively identified as Katherine Swynford, looks too young to be a woman of at least forty-six; her position next to Katherine Swynford, who has an arm around her, and in front of the man who may be John of Gaunt, suggests she was perhaps their daughter, Joan Beaufort; indeed, her image bears a close resemblance to Joan Beaufort's tomb effigy, which suggests that the painter had seen his subjects.

Other evidence supports this identification: In the fifteenth century the manuscript was owned by Joan's daughter, Anne Neville, Countess of Stafford, having probably been bequeathed to her by Joan, Chaucer's own niece, for whom it had almost certainly been made.[7] It would therefore be natural for Joan's parents to be conspicuously depicted in it, and for Joan to be shown with them. Later evidence (which will be discussed elsewhere) strongly suggests that Joan was committed to rehabilitating Katherine's reputation, and emphasizing her mother's importance as second lady in the realm by having her portrayed as the most prominent female figure in the picture would be a logical consequence.

Bearing this in mind, there are sound reasons for believing that this ermine-and-blue-clad lady in the *Troilus* frontispiece is Katherine, and thus we may have come, at last, face-to-face with her. If so, she was fair-haired and buxom, with a tiny waist, high stomach, and wide hips, a woman ideally proportioned to suit fashionable notions of the female figure in that era. Her neck was long, her face round with a high forehead, and her hair elegantly swept up and pinned beneath a golden coronet, which in itself identifies her rank. If she looked as voluptuously handsome as this when she was in her late forties, it is easy to see why John of Gaunt had been so taken with her charms a quarter of a century earlier, and why her beauty became legendary.

Much of what we can glean of Katherine's character and interests has to be inferred from the fragmentary sources that have come down to us; we have to look beyond the scathing criticisms of monastic chroniclers shocked by her liaison with the duke to the sounder evidence found in less sensational records. It is noteworthy that her worst critics, Thomas Walsingham and the anonymous author of the *Anonimalle Chronicle*, were men who did not know her personally, while Walsingham had an ulterior motive for reviling her, as will become clear. Henry Knighton, the Leicester chronicler whose house was under the patronage of John of Gaunt, and who may well have met Katherine, has nothing bad to say about her personally, and it is clear that she maintained good relations with the Chapter of Lincoln Cathedral throughout her adult life, and that they were happy to lease a house to her during the years of her ill fame.[8]

In fact, most of what we can surmise or know of Katherine Swynford suggests she was a remarkable, attractive, fascinating, and sympathetic woman. An early request for a private altar strongly suggests a devout religious faith instilled in childhood. In contrast, her long love affair with John of Gaunt implies allure, sensuality, charm, loyalty, emotional depth, and perhaps forwardness and a degree of ambition. She must have relished the material benefits that were to come her way as a result of John's devotion, but she does not seem to have been the most demanding of mistresses, and it is doubtful that she was much driven by mercenary motives: Her love for John was to survive concealment, long separations, social ostracism, and public vilification, which argues that it was deep and true. Her admirable discretion and tact helped smooth the path of the lovers, and when tragedy and loss struck, she had sufficient wisdom and strength of character to survive with dignity. We will learn that she cherished strong family ties and was concerned about how others saw her. She was to prove capable, responsible, caring, and successful in nearly all her enterprises.

A warm and kindly heart may be evident in Katherine's lasting love for John and in her apparent affection for children, her own and all those who came into her orbit. She was clearly good with the young and had, it seems, an innate sensitivity that made it possible for her to create unity from disparity—witness the successful bonding of the legitimate heirs of the House of Lancaster with Katherine's own children, her bastards by John of Gaunt, and the Chaucers, bonds that surmounted the barriers and taboos created by adultery, death, rank, and illegitimacy. Much of this was doubtless due to the powerful influence of the duke, but we must surely also give Katherine a great deal of the credit for it.

All this suggests that she learned much from the examples and influence of Queen Philippa and Duchess Blanche. Froissart said of her in later life that she was "a woman of such bringing up and honorable demeanour" that she was "well-deserving" of the respect of those about her. The undoubted esteem in which she was held in the Lancastrian household, and by three kings of England, argues that her integrity and other qualities were recognized, and that she was skilled in courtly accomplishments, sophisticated in her tastes, sociable, courteous, literate, intelligent, and a good conversationalist. Katherine would have to be most of these things to become such a respected member of the duchess's entourage, and later to attract and hold the attention of the duke. She would also have absorbed the cultivated ambience of the ducal court, in which John of Gaunt actively promoted the education of women and encouraged a love of learning in his wives and daughters.[9]

It was not unusual for members of royal households to marry each other, nor was it surprising that the husband chosen for Katherine de Roët, a servant of the Duchess of Lancaster, should have been a retainer of the Duke of Lancaster. His name was Sir Hugh Swynford,[10] and he was lord of the manors of Coleby and Kettlethorpe in Lincolnshire. The choice of Hugh Swynford suggests that the marriage was arranged by the duke himself at his wife's insistence. Possibly Queen Philippa was consulted, for it was she who had placed the Roët girl with the Lancasters. Marriage to one of John of Gaunt's retainers would certainly have strengthened Katherine's ties to the House of Lancaster.

The Swynford family was an old one, although claims that its ancestry could be traced back to Anglo-Saxon times[11] are unsubstantiated. Hugh's forebears probably came from Swinford—originally Swine's Ford—in Leicestershire, but there is no record of them there in Domesday Book. The family had many branches, and there are numerous references in medieval records to its early members, but attempts to discover their exact relationships and make any sense of the family genealogy prior to the fourteenth century have so far proved largely fruitless.[12]

The only one of Hugh's forebears of whose relationship to him we can be certain is his father, Thomas Swynford, who was probably the son of Robert de Swynford of Burgate, Suffolk, whose arms were the same three gold boars' heads on a field of silver as Hugh Swynford displayed.[13] By 1343, Sir Robert Swynford had sold the manor of Burgate; this would have left his heirs landless and might well explain why, in August 1345, Sir Thomas

Swynford acquired from the de Cuppledyke family[14] the manor of Coleby in Lincolnshire, which he held in chief of the King and in part of John of Gaunt, in whose Honor of Richmond it lay.[15]

Sir Thomas married Nichola, the widow of Sir Ralph Basset of Weldon.[16] From the mid-1340s until 1356 we find him appointed in turn to the shrievalties of Bedfordshire, Buckinghamshire, and Rutland, while in 1344 he was a commissioner of the peace in Bedfordshire, and in 1345–47 an escheator for that county and for Buckinghamshire.[17] Far from keeping the peace, he appears to have rather thrown his weight about: In 1356, he and his falconers caused chaos hunting pigeons on the manor of Barton, in defiance of the reeve's protests.[18]

That year, Thomas bought from John de la Croy (or Croix) the manor of Kettlethorpe in Lincolnshire,[19] which was to become the chief seat of the Swynfords until 1498; it would also be Katherine's marital home and become forever associated with her. Kettlethorpe was not far from Coleby, which Thomas had held since 1345. In 1357, Thomas and Nichola settled permanently in Lincolnshire,[20] where Sir Thomas again served as a commissioner for the peace.

Hugh Swynford—who is incorrectly named as Otes Swynford in Weever's description of the inscription on Paon de Roët's tomb in St. Paul's, in which Philippa de Roët is erroneously called Anne—had been born in 1340 at the latest; his father's Inquisition Postmortem of December 1361, taken in Lincoln, gives his age as twenty-one years and more.[21] This made him at least a decade older than Katherine, and possibly the same age as his master, the duke.

Hugh was a soldier by profession—"a shrewd and terrifying fighter"[22]— and would appear to have begun his career in royal service as a retainer of the Black Prince, for in 1356 he fought under the prince at Poitiers, and perhaps was knighted afterward. It was probably after the Black Prince removed to Aquitaine in 1361 that Hugh had transferred to the retinue of his feudal overlord, the Duke of Lancaster, to whom he owed knight's service.[23] It was as well that he did, for when his father, Thomas Swynford, died on November 3, 1361,[24] Hugh came into only a poor inheritance and would have badly needed the money he received as the duke's retainer and any profits he could make from campaigning. Almost certainly he would also have begun looking about him for a wife to bear him heirs and hopefully boost his social standing and his finances. Hugh had little to offer beyond his knightly status, so

Katherine de Roët, the alluring object and recipient of royal esteem and favor, with her family connections and her inheritance in Hainault, would probably have appeared an ideal choice.

For a long time, historians, basing their conclusions on the likely birth date of her son, assumed that Katherine was married to Sir Hugh Swynford around 1366–67. Yet we know that she was the mother of a daughter named Blanche, who was old enough to be placed in the train of the Lancastrian princesses before 1368, and it appears that Katherine was probably also the mother of one Margaret Swynford, who was of sufficient age to become a nun in 1377.[25] Of course, girls sometimes entered convents in their tender years—witness Mary, a daughter of Edward I, who became a novice at Amesbury Abbey in 1284, at the age of six; or Bridget, the youngest daughter of Edward IV, who was perhaps seven when she was placed in Dartford Priory around 1487. But it was more usual for girls to be adolescents of thirteen or fourteen at the time of their reception.[26] It would seem that there was a tradition of offering Roët daughters to God—witness the cloistering of Elizabeth de Roët and the eldest daughter of Katherine's sister Philippa; therefore, if Margaret became a nun at the usual age, and Blanche was the eldest child of Katherine and Hugh, it is likely that the Swynfords were married no later than 1362, not long after Hugh came into his inheritance and Katherine reached marriageable age. Certainly they were joined in wedlock before January 24, 1365, as an entry of that date in Bishop Buckingham's register refers to Katherine by her married name.[27] Their marriage may have taken place in one of the ducal chapels—even perhaps the magnificent chapel of the Savoy.[28]

Once married, Katherine's arms of three silver wheels on a red background would have been displayed impaling those of her husband, which were three golden boars' heads on a black chevron with a silver background. These are the arms that appeared on her seal of ca. 1377, which no longer survives.[29]

It used to be said[30] that Katherine married into an ancient landed aristocratic house. Although it is true that the Swynford family was old-established in Lincolnshire, Northamptonshire, Huntingdonshire, Essex, and Suffolk, it was hardly landed and certainly not aristocratic, for its members never rose above the rank of knight. In fact, Hugh was impoverished. He held only two manors, neither of which was profitable, and both had been recently acquired by his father[31]—hardly ancient wealth by any reckoning, as Katherine was to discover when Hugh first took her to his manor house at Kettlethorpe, which after his marriage he held jointly with his new wife of the King and John Buckingham, Bishop of Lincoln.[32]

Kettlethorpe was to become inextricably linked to Katherine in her own lifetime; for forty years she was known as the Lady of Kettlethorpe, and her memory is very much alive there today for the many visitors who make the journey—some would say pilgrimage—to this pretty, quiet, but rather isolated Lincolnshire village, which is situated about twenty feet above sea level and lies twelve miles west of Lincoln, just north of the border with Nottinghamshire. The River Trent flows west of Kettlethorpe, and the Fossdyke meanders along its eastern and northern boundaries. It is "a romantic spot, embowered by trees."[33]

The manor took its name from a Viking said to have settled there in the ninth century, Lincolnshire being part of the Danelaw in Saxon times. His name was Ketil, and the place he lived in became known as Ketil's Thorpe (or village), which over time became corrupted to Kettlethorpe. There is no mention of the settlement in Domesday Book, so it must have been very small, if indeed it still existed in 1086, in which case the story of the Viking settler may have been an oral tradition preserved in local places such as nearby Newton-on-Trent, which is on record as a Domesday village. In fact, there is no mention of Kettlethorpe in historical documents until 1220. The de la Croy family had come into possession of it by 1287.

The present Kettlethorpe Hall incorporates fragments of the medieval house that Katherine knew, and is still surrounded by a moat. All that survives of the original hall are interior walls in the two barrel-vaulted cellars, the remains of a passage from those cellars that is reputed to have led to the church opposite, a blocked fourteenth-century doorway and some stonework on the southern elevations, a few carved heads, and, standing apart, a ruined yet imposing fourteenth-century embattled and buttressed stone gatehouse with sunken moldings, a survival probably from the 1370s, when Katherine was converting Kettlethorpe into a residence of some magnificence. The gatehouse was reconstructed in the early eighteenth century, but not entirely successfully: The lower stones were reassembled authentically enough, but the upper parts owe much to the imagination of the builder who carried out the restoration. To the left is a medieval mounting block, three steps high. We might imagine Katherine standing by it with a stirrup cup, bidding Sir Hugh farewell as he rode off to war.

When Katherine came to Kettlethorpe, after living in luxurious royal palaces since her childhood, she must surely have been dismayed by its poverty. The place was in serious disrepair. Even in 1372, after having lived there on and off for the best part of a decade, it was "ruinous, and the land sandy and stony and out of cultivation"; the only crops it would support were hay, flax, and hemp, while the meadow was frequently flooded by the overflow from the nearby River Trent.

As lord of the manor, Hugh had the right to appoint priests to the twelfth-century parish church of St. Peter and St. Paul that stood to the north of the house,[34] a privilege that Katherine herself would one day exercise. In March 1362, Hugh presented one Robert de Northwood as rector. Katherine would have had frequent dealings with Northwood, who may have acted as her confessor when she was at Kettlethorpe; and because the manor population was small, she probably came to know everyone else quite well too.

Kettlethorpe had appurtenances in the nearby villages of Laughterton, Newton-on-Trent, and Fenton, all of which lay about a mile distant in different directions. In all, the Swynford holdings in the area comprised around three thousand acres, most of which was forest—prime hunting ground for the lords of the manor.[35] And we may be certain that when she was not pregnant, Katherine, like most ladies of rank, rode out with her husband and helped to put food on the table.

Kettlethorpe was Sir Hugh Swynford's chief residence, but not far off was his manor of Coleby, spectacularly perched high up on the Lincoln Cliff escarpment, commanding beautiful views of the Witham valley. It lay seven miles south of Lincoln, to the west of Ermine Street, the old Roman road that ran from London to Lincoln and York. The manor, which Hugh and Katherine now held jointly, was divided into two equal parts, each comprising roughly ninety acres of land and fifteen acres of pasture. In 1367 it was recorded that the part of this manor known as the South Hall, or Southall, which yielded 54s.4d (£785) each year in rents paid by free tenants, was held of John of Gaunt as Earl of Richmond by service, or rent, of 2s (£29) per annum or "a sorrel sparrowhawk." The other part of the manor, the North Hall, or Northall, was held in chief of the King, by service of half a knight's fee; as far back as 1086 the manor of "Colebi" had been recorded in Domesday Book as the property of the Crown. Earlier, like Kettlethorpe, it had been a Danish settlement, under a man called Koli, from whom it took its name; and earlier still, it may have been colonized by the Romans, for it is near Ermine Street and Roman coins have been found in the vicinity. Much later, in the twelfth century, the manor had been held by William the Lyon, King of Scots. At that time, a Gilbertine priory dedicated to St. Katherine was established in the village. A windmill—probably one of several—was in existence in 1361.

Hugh could never have relied on receiving the rents due from his Coleby tenants, for there was little prospect of any yield, let alone a surplus, from the land, which was poor. In 1361, when he inherited it, Coleby was a dismal place, worth only 37s.10d (£601), less than a third of its value than when Sir Thomas Swynford bought it in 1345. "The soil is hard, stony, and uncultivated because of its barrenness, the dovecote and windmill are in ruins," and no profit could be raised from them until they were repaired; the meadow was hard, choked with brambles, and too dry to be of any benefit.[36] Given these circumstances, Hugh's tenants may not always have found the means to pay their rents, which might explain why, a decade later, in 1372, the manor was still barren and impoverished and worth nothing.

Apart from the Saxon church with its later medieval additions—the spire is fifteenth century—no buildings from Katherine's time survive in Coleby. The earliest is Old House in the High Street, which is Tudor. The original manor house was the North Hall, which lay two hundred meters north of the village and had been built in the eleventh century by the then lady of the manor, Judith of Boulogne, Countess of Northumbria and Huntingdon, a niece of William the Conqueror and the ancestress of William the Lyon. The present Coleby Hall, built in 1628, stands on the site of the North Hall, and its walls were raised on the stone foundations of the earlier building. In 1372, in a royal writ assigning Katherine her dower, the North Hall was described as having at the west end of its great hall "a chamber called the West Chamber," a wardrobe for the storage of clothes, jewels, and other personal items, and le faux chambre, which literally translates as "the false room"; one is tempted to wonder if this was just an alcove (which is not a proper room) or if there was a concealed room leading off the West Chamber. Underneath these chambers were cellars for the storage of provisions. There was a kitchen, which was perhaps at the eastern end of the hall, a cow house, and an adjoining croft known as Belgarthes: "the fair sward." The western chambers of the hall overlooked part of the garden. Nearby was the Saxon church of All Saints.[37] It was a far cry from the Savoy.

Only a few miles from Kettlethorpe and Coleby lies the great city of Lincoln, which Katherine came to know—and probably love—very well: Her husband's family was well-known in its civic society, she herself would reside there for several years, and at least one of her children was born there.

In the fourteenth century Lincoln was a rich and prosperous city, dramatically situated on a high ridge. It was dominated by its castle, built by William the Conqueror in 1068, and its spectacular cathedral. Between the two lay the upper town center—"the Bail"—and surrounding the cathedral was the walled close with its substantial clergy houses and splendid twelfth-century Bishop's Palace, which boasted three halls. The close was accessed from the Bail through the now-ruined Exchequer Gate. Just beyond the gate, Steep Hill sloped dizzyingly down to the lower parts of the town, which were known as "the City," and on that hill stood two twelfth-century Norman houses, one of them the famous Jew's House, as well as several other notable buildings. The medieval Guildhall stood near the bottom of Steep Hill. Lincoln was a great trading center, annually hosted six fairs, and boasted fifty churches.

Lincoln Castle, in which extensive Norman buildings still survive within the walls, was then surrounded by deep ditches and high banks. Its main entrance was to the east, facing the Exchequer Gate, while the western gate of the castle led to open countryside. The shell keep was known as St. Lucy's Tower, and stood on a mound raised around 1200. In the thirteenth century a vaulted, horseshoe-shaped tower known as Cobb Hall had been inserted into the north curtain wall of the castle. In Katherine's day the castle precincts were part of the Bail.

Lincoln Cathedral was at that time the third largest in England. The original Norman structure was destroyed by a fire in 1141 and an earthquake in 1185, and rebuilt from 1192 onward in the Early English style by St. Hugh, Bishop of Lincoln. In Katherine's time the cathedral was a massive edifice with three Perpendicular towers and a magnificent west front adorned with myriad sculptured figures; solid on its high hill, it soared majestically over the city and could be seen for miles around. Pilgrims came flocking to make their devotions at the wondrous silver shrine of St. Hugh, a masterpiece of intricate stone tracery encrusted with precious metals and gems, which reposed in the beautiful Angel Choir at the cathedral's east end; this choir had been built in the 1260s and was named after the carved angels with which it was lavishly decorated. For Hugh Swynford, the shrine of his patron saint must have been a very special place, to be visited often, while for Katherine the cathedral had an altar to her own name saint[38] and housed two precious objects of special devotion: a finger that had reputedly belonged to St. Katherine and a chain with which the saint is said to have bound up the Devil.

John of Gaunt also had strong links with Lincoln. At the age of two he had been granted the earldom of Richmond, which incorporated lands in Lincolnshire. At three he had come to Lincoln Cathedral with the King, his father, and his brother the Black Prince, and admitted to its confraternity, a group of lay benefactors who were prayed for by the cathedral clergy in gratitude for their gifts;[39] John was to prove very generous to the cathedral over the years, and in his will would refer to "a certain devotion" he cherished for its patroness, the Virgin Mary. In the Angel Choir lay the visceral tomb of his great-grandmother, Eleanor of Castile, the beloved wife of Edward I.[40] At twenty-one John acquired the earldom of Lincoln itself, with its vast estates, in right of his wife Blanche; in this capacity he grew familiar with the great and gentle families of the shire, and numbered several of their members among his retinue. He would in time forge even closer links to Lincoln and the surrounding area through his involvement with Katherine Swynford.

As Earl of Lincoln, John was hereditary Constable of Lincoln Castle, yet it is not known if he ever lodged in the castle on his brief visits to the city or if he stayed in the Bishop's Palace, a house in the cathedral close, or one in the town. It was perhaps the latter, since the castle could only offer somewhat outdated accommodation.[41]

Tradition long had it that John of Gaunt owned a palace in Lincoln, an ancient stone mansion that stood to the west of the High Street in Wigford, a southern suburb of the city. The "palace" was situated on the west side of the churchyard of the Guild of St. Anne, which adjoined St. Andrew's Church. According to a 1726 engraving by Samuel and Nathaniel Buck, it was a medieval house with stone pinnacles and windows of the Decorated period; beneath a gable in the center of the extended battlemented front facade was affixed a carved free-stone shield bearing the arms of John of Gaunt, surmounted by his helm and mantling. Another old print reveals that the south range of this house was built in the later Perpendicular style, possibly in the fourteenth century. It boasted buttresses, a battlemented cornice, and square-headed two-light windows. All this would be commensurate with the house having existed in John's lifetime; it was probably altered during the centuries since his death. Buck tells us that "the castle was his, but standing much exposed to cold winds, and a place of office for the public service"; because of these drawbacks, "that prince probably built this below the hill for warmth, and for the use of his family and domestics, while he resided in this most ancient city." Buck claims that John stayed here mainly in his latter years, and unsurprisingly, Katherine Swynford is also said to have had the use of the house.[42]

There is little contemporary evidence to connect John of Gaunt with this building, nor did the early sixteenth-century antiquarian John Leland associate him with it; instead, he says this "goodly house" belonged to the Suttons, who were the richest and most prominent mercantile family in Lincoln in the late Middle Ages and held lands of the duke in the county. However, in 1586 the house was called "John of Gaunt's Palace" by William Camden, the Elizabethan antiquary who spent fifteen years researching the historic buildings of England,[43] and both Buck and the antiquary William Stukeley, writing in the 1720s, refer to it by that name. But later, in 1784, a Swiss artist, Samuel Hieronymous Grimm, labeled his drawing as "the pretended house of John of Gaunt at Lincoln." Today, historians are inclined to believe that it did not have any connection with the duke.[44]

John of Gaunt never stayed in Lincoln long enough to justify the building of a residence there, and there is no reference to this house in his registers, but these are of course incomplete. Yet it was certainly his coat of arms that Buck engraved, and it is indeed possible that it was for reasons of comfort that John lodged in this house whenever he was in the city. That does not mean it belonged to him; the evidence suggests that he probably stayed there as a guest of his vassal, John de Sutton, who died in 1391, and then of Sutton's son Robert. John de Sutton, who was Mayor of Lincoln in 1387, certainly knew Katherine Swynford, because that year he witnessed a grant to her;[45] he was probably the owner of the house in Wigford, and was no doubt proud to display on it the arms of his overlord and honored guest. It may be significant that the mansion boasted some of the innovative Perpendicular architectural features that were becoming fashionable at the end of the fourteenth century, the period when Buck says the duke stayed there most frequently. One would expect to find such novel features only in the house of some great and wealthy man who was eager to offer his lord the best accommodation that money and influence could provide.[46]

These were the places that Katherine now called home: the impoverished manors of Kettlethorpe—for which she nevertheless conceived an enduring affection—and Coleby, where no trace of her remains, suggesting—perhaps understandably, in view of its penury—that she was rarely there. And of course Lincoln, where she was to live in far greater luxury than she could ever have dreamed at the outset of her marriage to Hugh Swynford.

What can we know or surmise about the marriage of Katherine and Hugh?

Katherine was very young when they were wed, and Hugh was a soldier who would serve abroad on campaigns for long periods. There is no evidence to show whether the couple was happy or unhappy, although it is unlikely that Katherine found with her husband the kind of love that was between John of Gaunt and Duchess Blanche. Marriages such as Katherine and Hugh's were matters of business or policy that took little account of personal feelings. Hugh wasn't wealthy—far from it—but could provide Katherine with his knightly rank and social standing; on the other hand, living in poverty may well have put a strain upon the relationship. But although it is unlikely that Hugh had received much of a dowry from Katherine, if any at all, he had the advantage of a connection with a noble family—which would surely have inspired respect for his wife—and the prospect of her inheritance in Hainault, which may still have been in the hands of her father or brother at this time, for Hugh is not known to have attempted to take possession of it; and even if it had come to him on his marriage to Katherine, he was preoccupied with war and with rescuing his own estates from ruin, and would probably not have had the resources to administer and farm land in another country.

For Katherine, though, Kettlethorpe must have come as a shock after years of living in royal households where comfort and a laden table were taken for granted. It would appear that she faced this challenge with equanimity and resource, taking her responsibilities as lady of the manor seriously, which argues a certain strength of character. She would also have had to learn to juggle the demands of being the chatelaine of a knightly household and serving in the Lancastrian ménage with successive pregnancies and a growing family. Being married at such a young age, like many girls of her caste, she had to immediately face the sometimes brutal realities of childbirth, living as she did in an era of high maternal and infant mortality; in this respect she appears to have been quite hardy, for she was to survive at least seven or eight pregnancies with no apparent ill effects.

So in every aspect that mattered, Katherine made a success of her marriage. She clearly did her duty as a wife; she actively immersed herself in the life of the manor of Kettlethorpe to such an extent that for many years she would be known primarily as the Lady of Kettlethorpe; she fit seamlessly into her husband's social circle in Lincoln and the county at large, doubtless also mixing with his Swynford relatives and their connections by marriage; and she dutifully bore her husband the children that all men of property desired.

Their eldest child was probably Blanche, who is known to history through references in a papal petition, the duchy records, and a grant of wardship in *John of Gaunt's Register*. She was old enough by 1368 to be placed in the chamber of the Lancastrian princesses, probably as a playmate, and in view of the likely date of birth of her younger sister Margaret, must have been born no later than 1363. Margaret was the daughter who became a nun in 1377,[47] and she probably arrived in 1364; Katherine was in attendance on Duchess Blanche in January 1365,[48] and later that year she perhaps became pregnant with her third child.

Margaret may have been named for Margaret of Hainault, her grandfather's patroness. There is no actual record of her parentage, but several factors point to her being the daughter of Katherine and Hugh Swynford: first, her surname; second, the fact that she became a nun at Barking, one of the most exclusive abbeys in the land, and was nominated by the King himself, which suggests the influence of John of Gaunt, who was then the lover of Katherine Swynford; third, that the King, at the same time, nominated to St. Helen's Priory in London Elizabeth Chaucer, who was probably the eldest daughter of Katherine's sister Philippa—which suggests a link between the two girls, and more influential maneuevring behind the scenes; fourth, the possibility that Elizabeth Chaucer was later transferred to Barking because her cousin Margaret Swynford was there; fifth, there is evidence that two of Katherine's sons by John of Gaunt patronized Barking Abbey, in which Margaret, who was probably their half sister, lived;[49] and last, the likelihood of Margaret's birth occurring at a time when Katherine was bearing children to Hugh Swynford.

It has been suggested that there was a third daughter, Dorothy. According to Thomas Stapleton, writing in 1846, Dorothy married Thomas Thimelby of Poolham near Horncastle, Lincolnshire, who was Sheriff of Lincolnshire in 1380 and died in 1390, but that claim is usually dismissed on the grounds that the name Dorothy was not used in England until the sixteenth century. That is incorrect: Although uncommon, there are instances of English girls being named after the fourth-century Christian martyr St. Dorothy of Cappadocia in medieval times, and she features in stained glass and screen paintings in England, particularly in the late fourteenth and fifteenth centuries. In fact, her legend had been known in England since Saxon times. St. Dorothy's feast day is February 6, which was perhaps the birthday of Katherine's daughter (who was possibly born in 1366), and might account for the unusual choice of name.[50]

Evidence to support Stapleton's unsubstantiated claim is perhaps to be found in Irnham Church, where the coats of arms of the Thimelbys, Belesbys, Luttrells, and Sir Hugh Swynford are to be found in abundance on tombs and in stained glass. All were prominent Lincolnshire families, and all were linked by marriage.[51] Given the armorial evidence in the church, it is not therefore beyond the bounds of possibility that Thomas Thimelby married Dorothy Swynford, the daughter of Hugh and Katherine, or that he had children by her, for there were Thimelbys still living at Poolham in the early seventeenth century.[52]

The dates of birth of the Swynford girls are not recorded—those of royal daughters born in this period are hard enough to come by, let alone those of knightly birth. It was often the medieval married woman's lot to bear a child each year, since there was no effective birth control, so it was easily possible for Katherine to have borne Hugh four children in up to a decade of married life, even taking into account the periods he spent abroad. Since many children died in infancy, and the young were seen as marriageable assets, it was thought desirable among the landed classes to have as many as possible, so perhaps Katherine had unrecorded infants who did not survive.

In 1396, while affirming to the Pope that he had not committed adultery with Katherine during the lifetime of her husband, John of Gaunt revealed that he had stood godfather to one of her daughters by Hugh: "Duke John had lifted from the sacred font a daughter of Katherine, begotten by another man."[53] In so stating, John was admitting an impediment to his marriage to Katherine, the creation of a fraternal bond of brotherhood, or compaternity, that effectively made them spiritually brother and sister. John also affirmed that "the impediment of the aforesaid compaternity" was "not notorious but rather occult," meaning that it was private or secret. This secrecy has seemed puzzling to some, since it suggests there was some sinister reason for preventing John's sponsorship from becoming public knowledge, and one conclusion of several writers was that he was the baby's real father. This is highly unlikely. Apart from it being plainly stated in the petition that the baby was "begotten by another man," and the fact that a man could not stand godfather to his own child,[54] John was later willingly to acknowledge four bastards by Katherine, who were all given the surname Beaufort. Why, therefore, should he not have acknowledged a fifth, and also given it that name? Even if this child had been born before the others, in Hugh's lifetime, there was no reason for concealment in 1396, and anyway, in his petition to the Pope, John admitted everything about his relationship with Katherine, even his own adultery; he kept nothing back.

In the circumstances, it would have been foolish and incomprehensible to do so. This petition was of the utmost importance. John wanted the Pope to confirm his marriage to Katherine and so legitimize their children. Had he lied in that petition, it would have been self-defeating and catastrophic, for he risked receiving a flawed judgment from the pontiff that would have nullified the validity of both the marriage and the legitimation process, not to mention imperiling his immortal soul by the anathema that would automatically have been visited upon him for lying. It is unthinkable that an intelligent and honorable man such as the duke, who was clearly setting his affairs in order and safeguarding the future of his children—and who would have known what was at stake, both materially and spiritually—should deliberately misrepresent his case to the Pope and court damnation by so serious an omission. For even in the educated medieval mind, the prospect of divine judgment, Purgatory, and Hell itself loomed large and terrifying. For this reason we must accept what John wrote in that petition as the truth.

The reason for keeping John's private sponsorship of Katherine's child a secret surely lies in the fact of the compaternity that resulted from it: By becoming her infant's godfather, he effectively placed himself within the forbidden degrees of affinity to Katherine, for compaternity bound parents and sponsors together in kinship and created a barrier to them marrying or having sexual intercourse. His sponsorship would initially have been a kind gesture on the part of a good lord, an example of the patronage he extended to those who served him and his family well; it may have followed Katherine giving birth at one of the ducal residences, perhaps prematurely; it might have been at Blanche's request. And we may suppose that the baptism was only relatively ("rather") occult,[55] a private affair attended just by the duke and duchess, a few members of their households, and the proud parents. It was only later, when Katherine became John's mistress, that the compaternity became a matter for concealment, for the lovers were no doubt aware that it laid upon them an additional burden of sin above that of adultery, and could only have intensified the scandal their affair was causing.

It has been convincingly suggested that it was Blanche Swynford to whom John stood godfather. In this capacity, he bound himself to take some responsibility for her spiritual needs and her material well-being, and his exalted rank would have conferred on her a special status. John seems to have ably fulfilled his obligations: In 1375 he granted Katherine the wardship of the heir of Sir Robert Deyncourt and the marriage of that heir for her daughter Blanche,[56] thus effectively providing for Blanche's future as she approached marriageable age. And if John was her godfather, the name Blanche, in honor of his wife—who might well have stood godmother— was a natural choice. Duchess Blanche too seems to have taken a special interest in the little girl, for before 1368 she placed Blanche Swynford in the chamber of her own daughters.[57] All these factors suggest that Blanche was the eldest child of Katherine and Hugh.

Like other married couples in the Lancasters' service, the Swynfords divided their time between the ducal court and their own estates, which were run by stewards and other feudal officials in their absence. Hugh would spend a considerable part of their married life campaigning in France and

Spain, while Katherine—in between confinements—continued to serve the duchess. Given the familial nature of the Lancastrian household, she would have been permitted to have her growing children with her, to be brought up in company with the ducal children.

Caring for the infants of the duke and duchess was probably a large part of Katherine's duties as a chamber servant.[58] Young Philippa and Elizabeth were growing sturdily. The elder John was probably dead by April or May 1366, when his brother and namesake was born: On May 4 that year, one Robert de Walkyngton was lavishly rewarded with £6.13s.4d (£2,237) for bringing the news of the second John's birth to his grandfather, the King.[59] But the second John also died young—probably after April 1367[60]—as did Edward of Lancaster, who had been born around 1365 and named probably for the King, and who departed this life soon afterward. With the duchess frequently pregnant, recovering from childbirth, or grieving over the loss of an infant, Katherine would have been kept busy. And she would surely have been caught up in the emotional life of the household, rejoicing in the births of new babies to the duke and duchess, sharing in their pain when their infants died, and doubtless observing the enduring love and devotion between them.

That Katherine had a genuine religious faith cannot be doubted. Shortly before January 24, 1365, John Buckingham, Bishop of Lincoln from 1363 to 1398, granted her, as *ancille* to the Duchess of Lancaster, the privilege of having divine Service—the canonical offices of the Church—celebrated privately until Pentecost of that year, whenever she visited Leicester.[61] The bestowal of such a privilege, by a bishop who doubtless came to know Katherine since she had married Sir Hugh Swynford and become prominent among the Lincolnshire gentry, proves that she was not only pious but an important and well-respected member of the duchess's household. The performance of the divine offices would necessitate her having some personal space to facilitate it, such as a chapel, an oratory, or even a private chamber, and she would have also needed a portable altar—a luxury item in those days. Servants in royal and noble households in the fourteenth century lived communally, sleeping in dormitories or in the chambers of their lords or ladies; privacy was the preserve of the rich. The fact that Katherine was granted this privilege and enjoyed sufficient privacy to take advantage of it, together with the duke acting as godfather to her child and later rewarding her for good service to his wife, singles her out as one who was very highly favored by her employers.

That said, it is unlikely that Katherine got to exercise her pious privilege. The ducal household was at Bolingbroke in Lincolnshire until April 18, 1365, then it moved south to the Savoy; it was still in residence there on June 4, and did not arrive at Leicester until June 14, sometime after Pentecost,[62] and too late for Katherine to have her private services.

By September 12, 1366, Philippa de Roët, Katherine's younger sister, had become the wife of Geoffrey Chaucer, now a Yeoman of the Chamber to Edward III; Chaucer must have been newly appointed to this post because his name does not appear in a comprehensive list of members of the royal household compiled in the summer of 1366;[63] he was to hold it until 1372.

On that September 12, Edward III issued letters of patent granting a life annuity of 10 marks (£1,119)—to be paid twice yearly—to Philippa "Chaucy."[64] A Chancery warrant of the same date describes her as "Philippa Chaucer, one of the *damoiselles* of the Chamber of our very dear companion the Queen."[65]

Like Katherine and Hugh Swynford, the newly married Chaucers were both busily employed in a royal household; as we have seen, marriage between royal servants was not uncommon.[66] Philippa's duties increasingly involved looking after the ailing Queen, while Geoffrey, when not serving the King on a personal basis, was to be entrusted with several sensitive diplomatic missions. On June 20, 1367, Edward III granted "our beloved yeoman" Geoffrey Chaucer a pension of 20 marks (£1,926) a year for good service.[67] His status is variously described, but the titles used—yeoman, valet (Latin, *valettus, valettorum*), or esquire (French, *esquier*) of the King's Chamber— were interchangeable at that time, and all meant the same thing: a civil servant who performed confidential duties for his master as well as a wide range of tasks including the purveying of goods, the conveying of money, the making of beds, setting of tables, or lighting of torches, as directed by the Chamberlain of the Household.[68] Chaucer's manifold talents were already held in high regard by the royal family, and the likelihood is that his role as yeoman encompassed more responsible duties; there is evidence that in the spring of 1366, the year before he took up his new post, he was sent to Spain on a secret diplomatic mission probably connected with dynastic turmoil in Castile,[69] a matter that was to bear heavily on the fortunes of John of Gaunt.

And in 1368, Chaucer was sent to France on official business.[70] We might conclude, therefore, that his duties at court were by no means limited to domestic chores.

Geoffrey was remarkably clever and possessed great charm, but his appearance belied that. Surviving pictures of him in later life show a rotund little man of about five-six with brown hair, a forked beard, and dusty black garments. He was wise, tactful, discreet, shrewd, and observant, and his understanding of human nature profound. A well-read, objective scholar, a curious observer of life, he loved delving into the mysteries of science, astrology, philosophy, and religion.

Thanks to his abilities and his discretion, Chaucer was able to use his talents in a variety of capacities and was often rewarded handsomely; his marriage to the daughter of a knight, a girl above him in station, was a measure of his early success. He knew Latin, Italian, and French, and would undertake seven more diplomatic missions abroad for the King in the 1370s; in Italy, during that decade, he would perhaps meet those great literary colossi Petrarch and Boccaccio. In England, his royal service, and his marriage, gave him privileged access to the royal family.

Geoffrey's greatest gift, of course, was the ability to write wonderful, rich, witty, earthy verse in the English language, a departure from the usual French poetry beloved in courtly circles. Yet the classical and allegorical themes of some of his works show that they were indeed meant to be circulated, read, and enjoyed at court by a cultivated audience, and it would appear that at least by 1368, Geoffrey had already earned himself a reputation as a maker of verses, and that his compositions were admired by John of Gaunt and Blanche of Lancaster. His younger contemporary, the poet John Gower, tells us that "in the flower of his youth," Chaucer was already enthralling the country with "ditties and glad songs." He was not the first to write verse in English—although he was the first to use iambic pentameter, "the golden couplet"—but he was responsible for popularizing poetry in the vernacular, and in so doing, ensuring that in the decades to come, English would become the accepted literary language in England.

Geoffrey and Philippa were probably married well before September 1366. Their first child was almost certainly the daughter who would enter St. Helen's Priory, London, in 1377; her name at that time was recorded as "Elizabeth Chausier." Her parentage is indicated by her surname (there was no regularity of spelling then), her likely date of birth, her placement in a convent that lay a stone's throw from her father's lodgings in Aldgate, and the fact that in 1381, John of Gaunt most generously dowered an "Elizabeth Chaucy," who was almost certainly the same person, to the highly select Barking Abbey at a time when her aunt, Katherine Swynford, was his mistress. Elizabeth may even have been named after another aunt, the nun Elizabeth de Roët; as has been noted, the placing of Elizabeth de Roët, Margaret Swynford, and Elizabeth Chaucer in convents may well indicate a family tradition of offering Roët daughters to God.

Given that she first became a nun in 1377, Elizabeth was presumably born no later than 1365, the year after Chaucer perhaps returned from Ireland. Thus, her parents had probably married in 1364, possibly as soon as Philippa de Roët reached twelve, the minimum canonical age for girls to marry and have sex. The marriage was probably arranged by the Queen herself, who doubtless felt responsible for seeing the younger Roët girl safely disposed in wedlock and her future provided for. Within two years of it, Chaucer became a wealthy man, for his father died in 1366, leaving him all his property.

There was possibly a second daughter of the marriage, and improbably a third. An Agnes Chaucer, who may have been a daughter or granddaughter of Geoffrey and Philippa, and was perhaps named for Chaucer's mother, is listed as one of the *damoiselles* of the Queen at the coronation of Henry IV in 1399;[71] however, Henry IV was a widower at the time of his coronation, and his second wife, Joan of Navarre, was not crowned until February 1403, so there is something amiss here. And it was not until the seventeenth century that it was asserted that Chaucer had a daughter called Katherine—there is no contemporary record of her, so it is unlikely that she existed.[72]

Living with a genius cannot always have been easy for Philippa. Geoffrey owned sixty books—an amazing number for a man in his position—and he spent much of his leisure time reading them or foraging about in the many libraries in London. It has been suggested that he drew on his own experience when he depicted the frustrated Wife of Bath ripping up and burning her husband's books so he would have more time for sexual dalliance. Yet although Geoffrey claimed to be primarily a bookish man, he was also a career civil servant, and perhaps came to have less and less time to spare for his wife. He could be devastatingly cynical, and a passage in *The Boke of the Duchesse* suggests he was also a compulsive worrier who would lie awake at night fretting.[73] Thus, the married life of Geoffrey and Philippa may not have been particularly harmonious. Late in life, after Philippa had died, Chaucer composed a humorous poem, "L'Envoy à Bukton" (ca. 1396), for a bachelor friend of his, warning him of "the sorrow and woe that is in marriage." It was, he claimed, a deadly peril for all men, and he expressed the wish that his warning would prevent Bukton from rushing madly into the dire captivity of wedlock:

> God grant you your life freely to lead
> In freedom—for full hard it is to be bond.

From his tone, we might conclude that he had many regrets about his own marriage upon which he did not like to dwell. He ends by saying he is resolved not to fall into "the trap of wedding" again.

We might infer from this, and other circumstances yet to be revealed, that his marriage had not been happy, a theory that may be supported by internal evidence from Chaucer's own verse. He is not known to have dedicated a single poem to Philippa, and most of his allusions to married life are cynical, ironical, and disrespectful, hardly what one would expect from a man who enjoyed a loving relationship with his wife. Furthermore, Chaucer tells us in *The Boke of the Duchesse*, *The House of Fame*, *The Parliament of Fowls*, and *Troilus and Criseyde* (to name a few) that he has no experience of love apart from what he has learned from books—"I know not love in deed"— and his image of himself is that of an unprepossessing failure as a lover, one who is devout and chaste because he has been banished from love's courts. This self-deprecating portrayal may not be entirely truthful—how many men would wish to portray themselves as hopeless in bed?—and it could be merely the product of Chaucer's ironic humor, while his literary take on marriage might just reflect prevailing trends in popular humor. For in "The Man of Law's Tale," he reveals that, despite his protestations elsewhere, he knows just how spiritually transcendental love between a man and a woman can be:

> And such a bliss is there betwixt them two
> That, save the joy that lasteth evermore,
> There is none like that any creature
> Hath seen or shall, while that the world may endure.[74]

These read like the words of a man who has experienced such joy, yet although they refer to marital love, it is unlikely that Geoffrey and Philippa themselves enjoyed that kind of relationship, especially since Chaucer makes it clear he thought marriage a burden to be borne. No, his experience of love was of another kind entirely. In *The Boke of the Duchesse*, written probably in 1368, he reveals that he has been possessed with a great passion for an unnamed lady for no fewer than eight years. If this is true—and one theory will be discussed in the next chapter—then this passion must have predated his marriage, and may well have contributed to its failure.

All we know of Philippa herself is that, according to her countryman Froissart, she had a fine sense of protocol, which she must have learned in the course of her upbringing in the Queen's household, and which would have served her well at court. Given the differences in their status, she may have looked down on her husband and inwardly despised his humbler birth; after all, he was just the son of a vintner, while she was the daughter of a knight, and in her veins there probably ran the blood of ancient royalty. Her sister Katherine had married a knight, and Philippa perhaps felt she had not done as well. The fact that she married beneath her is another argument in favor of her being the younger sister.

Philippa Chaucer may have been discontented with her marital lot to begin with, or she might gradually have become disillusioned. The demands of their official duties dictated that she and Geoffrey were frequently apart, and both possibly came to welcome this. Philippa was perhaps shrewish and sharp-tongued, for in *The House of Fame*, Chaucer has himself worshipping at the shrine of St. Leonard, patron saint of henpecked husbands. And he speaks of a dream in which he is seized by an eagle's talons and awoken by the eagle's insistent cry, "Awake!" which it speaks:

> *Right in the same voice and pitch*
> *That useth one I could name;*
> *And with that voice, sooth for to say,*
> *My mind came to me again,*
> *For it was goodly said to me,*
> *So nas it never wont to be.*

We might infer that the voice that awoke the poet was that of his wife. For once, though, she has spoken kindly to him, unlike her usual tone. In

"The Franklin's Tale," Chaucer may have been thinking of the deterioration of his marriage, and perhaps of a continual battle for conjugal supremacy, when he expresses the opinion that:

> Love is a thing as any spirit free.
> Women, of kind, desire liberty,
> And not to be constrained as a thrall;
> And so do men, if I sooth say shall.
> Look who that is most patient in love,
> He is at his advantage all above.

Of course, Chaucer, like many writers, may not have based his works on his own life and experiences, but on his observations of others, the books he had read, or his own imagination. In assessing the nature of his marriage, we are entirely in the realms of speculation and educated guesses and can conclude nothing concrete.

Marriage to Philippa de Roët must inevitably have brought Chaucer into contact with his sister-in-law, Katherine Swynford, and also, no doubt, with the Lancastrian household. He was, of course, already known to the duke and duchess, and we might infer from *The Boke of the Duchesse* that he was on friendly if formal speaking terms with both of them. There is also some evidence to suggest that for much of his life Chaucer enjoyed John of Gaunt's patronage. Although there is no evidence to show that he was ever employed by the duke, he later received a pension from him, in addition to the one he received from the Crown, and may well have owed some if not most of the preferments that came his way to John's influence. His connection by marriage to Katherine Swynford, as well as his own talents and character, must in time have accounted to some degree for the duke's favor.

The marriage of her sister to a valued member of the King's household would inevitably have strengthened Katherine's ties with the court.[75] And she would certainly have benefited personally from a close kinship with Chaucer, whose wisdom, humanity, and erudition would surely have made an impact on her young and impressionable consciousness. Her mind would have been broadened by his verses and tales, her imagination aroused, and her understanding of life challenged by his thoughtful insights.

♦   ♦   ♦

In 1366 an event took place in Castile, a kingdom that spread across much of what is now Spain, that was to have far-reaching consequences for John of Gaunt, and for Katherine Swynford too. That event was the deposition of King Pedro I, known as "the Cruel." His nickname was not undeserved, for he was a hard and sinister man of uncontrollable passions. Since his accession in 1350, he had ruled as an autocratic and bloody tyrant, determined to crush the power of his volatile and anarchic feudal nobles. He caused much scandal by protecting Jews and keeping a Jewish mistress, and by employing infidels as his personal guard, predictably making many enemies in the process.

In 1353, Pedro had married Blanche of Bourbon, sister-in-law of the future French king, Charles V. Immediately after the wedding, though, Pedro repudiated their marriage, immured Blanche in a dungeon, and continued his longstanding liaison with his mistress, Maria de Padilla, whom he now claimed to have secretly married before he went through the ceremony with Blanche; so persuasive was he that the Castilian Cortes did in fact recognize Maria's children as his heirs, but sadly, their only son, Alfonso, died at eleven in 1362, his mother passing away the same year. Blanche had died in suspicious circumstances in 1361, and the evidence strongly suggests that Pedro had her poisoned. That was certainly what people were saying at the time, and if true, it was an ill-judged deed, for her death alienated the French and prompted the Pope to excommunicate Pedro for the murders of his wife and his many political opponents. These factors drove him to seek the friendship of the English.

It availed him little to begin with, because in 1366 he was overthrown by his bastard half brother, Enrique of Trastamara, backed by Charles V of France, who saw in Enrique a future ally against England. The newly crowned Enrique II, a vigorous, able, but unscrupulous man, was one of ten children born to Pedro's father, Alfonso XI of Castile, by his powerful mistress, Leonor de Guzman, whom Pedro had executed as soon as his father succumbed to the Black Death in 1350. Thus, Enrique had good cause to seek vengeance, and of course he was not the only man who had a score to settle with this "vile evil-doer," as Walsingham called him.

Pedro fled to Corunna, where he sent a desperate appeal to the Black

Prince for aid. The prince responded, determined not so much to uphold Pedro's legitimate claim to his throne and restore him by force as to crush the alliance between France and Castile, which placed Aquitaine under threat from both north and south, and England at risk of invasion by the powerful Castilian navy. Edward III readily sanctioned such an enterprise, and John of Gaunt offered military support. The two princes—mindful of the prophecy that the leopards of England would one day flutter over the battlefields of Spain—now prepared to make war on the usurper, raising armies in Aquitaine and England.

Meanwhile, Pedro and his three daughters by Maria de Padilla—Beatrice, thirteen; Constance, twelve; and Isabella, ten—had taken refuge at Bordeaux in Aquitaine, where they were accorded every courtesy by the Black Prince, and accommodated in the Abbey of St. Andrew. Pedro showed himself exceedingly grateful, and solemnly promised the prince, on oath, that once he was restored to his throne, he would reimburse him for the entire costs of the venture; he would leave his daughters at Bordeaux as surety for this.[76]

In November 1366, Hugh Swynford received letters of protection commanding him to join the Duke of Lancaster in Guienne.[77] In September, John of Gaunt had arrived at Bayonne in Gascony with a thousand archers and men-at-arms, and in November he traveled through Aquitaine to rendezvous with his brother the Black Prince. Soon afterward Hugh must have taken ship from England to Gascony and caught up with the Duke's army.

Both Duchess Blanche and Katherine Swynford were pregnant when their husbands rode off to war. They would not see their lords again for more than a year. By Christmas 1366, Blanche had established herself at Bolingbroke Castle, four miles west of Spilsby and twenty-six miles east of Lincoln, where the King joined her for the Yuletide festivities. The twelfth-century castle lay in the hilly Lincolnshire wolds, in what is now the village of Old Bolingbroke, and Katherine would almost certainly have visited it as part of the Lancastrian entourage. Seven months pregnant, with her lord overseas and her home not far away, she might well have been in attendance on the duchess at Bolingbroke on this occasion. The castle had become part of the Lancastrian patrimony in 1311; it was a strong square fortress, with round towers at each corner, a moat fed by springs, a "very stately" entrance "over a fair drawbridge," and an imposing Norman church nearby, the south

aisle of which had been built by John of Gaunt in 1363. The duchess and her
retinue would have been accommodated in the comfortable timber-framed
domestic range of buildings in the courtyard.[78]

Katherine had moved to Lincoln by the middle of February 1367. It was
in a house there that she bore Hugh a son and heir, who arrived on February
24, 1367, the feast of St. Matthias the Apostle, and was baptized Thomas
after his grandfather and one of his sponsors, Thomas de Sutton, a cathedral
canon, who was doubtless a relative of the powerful John de Sutton; the
other male sponsor was John de Worksop, also a canon of Lincoln.[79] Hugh's
Inquisition Postmortem of June 1372 states that his son Thomas was then
four, so it is often claimed that his birth took place in February 1368, but
Hugh probably did not return to England until October 1367, so that is
hardly possible. As has been demonstrated, dates of birth recorded in Inquisitions Postmortem are often inaccurate.[80]

This is manifest in the Inquisition taken to establish Thomas Swynford's
age between June 22, 1394, and June 22, 1395.[81] No fewer than twelve witnesses came forward to declare that he had been born in 1373, fifteen months
after his father's death and a year after he had been described as four years old
in Sir Hugh's Inquisition Postmortem. All had apparently been present at
young Thomas's baptism, which took place on February 25, 1367, the day
after his birth, at the Church of St. Margaret in the cathedral close. This is
the first record of an association between Katherine Swynford and Lincoln
Cathedral and its close, with which she was often to be linked in the future,
and the choice of two members of the Cathedral Chapter as sponsors suggests that she was already well known to and highly regarded by that body.

The eleventh-century church of St. Margaret no longer survives, having
been pulled down around 1780. It stood on a green in the precinct of the
Bishop's Palace, between Pottergate and the cathedral, opposite the house in
the close in which Katherine would one day reside. The church was surmounted by a squat Norman tower and had an Early English window at its
east end.[82]

The witnesses at the baptism included John Liminour of Lincoln, who
may have been a limner (a painter of miniatures in illuminated manuscripts),
for he recalled bringing a missal and another book to the church and selling
them there to John de Worksop; John Plaint and John Balden, servants to
Thomas de Sutton; Roger Fynden, chamberlain to John de Worksop; John
Sumnour, Nicholas Bolton, and Richard Colville, all of Lincoln, the last of

whom had been charged by Katherine's steward to bring home twenty-four bows for distribution to members of her household, doubtless for archery practice, skillful strategic use of the longbow being one of England's great strengths in the war with France; Henry Taverner, who recalled the occasion well because his first son was baptized on the same day; and Gilbert de Beseby, Katherine's chamberlain. The testimony of these people provides interesting details about a medieval baptism: we see Thomas Boterwyk, the parish clerk, reverently conveying the holy oil, or chrism, from the altar to the stone font; John Plaint carrying a flame to light the candle; two men holding basins of water and towels so the godfathers and godmother (her identity remains unknown) could wash their hands after the ceremony; William Hammond, a servant of John de Sereby of Lincoln (who would sell land to Katherine in 1387), falling and breaking one of the two jars of red wine he was carrying into the church, and being beaten for it by his master; and Katherine's chamberlain bearing cloths of silk and cloth of gold in which to wrap the baby after his christening. Such fabrics were extremely costly, and their appearance at this ceremony perhaps suggests that they had been generously provided by the Duchess Blanche; certainly an impecunious knight such as Hugh Swynford could not have afforded them.

There may be another explanation, though. This information was all provided in 1394–95, about twenty-eight years after Thomas's birth, and the witnesses were to a man inaccurate in one important detail, for it has been demonstrated that Thomas could not have been born in 1373. We should consider, however, that in 1394–95 most of these witnesses were in their fifties, sixties, and even seventies—old by medieval standards—and some may have been forgetful, or followed the testimony of the rest, or—which may be significant—even confused Thomas's baptism with another that did take place in 1373, in the same church. And that later baptism may have been of John Beaufort, the eldest of Katherine Swynford's children by John of Gaunt, for which rich cloths would undoubtedly have been provided. Certainly, as Cole points out, none of these witnesses intended that their testimony should in any way impugn Thomas Swynford's legitimacy. Their main purpose was to demonstrate that he was now over twenty-one and able to take up his inheritance as his father's heir. There were plenty of Swynford relatives to challenge his title, should any question of bastardy have arisen, but there is no evidence that any ever did.[83]

The birth of a Swynford heir must have been a great triumph for Katherine, especially after bearing two or perhaps three daughters; it meant that if the baby survived, Hugh's family name would be carried on and his lands inherited by his son.

Meanwhile, John of Gaunt had joined the Black Prince and his army at Dax on January 13, having paused briefly in Bordeaux to pay his affectionate respects to his sister-in-law, Princess Joan, and to greet her new son, Richard, to whom she had given birth there on January 6, the Feast of the Epiphany.[84] Richard of Bordeaux was the second son of the prince and princess, the elder, Edward of Angoulême, having been born on January 27, 1365; Edward, of course, was the next heir to England after his illustrious father.

In February, in bitter cold and heavy snow, the two armies made the hazardous crossing of the Pyrenees into Castile, where on April 3, 1367, they won a spectacular victory over Enrique of Trastamara at the Battle of Najera, near Burgos, during which John of Gaunt, in command of the vanguard, acquitted himself very courageously; according to Chandos Herald, "the noble Duke of Lancaster, full of virtue, fought so nobly that everyone marveled at beholding his great powers and at how, in his high daring, he exposed his person to danger." Earlier, he had earned stout praise for his alacrity in repelling a surprise attack by the French in the Pyrenees. After Najera, when sixteen thousand men lay dead in the field, the Black Prince wrote to his wife: "Be assured, dearest companion, that we, our brother of Lancaster, and all the great men of our army are, thank God, in good form."[85]

Doubtless the Duchess Blanche also would have been relieved to receive this news. On the very same day as the victory, she bore John of Gaunt a healthy son at Bolingbroke, who was named Henry in honor of her illustrious father. The choice of name suggests that his elder brother John was still alive.[86] It is unlikely, given that her own baby was less than two months old, that Katherine Swynford attended the duchess in her confinement, and she was probably then at Kettlethorpe or still in Lincoln. The house in Lincoln in which she gave birth has not been identified; given that she later occupied two properties in the cathedral close, and that her son was baptized in the church in the close, it was probably in that area, and she was perhaps staying there as the guest of one of the cathedral canons.

On May 2, the Black Prince and the Duke of Lancaster entered Burgos, the chief city of Castile, in triumph. Pedro was formally restored to his throne, and the English princes and their troops settled down to wait for payment of the money he had sworn to pay them. They waited in vain, for Pedro repeatedly refused to keep his promise, much to the Black Prince's fury; all that was handed over in reimbursement was a large, uncut ruby.[87] The delay was ultimately to prove disastrous, for in the burning heat of that summer, there was a fearful outbreak of amoebic dysentery in the English encampment, with the prince himself fatefully struck down and four-fifths of his men perishing. By the autumn he was no better, and also suffering from dropsy, while his surviving soldiers were thoroughly demoralized. To add to his troubles, Enrique was busily laying waste to Gascony, so the prince and John of Gaunt had no choice but to return there. John arrived back in England at the beginning of October,[88] and with him, we may presume, was Hugh Swynford. Both men must have been pleased to be reunited with their wives and delighted to make the acquaintance of the sons born in their absence.

Around 1367–68, Philippa Chaucer also bore a son, another Thomas,[89] whose paternity has been the subject of much debate. In the late sixteenth century Thomas Speght reported that "some hold opinion (but I know not upon what grounds) that Thomas Chaucer was not the son of Geoffrey Chaucer, but rather some kinsman of his whom he brought up." This is unfortunately too vague to constitute convincing evidence of Philippa's infidelity, but in recent years it has been suggested that she, as well as her sister Katherine, was John of Gaunt's mistress, and that he was the father not only of Thomas Chaucer, but also of Elizabeth Chaucer.[90] The grounds for this are threefold.

First, only the arms of Philippa de Roët feature in the twenty shields that adorn Thomas Chaucer's tomb at Ewelme in Oxfordshire; those of Geoffrey Chaucer are nowhere to be seen, and the Roët arms are quartered with those of Thomas Chaucer's wife, Maud Burghersh.

Second, in 1381, John of Gaunt paid a very handsome dowry to the prestigious Barking Abbey to cover the expenses of admitting Elizabeth Chaucer. As with Blanche Swynford, some writers have concluded that the duke was making generous provision for the future of his bastard child.[91] Barking Abbey was a most exclusive house; its abbess was foremost among all the abbesses in the realm and enjoyed the status of a baron—but for her sex, she could have sat in the House of Lords. Places in the novitiate at Barking were therefore much sought after for the daughters of noble families, but admittance usually depended on large sums changing hands and a royal recommendation. For the daughter of a mere civil servant, who could hardly afford the required dowry, to be accepted was a rare achievement, hence the interest it has attracted among historians.[92]

Third, there is the matter of John of Gaunt's generous gifts to Philippa Chaucer. On three recorded occasions, each at New Year—when gifts were customarily exchanged—in 1380, 1381, and 1382, he presented her with beautiful silver cups.

Advocates of the theory that John of Gaunt was the father of Philippa Chaucer's children would have us believe that he took first one of the Roët sisters, Philippa, as his mistress, presumably around the period 1364–67 or thereabouts, and later the other, Katherine. If so, Philippa would have been very young at the time the liaison began, probably no more than twelve or thirteen, hardly old enough to be of much interest to the twenty-four-year-old Duke. It has also been suggested that she was married off to a complacent Geoffrey Chaucer to give her a veneer of respectability and that Chaucer was willing to play the father to the duke's bastards; this would explain why his marriage to Philippa was not overtly happy. It would also mean that John was persistently unfaithful to Blanche over a period of perhaps four years, which is at variance with what we know of their marriage, for not a breath of scandal touched it at the time, and there is no evidence of any infidelity on his part. Nor did he ever acknowledge any of Philippa's children as his own, although he did recognize Katherine's bastards and Marie de St. Hilaire's daughter. And he was not in the habit of marrying off his mistresses so he could conceal his paternity of their children.

Most pertinently, any sexual relationship with Philippa Chaucer would have placed John even more firmly within the forbidden degrees of affinity to Katherine Swynford, rendering his relationship with her scandalously incestuous, in an age in which incest was a criminal act for which some offenders were burned at the stake.[93] If such a relationship had existed, it is astonishing that no disapproving chronicler made political capital out of it, or even mentioned it, for there were those who were continually to castigate the duke for his immorality, and who would have pounced gleefully on any scandal involving him. Furthermore, the only canonical impediment that John asked the Pope to dispense with in 1396 was the compaternity created by his being godfather to Katherine's child. Again, it is unlikely that he would have imperiled his immortal soul, and Katherine's, by courting automatic excommunication. He also risked nullifying the dispensation he was seeking by not declaring to the Pope such a serious impediment as incest; John, a man of the world, would have known that divine law prohibited him from marrying his mistress's sister. No dispensation had ever been granted in a case like this, so there was no question that such a marriage would have been incestuous and invalid.[94] Hence we must conclude that John was not the father of Philippa Chaucer's children, that he never had sexual intercourse with her, and that Thomas Chaucer and his sister Elizabeth were Geoffrey's children.

Interestingly, of those twenty shields on Thomas Chaucer's tomb, the only male ones are those of the Beauforts, the sons of John of Gaunt by Katherine Swynford. The other seventeen are those of female relatives from some of the greatest families in the land. We can conclude, therefore, that Thomas Chaucer, and no doubt his daughter Alice (the wife of William de la Pole, Earl of Suffolk), who was responsible for the building of his tomb, preferred to stress their royal and noble connections rather than the mercantile ones, and since Thomas's mother had been the sister of the Duchess of Lancaster, it was natural that he should place the duchess's arms on the tomb, and omit those of his father, who, for all his literary reputation, had no claim to nobility.[95]

The dowering of Elizabeth Chaucer should be seen as an act of generosity on the part of John of Gaunt to his mistress's niece, who was also the daughter of two people who had given excellent service to his family. Such liberality was a mark of the duke's character. Clearly he thought highly of Philippa Chaucer, who had served his mother so devotedly and would later render the same good service to his wife, and his philanthropic gesture to Philippa's daughter should therefore be viewed with no more suspicion than Countess Margaret's dowering of Elizabeth de Roët.

With regard to John's gifts to Philippa, these were probably innocent tokens of appreciation of the good service rendered to his mother and his duchess by a lady who was not only the wife of a man he liked and admired, but also the sister of his beloved mistress, whose other relatives also enjoyed his favor. Katherine seems to have been fond of her sister—Philippa was to live in her house in later years—and John's favor to Philippa may have been prompted by her. Other ladies of his wife's household, and members of his own, received similar gifts from the duke, so there is nothing particularly special or significant about his gifts to Philippa. And while John of Gaunt was extremely generous to his acknowledged bastards, he was far less munificent to Thomas Chaucer, which would have been strange had Thomas really been his son.[96]

Thus there are no credible grounds to substantiate the theory that John of Gaunt committed the sin of incest: that when he took Katherine Swynford as his mistress, he had already enjoyed a sexual relationship with her sister.

FOUR

Mistress of the Duke

D eath stalked Katherine's world in the years 1368–71. First, around July 24, 1368, her older sister, Elizabeth de Roët, died in her convent at Mons.[1] Unless Katherine was in touch with unrecorded relatives in Hainault, she might not for some time have learned of or been greatly affected by the passing of this sister with whom she can barely—if at all—have been acquainted. But the death of Blanche of Lancaster on September 12, 1368, at Tutbury Castle in Staffordshire[2] would have had far more impact and surely brought her much grief and distress, for Blanche had held her in "great affection," and Katherine in return had given her "good and agreeable service," for which she would in time be handsomely rewarded.[3] It also seems to have brought to an end her service in the Lancastrian household.

It was possibly around August 1368 when Blanche bore her last child, a third daughter, baptized Isabella, who shortly afterward was "swiftly summoned out of this world to the seat of the angels."[4] Blanche was then twenty-six and had borne seven children in nine years of marriage. The fact that she died the month after this latest birth suggests that she suffered complications in labor or contracted puerperal fever, a major cause of maternal deaths and a common occurrence in an era when the transmission of infection from a midwife's dirty hands, or other unhygienic practices, was not understood. John of Gaunt was with his wife at the end, and that same day he wrote from Tutbury to his "faithful friend" and neighbor Thomas Appleby, Bishop of Carlisle, bidding him order masses for the salvation of the soul of Blanche, "who has died."[5]

"Put a tomb over my heart, for when I remember, I am so melancholy," mourned Froissart. "She died young and lovely."[6] He wrote this the following year, and because of this historians believed until recently that Blanche perished of the plague on September 12, 1369, at Bolingbroke Castle. But the date clearly stated on the duke's letter in Bishop Appleby's register makes it clear that Blanche died in 1368.[7]

John of Gaunt was apparently devastated by the loss of his wife. Their love had been enduring, and throughout their nine-year marriage there was no hint of discord or infidelity, while the frequency of Blanche's pregnancies argues for a healthy sex life. Blanche's memory was clearly cherished by John, for he was solemnly to observe the anniversary of her death for the rest of his life, and more than thirty years later would direct in his will that he be buried beside her—the wife who brought him his great inheritance, the mother of his heir, and his first love.

We do not know if Katherine was in attendance at Tutbury when Blanche died, but with the rest of the duchess's household, she would have been issued with black mourning garments and summoned to accompany the funeral cortege, which was escorted south by a thousand horsemen. Carried beside the coffin was a seated effigy of the deceased in her robes of state, probably made of wood, and apparently looking very lifelike. Katherine perhaps witnessed the unseemly row between the Abbot of St. Albans and the Bishop of Lincoln over who should take precedence in St. Albans Abbey in Hertfordshire, where the duchess was to lie in state for a requiem mass,[8] just as she would witness a similar row on another tragic occasion just over twenty years later. She may also have been present when her late mistress's body was interred "on the north side of the quire,"[9] near the high altar, in St. Paul's Cathedral in London.

Old St. Paul's, which was destroyed in the Great Fire of 1666, was the largest building in medieval England. It was completed in 1220, on the site of an earlier church founded around 607 by King Ethelbert of Kent, which burned down in 1087. The new stone cathedral in the Romanesque style was truly awe-inspiring: "The height of the steeple was 520 foot, and the spire was 260 foot. The length of the whole church is 720 foot. The breadth thereof is 130 foot, and the height of the body of that church is 150 foot." Thus the building was longer than the present St. Paul's Cathedral, and its spire higher than that of Salisbury Cathedral, the highest in England today.[10]

Blanche's was the first royal burial in St. Paul's since that of Saxon King Ethelred II in 1016; in Katherine's day, his massive stone sarcophagus could still be seen in the north quire aisle. The cathedral also housed the magnificent shrine of St. Erkenwald, a seventh-century Bishop of London, which stood behind the high altar.

When a royal lady died, her household was usually disbanded, for it was not considered fitting for her female attendants to remain in a widower's establishment. Yet there was a pressing need for someone to take care of the three young children left motherless by Blanche's death, and it has been suggested by several writers that Katherine, who was clearly good with children and highly regarded in the Lancastrian household, stayed on in the nursery. If so, she cannot have been there in any exalted capacity, for it is clear that other ladies were looking after the ducal offspring.

In 1369 the duke appointed his and Blanche's cousin, Alice FitzAlan, Lady Wake,[11] to look after Henry, Philippa, and Elizabeth; Lady Wake, who was paid £66.13s.4d (£18,795) in 1369 just for looking after Henry and his household, was still in charge of them, and acting as their governess, in November 1371. Furthermore, in 1370, John of Gaunt rewarded Alyne, the wife of his squire, Edward Gerberge, with a handsome pension of £100 (£24,779) per annum for "the painful diligence and good service she has rendered to our very dear daughter Philippa during the death of our beloved companion."[12] We can infer from this that eight-year-old Philippa was perhaps with Blanche at the end, that her mother's death affected her very badly, and that Alyne Gerberge played a far more important role in comforting her than Katherine Swynford did, which suggests that Katherine was not at Tutbury when Blanche died. The size of the annuity paid to Alyne is commensurate with her having been appointed to look after Philippa after Blanche's death.

Clearly she was a trusted servant, for "our well-loved *damoiselle*" Alyne was later appointed by John of Gaunt to serve his second duchess.[13]

We do know, however, that Katherine's daughter Blanche remained in the ducal household as a *damoiselle* to Philippa and Elizabeth of Lancaster until at least September 1369,[14] which seems appropriate for a girl who was the probable godchild of the duke and duchess. But as none of the John of Gaunt registers survives for the period 1369–72, we have no way of knowing how long Blanche Swynford remained with the ducal princesses after 1369.

It might be more realistic to suppose that, rather than remaining with the duke's children, Katherine, who had a growing family of her own, returned to Kettlethorpe to bring them up and attend to her duties as chatelaine and custodian. Her long-term reputation as the Lady of Kettlethorpe would surely not have been so well-established had she spent long periods absent from the manor.

Geoffrey Chaucer had been sent to France and Italy on diplomatic business on July 17, 1368, so was not in England when Duchess Blanche died. On his return, before October 31,[15] he evidently found John of Gaunt paralyzed by grief, which spurred him to write his celebrated elegiac memorial for Blanche, *The Boke of the Duchesse*, as much to comfort her widower and bring him to an acceptance of her death as to commemorate her beauty and virtue—and perhaps to console himself.

In this, his first major poem, Chaucer conjures up a dream sequence of an allegorical royal "hunting of the hart"—the pun was intentional—in which he, the narrator, becomes separated from the hunting party and wanders into a forest, where he espies a tragic sight:

> *I suddenly saw a man in black*
> *Reclining, seated with his back*
> *Against an oak, a giant tree.*
> *"Oh Lord," I thought, "who can that be?"* . . .

Chaucer's readers would have recognized at once that it was the grieving Duke of Lancaster; we have already seen how, scattered through the poem, are punning allusions to "John," "Lancaster," "Richmond," and "Lady White" (for Blanche). Chaucer borrowed his theme from Guillaume de Machaut, but his subject was poignantly close to home.

The young knight, who "was wholly clad in black" and displayed "a complexion green and pale," was hanging his head and sighing, "and with a deathly mourning cried a rhyme of verse in lamentation to himself, more pitiful and charged with woe than I had ever heard. It seemed remarkable that Nature could suffer any living creature to bear such grief and not be dead." Seeing him "in state so grim," the narrator greets him, which prompts an outpouring of woe. The knight wonders why "his misery had not made him die"; his sorrows were so manifold and sharp, he says, they "lay upon his heart ice-cold . . . He'd almost lost his sanity." Then, realizing he is talking to a total stranger, he pulls himself together and greets him courteously.

Encouraged by the curious narrator, and thanking his "gentle friend" for his "kind intent," the knight opens his heart. Speaking kindly and frankly, "without false style or sense of rank," and seeming approachable, wise, and reasonable, he says he wishes he had not been born, that he weeps when he is alone, and that his days and nights are detestable, "for I am sorrow, and sorrow is I."

"My bliss is gone, my joy is lost for evermore," he cries, "and there exists no happiness." Without revealing what tragedy has overtaken him, he tells the stranger how he had won the love of his lady, despite being rebuffed several times. He says he had fallen in love at a tender age, and that that love is with him still. He describes, in minute detail, his lady's beauty and virtues. "I seem to see her evermore," he declares. "She was my hap, my heal and all my bliss . . . While I live, I'll evermore remember her." Eventually, the narrator asks, "Where is she now?"

"She is dead!" comes the bitter reply.

There is no more to be said; "all was done," and the hunters can be heard approaching. A bell strikes, and the narrator awakens to find it was all a dream. But the outpouring of memories of the cherished one who had gone and the love she shared with the man in black would have been cathartic in itself for John of Gaunt, and hopefully helped him come to terms with his grief, which was surely Chaucer's intention.

The voice in which Chaucer narrates the poem is unusually emotional; clearly the death of the young duchess had hit him hard too, occasioning genuine sympathy for the bereft widower. The social gulf between the griever—the King's son—and the comforter—the King's esquire—is apparent in the formal, deferential, and tentative manner in which the narrator approaches the man in black, but their easy discourse suggests an established rapport between two men who already knew, liked, and respected each other. Some commentators have claimed that *The Boke of the Duchesse* is purely a poem in the French poetic tradition and does not bear much relation to real events, but that is perhaps too narrow a view, for why should Chaucer have used all those allusions and puns to make it very clear to his readers that the "man in black" was in fact the grief-stricken Duke of Lancaster?[16] Furthermore, in the prologue to a later work of Chaucer's, *The Legend of Good Women*, reference is made to his having written a poem originally entitled *The Death of Blanche the Duchess*.[17] What could be clearer than that?

There may have been another reason for the emotional tone of the poem. In it, Chaucer intriguingly—and very obliquely—reveals that for eight years he has suffered a secret and unrequited desire for an unnamed lady. Only she can cure him of his "malady," but "that hope is gone." Therefore he knows, from personal experience, what loss is. "It must be endured," he says.

Historians have endlessly speculated who this lady was, some even claiming it was Blanche herself, which was certainly possible in those days when the conventions of courtly love permitted esquires to conceive passions for highborn ladies far above them and beyond their reach; and the reference to his hope being gone might refer to the death of his revered lady. If so, Chaucer had first fallen for her charms around 1360, soon after her marriage to John of Gaunt. Such a theory would account for his obscure wording of this passage, since he could never have dared publicly to confess such a love. And it would explain the emotional tone and empathy of the poem. Never again would Chaucer refer to himself in the guise of a lover.

G rief-stricken he might be, but political advantage dictated that John of Gaunt could not be allowed to remain a widower for long. He was too great a prize in the matrimonial market, and Blanche had not been in her grave two months before Edward III and Queen Philippa opened negotiations for a second marriage for their son. In November, John was proposed as a husband for Margaret, heiress to Louis III, Count of Flanders, a match that would have brought him a principality and provided England with a buffer state against the hostility of France. It was an irresistible prospect, and one on which John, however tragic his grief, could not have turned his back.

But the count rejected the offer, preferring to court the French, and in 1369 Margaret was married to Philip the Bold, Duke of Burgundy, brother of the French King Charles V.[18]

It has been credibly suggested that Chaucer probably wrote the 1,334 lines of *The Boke of the Duchesse* before these negotiations were opened, rapidly polishing off his masterpiece in the short weeks between his return from France and an approach being made to Flanders.[19] The intense immediacy and poignancy of the poem and its consolatory aspects suggest that it was indeed composed in the desolate aftermath of Blanche's death. John Stow claims—perhaps basing his information on sources now lost to us— that it was written at John of Gaunt's request, which is possible; however, there is no contemporary evidence for this, or any record of the poem being dedicated or presented to the duke. Claims that it was written for recital at one of the annual memorial services for Blanche may be a little far-fetched, considering its length and the fact that no one ever remarked upon this unusual addition to the ceremonies.

We may, however, be almost certain that the poem was intended for private circulation within the Lancastrian household and even in the court itself, for three copies have survived, which suggests there were more made; furthermore, the reference to the poem in the prologue to *The Legend of Good Women* indicates that it had attained some fame. It would certainly have been known to the members of Chaucer's own family, and it was possibly thanks to Chaucer's kinship to Katherine Swynford, as much as to his links to the court, that he learned of the magnitude of John's grief. Who else but Katherine would have been so well placed to tell him about it? Unless, of course, it was the duke himself and the poem is based on a real-life conversation that Chaucer set within a dream sequence to comply with contemporary literary conventions. Chaucer, as Pearsall points out, was a mere esquire at this time; he would surely not have presumed to write this intimate poem dealing with such private matters without some indication it would be well-received by the mighty Duke of Lancaster. The interaction between the two characters in the poem suggests that, whether the duke commissioned it or not, there was a rapport between him and Chaucer, and an element of patronage involved on his part. Yet whatever the circumstances in which the poem was composed, it does convincingly convey the deep and anguished grief that John of Gaunt undoubtedly suffered for Blanche of Lancaster.

·   ·   ·

In 1369 there was a third outbreak of the Black Death. It began in March, the same month that Pedro the Cruel, King of Castile, was ambushed and murdered by Enrique of Trastamara at Montiel. Instead of being decently chested and buried, the body was decapitated and left unburied, which outraged Castilian sensibilities. It was several days before the head was sent to Seville for public exhibition and the body interred. Immediately afterward, Enrique II usurped the throne, ignoring the legitimate rights of Pedro's two surviving daughters—Beatrice had taken the veil and died in 1368. Constance, the eldest, now succeeded her father as de jure Queen of Castile, but she and her sister Isabella were still in exile at Bayonne in Gascony as hostages of the Black Prince, and there seemed little prospect of her ever enforcing her claim to the Castilian throne and the crown Pedro had bequeathed to her.

Only a week after Pedro's murder, Charles V of France, having rejected the Treaty of Brétigny, declared war on England. Late in May the French clawed back all the land held by the English in Ponthieu and began amassing a great invasion force. In retaliation, in Parliament, an incensed Edward III again assumed the title King of France. This fresh outbreak of hostilities was to impact hugely on the lives of Katherine, Hugh, and John of Gaunt. On June 12—at a time when the plague hit London and the court had taken refuge at Windsor—the duke was appointed King's Captain and Lieutenant in Calais, Guisnes, and the surrounding country. This was his first independent command, and on July 26 he arrived in Calais with an army in which Geoffrey Chaucer and probably Hugh Swynford were serving, and spent August and September campaigning in France.

When John sailed from England, he left his mother, Queen Philippa, "dangerously sick" with what was described as a dropsy;[20] she seems to have been seriously ill for some time before then, since her tomb effigy had been ordered prior to January 1368.[21] Among those in attendance on her at Windsor was Philippa Chaucer.[22] On March 10, 1369, along with fifteen other damoiselles, Philippa had received furs and cloth for a new gown, but there was little chance to appear in public richly clad for by July the Queen was bedridden and needing the constant ministrations of her women. She died on August 14, "to the infinite misfortune of King Edward, his children, and the whole kingdom."[23] "I wring my hands, I clap my palms!" wrote an anguished Froissart, recalling also the death of Blanche of Lancaster a year earlier. "I have lost too many in these two ladies."[24]

On September 1, Edward III commanded Henry de Snaith, guardian of "our Great Wardrobe," to provide mourning garments for his family and the late Queen's servants. Among these were twelve ells of black cloth and some furs for little Blanche Swynford, who is described as a *damoiselle* of the daughters of the Duke of Lancaster; she received the same cloth and furs as allocated to her young mistresses and other high-ranking ladies, which suggests that Queen Philippa had retained an affection for the family of Katherine de Roët, her young compatriot, whom she had brought up and seen well placed and honorably married, and that the King too was fond of Katherine, for Philippa Chaucer—who had been in the Queen's service for some years—received only six ells of cloth, while Chaucer got just three.[25] As for Katherine, still perhaps sorrowing over the death of Duchess Blanche, the loss of her kindly and inspirational guardian, who had acted as a mother to her, must have left her feeling bereft.

The news of the Queen's death hit John of Gaunt hard too, for he loved and honored both his parents, and would still have been grieving for his late wife. Froissart tells us that "information of this heavy loss was carried to the English army at Tournehem, which greatly afflicted everyone, more especially her son, John of Gaunt." Until his death, John cherished "a gold brooch in the old fashion, with the name of God inscribed on each part of it, which my most honorable lady mother, whom God preserve, gave to me, commanding me to guard it with her blessing."[26]

On September 12 the first obit (a service marking the anniversary of a death) for Duchess Blanche was solemnly observed at St. Paul's, in the duke's absence. Her anniversary would be celebrated every year for the rest of John's lifetime and beyond, further evidence of his love for her and his grief at her loss. Whenever he was unable to attend, the great officers of his household stood proxy for him. By September 1371 a chantry chapel had been established above Blanche's burial place in St. Paul's, and soon afterward an altar was built and two salaried chaplains appointed to celebrate daily masses for the repose of her soul.[27]

In October, thanks to dwindling supplies, plague, and the arrival of wintry weather, John of Gaunt was forced to abandon his French offensive.

By the end of November he was back at the Savoy, and Sir Hugh Swynford was probably riding north to Lincolnshire to attend to his estates and be reunited with his family.

John of Gaunt kept the Christmas of 1369 at Langley in Hertfordshire with his father the King; it must have been a sad time for the bereft royal family, with the late Queen still unburied. Philippa of Hainault's magnificent state funeral took place on January 29, 1370, six months after her death—such things took time to arrange. Philippa and Geoffrey Chaucer would certainly have been there, and it may not be too fanciful to wonder if Katherine Swynford herself was among the mourners, for she had been brought up by the Queen and was her countrywoman. After being drawn in procession through streets specially cleared of mud and filth, Philippa's body was interred near the shrine of St. Edward the Confessor in Westminster Abbey, in earth brought to England from the Holy Land; a fine tomb was later built to her memory, with her lifelike effigy by a Netherlandish sculptor, Hennequin of Liège, resting upon it.

After the obsequies were completed, Katherine perhaps returned to Kettlethorpe. As Chaucer remained in service at court, her sister may have gone to live in his family house in London, with their growing family, for there was no place for her in the royal household now that the Queen was dead.

The political events of 1370 were to have a profound effect on Katherine's future, so it is worth leaving her at Kettlethorpe for the time being, and looking at what was happening in the wider world.

After Queen Philippa's death things went badly for the aging Edward III. In 1370, Aquitaine came under threat from Charles V, who had allied himself with Enrique II of Castile. The harsh rule of the Black Prince had driven his Gascon subjects to appeal to the French king for aid, and as the prince's overlord, Charles V had summoned him to Paris to account for his cruelties, but he was too ill to comply. In retaliation, the French closed in on the duchy.

Again John of Gaunt raised an army, this time to assist his brother in repelling the invader, and once more Sir Hugh Swynford was summoned to attend his lord. Did Katherine have a presentiment, as she saw him off on his way to join the Duke at Plymouth, that she would never see her husband again? She had perhaps often entertained fears of this kind, for war was a dangerous business, and those who escaped death at the hands of the enemy often perished as a result of the dysentery and disease that could decimate armies.

John of Gaunt's fleet sailed at the end of June, and once again Geoffrey Chaucer was with it, in company with his brother-in-law, Hugh Swynford.

John would have been shocked at the change in his once magnificent brother, who was waiting for him at Cognac. The Black Prince was virtually bedridden, suffering from what Froissart calls "an incurable illness," the malady that had laid him low for three years now, since he contracted amoebic dysentery in Castile. He could no longer ride a horse, and it was reported to Charles V that he had a dropsy from which he could never recover.[28] Modern medical opinion holds that this was symptomatic of nephritis, an inflammation of the kidneys that causes swollen legs, ankles, eyes, and genitals, due to a build-up of fluid.[29] The prince's condition, and the humiliation and frustration engendered by weakness and helplessness, had turned him into an embittered man.

On August 24, the city of Limoges voluntarily—and treasonably—surrendered to the French. The Black Prince's fury was lethal, his retribution savage. He laid siege to the city, and when the walls were breached on September 18, ordered it to be sacked, directing that neither man, woman, nor child be spared. The carnage went on relentlessly for two days, as the invalid prince watched from a horse litter, urging his men to ever worse atrocities. Soon the ruined streets were piled high with hundreds of corpses and running with blood.[30] Never again would Edward of Woodstock's glorious reputation shine as fair.

John of Gaunt was present at the fall of Limoges, in command of the English forces during the siege, and it was as a result of his brave efforts that the city capitulated. Froissart implies that John supported his brother in inflicting the atrocities committed after the siege: "I do not understand how *they* [author's italics] could have failed to take pity on people who were too unimportant to have committed treason," he opined, "yet they paid for it, and paid more dearly than the leaders who had committed it." But Froissart may not be correct—he certainly exaggerated by tenfold the number slaughtered—for afterward it was thanks to John's intervention that the bishop who had surrendered Limoges to the French was able to escape the Black Prince's vengeance.

After Limoges the prince realized he no longer had the strength to govern his principality and reluctantly decided to relinquish his command to his brother. On October 8, referring to "the very great affection and love" he cherished for John, he created him Lord of Bergerac and Roche-sur-Yon,[31] and three days later, surrendered to him the lieutenancy of Aquitaine. His burden laid down, he retired to Bordeaux.

In January 1371 the prince's physicians urged him to return to his native air of England without delay if he wished to preserve his life. His misery was compounded that same month by the death of his five-year-old heir, Edward of Angoulême, at Bordeaux. Yet so ill was the prince that the bereaved parents dared not let even their terrible grief delay their departure. Leaving John of Gaunt to arrange their child's burial,[32] the prince and princess returned to England with their surviving son Richard at the end of January. When they made land in Devon, they were obliged to rest for five weeks before the prince could face the journey to Berkhamsted Castle, and when they arrived there, he took to his bed. From that time, he was a broken man.

For the next six months John of Gaunt ruled Aquitaine, holding it successfully against the French. Then, in July, in accordance with the terms of his office, he relinquished his command and handed over his authority to Jean de Grailly, Captal de Buch.[33] The duke now had his sights on a richer prize than Aquitaine. The daughters of Pedro the Cruel, Queen Constance and her sister Isabella, had remained in exile under the protection of first the Black Prince and then John of Gaunt, consigned to a humble existence in a village near Bayonne. Their position was an invidious one, for although royal, they were outcasts from their homeland, dependent on the charity of the English, whom their father had betrayed, and surrounded only by a few of their own people. "The girls had suffered considerably, on account of which they were the objects of great pity."[34] Now all that was to change.

On August 10, John of Gaunt took up residence at Bordeaux, the capital of the duchy. English princes sojourning in Bordeaux resided in the ancient Ombriere Palace, in which the royal apartments were located beyond the Porte Cailhau in a tall keep known as the "Crossbowman," which was surrounded by courtyards with tiled fountains and beautiful semitropical gardens.[35] Once settled in this beautiful place, John gave some thought to what should become of Constance and Isabella, with whom he must have had a passing acquaintance over the years. He knew that Constance had been willed the throne of Castile by her father, King Pedro, and was regarded as its legitimate queen by his followers. All she lacked was someone to take up her cause, and for the man who could successfully do so, there would be rich prizes indeed.

Sometime during that sun-drenched summer of 1371, Guichard d'Angle, Marshal of Aquitaine and a trusted friend, diplomat, and member of the duke's council, who had been held prisoner by Enrique of Trastamara for two years, suggested to John that he marry Constance and claim the crown of Castile in her right,[36] a suggestion he would surely not have made without knowing that the idea was already in the duke's mind, and perhaps in Edward III's too. The Gascon barons backed the proposal. Such a union made good political sense: Not only would it bring John a throne and a kingdom, which he had perhaps long desired, but it would also break the alliance between Castile and France, which was posing a very real threat to England and her chances of winning the war. The proposal "pleased [the duke] so well that he sent without delay four of his knights for the young ladies."[37]

For Constance, regaining her throne and laying King Pedro's bones properly to rest in his native earth appear to have been sacred duties, for she cherished the memory of her father. Her strong loyalty is perhaps reflected in Chaucer's generous portrayal of Pedro in "The Monk's Tale," and we may suppose that the poet was used to hearing all about the murdered king's virtues and death from his wife Philippa, who in turn must have heard it again and again from Constance, whom she was to serve for years. Thus, ignoring the more brutal realities of Pedro's rule and character, Chaucer could write:

> O noble, O worthy Pedro, glory of Spain,
> Whom Fortune held so high in majesty,
> Well ought men thy piteous death complain!

Mindful that her father had long desired his daughters to be married to sons of Edward III, Constance accepted the Duke of Lancaster's proposal with alacrity, confident that such a great prince would be successful in helping her achieve her cherished aims. Realistically, though, that was a remote prospect, for with the backing of France, Enrique of Trastamara had become even more entrenched in Castile.

Constance was in every way an ideal choice of a royal bride: She was young, beautiful, and devout, and brought to the marriage the promise of a kingdom. Her tragic plight appealed to John's sense of chivalry: Guichard d'Angle had played on that when he pointed out that marrying her "would offer comfort and aid to these girls, daughters of a king, who are forced by circumstances to live in their present state." It was these words that had "softened the heart of the duke."[38] Yet Constance was no stereotypical maiden in distress: For all her youth (she was seventeen) she had her father's pride, his singularity of purpose and tenacity, and the passionate, grieving love that only an exile can feel for his or her native land.[39]

We have only two surviving manuscript pictures of Constance. One is in a late fifteenth-century manuscript in the Bibliothèque Nationale, Paris, and shows her with John of Gaunt at the surrender of Compostela in 1386. The other, in a genealogy executed between 1493 and 1519, shows the descent of the royal House of Portugal, which includes members of the family of John of Gaunt:[40] Constance wears a red velvet gown with a full skirt and blue kirtle typical of Castilian dress of that later period, and an anachronistic horned headdress; her hair is black, parted, and looped to either side of the face in the style that would be favored by Queen Isabella of Castile; and her features are florid, with a long nose. This illustration may have been based on one in an older manuscript that has been lost, for the headdress is partly of the fourteenth century.

Constance and John were married on September 21, 1371, at Roquefort-sur-Soulzon,[41] a small town nestling on terraces on the side of a rocky outcrop near Mont-de-Marsan in the Aveyron, just south of Bordeaux; since the first century BC, the distinctive Roquefort cheese had been produced there and matured in the local caves. John's wedding gift to Constance was a gold cup "fashioned in the manner of a double rose with a pedestal and lid, with a white dove on the lid,"[42] while Constance gave him the finest gold cup he ever possessed.[43] It would be no exaggeration to say that from the day of their marriage, the conquest of Castile would be the major preoccupation of John's life.

On September 25, after some brief celebrations in Bordeaux,[44] the duke and his new duchess arrived at the port of La Rochelle, and there requisitioned a salt ship bound for England, obliging the master to offload his cargo to make room for their retinue and chattels.[45] John was attended by a train of Castilian knights wearing the Lancastrian livery, and Constance by a bevy of Castilian ladies. They docked at Fowey, near Plymouth, on November 4, and rested at Plympton Priory from November 10 to 14.[46] Two days later the duke and duchess moved on to Exeter, where they offered 20s. (£335) in the cathedral.[47] John then left Constance and rode to London to make ready for her arrival; he was in residence at the Savoy, and reunited with his three children, by the end of the month,[48] when he went "to report to the King."[49] Then in December, after paying his respects at Blanche's tomb in St Paul's, he traveled down to Kingston Lacy in Dorset, where he and his bride kept Christmas, feasting on venison and rabbits.[50]

John was back at the Savoy by January 22, having arranged for Constance to journey up to London at her leisure. Her long sojourn in the West Country had perhaps been necessitated by her suffering the discomforts and sickness of early pregnancy.

Hugh Swynford had not accompanied his lord back to England. He died "beyond seas" in Aquitaine, "on the Thursday after St. Martin," November 13, 1371.[51] The fact that he did not follow the duke north in September argues that he was already too ill to do so. The news of his death would have taken some weeks to reach Katherine, but probably arrived in time for her to spend a dismal Christmas facing up to early widowhood and the prospect of bringing up her children alone on a pittance, for Hugh's finances and affairs had been left in little better shape than when she married him.

The medieval church at Kettlethorpe has long since largely disappeared, and with it any fourteenth-century tombs and memorials, so there is no way of knowing whether Hugh's body was brought back to England and interred there, but given his parlous financial state, he may well have been buried in Aquitaine.[52] Whether he was laid to rest in Kettlethorpe Church or not, a requiem mass would surely have been held there for him, with Katherine in attendance.

Katherine was only about twenty-one when she was widowed, yet custom required her to put on nunlike mourning garments consisting of a black gown and cloak and a white wimple; the constricting barbe that covered the chin and spread like a cape across the shoulders mercifully had not yet come into fashion. She would wear these weeds until the expiration of her first year of widowhood, after which she might remarry with propriety.[53]

It would appear that John of Gaunt came to her rescue, and that learning of her plight, and doubtless recalling her good service to Blanche, he invited her to serve his second duchess in a similar capacity. Philippa Chaucer, likewise redundant because of the death of a royal mistress, was also appointed to serve Constance as one of her many married *damoiselles*; on August 30, 1372, at Sandwich, John of Gaunt awarded her an annuity of £10 (£3,347) "by our especial grace for the good and agreeable service that our wellbeloved *damoiselle* Philippa Chaucer has done, and will do in the future, for our very dear and well-loved companion the Queen."[54]

There is no record of Katherine being in Constance's household until March 1373, but given the fact that the King and John of Gaunt were helping her financially in the spring of 1372, and that she was in attendance when Constance bore a child probably in the summer of that year, it is likely that she was engaged with her sister when the duchess's establishment was set up between January and April. Katherine's former experience as a longterm, much loved member of Duchess Blanche's household would have left her uniquely qualified to serve the young Constance, and that she was chosen to convey news of the birth of Constance's child to the King suggests that her position was of some prominence.

Philippa Chaucer's appointment to the Lancastrian ménage while her husband remained in royal service, and the fact that she was now often to be resident at Hertford Castle or Tutbury Castle, and would remain with the duchess for some years to come, meant that henceforth she and Geoffrey would see much less of each other. This may be a further indication that their marriage was unhappy, and also that Philippa was done with childbearing. Having spent most of her life at court, she probably preferred the social cachet conferred on her by her return to royal service to living in obscurity as the wife of a royal esquire; she had perhaps not liked living in London, where foreigners were regarded with suspicion and even hostility. Chaucer himself may have welcomed this new arrangement with amicable resignation, seeing his wife when their duties permitted and agreeing to pool their financial resources; from 1374, he went in person to collect Philippa's pension from the Exchequer.[55]

On January 30, Edward III's council formally recognized John of Gaunt as King of Castile and León; henceforth, John would be known as "Monseigneur d'Espaigne" rather than "Monseigneur de Lancaster"; he would sign his letters in regal Castilian style as *Nos el Roy* (We, the King) and his seal would bear the royal arms of Castile and León impaling those of England. He would now be deferred to as if he were a reigning sovereign, and the etiquette observed at his court would have reflected this.

John's zeal for winning a foreign kingdom for himself was to cost him much trust and popularity in England, where people suspected him of disloyalty to the Crown and speculated that his ambitions might not be satisfied with the throne of Castile. Unlike him, many lacked the foresight to see that with an English king reigning in a friendly Castile, France would lose a valuable ally, Castilian naval raids would cease, and England's chances of achieving some success in the war would be vastly improved. Furthermore, for many years to come John was to subordinate his dynastic ambitions in order to give priority to prosecuting the war with France on England's behalf, and not only because there was no money to pay for an offensive against Castile. Only time would prove that his loyalty to the English Crown was never in doubt, but to many of the xenophobic and increasingly nationalistic Commons, to whom all foreigners were "strangers" and therefore suspect, he was at best pursuing personal aggrandizement and at worst a traitor.

This would not have mattered so much had not John become the chief influence over the King. Because of Edward III's escalating physical and mental decline, the Black Prince's infirmity, and the death of Lionel of Antwerp in 1368, John was now the most important and powerful man in the realm. It was to him that men looked for political leadership, at a time when England's great victories against the French were long past and the war was going disastrously. There were frequent enemy raids on the south coast and consequent disruptions to trade, while a population ravaged by plague was increasingly burdened with the crippling taxes needed to pay for the war. At the same time, Edward III's once brilliant court was degenerating into corruption. It would not be long before both Lords and Commons looked about them for a scapegoat and pointed a finger at John of Gaunt. Hence he would become widely hated throughout the kingdom, which would ultimately have repercussions for Katherine herself.

John's unpopularity was unfairly linked in the public mind to that of the King's mistress, Alice Perrers, the married daughter of a Hertfordshire knight, who was now queening it over the court. Edward had first taken her to his bed perhaps as early as 1364, when she was one of Queen Philippa's *damoiselles*, and soon, despite her not being beautiful and lacking a good fig-

ure,[56] "Alice had been preferred in the King's love before the Queen." Since
Philippa's death, Alice had gained ascendancy over her royal lover, who was
now descending into a childlike dotage and was rarely seen in public; claims
that his decline resulted from the gonorrhea with which she had infected
him have never been substantiated. She bore her royal lover a son and two
daughters, and over the years wheedled out of him jewelery worth at least
£375 (£105,723), an annuity of £100 (£28,193), twenty-two manors, land in
seventeen counties, and a London town house.[57] It is not surprising therefore that she has been seen as the model for the acquisitive and corrupt Lady
Meed in William Langland's poem, *The Vision of Piers Plowman*:

> I . . . was ware of a woman, wonderfully clad,
> Her robe fur-edged, the finest on Earth,
> Crowned with a crown, the King hath no better,
> Fairly her fingers were fretted with rings,
> And in the rings red rubies, as red as a furnace,
> And diamonds of dearest price, and double sapphires,
> Sapphires and beryls, poison to destroy.
> Her rich robe of scarlet dye,
> Her ribbons set with gold, red gold, rare stones;
> Her array ravished me: such riches saw I never.

By 1372, Alice's reputation was notorious; she was shameless, rapacious,
and ruthless, and exploited to the full her dominance over the senile King.
She persuaded him to let her wear the queen consort's jewels, presided with
him over a tournament in Smithfield, decked out as the "Lady of the Sun,"
controlled the flow of royal patronage to the benefit of her favorites, and
caused outrage by overseeing the proceedings at the Court of King's Bench
in Westminster Hall from the sovereign's marble throne, intervening to secure favorable judgments for her friends. "This Lady Alice de Perrers had
such power and eminence that no one dared prosecute a claim against her."
The public were scandalized, and some accused Alice of using witchcraft to
achieve her aims, as they were one day to accuse Katherine Swynford. "It is
not fitting or safe that all the keys should hang from the belt of one woman,"
fulminated Thomas Brinton, Bishop of Rochester, while Thomas Walsingham castigated Alice as "a shameless doxy," "an infamous whore," and "a thoroughly bad influence." Alice's career illustrates just how influential—and

ruinous to a prince's reputation—a royal mistress could be, a salutary lesson from which Katherine Swynford's conduct when she herself came to be a royal mistress suggests she had learned much.

Before Alice Perrers, the mistresses of English kings had made only fleeting appearances in history. Their names are more often than not the stuff of legend or passing references in official documents, and none was particularly influential. Even fair Rosamund de Clifford, for whom Henry II planned to divorce Eleanor of Aquitaine in the twelfth century, played a passive role. Prior to the fourteenth century, such women lived obscure lives, enjoying brief liaisons with monarchs, bearing royal bastards, and occasionally meriting a mention in a chronicle.

But Alice Perrers broke the mold. With Edward III's blessing and the backing of her allies—William, Lord Latimer, John, Lord Neville of Raby, and the powerful London financier, Richard Lyons—she controlled not only access to the King, but also the flow of royal patronage, and thus secured for herself a position of the greatest influence. John of Gaunt may not have liked her, but along with many other eminent figures of the day, including the Pope himself, he respected her abilities and tolerated her for his father's sake—indeed, he was later to protest that he was powerless in the face of her hold over the King—and in May 1373 we find her serving Duchess Constance alongside Philippa Chaucer at the Savoy, and receiving gifts from the duke.[58]

On February 10, 1372, Constance made her state entry into London and was formally welcomed as Queen of Castile by the Black Prince, who had risen from his sickbed and struggled onto a horse for the occasion. He was accompanied by "several lords and knights, the Mayor of London, and a great number of the Commons, well-dressed and nobly mounted," who conducted the new duchess "through London in a great and solemn procession. In Cheapside were assembled many gentlemen with their wives and daughters to look at the beauty of the young lady." This statement suggests that Constance's physical charms were already renowned.[59] "The procession passed in good order along to the Savoy," where John of Gaunt was waiting to greet his wife.[60] The Black Prince's welcome gift to his sister-in-law was a golden brooch or pendant depicting St. George, adorned with sapphires, diamonds, and pearls, while the King presented her with a golden crown set with diamonds and pearls.[61]

Soon afterward, Constance took up residence at Hertford Castle, where her three Lancastrian stepchildren were sent to join her; in 1372 they shared a common chamber, or household, for which their father allocated 300 marks (£33,471) annually to cover their expenditure. Henceforth, they would be attended and attired as befit the children of a king.[62] The appointment of Alyne Gerberge as a *damoiselle* to Constance[63] suggests that she was still looking after Philippa of Lancaster. By now Katherine Swynford and Philippa Chaucer were probably also part of the duchess's household, and both are likely to have had their children with them. Once again Katherine's duties probably involved helping to care for the ducal children, who must have known her well, and had perhaps welcomed her back warmly.

In March and April 1372, John of Gaunt made a generous settlement on his wife, assigning her 1,000 marks (£111,569) per annum for the expenses of her wardrobe and chamber. He also presented her with costly gifts: rich furs, lengths of cloth of gold, nearly four thousand loose pearls (probably for embellishing her gowns and making buttons), a small circlet of gold encrusted with emeralds and balas rubies, a golden filet set with four balas rubies, and twenty-one pearls set in gold rubies. All were delivered by the Clerk of the Wardrobe to Alyne Gerberge.[64]

This was no more than any royal duke would be expected to do for his bride. But John's generosity might have been prompted by his conscience, for despite his recent marriage, he had taken a mistress: On May 1, 1372, at the Savoy, he gave Katherine Swynford the handsome sum of £10 (£3,347), his first recorded gift to her.[65] This and other evidence strongly suggests that the love affair that was to change the course of English history had begun.

We do not know for certain when John and Katherine became lovers, but their affair had certainly begun by the late spring of 1372. In determining the date of birth of John Beaufort, the first of the children born to them, we may also discover the likeliest date for the commencement of their relationship. According to the grant of an annuity made to him by Richard II on June 7, 1392, John Beaufort was then in his twenty-first year;[66] thus, he was supposedly born between June 1371 and June 1372. But the dates are problematical. John of Gaunt went to Aquitaine in late June 1370, and did not return until November 1371. To have been born within the stated period, John Beaufort had to be conceived between September 1370 and September 1371; however, his father was abroad for the whole of that period, and in September 1371 he married Constance of Castile.

It could be conjectured that Katherine joined Hugh Swynford overseas, once it was known that he expected to be in Aquitaine for some time, and that the attraction between her and John of Gaunt flourished in the south of France. But that is an unlikely scenario. The wives of soldiers rarely accompanied them abroad; only laundresses and prostitutes followed armies, and any other woman who did so was putting her reputation at risk. And Katherine was the wife of a landed knight, however poor; her task during his absence was to oversee his estates in England and rear their young family.[67]

Even if Katherine had been in Aquitaine with Hugh, there is virtually watertight evidence that her affair with John did not begin until after she was widowed. In John and Katherine's petition to the Pope of September 1, 1396, they asserted that sometime after John had stood godfather to Katherine's daughter, "the same Duke John adulterously knew the same Katherine, *she being free of wedlock* [author's italics], but with marriage still existing between the same Duke John and [his wife] Constance, and begot offspring of her."[68] The compelling reasons for accepting the statements in this letter as the truth have been previously stated, and therefore we must accept that Katherine was no longer married to Hugh when she became John's mistress and conceived a child by him, although he was already married to Constance.[69]

That means they could not have become lovers until November 1371 at the earliest, and makes nonsense of claims that they had begun their affair in the lifetime of Duchess Blanche,[70] and of Froissart's assertions that Katherine "had been mistress of the duke both before and after his marriage with the Princess Constance" and while Hugh Swynford was alive. "Both during and after the knight's lifetime [he claims] Duke John of Lancaster had always loved and maintained this Lady Katherine." Since Froissart incorrectly states in the same passage that John and Katherine had three children, not four, his sources can hardly have been reliable.[71] He was, after all, writing long after these events.

John and Katherine's statement to the Pope also exposes as blatant propaganda Richard III's proclamation of 1485, which was designed to impugn the claim to the throne of his rival, Henry Tudor, who was descended from John of Gaunt through John Beaufort: Richard asserted that Henry "was descended of bastard blood both of the father's side and of the mother's side . . . His mother was daughter unto John [Beaufort], Duke of Somerset, son unto John [Beaufort], Earl of Somerset, son unto Dame Katherine Swynford, and of her in *double* [author's italics] adultery begotten, whereby it evidently appeareth that no title can or may be in him."[72] Richard conveniently ignored the fact that he himself was descended from John of Gaunt through Katherine Swynford.

It is very unlikely that Katherine was at the Savoy when John returned there in November 1371. It is more probable that she came to his remembrance when he heard of the death of Hugh Swynford, which was perhaps what prompted him to find a place for her in his new wife's household. It was quite possible that the news of Hugh's death reached England in little over two weeks—in 1386 it took John of Gaunt sixteen days to sail from England to Spain. The duke must have heard of it by late January, when he was back at the Savoy and probably engaged in assembling a household for his wife, ready for her arrival in London. Since Hugh was his retainer and vassal, John would have naturally taken an interest in his widow and dependants, and the disposal of his estates, and it would have been quite legitimate for Katherine to inform him of the dire financial straits in which she now found herself, and appeal to him for aid.

He had probably not seen Katherine for about three years, and maturity and vulnerability may have made her appear more beautiful and alluring; for him, she must have had too those indefinable qualities known as charm and sex appeal. Was it her fair Hainaulter beauty that appealed to him? Did it remind him of the "full feminine visage" of his mother, Queen Philippa, or the white-blond rounded loveliness of his late wife Blanche, or the charms of Marie de St. Hilaire, another Hainaulter? If these are indicative of John's taste in women, then the theory that Katherine herself was fair and voluptuous appears even more credible. Certainly for John, Katherine's extraordinary beauty eclipsed the charms of Constance. But even if the first attraction was physical, the enduring nature of his love for her must have been rooted in far more than beauty and sex, for she was intelligent, cultivated, and accomplished, and could thus share in his sophisticated tastes and interests. Theirs must have been what Shakespeare later called "a marriage of true minds."

Much of what Katherine saw in John is obvious: He was royal, authoritative, and powerful, a heady and sexy combination, especially when combined with aristocratic good looks, a tall, lean, and muscular body, a cultivated mind and attractive personality. More than that, he was a man who knew about love, and who had been brought up to treat women chivalrously and with respect.

John had not found love with his bride. There is no way of knowing whether they were incompatible from the start, or if Katherine's appearance in his life so early in the marriage put paid to any chance of him growing closer to Constance. For despite its auspicious beginnings, John's second marriage appears never to have been particularly happy. There is no evidence of any real love or affection between him and his wife, just mutual courtesy and respect, and although Constance was beautiful, she does not seem to have inspired any passion in her husband. In fact, the young duchess, far from dwelling on thoughts of love, was more probably consumed with a deep hatred for the usurper who had murdered her father and seized his throne,[73] and apparently saw her husband chiefly as a means of regaining it. It does not seem that she made much attempt to integrate in England, and was rarely at court; in her youth she had led a narrow, miserable existence, and even after her marriage, although she kept regal state, she preferred to live in seclusion with her Castilian ladies in the Spanish manner, residing mainly at the duke's magnificent castles at Hertford and Tutbury,[74] biding her time until she could return to her native Castile.[75] Perhaps she found the English climate uncongenial or the people strange and unintelligible. Communication with her husband was probably inhibited by the fact that she spoke little English and he only limited Castilian: Seventeen years after their marriage, he had difficulty in following an oration in that language.[76] Not that they would have had much in common, apart from Castile, for unlike Katherine, Constance was more pious than accomplished. All John seems to have shared with her was a burning ambition to regain her throne, and thus he would often defer to her judgment when it came to Castilian affairs. In every other respect he belonged to Katherine Swynford.

Katherine, in contrast, had a shared history with the duke; having lived in his household for many years, in attendance on his wife and children, she probably knew him quite well, and she had witnessed his devotion to Blanche, whom she herself seems to have loved and revered. Possibly the recall of those happy times created a shared bond between Katherine and

John; each had memories to treasure, and the poignant remembrance of grief. But it was now more than three years since Blanche's death, long enough for her widower to have recovered sufficiently to love again.

John's early experience of love and his happy first marriage would have awakened him to the joy in sharing his private life with a responsive woman, and we may see his need for Katherine as a tribute to Blanche, and perhaps an attempt to recreate the idyllic domestic joys of his youth. And the fact that Katherine was a Hainaulter, and possibly a distant relative, was probably an added bond: John himself was half Hainaulter through his mother, and throughout his life was to demonstrate that affinity by showing friendship to the Low Countries.

The most probable theory is that Katherine and John became lovers soon after she moved into Constance's household in the spring of 1372, when he was thirty-two and she about ten years younger and helping to look after his children. In this context, Armitage-Smith's delightfully Edwardian suggestion that the duke's visits to the nursery facilitated a rapidly growing intimacy may be accurate. The speed with which the supposedly grieving widow fell into John's bed suggests that her marriage had never been much more than a convenient arrangement, and that her sorrow for Hugh did not run deep. After all, she had not seen him during the sixteen months before his death, during which time she might well have grown used to living without him. And we might also wonder if Katherine had for years cherished a secret, unvoiced desire for John.

After his grant of May 1, 1372, there is further evidence of John's interest in "our very dear *damoiselle* Katherine de Swynford," and his concern for her financial problems, a concern far in excess of the usual consideration shown by an overlord to the widow of one of his knights. On May 15, 1372, again at the Savoy, he generously increased her permanent annuity from the Duchy of Lancaster (which originally must have been awarded during or after her years in Blanche's household) from 20 marks (£2,231) to 50 (£5,578), on account of "the good and agreeable service she has given to our dear companion [Blanche], whom God pardon, and for the very great affection that our said companion had for the said Katherine."[77]

When a vassal died leaving an underaged heir and a widow provided with a dower, his estates and property were normally taken into the hands of his overlord, who would then administer them as he thought fit until the heir attained his majority;[78] the wardship of that heir was assigned or sold to the person designated to raise him, and such arrangements could be very profitable for all concerned. Sir Hugh Swynford's estates had therefore reverted for the time being to the King and the Duke of Lancaster, but—unusually—both now broke with custom and acted swiftly to ameliorate Katherine's financial plight.

On June 8, Edward III stepped in, doubtless at John's behest, and ordered his escheator to assign Katherine her dower, on condition that she swore an oath not to marry without the King's license; that dower was formally assigned on June 26, after she took that oath.[79] By this means she gained control of Kettlethorpe during the minority of her son. On June 20, at the Savoy, again on account of the "good and agreeable service" she had rendered to Blanche, John granted "our well-loved Lady Katherine" wardship of all the lands and tenements that her late husband had held of the Honor of Richmond in Lincolnshire, "which is now held of us because of the minority of Thomas, son and heir of the said Sir Hugh." Katherine was "to have and hold" these lands "with all the profits appertaining to them from us and our heirs till the full age of the said heir, with nothing to render to us or our heirs." The only exceptions were the marriage fee due when Thomas took a wife and "what is due to the Church," which refers to Hugh's two advowsons, the right to appoint priests to the churches of Kettlethorpe and Coleby.[80] Thus Katherine gained control of one-third of the manor of Coleby.

On June 23, John made Katherine a further gift of three bucks, which he had probably killed himself while hunting near Hertford, and on June 28 he ordered that she be provided with oaks from his estates, presumably so she could undertake building repairs and improvements at Kettlethorpe.[81]

The Inquisition Postmortem on Sir Hugh Swynford was taken soon after April 25, 1372, at Navenby, nine miles south of Lincoln, and on June 24 in Lincoln itself.[82] Thomas Swynford, "aged four years and more," was recognized as his father's heir, but Kettlethorpe and Coleby were still in a poor state and worth little or nothing.[83] Again Edward III and John of Gaunt came to Katherine's rescue. On September 12, 1372, in return for a fee of £20 (£6,694) to be paid at the Exchequer, the King granted Katherine the remaining two-thirds of the manor of Coleby, and the marriage of her son until such time as he reached twenty-one.[84]

Thanks to his influence over his father the King, and through his own generosity, John had provided handsomely for Katherine, ensuring her rights to the control of Hugh's estates and the disposition and upbringing of her son, and by granting her a substantial annuity. The bountiful care and consideration shown to her by John of Gaunt and the King, and the speed with which her affairs were settled, is proof that she was very highly regarded in royal circles, and is also indicative of her being in regular contact with the duke, as a member of his household and, indeed, probably much more than that. Ever a man to take his responsibilities seriously, John had done his best to ensure that she and her children did not suffer want, but there was more to his generosity than this: By the summer of 1372, Katherine was almost certainly expecting his child, and he no doubt wished to provide handsomely for them both.

Katherine was not the only woman who was to bear the duke an infant: Duchess Constance was also pregnant, and on June 6, at the Savoy, her husband sent orders to Sir William de Chiselden, his receiver of Leicester, to send for "Elyot the wise woman" ("wise woman" being a common term for a midwife) to attend "our well-loved companion the Queen" at Hertford Castle "with all the haste that in any manner you can."[85] Elyot had delivered one or more of Blanche of Lancaster's babies—John mentions in 1372 that she had attended "our dearly loved companion, whom God keep in His command"; his reference to "our well-beloved Elyot, midwife of Leicester," and the payment of an annuity to "Eleyne, midwife" (who must be the same person) out of the revenues of Leicester in 1377–78[86] suggest he had enduring confidence in her, for she was also to assist during at least one of Katherine Swynford's confinements.[87]

John had sent to Chiselden his "well-loved esquire" John Raynald, "who will inform you fully of this matter" and who was to accompany Elyot to Hertford. Considerately, John stipulated that Chiselden was to order for her journey "a chariot or a horse or any other manner that seems best to you for her ease."[88] The urgency implied in the duke's commands suggests that the birth of Constance's child was reasonably imminent—he would have had to allow a week or more for his orders to reach Leicester and for Elyot to travel to Hertford—and that this pregnancy had resulted from the bride conceiving soon after her marriage in September. This would account for her remaining in Devon and Dorset from November to February, at that stage of pregnancy when morning sickness and debility are at their most troublesome. The date of her child's birth is not recorded, and since it was not until March 31, 1373, that Edward III rewarded Katherine Swynford with 20 marks (£2,231) for bringing news of it to him,[89] several historians are of the opinion that the birth occurred nearer to that date. However, given the other circumstances, the fact that months could elapse before royal rewards were actually paid or recorded, and the delay in payment perhaps accounted for by Katherine's absence from the Lancastrian household for some time due to her own pregnancy, it is more likely that Constance's child was born in the summer of 1372 at Hertford Castle. Gifts of wine were sent to Hertford that summer, and the duke was there on July 7, probably to see his new child.[90]

Disappointingly—for the royal parents were doubtless anxious for a boy to inherit the crown that John meant to wrest from Enrique of Trastamara— the baby was a girl. She was named Katherine—or Catalina, as her mother called her, and as she would one day be known in Castile—and styled Katherine d'Espaigne. Her Christian name had never been used by the Castilian royal family, and was rare in the House of Plantagenet, so one is tempted to wonder if John of Gaunt chose it, and why. Was the choice prompted by Katherine Swynford, out of devotion to St. Katherine? Or was John himself so entranced with Katherine that he was blind to the implications of using her beloved name for the child his wife had borne him? Of course, the choice of name may have sprung from some other association entirely: St. Katherine may have been one of Constance's favorite saints, as well as John's.

Katherine's conveyance of the news of Catalina's birth to the King suggests that she was in attendance; having borne at least four children of her own at a young age, she would have been able to reassure and support Constance through her ordeal. But as soon as her own pregnancy became obvious, a pregnancy that could not have been her husband's doing, she was obliged to resign her post and return to Kettlethorpe.

The war with France was not going well at this time. The French were making inroads into Aquitaine and attacking Brittany. In June, at Hertford, in order to retain the friendship of a valuable ally against France,

John surrendered the earldom of Richmond to John de Montfort, Duke of Brittany, in whose family it had previously been for centuries, receiving other lands in exchange. That same month, Edward III resolved on a naval offensive against France, whereupon, on July 1, John undertook to serve overseas for a year.

John was probably at Wallingford Castle on July 11,[91] attending the marriage of his younger brother, Edmund of Langley, Earl of Cambridge, to Constance's younger sister, Isabella of Castile, an alliance that had been arranged by John of Gaunt to bolster England's links with the future monarchy of Castile and to "save [Isabella] from her enemies."[92] It was also seen as a way of preserving England's claims to Castile should Constance die in childbirth.[93]

On the same day as the wedding of Edmund and Isabella, John of Gaunt summoned all his retainers to attend him on the coming campaign, then went north for a few weeks' hunting in Leicester Forest before joining his army at Sandwich before August 18.[94] There, on August 30, he granted the annuity to Philippa Chaucer in recognition of her past and future services to Duchess Constance. We might conclude that Philippa had been instrumental in helping her young mistress to settle in a strange land, and perhaps assisted her during her pregnancy and confinement and was helping to look after her baby; and we might wonder if John's grant to her was at Katherine's behest.

On August 31, John sailed for Gascony with his father the King and the Black Prince, for both of whom this would be their last military adventure; and for Katherine and John, the first of many partings occasioned by the war. The expedition was a disaster, with ships smashed or blown off course by contrary winds and gales and many lives lost, and after two hellish storm-tossed months in the Channel, the remains of the fleet limped home, having accomplished nothing.

During John's absence, Katherine would have been preparing for her coming confinement. Her baby probably arrived in the winter of 1372–73;[95] by this reckoning, John Beaufort's age, as given in Richard II's grant of 1392, must be inaccurate. In which case, if Constance gave birth in the summer of 1372, Katherine's pregnancy would not then have been apparent; she had probably left the duchess's household soon afterward and returned to Kettlethorpe. Her child was perhaps born there. The delivery of oaks in June 1372, on the duke's orders, might have been intended for the refurbishment of the manor house, to make it a fit place in which Katherine could bear or rear his child; if the calculations above are correct, it was around June that her pregnancy became a certainty. It is possible, though, that Katherine actually gave birth to this son in Lincoln, and that he was the child for whose baptism in February 1373 rich cloths were provided.

In childbed, Katherine succeeded where Constance had failed, for she had borne a son, a boy who would be known as John Beaufort of Lancaster;[96] named John for his father, with whom he was always to be "a great favourite,"[97] and Beaufort after the lordship of Beaufort in Champagne, once held by the duke as part of his Lancastrian inheritance.[98] In 1369, John of Gaunt had lost Beaufort to the French through the treachery of one of his vassals,[99] thus it was a safe name to give to his bastard son by Katherine Swynford: It was a name associated with the duke, yet the lordship was no longer part of—and could not therefore prejudice—the inheritance he would leave his lawful heir.[100] It was often claimed[101] that John's children by Katherine Swynford were born at Beaufort Castle, but that would not have been possible, for he had sold it years before, and never visited it anyway.[102]

John Beaufort's early years were probably spent at Kettlethorpe. The pattern of the duke's grants to Katherine, some of them concerning its refurbishment, some of them handsome gifts, may indicate the dates of birth of their other children, and certainly suggests that the manor was being made a fit place for them to be brought up in. Kettlethorpe was a remote village with a tiny population, an ideal setting for discreet confinements and the raising of royal bastards whose existence was better kept secret—for the present.

Certainly the lovers were discreet, at least to begin with—had they not been, the world would soon have known of their affair, and we would not have to rely on inference and speculation in determining the circumstances in which it began. Costain argues that it was Katherine who insisted on secrecy in the early years of the liaison—she was, after all, newly widowed—but there were political imperatives to be considered too: John would not have wished to openly dishonor his new wife when all his hopes were centered on claiming the crown of Castile in her right. Thus, the need for discretion was probably mutual, and it ensured that for some years to come his affair with Katherine was conducted in secrecy and with great circumspection.

FIVE

Blinded by Desire

The love and friendship between John of Gaunt and Katherine Swynford was to endure for more than a quarter of a century. For great lords, marriage was normally a political affair and love a private one.[1] The Church and the public at large might frown on extramarital liaisons, but they were an accepted part of aristocratic life, given that love rarely followed marriage. Because John's liaison with Katherine was to last so long, many people in court circles must have come to regard it as unremarkable. In the meantime, John would treat his young wife with respect and courtesy, for she was his duchess and a queen in her own right; but clearly his heart was Katherine's, and would probably remain so until death.

It was quite permissible, in a world in which courtly love held sway over relationships between the sexes, for a man like John of Gaunt to pay open court to a lady who was not his wife. But Katherine was a widow, who for the first year of her widowhood was expected to be unattainable; she was of far lower degree than he, for all that she might have been distantly related, and had nothing more than herself to offer him; and John was a newly married man. Yet where Katherine was concerned, he seems to have been unable to restrain his passion: "He was blinded by desire, fearing neither God nor shame amongst men."[2] Was Chaucer thinking of his sister-in-law and John of Gaunt in the 1380s, when he wrote, "You wise ones, proud ones, worthy ones and all, never scorn love . . . For love can lay his hands on every creature . . . The strongest men are overcome, and those most notable and highest in degree."[3] John's younger brother, Thomas of Woodstock, would later put it more succinctly, calling him (says Froissart) a "doting fool" for loving Katherine Swynford so utterly and so enduringly.

Yet, sadly for those romantics who would prefer to believe that the duke stayed true to Katherine within the limits of their adulterous relationship, there is some evidence that he had fleeting sexual encounters with other women during the course of it. In 1381 he was publicly to confess that he had committed the sin of lechery with Katherine herself "and many others in his wife's household."[4] Certainly this reputation for lechery endured. Francis Thynne, Lancaster Herald under Elizabeth I, and a commentator on Thomas Speght's edition of Chaucer,[5] asserted that John of Gaunt "had many paramours in his youth, and was not very continent in his age." In The Boke of the Duchesse, on which Thynne must have based his assertion, Chaucer has John recalling that from his youth he had "paid tribute as a devotee to love, most unrestrainedly, and joyfully become his thrall, with willing body, heart and all." When contemporary chroniclers spoke of the duke as a lecher and "great fornicator," they may not have been commenting solely on his liaison with Katherine Swynford, as is often claimed. Then there is some fifteenth-century evidence that John died of a venereal disease, which—if true—he is unlikely to have contracted as a result of long years of fidelity to the same mistress.[6] Even if this evidence is unsound, the fact that the allegation was made at all is proof that, forty years after his death, the charges of promiscuity were remembered and believable.

In his confession of 1381, John's reference to "his wife" can only be to Constance; there is no evidence that he was unfaithful to Blanche, although it is of course possible. Thynne and Chaucer were obviously referring to John's early amorous encounters. Today, we know only of his affair with Marie de St. Hilaire, but there were seemingly others; possibly the occasional grants to various ladies in the Register are rewards for favors bestowed. Thynne's comment about John not being continent in his age probably refers to his notorious relationship with Katherine Swynford. But the duke's own confession, and Chaucer's portrayal of him as a man who unrestrainedly pursued sexual pleasure, suggest that he found it hard to remain physically faithful. During the years of his affair with Katherine, they were often apart, and he would have had many opportunities for straying. His taking many women of his wife's household to bed supports the theory that he and Constance did not enjoy a satisfying conjugal relationship—they had just two, possibly three, children in twenty-three years—and suggests that on his visits to her, he often abstained from her bed and assuaged his needs elsewhere. For great lords, such casual dalliance was easy, and many regarded it as their privilege; in aristocratic society, these things were accepted. Fidelity and the pursuit of the courtly ideal were conceits that masked the indulgence of lust. And probably John's amours were fleeting and purely physical—and made no impact on his obviously deep feelings for Katherine Swynford.

Katherine may only have found out about these casual affairs in 1381, after John made his public confession. Throughout their years together, he appears to have treated her with dignity, discretion, and generosity, and perhaps never admitted to what he considered to be insignificant lapses.

The medieval Church, however, essentially regarded all sexual acts as potentially sinful, following St. Augustine, who wrote: "There is nothing that degrades the manly spirit more than the attractiveness of females and contact with their bodies." St. Paul's dictum, "It is better to marry than to burn," implied that celibacy was the ideal state. Even within marriage, sex was meant to be only for the purpose of procreation: According to the ascetic St. Jerome, a man and wife who indulged in carnal lust for pleasure were no better than adulterers, for "in truth, all love is disgraceful, and with regard to one's own wife, excessive love is. The wise man must love his wife with judgment, not with passion. Let him curb his transports of voluptuousness, and not let himself be urged precipitately to indulge in coition. Nothing is more vile than to love a wife like a mistress." Certain sexual positions were forbidden, as were masturbation and coitus interruptus, and those found guilty of indulging in oral sex might incur a penance lasting three years. You could not make love on Sundays, holy days, or saints' days, or during Lent, pregnancy, or menstruation. For the devout, married life must have been a continual battle with temptation.

There was therefore no hope that the Church would ever officially look upon the adulterous relationship of John and Katherine with anything other than disapproval; each would have been regarded as equally guilty, and irrevocably damned.

In practice, however, attitudes were more lax. By the fourteenth century the promiscuity of the clergy had become a byword, and many in holy orders took a relaxed and worldly view of immorality. Whereas in the thirteenth century adulterers had been publicly whipped, they were now more likely to be forced to do public penance, going in procession to church wearing just a sheet and carrying a candle. But no one ever called for the mighty Duke of Lancaster and his mistress to be punished in such a humiliating way.

The laity were generally tolerant of sexual license, albeit in men, blaming it on the frailty and insatiability of women. Chaucer's *Canterbury Tales* and Boccaccio's *Decameron* reveal just how licentious fourteenth-century society was, and how relaxed with regard to fornication. The aristocracy were sophisticated to a degree in their attitudes to sex outside marriage: It was accepted that titled men took mistresses or had casual sexual encounters. The royal court, as we have seen, was a hotbed of promiscuity, due to the financial inability of many young knights or gentlemen to marry. But where the wives and daughters of the nobility were concerned, chastity was the order of the day, for dynastic bloodlines and inheritances had to be protected, and soiled goods were of little value in the marriage market. Thus, the purity of noblewomen was jealously guarded. Females of lower rank were considered fair game and more responsive than their betters, and any gently born woman who so far forgot herself as to have an affair outside wedlock usually lost her reputation irrevocably. It is easy to see, therefore, why Katherine Swynford was so bitterly disparaged in the monastic chronicles.

When it came to bastardy, the world could be a cruel place. A bastard could not officially inherit lands or titles, nor obtain preferment in the Church. Yet these barriers could be circumvented by bequeathing property or by dispensations, and when it came to the aristocracy, much could be gained from a sympathetic monarch. Moreover, being the bastard child of a great lord conferred nobility, inspired deference, and entitled one to bear the paternal arms differenced with a bend sinister denoting illegitimacy. The infant John Beaufort's arms were the leopards and lilies of England on a bend, mounted on a shield of blue and white, the Lancastrian colors. Fathers were seen as having a duty to provide equally for their legitimate and illegitimate children.[7]

Katherine must have embarked upon her affair with John of Gaunt knowing exactly what she was doing and aware of the risks she was taking and the penalties that society could impose. That she chose to be his mistress in light of this knowledge suggests that she loved him enough for the consequences not to matter, and that this and the protection, security, and benefits such a relationship could afford her were not only welcome to her, but of more importance than the stigma attached to being a partner in adultery and losing her reputation.

Much of what we know of Katherine Swynford's years as John of Gaunt's mistress is recorded in *John of Gaunt's Register*, which survives for the periods 1372–76 and 1379–83. This covers much of the period in question, although three vital years are missing, as are the years following their parting. These missing records would surely have contained more clues to the truth of the relationship between Katherine and John, so their loss is only to be lamented. Nevertheless, as will shortly become clear, there is much that can be inferred from the information that *has* come down to us.

John of Gaunt spent Christmas of 1372 at Hertford Castle with Constance. Game from Ashdown Forest in Sussex and five dozen rabbits from Aldbourne were delivered there for the Christmas feasts, while the duke's valet brought him cloth of gold, furs, silk, and linen from his wardrobe at the Savoy.[8] On Christmas Eve, Alyne Gerberge was dispatched to the Savoy to collect some jewels and precious stones that the duke intended to give as New Year gifts, as well as jewels given by Edward III and the Black Prince to Duchess Constance, who doubtless wanted to wear them during the festive season. It is tempting to speculate that some of the other jewels were intended as presents for Katherine Swynford, whose New Year gifts from her royal lover were almost never recorded in his *Register*. Her presents were probably paid for out of the large sums of money the duke frequently arranged to be "given into my own hands for my own secret business."[9] Philippa Chaucer's gifts were recorded, however, and at this New Year of 1373 she received six silver-gilt buttons attached to an embroidered strip of fabric called a "buttoner,"[10] which indicates that, after less than a year in Constance's service, she had become highly regarded by both the duke and duchess. Her life would now have been centered mainly upon the Lancastrian household, which was as well, because royal duties were keeping her and her husband increasingly apart: Chaucer was in Italy at this time on official business, and would not return until the following May.

John was still at Hertford on January 10, 1373, but soon afterward he moved to the Savoy, where he remained until June, apart from a brief visit to Hertford in early February to celebrate the Feast of the Purification of the Virgin Mary with his wife.[11] Katherine Swynford, meanwhile, had given birth to John's child, but was probably back at the Savoy by March 31, for it was on that date that Edward III rewarded her for bringing news of Catalina of Lancaster's birth to him the previous year.

Writing after 1378, the chronicler Knighton describes Katherine as being in Duchess Constance's household. Certainly she would have been there from time to time, but probably not as a lady-in-waiting, for none of the many grants to her by the duke would be made in consideration of her good service to his second wife, although several were awarded in regard to her devotion to his first. Instead, John had found another post for Katherine that would facilitate her being near him as often as possible, and be eminently suited to her character and talents. He appointed her *magistra*—which means mistress, directress, leader, or, more loosely, governess—to his daughters: Philippa, now thirteen; Elizabeth, ten; and perhaps to his six-year-old heir Henry too, until a governor was appointed for the boy in 1374. Effectively, Blanche's children would now have two stepmothers—Duchess Constance and Katherine Swynford, who was mistress in different senses to them and their father.

We do not know the exact date on which Katherine was appointed governess, and it has been suggested that she had fulfilled this role while in Blanche of Lancaster's household. But she would have been quite young at that time and frequently pregnant; moreover, continuity would have been an important factor, and there is no evidence to show that she was employed by the duke between 1368 and 1372, when it appears that others were caring for the ducal daughters. An undated letter of ca. 1376 from a woman called Maud to John of Gaunt identifies Maud as a former nurse to young Philippa,[12] and in 1370, Alyne Gerberge was rewarded with a lifetime annuity for caring for Philippa in the aftermath of Blanche's death. In November 1371 we find that Lady Wake was serving as governess to all three of the Duke's children.[13] But she would not have been able to remain in the post of governess for long because she was preoccupied with bearing her husband a dozen children throughout the 1370s and 1380s. So by 1373 there was definitely a vacancy to be filled.

Katherine had the requisite skills and experience, and certainly helped to look after Blanche's children during their mother's lifetime, a factor that John must have taken into account when choosing her as his daughters' governess, because in everything that mattered, she was going to be a mother to them. John's children were still sharing a joint household in 1372,[14] so the likeliest date for Katherine's preferment was after the birth of John Beaufort, around the spring of 1373. It may be that the children had been looked after in the interim by the *damoiselle* Amy de Melbourne, who was rewarded in 1375 by John of Gaunt for her care of them, or that Amy was an assistant to both Lady Wake and Katherine Swynford. From 1372, Amy and Alyne Gerberge were entrusted to look after the jewel coffers of the duke's womenfolk, and Alyne was then not only caring for Philippa, but also dressing Duchess Constance's hair and setting her coronet in place. We know that the duke thought highly of Amy because he sent her a pipe of wine each Christmas from 1372 on.[15]

Katherine's appointment as governess was timely, because John was traveling abroad and expected to be away for some time. The war was going catastrophically, and England needed to intervene quickly, otherwise Aquitaine—that precious jewel in the Plantagenet crown—would be irrevocably lost. On March 1, 1373, John had begun to gather an army, having sealed an indenture to go campaigning in France for a year. By then Katherine must have faced up to the painful fact that the demands of his position, and the likely necessity for her to spend long periods in the country discreetly bearing his children, might mean that they would often be apart.

On April 23 the duke gave orders for Tutbury Castle, which had been damaged in a storm, to be put in good repair, so his wife and children could reside there during his absence in France.[16] Tutbury, where Blanche had died, was a mighty fortress perched high above the banks of the River Dove, and lay eleven miles southwest of Derby. John, who often stayed there for the excellent hunting in the vicinity, had built the red sandstone gatehouse in 1362, and carried out many works there over the years, to make the castle a fitting residence for his queen. Below the castle stood St. Mary's Priory, a Benedictine house under the Duke's patronage.[17]

By now Katherine had perhaps taken up her duties as governess. In the fourteenth century a "mistress's" role was to supervise the upbringing of the girls committed to her charge until the day they married, and to set a good and virtuous example for them to follow.[18] The emphasis was more on character training than the acquisition of skills, although learning the conduct expected of highborn females was important too. Formal education was not normally part of the governess's remit: Teaching the Scriptures and devotional works, reading, writing, English, French, and perhaps a little Latin would have been undertaken by household chaplains. Katherine, however, was unusual in that she had grown up in one of the most cultivated courts in Christendom and was part of an aristocratic circle in which learning in women was encouraged, so she herself may have imparted some of her own knowledge to the two princesses.

Above all, noble girls were to be protected from the snares of the flesh and the wiles of men, which was why so many were brought up in convents. In this respect, Katherine was perhaps not the wisest choice as governess, and her appointment may have led to a few knowledgeable eyebrows being lifted; but in all other respects she was eminently fit for the office, otherwise John of Gaunt would surely not have appointed her. In thrall as he was to Katherine's charms, he could never have compromised the education of his daughters, nor their moral welfare, for both were princesses of the blood and expected to make good political marriages. This argues that Katherine was discreet and did not flaunt her position in any way, and also that her intimate connection with John of Gaunt was not widely known at this time, nor her reputation compromised; otherwise, her appointment would have been cause for open scandal, which it was not. Chaucer may be referring obliquely to Katherine in "The Physician's Tale" where he wryly observes that governesses with a past were well-suited to be poachers turned gamekeepers,[19] but this was written years later, and does not reflect contemporary opinion in the early 1370s. Above all, with the crown of Castile beckoning, John would not have wished to offend his wife by his indiscriminate promotion of his mistress.

Katherine would have been responsible for teaching Philippa and Elizabeth the accomplishments that would befit them to adorn courts and rule their own establishments: courtesy, conversation, good carriage, dancing, singing, embroidery, courtly games, and household management. These were probably all skills in which she herself was more than proficient. Although she was only about twenty-three, Katherine was already the mother of at least four children, and experienced not only in the ways of courts, but also in running her own establishment at Kettlethorpe. Lady Wake, who was the same age, had been even younger when she looked after the Lancastrian siblings. Katherine was pious too, and this would have had some bearing on her influence over her charges. She was also responsible for their diet, their clothing, and the accoutrements of their chamber.

Although Katherine was indeed in many ways qualified for her post, it seems to have been something of a sinecure, for clearly she was not always resident with her charges, and it would appear that the demands of the duke and her own family came first. Thus, we must conclude that being appointed governess was in part a ploy to lend her respectability while ensuring that she could remain within the duke's orbit and be available when he needed her, not only in bed but also at board, because she probably acted as hostess and graced his table in the absence of the duchess. Yet there is evidence that she did spend a lot of time with Philippa and Elizabeth, that she indeed fulfilled her official role as their governess, and that even if she did so only on a part-time basis, she certainly had overall control of her charges. During her absences she seems to have delegated their care to others, such as Amy de Melbourne, while *John of Gaunt's Register* also records occasional payments to ladies with whom the two princesses were sometimes sent to stay.

Occupying an official position gave Katherine a legitimate reason for residing in one or other of the ducal households. Such evidence as we have indicates that her duties and commitments, official or otherwise, sometimes necessitated her lodging with Duchess Constance's household, which could not have happened unless Katherine was the soul of discretion and tact, given that John desired not to offend his wife, in whom he had invested all his political ambitions. Yet it appears that the duchess's Castilian ladies were already aware in 1373 that Katherine was John's mistress. Their gossiping so annoyed the duke that he packed them all off to Nuneaton Abbey, hoping the abbess would teach them discretion. By the end of 1374 they were chafing at the conventual regime at Nuneaton and begging to be allowed to leave, but it was not until 1375 that John relented and sent them to live in Leicester with some of his trusted retainers; later, he arranged marriages for a number of them.[20]

If her ladies knew what was going on between the duke and Katherine, the chances are that Constance did too. It has been suggested that her Spanish pride was affronted by Katherine, but it may be that the young duchess took a more realistic view of such matters. She herself, after all, was the daughter of a royal mistress, and she came from a royal house famed for its high rate of bastardy. Preoccupied as she was with regaining her throne, and preferring to remain secluded with her Castilian entourage, she was perhaps relieved to know that her husband's sexual needs were being met by another woman. Her later acknowledgment that she herself was at fault with regard to the failure of their marriage suggests she was aware that she had made little effort to be a loving wife, or had defaulted in some other way. If she never loved her husband, she could hardly blame him for seeking love elsewhere, and perhaps she was not unduly troubled by the fact that it was John's passion for Katherine that was preventing him from making a success of their marriage. Furthermore, in the years to come, Katherine's baseborn children by John would pose no threat to Constance's own legitimate issue. Nor, it appears, did Katherine ever seek to interfere with John's plans to conquer Castile, which was the most important thing in view in Constance's life, and which, during the first two years of her marriage, seemed a realistically attainable goal. Hence, Constance would have regarded her sojourn in England as purely temporary, and might well have reasoned that, once Castile was regained, she and John would live there, king and queen in their own realm, and that her position would be unassailable. Thus, Katherine could hardly have posed any real threat to Constance.

In May 1373 the duke's ships began assembling at Dover and Sandwich. John was very busy with his preparations, but on May 12, at the Savoy, he gave orders to John de Stafford, his receiver in Lincoln, that Katherine's allowance be paid promptly during his absence: "We want and we command that you pay immediately to our very dear and well-beloved Dame Katherine de Swynford her annuity given by us to her, taken from the issues you will receive and in the manner that our letters of guarantee had specified; and see to it that there is no delay at the term of the payment, and no default. These my letters are a guarantee."[21]

Katherine seems to have either visited or stayed briefly with John at his headquarters at the manor of Northbourne, a grange of St. Augustine's Abbey, Canterbury, that he had commandeered, which lay four miles west of Deal in Kent. Here he sojourned from June 27 to July 16. Katherine's presence at Northbourne underlines how important a person she now was in John's life, and shows that he wanted to spend as much time as possible with her before the long parting that lay ahead. Presumably he hoped she would join him in Castile once he was established as its ruler: Given the irregular domestic arrangements of previous Castilian kings, one mistress discreetly kept could hardly have offended public opinion.

It would appear that while Katherine was at Northbourne with John, she complained that his orders for the prompt payment of her allowance had not been obeyed, for on June 27, clearly angered, he wrote to John de Stafford commanding him to pay "our very dear and beloved Dame Katherine de Swynford the annuity that we have granted her; this must be paid to her in the manner ordered in the letter of guarantee. See to it that this is done without delay, and without any kind of excuse."[22] Either John de Stafford had just been dilatory in carrying out his orders, or—as Silva-Vigier suggests—he was being deliberately obstructive toward a woman of whom he did not approve.

Katherine must have said her farewells and departed on or soon after June 27, as it was before then that John promised to send gifts of venison and wood to her at Kettlethorpe. On that day, he informed the warden of his park at Gringley, Nottinghamshire: "We have granted to our dear and well-beloved Dame Katherine de Swynford, as our gift, two deer from one of our parks, and a third from another of our parks, as you will judge to be the best."

John de Stafford, perhaps still simmering with disapproval, was also commanded to dispatch to Katherine "six chariots of wood for fuel and three oaks suitable for building, which we have given to the said Dame Katherine; these are to be taken from one of our parks, which you will judge to be most suitable."[23]

Preoccupied as he was with military matters, John had yet found time to send some comforts to cheer his love during his absence. The oaks, of course, were to be used for the improvements she was making at Kettlethorpe,[24] which suggests she did not immediately go to her charges at Tutbury. On July 6, John gave orders for the supply of coal and wood to Tutbury Castle for "the Queen of Castile" and his four legitimate children.[25] The duke's womenfolk were to remain at Tutbury for a year; as governess, Katherine must have spent some time there during that period with Philippa and Elizabeth, while Philippa Chaucer seems to have been a constant presence in the household.[26]

he duke, who had been appointed Captain-General in France and Aquitaine on June 12, sailed to France late in July with an army of perhaps six thousand men, and there undertook one of the most astonishing and controversial actions of the Hundred Years War. On August 4 he began his famous—or notorious—*grande chevauchée* (great cavalry ravage) through France, marching his army unopposed from Calais to Bordeaux, his aim to relieve Aquitaine, then cross the Pyrenees and force Enrique of Trastamara to surrender his ill-gotten crown.[27] This was a daring show of strength designed to intimidate the French, divert them from mounting a naval offensive against England, and bait them into giving battle. But they held aloof, and during five months of terrible but futile marching, plundering, and looting, the duke took not a single fortress or town.[28] Unwilling to compromise his honor by turning back, he and his army pressed on farther and farther south, only to find themselves increasingly short of funds, food, and morale. As winter encroached, the way became hard and led them through the barren mountains of the Massif Central, where they encountered ambushes and bitter weather and the flood-ravaged lands of Aquitaine. Many men and nearly all the horses fell sick and died, armor and booty had to be abandoned, and even the knights were reduced to begging for bread.

At Christmas, having long since abandoned all thoughts of pressing on into Castile, and suffering from "great bodily fatigue" and the loss of his customary good spirits,[29] John limped into Bordeaux with an army tragically halved by death or desertion. All that now remained of the once mighty Plantagenet empire in France was Calais and the coastal strip between Bordeaux and Bayonne. Nevertheless, John had held off the enemy and probably saved Bordeaux; far from his military reputation being in the dust, as historians used to conclude, his great march was regarded by the French as "most honorable to the English."[30] In England, however, it came in for scathing criticism, and he was compared very unfavorably with his brother, the Black Prince.[31] In January 1374, John concluded a truce with the French, then immediately began planning another campaign, but in March, when the Pope intervened and demanded a new truce, hostilities were suspended.[32]

After an absence of nine months, John surrendered his lieutenancy of Aquitaine, and returned to England on April 26, 1374; he was back at the

Savoy on May 1, and stayed there until the middle of July.[33] Chastened and humiliated by the failure of his great *chevauchée*, and castigated for it by both his father the King[34] and the public at large, he would spend the next year in the political wilderness, taking little part in public affairs,[35] and doubtless making up for lost time with Katherine Swynford: It says much for the strength of their feelings for each other that their love had survived the long months of separation.

In private, however, John was preparing to take part in the new peace negotiations called for by the Pope. Increasingly, he was becoming convinced that there was no point in continuing with this ruinous war, and that peace was essential for the future prosperity of England. The following year he would emerge as the major advocate of a peace policy,[36] and would remain so for the rest of his life, but his views were to be at variance with those of the majority of his countrymen, who wanted victories and military glory, and regarded any overtures for peace as craven and shameful. Hence, John's unpopular stance would be yet another score to be notched up against him.

Geoffrey Chaucer had returned to England from Italy on May 23, 1373. On April 23, 1374, the King rewarded him for his good service with an annual gift of a pitcher of wine for life. But it was after John of Gaunt's return to the Savoy in May that Chaucer's fortunes were markedly advanced, lending support to the theory that, although John was never his overt patron, he used his influence behind the scenes to bring Geoffrey advancement and wealth. We might credibly conjecture also that Katherine Swynford had hastened—or was summoned—to be reunited with her lover at the Savoy, and that in the heady flush of those lengthening summer days, John heeded her when she pointed out to him that, despite years of loyal and dedicated service to the Crown, during which he had performed important diplomatic missions, her brother-in-law had received little in the way of reward. Katherine might well have heard this complaint repeated many times by her sister Philippa.

John acted immediately. On May 10, Chaucer was given a lifetime rent-free lease on a desirable property that straddled Aldgate in London, with rooms above the gate and a cellar below. Then, on June 8, he was appointed to the lucrative and prestigious post of Controller of Customs and Subsidies on Wool in the nearby Port of London, an extremely responsible position, given that taxes on wool exports provided England's highest peacetime revenue. Four days later he was also appointed Controller of Petty Customs on Wines. On June 13, John granted "our well-loved Geoffrey Chaucer" a standard esquire's life pension of £10 (£3,414) a year, partly in recognition of the good service that his wife had rendered both to "our very honored lady and mother the Queen, whom God pardon, and for our very beloved companion the Queen of Castile."[37] And on July 6 both Geoffrey and Philippa Chaucer received overdue back payments of their annuities.[38] It would be incredible if these grants owed nothing to the influence of Katherine Swynford. In fact, the links she and her sister forged between the illustrious House of Lancaster and the relatively humble Chaucer family were to ensure lasting benefits for the latter and rapidly propel its members up the social ladder.

Thus began what were for Chaucer the years of prosperity, years in which he would be busily occupied with his duties, yet find time to write more of the great works that would bring him lasting fame, notably the dream poems, *The House of Fame* and *The Parliament of Fowls*.

Another man who was rewarded for his services by John of Gaunt at this time was John Wycliffe, who received the living of Lutterworth in Leicestershire. Wycliffe was a brilliant Oxford doctor, theologian, and philosopher, who had served as a chaplain to Edward III; he was a highly intelligent and sophisticated man whose radical and controversial views on the abuses and corruption within the Church would make him notorious. He disapproved of career bishops, ecclesiastics who grew wealthy on the spoils of their office and exerted too much power, and he opposed the high taxes levied on behalf of an increasingly secularized Papacy. He believed passionately that Christians should live by the rules of Christ as set down in the Gospels, and not by regulations laid down by the Church. He denied that the Pope was the true head of the Church and regarded the priesthood as superfluous. Power, he argued, should lie with the king and the chief nobles, a view John of Gaunt enthusiastically endorsed.

John likewise wished to curb the power wielded by high-ranking churchmen, and by 1371 had become Wycliffe's patron. That year, he backed Parliament's calls to restrict public offices to laymen only. Wycliffe also believed that peace with France was essential, which may have influenced John's own views on this issue. The duke's admiration of Wycliffe's political stance led

The Troilus Frontispiece. The lady in blue kneeling second from
the left in the front may be Katherine Swynford.

Edward III and his eldest son, Edward, "the Black Prince." They were two of the greatest paragons of chivalry in Christendom.

Philippa of Hainault, Edward III's queen, who acted as a mother to Katherine Swynford from her infancy.

Joan, "the Fair Maid of Kent." Her marriage to the Black Prince caused some scandal.

John of Gaunt, Duke of Lancaster. This later portrait may be based on his tomb effigy. He was "a splendidly looking knight of noble stature."

Blanche of Lancaster, first wife of John of Gaunt. Chaucer calls her "the flower of English womanhood."

The wedding of John of Gaunt and Blanche of Lancaster in Reading Abbey, 1359. In this nineteenth century representation, Henry, Duke of Lancaster stands behind his daughter, and the man in black by the pillar is meant to be Geoffrey Chaucer.

The Savoy, London. No image of the lost palace of John of Gaunt on the Strand survives; this image shows the location of the palace and the Tudor Hospital of the Savoy, which replaced it.

Geoffrey Chaucer, the poet who married Katherine Swynford's sister Philippa, and was to benefit from Katherine's liaison with John of Gaunt.

The great hall of Leicester Castle.

The ruins of Leicester Castle. Leicester Castle was one of the chief Lancastrian residences. Katherine may have come here when she first entered the service of the Duchess Blanche.

Kettlethorpe Hall, Lincolnshire: the manor house of the Swynfords. The gatehouse and fragmentary remains incorporated in the Victorian house survive from Katherine's time.

Lincoln Cathedral. Katherine was to enjoy a long association with the cathedral and its clergy.

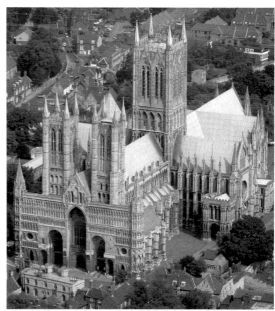

St. Margaret's Church, Pottergate, Lincoln (now demolished). Katherine's son, Thomas Swynford, was baptized here in 1367.

Kenilworth Castle. John of Gaunt's great hall is one of the finest surviving fourteenth-century rooms in England.

Constance of Castile, second wife of John of Gaunt. Within months of their marriage, Katherine Swynford had become John's mistress.

John Wycliffe reading his translation of the Bible to his patron John of Gaunt. Painting by Ford Madox Brown. Among those listening is Chaucer; the lady with the baby is perhaps meant to be Katherine.

After she became his mistress, John of Gaunt appointed Katherine Swynford governess to his two daughters by Blanche.

Philippa of Lancaster

Elizabeth of Lancaster

Henry of Bolingbroke, Earl of Derby (later Henry IV), John of Gaunt's heir.

Richard II: detail from the Wilton Diptych.

Both Richard II and Henry IV were to show friendship for Katherine.

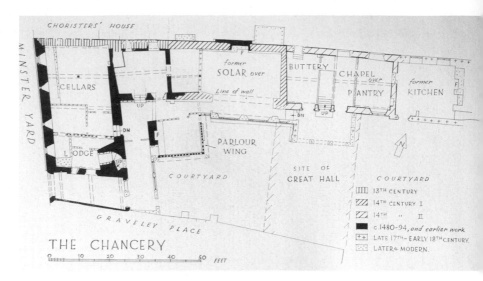

THE CHANCERY

13TH CENTURY
14TH CENTURY I
14TH " II
c.1480-94, and earlier work
LATE 17TH- EARLY 18TH CENTURY
LATER & MODERN

Plan of the Chancery, Lincoln. After the Peasants' Revolt of 1381, Katherine retired to Lincoln and leased the Chancery, a fine house in the cathedral close; for the next fifteen years, she would be based here and at Kettlethorpe.

The Chancery: Katherine's solar and chapel block, her screens passage and the site of her great hall. The timbered range is Tudor.

The supposed effigy of Philippa Chaucer in Old (East) Worldham Church, Hampshire.

The arms that Katherine adopted after her marriage to John of Gaunt. Throughout her life, Katherine showed great devotion to her patron saint, and adopted her wheel emblem in her arms as Duchess of Lancaster.

Mary de Bohun, wife of Henry of Derby, was close to Katherine.

Pontefract Castle, Yorshire. This Lancastrian castle was a favored residence of John of Gaunt and Katherine Swynford after their marriage. It may also have been the scene of an earlier parting.

Ely Place. A model of the great palace as it looked in the sixteenth century. Ely Place was the London residence of John of Gaunt and Katherine Swynford after their marriage.

St. Etheldreda's Church, the former chapel of Ely Place.

Richard II receives his child-bride, Isabella, from her father, Charles VI of France.
Katherine Swynford was to serve as companion to the young Queen.

The arms of John Beaufort

The arms of Cardinal Henry Beaufort

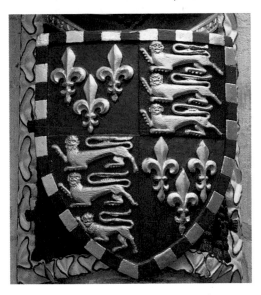

The Beauforts were Katherine's children by John of Gaunt, and from them descended the royal house of Tudor.

The arms of Thomas Beaufort

The seal of Joan Beaufort

John Beaufort, Earl of Somerset, and his wife,
Margaret Holland, from *The Beaufort Hours*.

John Beaufort: effigy
in Canterbury Cathedral.

Cardinal Beaufort: effigy in
Winchester Cathedral.

Portrait of a Cardinal by Jan Van Eyck. It is
possible that the sitter may be Henry Beaufor

Joan Beaufort's tomb effigy in Staindrop Church, Co. Durham. She is not buried here.

A drawing of Joan Beaufort's effigy at Staindrop.

Joan Beaufort and her daughters by Ralph Neville, Earl of Westmorland, from *The Neville Hours*. It has been suggested that a text in this manuscript reveals Joan's feelings about her bastardy.

The brass of Thomas Chaucer and his wife, Maud Burghersh. The armorial shields on this tomb have given rise to the theory that Thomas was Philippa Chaucer's son by John of Gaunt.

John of Gaunt in later life, from *The Golden Book of St. Albans*.

John of Gaunt, from the St. Cuthbert window in York Minster. This window may hold clues to the Duke's final illness.

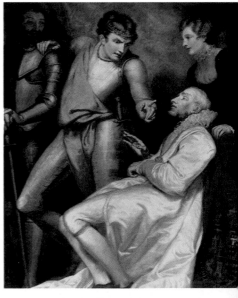

The dying John of Gaunt, by James Northcote. A romantic view, showing Katherine Swynford attired in the costume of the 1790s.

Katherine in widow's weeds,
from her lost brass tomb.

The Priory, Lincoln, and its vanished gatehouse.

During her second widowhood, Katherine leased another house in Lincoln's cathedral close, where she spent her last years.

The stone dresser from the former great hall of the Priory; it dates from Katherine's time.

The exterior of the Priory, as it is today. Katherine's long-demolished solar block was to the right of the building.

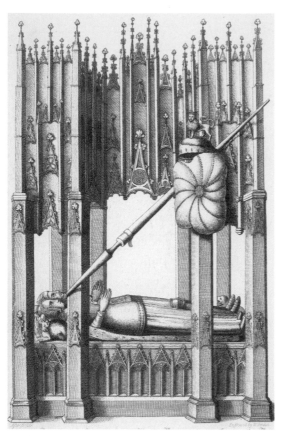

The lost tomb of John of Gaunt and Blanche of Lancaster in Old St. Paul's Cathedral, which was destroyed in 1666 in the Great Fire of London. These effigies were not the originals, which were replaced in Tudor times. An inscription on this tomb paid tribute to Katherine Swynford's famed beauty.

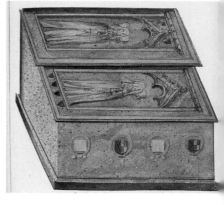

The tombs of Katherine Swynford and Joan Beaufort in their original positions in Lincoln Cathedral.

The tombs of Katherine and Joan in their present positions. Katherine's obit is still celebrated annually in Lincoln Cathedral.

some people to believe that he also supported the doctor's increasingly provocative opinions on the Church and its doctrines,[39] but this would have been surprising in a man with such ultraconservative religious views, whose actions show him to have been essentially opposed to most of Wycliffe's theological teachings.

John's willingness to champion and protect Wycliffe, and his enduring loyalty toward him, which was to provoke a backlash on his own probity and reputation, strongly suggest that he liked and respected his protégé, enjoyed discussing and debating political and religious issues with him, and believed him to be sincere and much misunderstood. But according to Knighton, it was he himself who was "deceived," and in the end, after years of defending the ever more controversial Wycliffe, even John would abandon him.

The Princess of Wales supported Wycliffe too; he was a familiar figure in court circles, and Katherine Swynford must have known him. It is easy to imagine this intelligent woman joining in his stimulating conversations with her lover, and although of course there is no evidence that she ever did so, it is more than possible. We do not know enough about her to surmise that she was in sympathy with Wycliffe's teachings, for in every known respect she was religiously orthodox. But maybe she was swayed by her lover on the doctor's political opinions.

In July 1374, John rode north to Tutbury to see his wife and children, then in early August he was at Leicester,[40] perhaps with Katherine. But he was back in London by September 11 to commemorate the sixth anniversary of Duchess Blanche's death, the first he was able to attend—for he had been abroad every previous year—and consequently the most splendid to date.

The magnificent obit took place on September 12.[41] On the evening beforehand, after Vespers in St. Paul's, the duke entertained the clergy at a banquet in the cathedral that consisted entirely of sweet confections and included ginger confits, aniseed, cinnamon, a marble plate of expensive sugar bonbons, sweetmeats, and nuts, and seventeen gallons of wine in earthenware jugs.

The anniversary itself began with a procession from the Savoy to St. Paul's Cathedral, which had been rendered suitably somber with funereal black hangings brought from the Savoy. Around Blanche's partially completed tomb there burned thirty-six new wax candles in place of those that had been lit there daily, and on the tomb stood eight metal bowls containing mortar lights. Further illumination came from the torches held by twenty-four poor men who had been given gowns and hoods in the blue and white Lancastrian livery colors and stood encircling the tomb. In the presence of the duke and his retinue, a senior canon, assisted by the massed cathedral clergy and choristers, celebrated high mass at the chantry altar. Afterward, the company returned to the Savoy for a further taste of the duke's famous hospitality, and consumed roasted beef, lamb, goose, pork, pigeons, pullets, and salted fish, some cooked with costly spices, followed by fruit, bread, and wafers, the food washed down with sixty gallons of wine and eleven gallons of ale. The total expenses for the obit were £40 (£13,657).[42]

In the years to come, Blanche's anniversary would remain an important event in the Lancastrian calendar, but the duke was not always able to attend, and the ceremonies were rarely as lavish as this one, some only costing £10 (£3,877).

Did Katherine Swynford grace the obit that took place in 1374? If the ducal children were present, she would have had a legitimate reason for being there, but there is no record of them attending; the names of only two of the guests are recorded.[43] Furthermore, the pattern of John's travels both before and after the anniversary suggests that his womenfolk and children were in the Midlands at the time, and it looks as if he made haste to rejoin Katherine afterward. For as soon as all was done, John rode north to Yorkshire, reaching his castle at Tickhill before September 22. By the following day he had moved south to his manor of Gringley in Nottinghamshire, and by September 25 he had traveled the thirty miles to Lincoln.[44] As Kettlethorpe was on the way, it is more than likely that he spent the night of September 24 there with Katherine.[45] On September 26, at Savenby, he ordered John de Stafford, his receiver in Lincoln, to pay a gift of 25 marks (£2,845) to Katherine "for services rendered."[46] This indicates that after John had ridden to London for the obit, she had traveled from Leicester to Kettlethorpe to await his coming, and rode forth with him when he left it. John had gone south to Stamford by September 29, and was back in residence at the Savoy from October to December.[47]

On December 10 the duke appointed a trusted esquire, Thomas Burton, as governor to his heir, seven-year-old Henry,[48] who was now too old to have a governess. The boy was given not only a tutor, but also a chaplain and a keeper of his wardrobe, and sent to live in the household of Lady Wake, his former mistress.[49] By 1376, Henry had been assigned a "military master" to teach him the arts of war, and his sisters were given their own chamber and wardrobe, a household within a household, with Katherine Swynford in charge of it.

At Christmas it would appear that Katherine was with John at Eltham, where he celebrated Yuletide and New Year with the King.[50] Since Alice Perrers was presiding over the court as unofficial queen, Edward III could hardly have complained about the presence of his son's mistress; in fact, he probably welcomed her, for he had known Katherine since her childhood, and his kindness to her at the time of her widowhood suggests that he liked her well. Her presence at court is indicated by a New Year gift from her lover: On January 1, 1375, "with my especial grace," John granted her the lucrative wardship of the lands and heir of his late retainer, Sir Robert Deyncourt, "and the right of the marriage of the heir for Blanche her daughter,"[51] his godchild. Sir Robert was possibly related to one of the duke's retainers, John Deyncourt, Constable of Kenilworth Castle,[52] whom Katherine probably knew quite well.

In fulfilling his obligations as her sponsor, the duke intended that Blanche Swynford, who at almost twelve was nearing marriageable age, should be wed to young Robert Deyncourt. On January 13 he gave orders to his steward, Oliver de Barton, to "carefully guard the heir till such time that Dame Katherine will send for him, when you will deliver him and the guard of the lands to her."[53] The wording of this warrant reveals John's respect for Katherine and his confidence in her acting autonomously. There is, however, no record of the marriage taking place, nor is there any further reference to Blanche Swynford in contemporary sources, from which we might sadly conclude that she did not live to see her wedding day. Robert Deyncourt, however, survived to press in 1387–92 for the restitution of his lands.[54]

On January 2, 1375, John rode to Hertford Castle to visit his wife, while Katherine presumably traveled home to Kettlethorpe. At Hertford, on his arrival, John issued an order to John de Stafford to pay Katherine one mark (£114), perhaps for a wager she had won over Christmas. On the same day, he granted her the more handsome sum of 50 marks (£4,709) per annum, possibly because she was pregnant again; this allowance was also to be paid by John de Stafford.[55]

John had returned to the Savoy by January 14, when he ordered de Stafford to send a tun (a large cask holding 252 gallons) of the best Gascon wine to "our very dear and well-beloved Dame Katherine de Swynford" at Kettlethorpe; "if none can be found, send a vat of the best wine from the Rhine that you can find."[56] This was a parting gift, for he was soon to go abroad again. Edward III had declared his readiness to make a truce with France, which was now a matter of necessity after Bayonne had fallen to the enemy; in February, John, who was to head the English embassy, was granted the diplomatic powers necessary to negotiate the truce, and by March 9 he was in Dover, ready to sail. John Wycliffe was in his retinue. The duke arrived in Bruges on March 24, and presided over the peace conference that lasted until June 27, when a one-year truce with the French was concluded. By July 15 he was back in England.[57]

The summer of 1375 was very hot, with a severe drought. Katherine appears to have spent these months at Kenilworth, and it was probably at this time that she bore the duke a second son, for in August he ordered that two chariots of wood for fuel be delivered to Elyot, the midwife of Lincoln. Elsewhere in the *Register* Elyot is referred to as a midwife of Leicester, but this grant suggests that she had moved to Lincoln to attend Katherine Swynford in childbirth when necessary and was being suitably rewarded.

John of Gaunt's Register for 1375 has references to two other women connected with Katherine. The first was Agnes Bonsergeant, a widow, who was rewarded with a life pension of 5 marks (£486) for services she had performed as Katherine's nurse;[58] this was the lady appointed by Queen Philippa to look after her young ward. As Professor Goodman points out, it was usual for princes to award pensions to their own nurses or those of their wives but virtually unheard of for a royal duke to remember the nurse of his mistress in this way, and an unmistakable indication of how deeply John had come to feel for Katherine and how important she was to him. It is also possible—with her pension being awarded at this time—that Agnes assisted at Katherine's confinement.

The *Register* also records an undated payment—perhaps in 1375—of 66s.8d (£942) to John, son of Hawise Maudelyn, "*damoiselle* of our very dear and beloved Dame Katherine de Swynford."[59]

Another grant made by John may also have marked a birth, for on July 24 he ordered Oliver de Barton, his seneschal in Nottinghamshire, and Richard de Lancaster, park warden of his manors of Gringley and Wheatley in that county, to send to his "beloved Dame Katherine Swynford or her attorney, sixty oaks suitable for building from any of our parks thought convenient, and which, in your judgment, will best profit her for the improvement of her houses at Kettlethorpe."[60] From this and the 1372 grant of oaks, it is clear that Katherine's program of improvements was well under way, and that John's new gift was intended to further assist her in making the manor a residence fit for their children. Also during 1375 he arranged for her to be paid 100 marks (£9,419), to be delivered into her own hands;[61] this was possibly provision for their two children.

This pattern of gifts and grants had occurred before, probably in connection with the conception and birth of John Beaufort, and was to be repeated in the future. In 1375 it perhaps marked the advent of a second Beaufort. The evidence is not conclusive, but the repetition of this pattern on each of four occasions may well point to Katherine's illicit pregnancies and the duke's discreet arrangements for the maintenance of their expanding family.

An undated warrant in *John of Gaunt's Register* possibly belongs to the period July 23–September 26, 1375 (or perhaps 1377), and might have formed part of this provision. In it, in consideration of the good and agreeable service she had rendered to Duchess Blanche, John granted Katherine "all the tenements that we own in our honor of St. Botolph"—this being a manor on the east side of the River Witham in the thriving port of Boston, Lincolnshire, which had been part of the Honor of Richmond since the time of William the Conqueror. The tenements (which could have been lands, dwellings, rents, or commercial premises) granted to Katherine had formerly been held by Geoffrey de Sutton, doubtless a connection of the prominent Lincoln family. Katherine was to hold these tenements and the profits from them from the duke and his heirs for the term of her life.[62]

Boston was a flourishing port at this date, second only to London in prosperity, and boasting fifteen merchant guilds; the beautiful parish church of St. Botolph, with its famous squat tower, the "Boston Stump," was rebuilt in the fourteenth and fifteenth centuries by mercantile wealth. In 1369, Edward III had established a staple for wool and leather in Boston, and trade with the Low Countries was booming. Much of the medieval town has long since disappeared, but although there are no records to show where Katherine's properties were, there are clues.[63]

All that we know for certain is that her tenements lay in the parish of St.

Botolph. In 1774, when its churchyard was extended, many old houses and shops were demolished. Hers may have been among them, but there is some evidence to suggest that she owned Gisors Hall, a substantial building that survived into the nineteenth century.

In 1372, before he relinquished the earldom of Richmond, John of Gaunt had held a "messuage"—a house with land and outbuildings—in St. Botolph called "Gisorshall."[64] Gisors Hall, probably built around 1245, stood in a part of town that centuries later would become South Square, a spacious and desirable residential area backing onto the river; the hall occupied the northwest corner plot. In 1282 it had been held of the Honor of Richmond by John de Gisors, after whom it was named. He belonged to an important merchant family that traded in Boston and London; in 1245 a John de Gisors had been Mayor of London. In 1282, Gisors Hall was a capital messuage comprising buildings, gardens, and a yard, set in two acres of land—an ideal town residence.

In 1810, when Gisors Hall was partly demolished and rebuilt as a granary, stone fabric from the old building was incorporated in the new. A drawing made of the granary in 1856 shows a double-gabled stone frontage with two medieval mullioned windows sporting ogee arches on the upper floor, with Victorian brickwork arches surmounting them. At ground level may be seen two double-arched doorways to allow access for carts bringing grain—a nineteenth-century feature—and an old Gothic doorway at one end.

Katherine's ownership of this property is suggested by the fact that in 1427, after the death of her son, Thomas Beaufort, it was recorded that he had had a messuage called "Gisours Hall" in Boston, with the customs and franchises thereto belonging, just as his father had had in 1372.[65] Quite clearly, Gisors Hall was no longer a part of the Honor of Richmond in 1427, so possibly it had been alienated and sold to Geoffrey de Sutton in the 1370s, then repurchased by John of Gaunt, who granted it to Katherine Swynford, who in turn bequeathed it to Thomas Beaufort.

Katherine's familial connections with Boston were enduring. Between 1400 and 1404 her sons, Thomas and Henry Beaufort, were admitted to the fraternity of the town's Corpus Christi Guild, of which Edward III, Philippa of Hainault, Duke Henry of Lancaster, the Black Prince, and

Blanche of Lancaster had also been members. (There was also an associated guild dedicated to St. Katherine; did Katherine Swynford ever pay her respects to her name saint's image in that guild's chapel in St. Botolph's Church?)

In 1500 a substantial house called Spayne's Place, in Boston, was recorded as being the property of Katherine's great-granddaughter, Margaret Beaufort, Countess of Richmond and Derby, the mother of Henry VII. In the fourteenth century the de Spayne family had been prominent merchants, guildsmen, and aldermen in the town, and Spain Lane is said to be named after them. However, there is no trace of Spayne's Place there, although it could have stood in Spain's Court, an opening on the south side; the ancient buildings that line the street were probably once the family's warehouses.

Given her connections with Boston, Katherine must have visited the town on several occasions and become acquainted with its leading burghers; she possibly had mercantile interests there, and might have known or visited Spayne's Place, but there is no evidence that she owned it or that it descended from her to Margaret Beaufort. On the contrary, in 1487 it was one of the properties of the earldom of Richmond, once held by Margaret's late husband, Edmund Tudor, that were granted to her by her son the King.[66]

Interestingly, according to an Inquisition Postmortem of 1546, Margaret Beaufort also held Gisors Hall. Unless it was returned to the Honor of Richmond at some stage, it might well have passed to her by descent through the Beauforts; Thomas Beaufort left no children, so his eldest brother's son, John Beaufort—Duke of Somerset, Margaret's father—was his heir. In 1545, Spayne's Place was sold by Henry VIII to the Corporation of Boston. How long it survived after that is not recorded.

The son probably born to Katherine in the summer of 1375—and therefore conceived during the duke's visit to Lincolnshire the previous September—was almost certainly Henry Beaufort, who was probably named after Henry, Duke of Lancaster. It has been suggested that Henry was the youngest of the children Katherine bore the duke: in 1398, in connection with being appointed Bishop of Lincoln, he was described as *admodum puer*—just a boy. But this was probably merely a derisory comment on his elevation to episcopal rank at the age of just twenty-three. The seventeenth-century genealogist, Francis Sandford, describes the arms of Henry Beaufort in Wanlip Church, Leicestershire, as having a crescent as a cadency mark, which in Sandford's day indicated a second son.[67] More tellingly, Henry is second in the list of the Beauforts in the Letters Patent legitimizing them in 1397.

In August 1375, John was at Leicester[68] with Katherine, and it was probably at this time that William Ferour, the Mayor of Leicester, spent 16s. (£226) on a gift of wine for "the Lady Katherine Swynford, mistress of the Duke of Lancaster," doubtless in the hope of securing her patronage; this payment is recorded in the civic records for the year 1375–76.[69] This approach by the mayor is the first evidence that her position of influence with the duke was becoming public knowledge. It also shows that the mayor thought an appeal to Katherine would be more successful than one to Duchess Constance; to this extent, as Professor Goodman points out, she had usurped the duchess's rightful place in Lancastrian affairs.[70] Nevertheless, there is no evidence that she exploited or abused her influence. On the contrary, she seems to have avoided embroiling herself in politics and kept very much in the background. Although there are very few known instances of her exercising any powers of patronage, the Leicester records show that Katherine occasionally used her influence for the benefit of others, while there is evidence to suggest that if she did ask favors from the duke, it was usually for her own family members, such as her brother-in-law, Geoffrey Chaucer, and her sister Philippa. But she was no Alice Perrers, feathering her nest at the Crown's expense: No chronicler ever accused her of such greed and rapacity, nor of the bribery and corruption that would bring Alice down.

Certainly Katherine profited materially from her relationship with John of Gaunt, but never excessively. His recorded gifts to her demonstrate his generosity, his care for her welfare, and his desire to please her; they made her wealthy, but not ostentatiously so, and were hardly lavish compared to Alice Perrers's ill-gotten gains. Nor did he abuse his political power or misappropriate public funds to indulge Katherine. In fact, she seems to have retained her autonomy as a widow and pursued her private financial and other interests when she was not with her lover, which was relatively often.

It is reasonable to suppose that Katherine accompanied John when he moved to Kenilworth later in August, and that this was only one of many visits she made to that imposing castle, which she must have come to know well.

Kenilworth, which lies four miles north of Warwick, was to be one of the most magnificent of the castles owned by John of Gaunt, who by 1377 had begun building a sumptuous range of apartments and lodgings there. This massive and important stronghold, built of golden sandstone, dated from the early twelfth century and had been extended and formidably fortified by King John—who surrounded it on three sides with a defensive lake called "the Mere"—and Henry III, whose mighty keep still stands. In 1265 the castle had fallen to the latter after a nine-month siege during the Barons' Wars, and in 1267 it was granted to Henry's younger son, Edmund Crouchback, founder of the House of Lancaster. Since then, it had remained one of the chief Lancastrian seats, and under John of Gaunt was to become a luxurious palace. He built the massive Perpendicular great hall, which still survives in a ruined state, and an extensive range of private apartments and domestic offices, also now ruined.[71]

John's great hall, or "New Chamber," which measures 90 by 45 feet, was accessed at one end by an external processional stair leading up from the inner court to an imposing main doorway decorated with fine stone panels and carvings, and set within a vaulted porch. The other end of the hall was graced by an oriel window; in the privacy of its embrasure, which had its own fireplace, would be set the duke's table, where he would eat with his family and friends; Katherine must have sat at board with him here on many occasions. The rest of his household dined at trestle tables placed along the length of the hall, which was heated by two vast fireplaces of carved stone and lit by four huge traceried windows with stone seats in the alcoves beneath. Anyone sitting there reading or sewing—as Katherine might well have done—would have benefited from the natural light such windows afforded. The vast timber hammerbeam roof has long disappeared, as has the wooden floor of the hall, but much remains of the once-vaulted undercroft, which was used for storing wine and provisions. From here, a northeastern doorway led to the three-story service block known as the "Strong Tower," which housed the kitchens, bakehouse, servants' quarters, and other domestic offices.

Adjacent to the great hall at the southwestern end were the duke's apartments, accessed through the Saintlowe Tower; this range overlooked the Mere. His family, knights, esquires, and, of course, Katherine would have lodged with him there. His great chamber, known as the "White Hall," was a rectangular room located on the first floor; this was where he gave audiences and received guests, seated on a throne on a dais beneath a canopy of estate bearing the royal arms of Castile. Gaunt's Tower, a four-story edifice that lay beyond the chamber block and projected over the lake, contained his private lodgings, or lesser chamber, which could be reached via a spiral staircase leading from a door in the inner court, although it must surely have been possible to access them from the great chamber. Gaunt's Tower also contained a chapel, and had garderobes on the ground and first floors. The garden outside was enclosed in September 1373,[72] possibly to allow the duke some privacy with his mistress, and along the causeway that now leads to a car park there was a tiltyard.

Work on Kenilworth continued on and off until 1394, cost the duke a princely fortune, and provided employment for numerous masons, carpenters, goldsmiths, and embroiders. In its finished state it was the embodiment of its owner's status, splendor, and authority, which was doubtless his intention, and in later years it replaced the Savoy as the showpiece of the Lancastrian inheritance. The great hall, which has been called one of the finest fourteenth-century rooms in England, is said to have inspired Richard II's remodeling of Westminster Hall in the 1390s.

I n September, when John moved south to tour the West Country,[73] Katherine returned to Kettlethorpe, and it is often erroneously claimed that she used her influence at this time to get the Fossdyke cleared.[74] This, the oldest canal in England, had been constructed by the Romans around AD 120, to link the River Trent at Torksey to the River Witham at Lincoln, eleven miles away, and during the Middle Ages became a major waterway for the transport of wool from Nottingham, Hull, York, and other places. But for thirty years now it had been silted up, and it was claimed that £1,000 (£282,562) were lost in trade as a result. During the Michaelmas law term of 1375 a Lincoln jury had made representations about this, pointing out that local landowners such as "the Lady Katherine de Swynford," whose manors and lordships abutted the Fossdyke, "ought and were wont to clean, empty, and repair" their own stretches of the dike, according to an ancient rota; but clearly they had long since ceased to perform their responsibilities in this respect. The protest fell on deaf ears. On May 15, 1376, a commission of oyer and terminer was appointed at Westminster "on complaint by the citizens of Lincoln . . . that the dike is now obstructed partly by riparian [i.e., riverside] owners [Katherine Swynford being one of them] who have meadows and pastures on both sides of the dike, taking across their cattle in summer to pasture, and also by grass growing therein in unusual quantities."[75] Far from agitating to have the canal cleared, Katherine and other landowners were taking advantage of it being silted up. Yet despite parliamentary intervention, nothing appears to have been done, for in 1384 another commission, headed by John of Gaunt himself, was appointed to solve the problem.[76] But even he was not entirely successful, for efforts were still being made to have the Fossdyke cleared in 1518, and the problem was only finally solved by an Act of Parliament passed in 1670.

By the end of September, John had returned to the Savoy[77] to prepare for yet another round of peace negotiations in Bruges. Having arranged for his three-year-old daughter Catalina to have her own chamber at Melbourne Castle, where she would be looked after by a Castilian lady, Juana Martyns,[78] he departed with Constance for Bruges at the end of October 1375.[79] Katherine was probably still at Kettlethorpe at this time.

John apparently took Constance with him because she was expecting his child; no doubt he relished the prospect of her bearing a son and heir to Castile while the eyes of all Europe were on Bruges. Prior to her confinement the duchess went on pilgrimage to the shrine of Saint-Adrien de Grammont,[80] but the boy she bore late in the year at Ghent—another John of Gaunt—appears to have been sickly, and died young, possibly in November 1376. Constance would hardly have traveled abroad at full term, so her baby was probably born several weeks after her arrival in Flanders, in early December. In that case, she must have fallen pregnant just before John left for Bruges in early March.

Constance would not conceive again for nearly ten years, when there were compelling political reasons to produce a son. Comparing this dismal record with that of Blanche of Lancaster, who bore seven children in nine years, and Katherine Swynford, who had at least four in the same time span, it can only be concluded that conjugal relations between the duke and duchess were now either very infrequent or had ceased entirely, probably because of John's passion for Katherine Swynford, and because of Constance's own antipathy. She seems to have been more preoccupied with her Castilian ambitions than with her husband, and she could not hope to compete with the other woman in his life, whose influence was so all-embracing.

John remained in negotiation at Bruges until at least January 20, 1376, then made a brief visit back to England before returning to the peace conference for the conclusion on March 1 of a new truce, which would prolong the first until April 1377 and bring hostilities to a halt.[81] The lavish ostentation, "rioting, reveling, and dancing"—all funded by public money—that attended John's embassy attracted much criticism from the chroniclers, who suspected that he was only advocating peace in order to enrich himself.[82] The duke and duchess sailed home at the end of March, and on April 23, John was at Westminster for the annual feast of the Knights of the Garter that Edward III hosted to mark St. George's Day. Five days later what was to become known as the "Good" Parliament met at Westminster, summoned because the King was in desperate need of money, and John of Gaunt found himself facing one of the worst crises of his career.

SIX

His Unspeakable Concubine

John of Gaunt was now the most hated and feared man in England. "Oh, unhappy and unfortunate duke!" fulminated Walsingham in 1376. "Oh! Those whom you should lead in war you betray by your treachery and cowardice, and those whom you should lead in peace by the example of good works you lead astray, dragging them to ruin!" People of all ranks were suspicious and envious of the duke's vast wealth and power, his incomprehensible—to the insular English—foreign ambitions, and the trappings of sovereignty that underlined his kingly rank. Churchmen abhorred his anticlerical stance and his patronage of John Wycliffe. His perceived military failures, his staunch advocacy of a peace policy, and the recent truce he had negotiated, outraged all those who felt that the English should be winning great victories over the French, as in the glory days of Edward III and the Black Prince. And the common people, long burdened by the crippling taxes levied to pay for no more than a series of humiliating losses in the war with France, blamed John for England's misfortunes. This mounting resentment, building for some time, was now about to explode.

No Parliament had been called since November 1373, and such was the importance of this new session that the desperately sick Black Prince had himself carried to Westminster for it. Meanwhile, the city was loudly resonating with "a great murmur of the people," and soon it became clear that the Commons were bent upon challenging the authority of the Crown itself, and that their chief targets were the corrupt influences about the King, foremost among them Alice Perrers, who were "neither loyal nor profitable to the kingdom." This unprecedented attack was to appear dangerously radical to the politically conservative duke, and his honorable but ill-judged attempts to protect his father's interests were further to undermine his standing in the land.

Edward III was too infirm to attend Parliament. Thus it was that in May the Commons dared to confront a "very ill-at-ease" John of Gaunt in the House of Lords.[1] They accused the government—and, by implication, John himself—of profiteering from the war, wasting public money, and corrupt practices. The King, they insisted, must "live off his own" in the future, and not burden his people with heavy taxes. John of Gaunt was inwardly infuriated by the insolence of these "degenerate hedge-knights of tallow," as he put it.

"Do they think they are kings or princes of this realm?" he raged in private. "Whence have they got their pride and arrogance? Have they forgotten how powerful I am? I will give them such a fright that they shall not provoke me again."[2] But such was the strength of parliamentary fervor that he had no choice but to back down and graciously agree to an inquiry into the royal administration, along with the impeachment of allegedly corrupt courtiers and the banishment of Alice Perrers from court for having fleeced the King of up to £3,000 (£806,547) a year, to his great damage.[3] Never before had a royal mistress suffered such public castigation. John saw this as an attack on monarchical authority itself, and his overriding priority was to crush it, but his transparent efforts to forestall these proceedings, and his high-handed attitude toward his adversaries, only served to antagonize them further.

He was certainly in touch with Katherine Swynford during this tumultuous time; she had perhaps joined him at the Savoy after his return from Bruges, and she probably conceived another child during that spring. Preoccupied though he was with the tortuous affairs of Parliament, John found time, on May 15, to appoint a commission to address the matter of draining the Fossdyke. His aim may have been to mollify the citizens of Lincoln while at the same time protecting Katherine's own interests.

When the Black Prince had himself carried into Parliament, he fainted several times and was forced to withdraw to his sickbed at Kennington Palace. Claims that he supported the Commons derive mainly from the overimaginative Thomas Walsingham and have been greatly overstated: He was far too ill to play any political role, and his overriding concern was to safeguard the rights of his nine-year-old son, Richard of Bordeaux. For six years now the prince had suffered the most debilitating and humiliating illness, with a recurrent "flux, both of seed and blood, which two infirmities made him so feeble that his servants took him very often for dead."[4] On June 7, 1376, aware that he was dying, he made his will, and his father, his wife, and his brothers gathered around his bed "amid great lamentations. No one there could keep from tears," and there was "great desolation at the sorrow of the King taking leave of his son forever."[5] The Black Prince died the following day, Trinity Sunday, leaving young Richard of Bordeaux as the heir to the English throne. The prince was later buried in a magnificent tomb executed by Henry Yevele in Canterbury Cathedral.

The Black Prince's death left John of Gaunt as the ailing Edward III's chief counselor and hence the most powerful man in the land. "The King no longer wished to be guided through his lords assembled in Parliament, and so he had recourse to his son, John of Gaunt, to guide himself and the realm. Until the death of the King, the duke acted as governor and ruler of the kingdom."[6] The general feeling was that John was too powerful, while some feared that he had sinister designs on the Crown itself. Walsingham claims that during the Good Parliament, John demanded that the French Salic Law, which barred women from succeeding, or transmitting a claim, to the throne, be introduced into England.[7] This would effectively have removed from the succession the heirs of his elder brother Lionel, who had left one daughter, Philippa, now the wife of Edmund Mortimer, Earl of March, by whom she had four children. The implication was that John wanted to be acknowledged heir presumptive after Richard of Bordeaux. For Walsingham, that was a step too near the throne, and therefore suspect, and he tells us that the Commons rejected the duke's petition, much to the triumphant glee of the Earl of March. But this episode may just be one of Walsingham's imaginative calumnies, for it is not referred to in other chronicles. However, Parliament did take the precautions of having Richard brought before it and acknowledged as heir apparent and of appointing a council of peers to ensure good government, designating several of their number to attend upon the prince and protect him from his dangerous uncle.

Sadly for the duke's reputation, it is Walsingham's so-called "Scandalous Chronicle" (his *Chronicon Angliae*) that records most of the events of this time. It is hopelessly biased. The waspish and vituperative Walsingham, incensed at and deeply suspicious of John's patronage of the increasingly outspoken anticlerical Wycliffe, went out of his way to record—and doubtless embroider—every evil bruit he had heard concerning the duke. He asserted that John was a traitor to his country and his house, guilty of underhanded intrigue, bribery, and murder; that he was a wicked uncle, intriguing to assassinate Prince Richard, or plotting with the French king to have the boy declared a bastard; that his military campaigns had failed because of his cowardice and corruption; that he led an immoral life—the only accusation founded on fact—and had treated his first wife shamefully. But if Walsingham knew that the duke had a mistress, he clearly did not at this time know her name, for if he had, he would surely have mentioned it. He resurrected the old calumny that, back in 1362, John had Blanche's sister, Matilda of Lancaster, poisoned so he could claim her inheritance. No accusation was too vile or far-fetched to be leveled at the hapless duke, and Walsingham was to continue this relentless campaign of character assassination until 1388. The sad thing was that many people were prepared to believe his allegations, with the consequence that John of Gaunt became the scapegoat for all the evils and insecurities plaguing the realm.

In fact, there is absolutely no evidence that John had sinister designs on the throne. He had given his oath to his dying brother to loyally serve Richard of Bordeaux, and he was always to honor it. He could indeed have challenged Richard's legitimacy, given Joan of Kent's checkered matrimonial history, but to his credit, he made no attempt to do so. Nor would the Black Prince have made his "very dear and well-beloved brother of Spain"[8] his chief executor if he believed that his son had anything to fear from John: This appointment, like so much else, bespeaks a deep respect and trust between the brothers.

There appears to have been a keen mutual regard between John and his widowed sister-in-law and cousin, Joan of Kent—which there surely would not have been had the shrewd princess for a moment entertained any suspicions of John's intentions. The welfare of the young heir was a matter of importance to them both: John clearly felt a strong sense of responsibility toward Richard, for he had sworn to protect him, and he had an affection for the boy as his revered brother's son. An interest in Wycliffe's teachings was another common bond with the princess.[9] Soon after the Black Prince's death, John saw to it that Joan's dower rights were confirmed, ensuring her financial security, while she, on her part, was to prove warmly supportive of him in the months to come. Lavish New Year gifts to her are recorded in *John of Gaunt's Register*.

On July 10, Parliament had the temerity to refuse the Crown's request for funds, and in retaliation, an angry Edward III dissolved it that same day. However, he "wholly laid down the government of the kingdom and put it in the hands of the duke, allowing him to do all he wanted."[10] John of Gaunt became effectively the uncrowned ruler of England. Before the month was out, John's overriding influence was made manifest, as he firmly asserted his authority and began steadily reversing and undoing all the work that Parliament had done, high-handedly reinforcing the supremacy of the Crown and making many enemies in the process, while establishing himself as the supreme champion and defender of royal power.

John then rode north to Pontefract Castle in Yorkshire, probably with Katherine in his train, and it was there, on July 25, that he granted her the wardship and marriage of the heiress of Bertram de Sauneby, in recognition of the "good and agreeable" service she had rendered and continued to render "to our dear daughters."[11] Again this grant may mark a new pregnancy.[12] When John returned to London in the early autumn, "he permitted the King to receive back into grace many who had been perpetually banished from his presence":[13] The courtiers displaced by Parliament were pardoned and restored to their former places, while Alice Perrers hastened back to the side of a grateful Edward III. On October 7 the ailing King made his will and named John of Gaunt as his chief executor.[14]

Nine councillors were dismissed. William of Wykeham, Bishop of Winchester and founder of Winchester School and New College, Oxford, had been active in leading the clerical opposition to the Crown in Parliament, and was to prove a lifelong enemy of John Wycliffe. Wykeham had been dismissed as chancellor in 1371, but recalled by the Good Parliament. He typified the career churchmen so detested by Wycliffe, while John of Gaunt was determined to target the wealth of the Church, which enjoyed immunity from taxation, and was incensed that Wykeham had supported Parliament to the detriment of the King. Thus it may have been the duke who prompted

Wycliffe to preach against Wykeham in London. But the new Bishop of London, William Courtenay, a young aristocrat of great ability and energy, was a supporter of Wykeham, and deplored John's perceived anticlericalism, while the Londoners themselves had their own grievances against the duke: They resented his interference in the city, believing that he cherished "an ancient hatred" against their jealously guarded liberties. In actuality, John was keen to protect the interests of struggling artisans and small craftsmen in the face of the financial might and monopolies wielded by the wealthy merchants and trade guilds.

In October, still relentlessly moving against his enemies, the duke accused William of Wykeham of misappropriating public funds, and presided over the judicial proceedings taken against him; on November 17, Wykeham was stripped of his temporalities and banished from court.[15] It was perhaps around this time that the duke's infant son by Constance died,[16] a tragedy that must have hit John hard.

That same month, Walsingham claims, John attempted to chasten the Earl of March by ordering him to Calais, but the earl refused to go, so he was forced to resign his office of Marshal of England, which was assigned by John on December 1 to his cousin Henry, Lord Percy,[17] one of the foremost northern barons, in a successful attempt to buy the latter's loyalty. It is more likely that March resigned the marshalship because he was needed in Ireland.[18] However, Peter de la Mare, Speaker of the Commons during the Good Parliament, *was* a target of the duke's wrath: He was sent to prison. In January, Adam Houghton, Bishop of St. David's, a friend of the duke and of his first wife, Blanche, was appointed Chancellor of England. In his prologue to *Piers Plowman*, William Langland refers scathingly to the "rout of rats" by "a cat of the court"—John of Gaunt—who:

> *. . . came where he liked*
> *And leapt over them lightly, and caught them at his will,*
> *And played with them perilously, and pushed them about.*

Meanwhile, on November 20, in belated response to the urgings of the Commons in the Good Parliament, Richard of Bordeaux had been created Prince of Wales. On Christmas Day the King hosted a great feast in Westminster Hall at which all the peers, led by John of Gaunt, knelt in turn and solemnly swore allegiance to Richard as the heir to the throne; then the boy was placed next to his grandfather at table, above the duke and the King's other children.[19] This was a tactical move, no doubt orchestrated by John himself, to demonstrate that he was no threat to Richard but loyally supported him as heir to the throne. On January 25, further underlining his commitment, John and his brothers attended a great open-air entertainment put on by the Londoners for the prince, with mummers in fantastic costumes parading by torchlight and prizes to delight a young boy.[20]

It was during that turbulent year of 1376–77 that Katherine Swynford received her first recorded payment, of £50 (£13,442), for the wardrobe and chamber expenses of Philippa of Lancaster. The duke also arranged for her to be paid £100 (£28,885) a year in equal portions, at Easter and Michaelmas, to meet these expenses, for which she was to issue letters of acquittance under her seal[21]—which sadly does not survive. This grant suggests that she was caring for her charges throughout the tumultuous period of the Good Parliament and its aftermath; Elizabeth, as the younger daughter, would have shared her sister's chamber. The duke ordered these payments to be made to William Oke, the clerk of his Great Wardrobe, so perhaps both governess and charges were in residence at the Savoy for much of the period. John's readiness to entrust such large sums to Katherine demonstrates his confidence in her integrity and her financial acumen.

The closeness and family solidarity increasingly and enduringly demonstrated between the Lancastrian children, the Swynfords, the Beauforts, and the Chaucers suggests they had all known each other from childhood, so it is quite likely that Katherine had her own children with her when she was acting as governess to the princesses, and that the Chaucer children were in evidence too, in Constance's household with their mother. It is not beyond the bounds of probability that Katherine's royal charges sometimes came to stay with her at Kettlethorpe, just as they sojourned from time to time in other households. These arrangements meant that all the children grew up in an environment in which learning, literature, poetry, religion, the arts, and intellectual debate were strong elements, and that they would have absorbed those influences from their infancy, with even the girls encouraged to participate, for John of Gaunt was the most enlightened of medieval men in that respect, and Katherine was herself a cultivated and intelligent woman. Furthermore, it is obvious that John's legitimate children were fond of Katherine, and readily accepted her children by their father as their half siblings, even embracing her Swynford children within the family circle.

The effects of such an upbringing are apparent in the success that all these children were to achieve in later life. That success, and the establishment of close and harmonious relationships within what could have been a highly dysfunctional family, must largely be a tribute not only to John of Gaunt's forceful character and influence, but also to Katherine's tact, humanity, and obvious gift for getting the best out of people.

All the evidence suggests that Katherine and John were good and caring parents whose children grew up to love and respect them. Judging by the gifts that attended their arrival, the births of the Beauforts were welcomed by the duke, who must have seen them as a means of extending his affinity and influence. But there was more to it than that. John, whose devotion to his offspring by Katherine was commented upon by Froissart, was to prove diligent in securing for them a place in society that befit their noble birth and in promoting their interests, while cautiously ensuring that these did not infringe upon the rights of his legitimate heirs, a policy that would have preempted any jealousy on the part of the latter. As for Katherine, "she loved the Duke of Lancaster and the children she had with him, and she showed it."[22]

In 1376, probably at the intercession of John of Gaunt, the Pope granted permission (an "indult") for "Catherine de Swynford," in the diocese of Lincoln, to have a portable altar in her lodgings,[23] which is surely further testimony to her piety, although we might wonder if the pontiff was aware of her adulterous relationship with the duke, or if her conscience was ever troubled by it. Could she have gone to confession, knowing she was committing a sin in the eyes of the Church every time she slept with him? Or did she confess these transgressions, sincerely intending each time not to commit them again, but failing miserably? We have no way of knowing.

Katherine's disappearance from the records during the turbulent latter months of 1376 was probably occasioned by advancing pregnancy: It is likely that she bore her third child by John in the early months of 1377.[24] This was a dramatic and highly publicized period in the duke's life, but nowhere is there any mention in the chronicles of Katherine, who may well have been in seclusion at Kettlethorpe or elsewhere at this time. It might be significant that, on February 25, Edward III licensed John to grant to Katherine for her lifetime the ducal manors of Gringley and Wheatley in

Nottinghamshire, which were jointly worth more than £150 (£52,428) per annum;[25] this grant perhaps marked the birth of a third child, and the rents from these manors were possibly intended to provide for its upbringing, as might have been the profits from the Sauneby wardship, granted by John the previous July when the pregnancy would have been confirmed. The duke also presented Katherine with a tun of wine at this time.[26] Armitage-Smith opines that it was Thomas Beaufort who was born early in 1377, but this third child was probably Joan Beaufort, Katherine's only daughter by John, perhaps named in honor of the Dowager Princess of Wales, who was demonstrating such kindness and friendship to the duke at this critical time. The usual date given for Joan's birth is 1379, but that would mean she was barely fourteen when her first child was born around 1393, and the pattern of grants is not repeated in 1379. An earlier birth date of 1377 is probably more realistic.

Joan might have been born at Kettlethorpe, but given the political situation at this time, her birth perhaps took place elsewhere, for John of Gaunt was so hated in the country that anyone connected with him was at risk—as would be proved dramatically in February 1377—and Katherine, as his mistress, was especially vulnerable. Professor Goodman, who places Joan's date of birth in 1379 with reservations, has suggested that she was delivered at Pleshy in Essex, the residence of Joan FitzAlan, Dowager Countess of Hereford, Essex, and Northampton. The countess was the daughter of Eleanor of Lancaster, a sister of Duke Henry, and she—like her late husband, Humphrey de Bohun (pronounced Boon)—enjoyed an enduring friendship with John of Gaunt. Her elder daughter Eleanor had just married Thomas of Woodstock, John's youngest brother, who would be created Earl of Buckingham on July 16, 1377. Given the fact that the latest Beaufort was christened Joan, and was later welcomed into the household of the countess's younger daughter Mary, it is indeed possible that she was born at Pleshy Castle near Chelmsford, and that the countess acted as her sponsor.[27]

The King confirmed the grant of Gringley and Wheatley at Sheen on March 4, 1377.[28] The acquisition of these two manors, both situated not far from Kettlethorpe, added considerably to Katherine's income; she was by now a fairly wealthy woman.

Gringley-on-the-Hill is a pretty village perched eighty-two feet above sea level, twelve miles to the northwest of Kettlethorpe, and boasts beautiful views over Nottinghamshire, Lincolnshire, and Yorkshire, and a church with a Norman arch, dedicated to St. Peter and St. Paul. To the east is Beacon Hill, the site of the original Saxon settlement. The medieval manor had been granted to John of Gaunt by Edward III,[29] and between 1372 and 1377 he kept the manor house and its chambers in repair.[30] There was good hunting to be had nearby: In his *Register*, the duke refers to "the West Park" and "our parks of Gringley." Katherine surely would have visited and stayed at this desirable property.

Wheatley, which is mentioned in Domesday Book and was granted to John of Gaunt by Edward III,[31] is now two villages, North and South Wheatley, but in Katherine's time it was a manor set in woodland and famous for the strawberries that grew there. It is situated three miles south of Gringley and nine miles northwest of Kettlethorpe.

At some unspecified date, possibly in 1377, Katherine was also granted the manors of Waddington and Wellingore in Lincolnshire. The entry in *John of Gaunt's Register* (which is erroneously dated 1354, at the Savoy) states that these properties were bestowed on her in reward "for the good and loving service which Lady Katherine Swynford has rendered to our late dearly beloved duchess."

Waddington lies about five miles south of Lincoln, and had formed part of the Lancastrian inheritance. Wellingore is five miles farther south, and ten miles east of Newark on the Lincoln road. Originally a Saxon settlement and Domesday village, it occupies a magnificent position on the Lincolnshire Cliff, with the old village built of light brown stone lying to the west, where the escarpment rises 260 feet above sea level; below is the valley of the River Witham. Apart from the heavily restored twelfth-century church, the ruined stone cross by the old main road is the only surviving medieval structure; the Manor House to the north and Wellingore Hall, set in extensive parkland to the south, both date from the eighteenth century.

Katherine was at Nottingham, or had business there, sometime during 1377, for her seal was used there by John, son of Walter de Dunham, in witness of a document.[32] John de Dunham was a prominent merchant and burgess of Bishop's (later King's) Lynn in Norfolk; he owned at least one shop there in the 1370s, and served as one of the town's chamberlains in 1377–78. His father, Walter, held the same office in 1340–41. The Dunham family was spread all over East Anglia and the East Midlands, while an earlier John de Dunham's will had been dated at Lincoln in 1346.[33] Katherine's links with the family probably arose through trading connections, for at some point she too owned a house in King's Lynn (see Chapter 10), while Dunham's use of her seal suggests a degree of friendship between them.

K atherine's fortunes may have been in the ascendant in 1377, but John of Gaunt's were under serious threat. His reversal of the decisions of the Good Parliament had made him even more hated and feared than before. It was probably around this time that his daughter Philippa's former nurse, a lady known only as Maud, wrote warning him that five friars of Canterbury "have wickedly and treacherously spoken of you, my very redoubtable lord." She beseeched him to protect himself "well from them and all others, in God's name."[34] Did Katherine tremble for her lover when she heard of such things?

Parliament had reassembled on January 27, with Prince Richard and John of Gaunt presiding. It has often been said that it was packed with John's supporters, but the evidence does not bear this out.[35] Nevertheless, due to the duke's influence, much of the legislation of the Good Parliament was formally reversed.

By this time disturbing rumors that John of Gaunt was a changeling were causing "great noise and great clamor" in London and the rest of the kingdom. They appear to have been spread by the banished William of Wykeham (although he was to deny that),[36] and/or his supporters, in a bid to topple the duke from power. It was asserted that in 1340, Queen Philippa actually gave birth to a daughter but overlaid and suffocated her. Fearful of confessing this to King Edward, she substituted the little corpse for a living baby boy, the son of a Ghent laborer, butcher, or porter (there are various versions of the story), this infant having been smuggled into St. Bavon's Abbey where the Queen had been confined; she named him John and brought him up as her own. Philippa was said to have admitted this in confession to William of Wykeham on her deathbed in 1369, insisting that, should there ever arise any prospect of John succeeding to the throne, the bishop must break the seal of the confessional and publicly reveal the truth, "lest a false heir should inherit England."[37]

There are inherent flaws in this story. First, there was a strong family resemblance between Edward III and John of Gaunt, who had typically Plantagenet features. And second, Queen Philippa was a lady of great integrity, unlikely to have contemplated such a deception; nor is there any evidence that Edward III was so fearsome a husband that she could not have told him of the tragedy that had supposedly occurred; on the contrary, theirs was an affectionate union, and he both loved and indulged her. Finally, had there been any substance in the story, surely the bishop would have openly proclaimed the truth, rather than stooping to spread scurrilous unsubstantiated rumors. Unsurprisingly, few believed the tale, although there were those who were ready to use it as a weapon against the duke. The rumors angered John himself, and doubtless hurt him, for he had cherished a high regard for his mother, but he did not stoop to contradict them. It would have been beneath his dignity to do so.

On February 2, Convocation—the assembly of bishops—met, and demanded that William of Wykeham be present among them. Bishop Courtenay now seized his opportunity to move against Wycliffe, who had openly preached against Wykeham; he was determined to silence Wycliffe's subversive views on the Church and its wealth, and summoned Wycliffe to appear before him to answer a charge of heresy. John of Gaunt rightly saw in this an attempt to disparage him too, for he shared those views, and he resolved publicly to champion Wycliffe's cause and discredit the bishops who had opposed him. He began by appointing four doctors of theology to undertake Wycliffe's defense.

February 19 was the day appointed for the trial of John Wycliffe. John of Gaunt and Henry, Lord Percy, backed by a band of heavily armed retainers, "stood shoulder-to-shoulder" with the reformer as he arrived at St. Paul's Cathedral, and forced a path through the large crowds of Londoners who had gathered there, Percy brandishing his staff of office and jostling the people aside. Bishop Courtenay was angered by the presence of the duke and the marshal, and a sharp quarrel erupted, with the bishop castigating Percy for manhandling his flock, whereupon the Duke retorted that Percy would conduct himself as befit the marshal whether Courtenay liked it or not. This incensed both the bishop and the people, who chose to interpret John's words as a further threat to the city's jealously guarded liberties, and the atmosphere grew dangerously heated.

Once the tribunal had assembled in the Lady Chapel, further harsh words were exchanged. Percy showed Wycliffe to a seat, but the bishop ordered him to remain on his feet throughout the proceedings, at which John of Gaunt uncharacteristically lost his temper.

"Lord Percy's motion is but reasonable," he insisted, "and as for you, my lord Bishop, who are grown so proud and arrogant, I will bring down the pride, not of you alone, but of all the prelacy in England." Courtenay told him to do his worst, provoking the stern warning that Courtenay need not think that his aristocratic relations would protect him from the day's repercussions, for they would be hard put to it to look to themselves. The bishop replied that he would trust in God, not in his relatives. Angered by the duke's threats, the people began loudly to heckle him. He warned them he would have them arrested if they persisted, but Courtenay threatened to excommunicate him if he dared to do so in his cathedral. Whereupon the duke muttered, "Rather than endure this, I should take him by the hair and drag him out of the church." It was probably said in the heat of the moment, but John's arrogance and his apparent determination to ride roughshod over the privileges of the Londoners were to prove his downfall. Incensed by his treatment of their bishop, and inflamed by a rumor that he intended to deprive them of their elected mayor and replace him with the marshal, the citizens exploded in anger, and the proceedings collapsed in chaos, with Wycliffe being hustled away by the duke and Percy and escaping ecclesiastical censure for the time being.[38] Nevertheless, he was now a marked man, irrevocably alienated from the hierarchy of the Church. As for John of Gaunt, far from directing the opprobrium of the Londoners toward the bishops, as he had intended, he had succeeded in turning it upon himself.

Percy now made matters worse by usurping the powers of a magistrate and imprisoning a London man in his official residence as marshal, which was seen as an even more outrageous attack on the city's liberties. The next day a rioting mob of Londoners rescued the prisoner and sacked Percy's house. Then they made for the Savoy in a murderous mood, bent on assassination. On the way they lynched a man who spoke up for John of Gaunt, and in Cheapside some insultingly hung the duke's coat of arms upside down, as if he were a traitor. They would have fired the palace itself had not Bishop Courtenay arrived and ordered them to desist. Fortunately, the duke and Percy were not there, but dining on oysters in Thames Street at the house of Sir John d'Ypres, a wealthy Flemish merchant who was an old friend of John of Gaunt's and stood high in the favor of the King. Warned by one of his knights that "infinite numbers of armed men" were out for his blood, and that "unless he took great heed, that day would be his last," John leapt up so hastily from the table that he painfully crashed the backs of his legs against the wooden bench. His host offered him wine, "but he could not drink for haste." He and Percy fled through a back gate, commandeered a boat across the Thames, and "never stayed rowing" until they reached Kennington, where Princess Joan was persuaded to act as mediator in the hope of calming the situation. She sent three of her knights to check the citizens, and because of the affection in which she was held, the mob gradually dispersed.[39]

The next day, when tempers had cooled, a deputation of Londoners went to Sheen to beg the King's forgiveness for the rioting, but insisted that John of Gaunt was to blame for all their troubles. Edward III promised he would uphold the city's liberties, and to mark his golden jubilee, he would later issue a general pardon. The only person exempted from it was Wykeham— in which the hand of John of Gaunt may clearly be perceived. In the end the mayor and his brethren had to get to their knees, beg the duke's forgiveness, and agree to his demand that they set up a marble pillar bearing the arms of Lancaster in Cheapside.[40] Parliament was dissolved the next day, and the political life of the nation began to recover its equilibrium.

That Edward III approved of the duke's actions is suggested by the lifetime grant he made him on February 28 of palatinate powers in the Duchy of Lancaster. This meant that John would enjoy virtually regal authority within those lands, and that the officers of the Crown could not trespass upon them. Lancaster was one of only three palatinates in England,[41] and had first been elevated to that status in 1351 for Duke Henry. The grant underlined John's preeminence among the nobility of England. On March 5 and 6 royal commands were issued on the basis of information supplied by him,[42] and that same month, John had Wykeham's temporalities granted to Richard of Bordeaux, thus cleverly affirming his loyalty to the prince and preempting any protests by his enemies. Edward III would have appreciated that, through the efforts of John of Gaunt, and at much cost to the latter, the royal authority had been largely restored, and that Richard would be the main beneficiary.

It is unlikely that Katherine Swynford had been in London to support her lover during these difficult weeks. She had probably just emerged from childbed, and the capital would have been a dangerous place for her, given her connection with the most hated man in England. She probably remained at Kettlethorpe, and would not rejoin John until the crisis had well and truly passed.

* * *

John spent Easter at Hertford, probably with Constance. He was gathering a fleet in the Port of London, in readiness for a new naval offensive against the French.[43] On April 20 he was back at the Savoy. Three days later, to mark the Feast of St. George, Edward III dubbed Richard of Bordeaux and Henry of Bolingbroke "Knights of the Garter."[44] By the following month, ten-year-old Henry, who was shortly to assume his father's title of Earl of Derby, was in the prince's retinue.[45]

Preparations for the offensive against the French had escalated by the end of May, but it was soon to be canceled. On June 18, Edward III pardoned William of Wykeham and restored his temporalities; Wykeham is said to have achieved this through bribing Alice Perrers.[46] Three days later, the old king suffered a stroke; its ravages may be seen in the dragging down of the mouth of the wooden effigy made for his funeral, which was taken from a death mask, and is the earliest of its kind to survive. He died at Sheen on June 21. Left alone with his corpse, Alice snatched the rings from its fingers and fled.[47]

Richard of Bordeaux was now King of England, and was proclaimed Richard II on June 22. But before that the ten-year-old king had responded to a petition from the Londoners asking if he would intervene to end the unhappy quarrel between them and the Duke of Lancaster. Later that day a civic deputation, fearful of reprisals on the part of the duke, went to Sheen to lay their case in full before Richard and his uncle. This led to a second formal reconciliation between the duke and the City of London, on June 27, with John graciously accepting the citizens' public apology for their behavior toward him.[48]

The accession of Richard II was greeted with rapturous acclaim. People believed that the boy king would usher in a golden age in which England, with a new champion at the helm, would recover her fortunes in the war with France, and her international prestige. Richard was an attractive child, with golden hair, blue eyes, and pink cheeks, intelligent and well-educated, and hopes were expressed that as he grew to manhood he would emulate his famous father. For the time being he was to be left under the care and guidance of his mother and his tutor, Sir Simon Burley.

As the King's senior uncle, and the greatest nobleman in the realm, John of Gaunt was now the most important public figure in England, powerfully influential with the young monarch. In fact, he was to be the dominant political player throughout Richard's reign, and the real ruler of the kingdom for several years of it. As such, he would prove a loyal subject of the King and the chief supporter and mainstay of the Crown. At the same time, he was actively pursuing his plans for an English invasion of Castile, with a view to breaking the Franco-Castilian alliance and setting himself up as de facto King of Castile. But Parliament proved reluctant to vote the necessary financial support; there were those who remained suspicious as to where the duke's ambitions would lead him, and others who still believed that naked self-interest was the real motive for his proposed enterprise.

It is possible that Katherine came up to London for Edward III's funeral, but if so, she cannot have seen much of the duke there, for he was very busy. Early in July he claimed the right, as High Steward of England, to perform various ceremonial roles at the coming coronation. In this capacity, he presided over the Court of Claims that was set up at Westminster, which adjudicated on the allocation of ceremonial duties, and he also organized the late king's funeral, which took place on July 5.[49] "To witness and hear the grief of the people, their sobs and lamentations on that day, would have rent anyone's heart."[50] As governess to the late monarch's granddaughters, and a respected former member of the late queen's household, Katherine was perhaps a witness to the funeral procession; she would not have been present in Westminster Abbey, as etiquette demanded that only male mourners attend the obsequies of a king. Edward III was buried near Queen Philippa, and a fine tomb bearing an effigy of him (perhaps sculpted by Henry Yevele) was later raised to his memory.

Setting aside his grief for his father, John now proceeded to make plans for the new king's coronation, the first for fifty years.[51] On July 15, with a smiling John of Gaunt and Henry Percy riding before him, and the crowds unexpectedly cheering them, Richard II, clad in white to symbolize his youth and innocence, made his state entry into London, riding in procession through a packed city made festive with hangings of cloth of gold and silver, colorful pageants, and free wine running through the conduits. The next day he was crowned at Westminster in a magnificent ceremony organized by

John of Gaunt; it was, enthused an optimistic Walsingham, "a day of joy and gladness, the long-awaited day of the renewal of peace and of the laws of the land." As Earl of Leicester, the duke carried Curtana, the blunted sword of mercy, in the procession, and afterward, as Earl of Lincoln, acted as the King's carver during the coronation banquet. By then the nine-hour ceremony had proved too much for the boy, who had to be carried from the abbey afterward; superstitious folk, seeing one of his slippers fall off, took it for a bad omen.[52]

Was Katherine a witness to some of these ceremonies? Hordes of people had descended upon London from all parts of the kingdom to watch the spectacle or take part, and John of Gaunt had summoned all his retainers.[53] As governess to his daughters, Katherine had an official reason for being there. However, it is unlikely that she would have had a place in the abbey itself. Only the wives of peers were admitted to watch the coronation ceremony, a privilege that had first been extended only as recently as 1308, in honor of Edward II's wife, Isabella of France. If Katherine saw anything of the coronation, it was probably the procession, perhaps from a privileged position.

On July 19 a council of twelve lords was appointed, which would serve under the nominal rule of the King. John of Gaunt and his brothers were not among them, nor was Henry Percy, although John's interests were well-represented by five of his adherents.[54] John's unpopularity precluded him from ruling as regent, and there was clearly a feeling among the lords that power should be shared, although the duke's ultimate authority was tacitly acknowledged, for the nobles went in constant fear of him on account of his "great power, his admirable judgment, and his brilliant mind." His influence was quickly made plain, for on July 20 the young king ratified the grants of Gringley and Wheatley to Katherine Swynford.[55] This was the first manifestation of Richard's lasting affection and esteem for Katherine, and it attests to his desire to please his powerful uncle. On July 24, John made Katherine a further gift of oaks for the repair of her houses at Kettlethorpe.[56] This, as well as subsequent evidence, suggests that she was in London at the time of the coronation, probably staying at the Savoy.

The King's desire to please his uncle and Katherine Swynford may be perceived in another generous gesture. On July 27, 1377, exercising royal privilege, Richard nominated Elizabeth Chaucer, Philippa's eldest daughter, to the thirteenth-century Benedictine priory of St. Helen's in Bishopsgate,

London. Around the same time, he nominated Elizabeth's cousin, Margaret Swynford, Katherine's daughter, to Barking Abbey, another Benedictine house.[57]

As noted earlier, Barking, originally founded in the seventh century, was one of the oldest, richest, and most prestigious abbeys in the land; two twelfth-century queens, Matilda of Scotland and Matilda of Boulogne, had been educated there, and the natural daughters of Henry II and King John had ruled as abbesses. Further, the Abbess of Barking had the status of a baron and ranked foremost among the abbesses of England. Only the daughters of the rich and influential were accepted as nuns of Barking, and all had to be nominated by the King.[58] So the admission of Katherine's daughter and her niece was an exceptional and signal favor that further demonstrates the young Richard's regard for Katherine, and almost certainly reflects the influence of John of Gaunt.[59] Yet despite the honor conferred, the surrender of her daughter to the cloistered existence of a Benedictine nun at such a tender age must have been hard for Katherine; at the same time, in dedicating a daughter to God, she was perhaps following a Roët family tradition, and no doubt believed it would earn her, and her firstborn Margaret, grace in Heaven.

The King's patronage of the Chaucers did not stop there. On March 26, 1378, he was to confirm Edward III's 1366 grant of an annuity to Philippa Chaucer.[60] That year, both she and Geoffrey were in receipt of substantial annuities totaling £63 (£24,464).

His state duties completed, John, realizing that the euphoria surrounding the new reign would soon evaporate and that he would probably be blamed for any failure on the part of the new council to tackle the endemic problems, as well as a fresh wave of French and Castilian attacks on the south coast,[61] obtained leave of the King to retire to Kenilworth, and then spent the summer and early autumn of 1377 hunting in Leicestershire and assessing the defenses of his castles.[62] Katherine was probably with him. The duke seems to have been in high good spirits, for it was supposedly at this time that, riding along the road between Bosworth and Leicester one evening, with only one servant in attendance, he saw laboring folk enjoying merry sports and dancing in a meadow at Rathby and dismounted to inquire why they were celebrating. When told they were celebrating Meadow

Mowing Day, an annual custom in those parts, he asked to join in and was made very welcome.[63]

John was back at Westminster in time for the opening of Parliament in October, and there, on his knees before the young king, made a dramatic plea in defense of his role in the recent political conflicts. None of his ancestors had been traitors, he declared, but good and loyal men, so it would be strange indeed if he himself were a traitor, for he had more to lose than any other subject in the realm. Therefore, if "any man were so bold as to charge him with treason or any dishonesty, he was ready to defend himself with his body." At this, the Lords rose to their feet in unison and begged him to desist from those words, since no one would wish to say such things of him, while the Commons insisted that he was free from all blame or dishonor, and that they took him for their "principal aid, comforter, and councillor."[64] Thus they defined the role he would fulfill in the years of the King's minority.

With the duke publicly exonerated and vindicated, at least superficially, Parliament instituted proceedings against Alice Perrers. Charges were laid that she had unlawfully interfered in the government of the kingdom and that she had controlled all channels of communication with the late king, even to the extent of eavesdropping through his bed curtains on his conversations. John of Gaunt was one of the chief witnesses against her, and in his testimony revealed that he had been powerless in his attempts to curtail her activities. She was sentenced to forfeiture of her property—some of which was given to the duke—and banishment.[65] Her trial caused a sensation and left the public with the impression that royal mistresses were greedy and corrupt creatures bent only on the acquisition of power and wealth, a perception that would soon rebound on Katherine Swynford.[66]

The duke was in Scotland for talks with the Scots in January 1378, but had returned to the Savoy by February 7.[67] On March 4 he received letters of protection for himself and his retinue, in advance of a new naval campaign to crush the French and Castilian fleets.

Late in 1377 the Pope had been moved to condemn the teachings of John Wycliffe, but thanks to the protection of John of Gaunt and Joan of Kent, the reformer was allowed to stay on at Oxford and pursue his work unmolested. Undeterred by papal censure, Wycliffe now wrote a series of works challenging the Church and its teachings, and in the spring of 1378 he published a controversial treatise on the Bible, which provoked Simon Sudbury,

Archbishop of Canterbury, to summon him before his court at Lambeth to answer for his heresy. Again, thanks to the intervention of Joan of Kent and John of Gaunt, the reformer escaped with a mild rebuke and was once more left in peace for a time. John's loyalty to Wycliffe in the face of mounting censure was staunch: Regardless of his own unpopularity and any consequences that might ensue, he kept the controversial doctor under his protection, declaring that he believed Wycliffe and his followers—who were disparagingly nicknamed Lollards, or "mumblers"—to be "God's saints," and "was an invincible guardian in all their needs, for otherwise they would have fallen into the pit of destruction."[68]

When the invasion fleet sailed on April 7, 1378, the duke was not with it. In his "Scandalous Chronicle," Walsingham asserts that there was growing condemnation "for his wicked and disgraceful behavior because he himself put aside respect for God's dread," and he alleges that John delayed his arrival at the port for months for fear of the enemy's fleet—the implication being that the duke was guilty of cowardice. At that point John first appeared in public with Katherine, an occasion that made their affair so notorious, and one that Walsingham did not hesitate to exploit in his prolonged and determined campaign to discredit John of Gaunt. Outraged, he claimed that having "deserted his military duties" and "put aside all shame of man and fear of God, [John] let himself be seen riding around the duchy with his unspeakable concubine, a certain Katherine Swynford, holding her bridle in public, not only in the presence of his own wife, but even with his people watching on in all the principal towns of the country." By this, Walsingham meant "the county," and he was probably referring to Leicestershire, where the duke was staying in March 1378.[69] By so brazenly flaunting his mistress, John "made himself abominable in the eyes of God."

Walsingham says the people were indignant and despairing at this scandalous conduct, and feared that the Almighty would soon vent His displeasure by punishing the whole kingdom for the duke's sinfulness, and he accuses the latter of betraying the King's youthful innocence and putting him and his realm in jeopardy.[70] Monkish chroniclers invariably wrote their accounts with a view to illustrating moral precepts and demonstrating that human failings had divine consequences; the objective study of current events and history, as we know it, was rare in medieval times. But Walsing-

ham may truly have reflected the opinions of a majority of the common people, who already blamed the duke for so many ills and whose views on his
private life might consequently not have been as accepting or forgiving as
those of the aristocracy or the court. Walsingham says that it was as a result
of his blatant and unashamed appearances with Katherine, whom he refers
to as "a witch and a whore," that "the worst curses and infamous invectives
started circulating against [the duke]." However, it may not have been the
sexual relationship between the lovers that caused the greatest offense, for
such affairs were common among kings and nobles, but the way he was un-
abashedly flaunting it publicly, to the injury of his virtuous wife, and—even
more pertinently to the class-conscious and xenophobic English—the fact
that Katherine was of comparatively lowly birth and a foreigner. Above all,
Katherine was tainted simply through being associated with the most hated
man in the kingdom.

Walsingham's passage quoted above is the only description that survives
of John and Katherine together;[71] it is also the first mention of Katherine's
name in any chronicle, and is evidence that she had now become notorious.
Although it is worth pointing out that no other chronicler mentions this
specific public display by the lovers, Katherine was from then on to be referred to elsewhere in disparaging terms. To the monkish author of the
Anonimalle Chronicle, she was "a she-devil and enchantress," a charge that
echoed Walsingham's branding of her as a witch, and was therefore highly
provocative and detrimental, and reveals just how perilous Katherine's position might have become. Thomas Brinton, Bishop of Rochester, castigated
the duke from his pulpit for being "an adulterer and pursuer of luxury,"[72]
while Froissart, writing decades later, thought Katherine "a woman of light
character." Even Henry Knighton, the pro-Lancastrian chronicler from
Leicester, who admired John of Gaunt, clearly did not approve of his mistress: "In his wife's household, there was a certain foreign lady, Katherine
Swynford, whose relations with him were greatly suspect." Knighton reveals
that members of the duke's household were very concerned about the effect
of their master's involvement with his mistress; they, as well as he, were
aware that it was his duty, as lord and master, to set a good moral example to
his servants, as the Church enjoined. John himself disclosed in 1381 that he
had been repeatedly warned by his clerics and his servants of the detrimental effect his relationship with Katherine was having on his reputation but
that he had chosen to ignore them.[73]

Not everyone disapproved. Katherine seems to have been held in lasting affection by the Cathedral Chapter of Lincoln and by the Mayor of Leicester, who, probably in company with a lot of people, took a pragmatic view of her dubious position. Between 1377 and 1379 he paid £3.6s.8d (£1,165) for a horse and £2.0s.6d (£708) for an iron pan (probably a large cauldron), both of which were presented to Katherine in gratitude for "expediting business touching the tenement in Stretton,[74] and for other business for which a certain lord besought of the aforesaid Katherine with good effect, and besought so successfully that the town was pardoned the lending of silver to the King in that year."[75] (The mayor seems to have had the better part of the bargain.)

In assessing Walsingham's stance on John of Gaunt's affair with Katherine Swynford, it is important to remember that he loathed and feared John for many reasons, and always seized upon every means to discredit him;[76] he was not above exaggerating the duke's faults or even making things up, and in his view John was foolish, unscrupulous, and "without conscience."

When it came to sexual matters, Walsingham was at his most inventive, claiming that the duke's character "was dishonored by every kind of outrage and sin. A fornicator and adulterer, he had abandoned lawful wedlock" and deceived both of his wives. "He not only dared to do such things secretly and privately, but also took the most shameless prostitutes to the beds of these wives, who, grief-stricken as they were, did not dare to protest." This assertion is uncorroborated elsewhere and entirely at variance with what we know of John of Gaunt; this particular calumny surely stems solely from the chronicler's desire to discredit the champion of the heretical Wycliffe, and it can be dismissed as pure character assassination, born of moral outrage and a fevered imagination.

Learning that John had publicly flaunted his relationship with Katherine gave Walsingham further ammunition against the hated duke. It has been claimed that his comments about Katherine were aimed primarily at John, and were not intended to cast aspersions on her character beyond the charge of immorality,[77] yet being branded an "unspeakable concubine" was damaging to the reputation of a woman who was, after all, governess to the Lancastrian princesses. Let it not be forgotten that adultery and promiscuity were then perceived to be far more sinful in a woman than in a man and carried a greater stigma. The fact that Katherine did not take a second husband for twenty-four years may have been a matter of personal choice—with the duke supporting her, she had no need to, although marriage could confer a veneer of respectability upon royal mistresses—but it may also indicate that there was a shortage of suitors due to her living in open adultery with the duke, and that her increasing notoriety lessened her chances of remarrying.

There can be little doubt that, once it became clear that his marriage to Constance had failed, and the crises of 1376–77 had passed, John and Katherine grew reckless and ceased to exercise the same discretion they had employed in the early years of their affair, and that the liaison was now public knowledge. The notorious reputation and conduct of Alice Perrers had prejudiced public opinion against royal mistresses, and it would not be surprising if people viewed Katherine too as an immoral and self-seeking woman and a corrupting influence on the duke, nor that they were incensed that Duchess Constance should be so slighted and insulted. For if she had not been too bothered before about her husband's mistress, with the affair now exposed, she was forced into an impossible position that gave her just cause for complaint, and could no longer discreetly turn a blind eye to what was going on. That cannot have improved relations between Constance and the duke, and it appears to have led to an informal separation. Later evidence suggests that Constance felt herself to be at fault with regard to the breakdown of the marriage, and in time it was she who begged for John's forgiveness, so there were apparently more factors at play here than his affair with Katherine, although that was probably the catalyst for the separation.

Given public sympathy for Constance, John of Gaunt's enduring reputation for lechery, as well as contemporary observations about and responses to his relationship with Katherine, there can be little doubt that the publicizing of their affair did indeed damage his political standing in England and ruined her reputation.

But it was certainly not Katherine who had kept John from sailing to France. On April 29, after seeing his wife and elder daughters admitted with Princess Joan to the confraternity of the Garter at Windsor, he was at a council meeting at Westminster,[78] and in May he was at the Savoy, busy commandeering the extra ships so urgently needed.[79] On May 20 he levied an aid for the knighting of his heir, Henry of Derby,[80] and early in June he attended another council meeting. Five days later the invasion fleet returned to England, but when, later that month, Castilian ships threatened St. Malo in Brittany, which was perilously close to home, John decided to take the offensive. On June 17 he was appointed King's Lieutenant in France and Aquitaine, and thereafter he divided his time between Southampton and the Savoy, making preparations for his attack and waiting for a favorable wind.[81] In July he appointed Henry of Derby Warden of the Palatine County of Lancaster, and soon afterward sailed for France with his navy. None of this sounds like idle dalliance with his mistress.

John spent August and September besieging St. Malo, to no effect. Repulsed by the Castilians, he returned ignominiously to England in September to face accusations of cowardice and incompetence.[82] "And the Commons of England began to murmur against the noblemen, saying how they had done all that season but little good."[83] There were wild and unfounded rumors that John had appropriated for himself the taxes voted by Parliament for the war, and even that he and Wycliffe were plotting the destruction of the Church itself.[84] It seemed that the superstitious predictions of divine retribution were being fulfilled, and that John's failure to take St. Malo was God's punishment for his sins.

B etween May 28 and September 19, 1378, Geoffrey Chaucer had been abroad on business in Lombardy. On May 21, before Geoffrey left, John of Gaunt arranged for Philippa Chaucer's royal annuities to be paid by the Sheriff of Lincoln and other officials from Michaelmas 1378.[85] From this we may infer that Philippa had taken up residence with her sister Katherine at Kettlethorpe. But what may have begun as a temporary arrangement ended up lasting for a minimum of four years, for until 1383, at least, Philippa's royal annuities were paid to her by the Sheriff of Lincoln and other officials in Lincolnshire;[86] furthermore, from 1381 to 1386 all customs receipts were divided between Chaucer and his wife. From this we may infer that the Chaucers had decided they were happier living apart.

It may be that they had finally agreed they were incompatible, yet there was possibly another woman involved, for in May 1380 there is an intriguing record of Alice Perrers's stepdaughter, Cecily Chaumpaigne, releasing Geoffrey from any action resulting from "my rape and other causes."[87] Rape in the fourteenth century was not necessarily a sexual crime: Although it could refer to sexual assault as well as forced intercourse, it could also mean abduction. Either way, it was a serious offense, punishable by hanging (and formerly by castration), and thus very rare.[88]

In this case, the rape—if it was that—may have involved penetration. We know that Chaucer had a son called Lewis, who was born probably in

1381; Lewis seems to have been a very bright boy because he was admitted to Oxford University when only about nine, and it was to "little Lewis my son" that Chaucer dedicated his *Treatise on the Astrolabe* in 1391; at that time, Lewis had reached "the tender age of ten years." Given the long gap between the births of Elizabeth and Thomas Chaucer and that of Lewis, it can be conjectured that Philippa was not Lewis's mother, and some historians have credibly suggested that he was Geoffrey's son by Cecily Chaumpaigne. If so, he was perhaps not the fruit of rape, but of an affair: Cecily, with the proverbial fury of a woman scorned, may initially have pressed the rape charge in the hope of gaining some financial provision for her child. But Chaucer brought forward four eminent witnesses in his defense: the King's chamberlain and two of his household knights, as well as the Collector of Customs, Chaucer's own superior.[89] Their testimony persuaded Cecily to drop the charge, but that there was some substance to her accusations is evident in Chaucer paying her £10 (£3,877) in compensation for her "rape" two months later.

We can only conjecture that it was this episode that drove the Chaucers apart. What seems likely is that Geoffrey and Philippa separated on reasonably amicable terms. In the 1380s it was he who usually went to the Exchequer twice a year to draw her annuity.[90] She remained a member of Constance's household, on very good terms with the duke and duchess.[91] However, her removal to Lincolnshire, although apparently primarily for personal reasons, came at a time when her sister's relationship with the duke had become notorious, and afforded her perhaps a welcome respite from the tensions in the duchess's chamber.

Philippa and Katherine now had much in common: Both were essentially *femmes soles*, both had dedicated a daughter to God, both were rearing sons called Thomas who were of similar age, and both were an integral part of the Lancastrian social circle, Katherine especially so. But while Katherine was the duke's mistress, Philippa loyally served the duchess, and historians have conjectured that Philippa could only have looked on her sister with disapproval, and that her loyalties were painfully divided between Constance and Katherine. Yet if so, Philippa would hardly have chosen to live for some years with Katherine at this time and in these circumstances. It may have been a case of loving the sinner while deploring the sin, but her removal to Kettlethorpe perhaps reflects the need of the younger and distressed sister for the support and companionship of the elder, who had in the past demonstrated great concern for her through the favors she obtained for her and her husband. And Constance, regardless of her feelings toward Katherine Swynford, seems to have liked Philippa for her own sake; they were, after all, much of an age, and Philippa seems to have rendered excellent service to her mistress.

It may have been Geoffrey Chaucer who disapproved of Katherine, despite all the favors her influence had procured for him. His disparaging remark about governesses with a past, and his panegyric lauding Pedro the Cruel, may well reflect his opinion of his sister-in-law and his loyalty to Constance.[92] In "The Man of Law's Tale," the heroine—tellingly called Constance—is a model of patience and piety who accepts "the will of Christ" in all the misfortunes and sufferings that are laid upon her.[93] This too may be a comment on the tribulations and virtues of Duchess Constance. Certainly Katherine does not feature largely—or features barely at all—in the surviving records of Chaucer's life, and it may be that, after his separation from Philippa, he had as little to do with her as possible. His attitude toward her may have been a further source of discord between the Chaucers.

With Philippa in residence at Kettlethorpe, it would surely have been a lively household. When she was not in attendance on the duchess, Philippa would have had her ten-year-old son with her. Thomas Swynford, probably a year older, and the young Beauforts were playmates for him. As there is no record of her marriage, we may suppose that Blanche Swynford, who would have been about fifteen in 1378, had already died, but possibly her sister Dorothy was still at home. John Beaufort was now about five, Henry possibly three, and Joan not quite two. It would have been a chaotic household, with all the building works going on at this time, and of course the lady of the manor was often away. Katherine was probably with John when he was at Leicester Castle on October 4, for on that day he issued letters patent permitting her to cut down oak trees at his manor of Enderby in Leicester Chase, "and to sell or carry this wood wherever she wishes, and use the profits for her own use."[94] It was probably used for the ongoing renovations at Kettlethorpe, which by now must have begun to look very imposing indeed; it was perhaps in this period that the great stone gateway was built.[95] To all appearances, Katherine's was now a lordly household, reflecting the wealth and social position of its mistress.

Katherine probably went home to supervise the new works she was planning when John rode south to Gloucester, where Wycliffe was allowed to address Parliament, which assembled there in late October. That was to be Wycliffe's political swan song. The following year, "this second Satan" would attack the sacrament of the Eucharist itself, whereupon the deeply orthodox duke began to distance himself from his former protégé—"he was deceived, as were many others."[96] In 1380, Wycliffe was ordered not to preach, and the following year his heretical views on transubstantiation were condemned by the Church. He had just completed his translation of the Bible into English, but his works were all condemned and banned in May 1382. By then John of Gaunt had severed all connections with him, and he had retired to Lutterworth, where he died of the effects of a stroke in 1384. His bones were exhumed and burned in 1419, under a heresy law that had not been in force in his lifetime.

Nevertheless, when Parliament, in 1395, proposed the burning of Wycliffe's Bible, John of Gaunt, with "great oaths," spoke up in its defense. "Other nations have God's law in their own mother tongue," he argued, "and we will have ours in English."[97] In this, he was way ahead of his time—it would be another 150 years before English Bibles were chained in churches for all to read.

After spending some months at the Savoy, John of Gaunt was again at Leicester in August 1379,[98] probably enjoying the pleasures of the chase. But he was back in London before September 12 for Blanche's obit at St. Paul's,[99] where an elaborate iron grille had been set up around her new tomb.[100] John must have left immediately after the obit for Kettlethorpe, where, only two days later, he made a grant to Katherine.[101]

This was probably a fleeting visit, for John was not among the witnesses to a deed dated that same day, September 14, the Feast of the Exaltation of the Holy Cross, and issued at Kettlethorpe in the presence of the rector, Sir Robert de Northwood; in it, John de Dovdale of Chaworth granted to Katherine and her heirs "certain tenements he had in the town and fields of Kettlethorpe and Laughterton." Some years later, on July 25, 1387, John de Sereby, citizen of Lincoln (who had been at her son's baptism), granted to "Lady Katherine de Swynford, Lady of Kettlethorpe . . . all his rent which he had in Kettlethorpe, Laughterton, and Fenton."[102] By using part of her substantial income to purchase small properties and plots of land in nearby villages, Katherine was prudently extending her holdings at Kettlethorpe and Coleby, and thus conserving and improving her son's inheritance.

John was at Kenilworth from October 27 to the second week in November, doubtless to see how his extensive renovations were progressing; they were evidently causing a lot of disruption, because when the duke came to Kenilworth for Christmas, he and his retinue had to lodge at Kenilworth Priory, where a floor was laid for dancing in the great chamber[103]—surely an unwelcome intrusion in the monastic regime. During his sojourn at Kenilworth in the autumn, John had ordered the payment of moneys to Geoffrey Chaucer; also, on November 6, he commanded his receiver in Lincolnshire to pay "our dear and well-beloved *damoiselle*" Philippa Chaucer's annuity.[104] These orders may have been prompted by Katherine, who had perhaps accompanied her lover to Kenilworth. John was again at Kettlethorpe with Katherine from November 14 to 16.[105] By November 17 he had ridden south to Newarke.[106]

It is doubtful if Katherine spent the Christmas and New Year of 1379–80 with John at Kenilworth,[107] for he would have presided over the festivities with Duchess Constance for form's sake, but Philippa Chaucer was almost certainly among the company, for among John's New Year gifts was a silver hanap (a cup with a lid) costing 31s.5d (£609) for her.[108] On January 2 a payment of 20s. (£368) was made to a messenger of Matilda de Montagu, Abbess of Barking, who had come to receive a gift for the abbess from the duke; it is tempting to speculate that this messenger brought a message from Margaret Swynford for her mother, and that a part of his handsome fee was intended for the young nun.[109] Constance had moved to Hertford by January 11, 1380, while John, who stayed at Kenilworth, later rode south to the Savoy, where he remained until March.[110]

John was at Windsor on April 1 for the magnificent wedding of the King's half sister, Maud Holland, to Waleran, Count of St. Pol.[111] On the following day he arranged for Catalina, his eight-year-old daughter by Constance, to be brought up in the household of Joan Burghersh, Lady Mohun, the widow of John, Baron Mohun, who had been a retainer of the Black Prince and died in 1375. The child was taken to Lady Mohun on June 8 and remained in her care until at least 1383, when the duke paid £50 (£20,360) for her expenses.[112] It was quite usual for children of the aristocracy to be reared in a separate establishment, since it was generally felt that parents might be too soft when it came to education and discipline.

Understandably, John did not show disrespect to his wife by placing her daughter with her two half sisters under the governance of his mistress. However, he was now effectively living apart from Constance; on May 12, at the Savoy, he ordered his receiver in Norfolk to pay 500 marks (£65,002) annually for her wardrobe and chamber expenses at Tutbury. In March 1381 he would augment this sum by a further 200 marks (£25,420) and then increase Constance's original settlement of 1,000 marks per annum (worth £125,221 in 1381) to £1,000 (£375,662).[113] These increases may well reflect the increasing political importance of "his dear wife the Queen," as his hopes for the Castilian throne grew more realistic; it may also have been in part the result of the pricking of the duke's conscience over his adultery with Katherine Swynford.

Meanwhile, on April 15, at Kenilworth, he handed over £100 "to Dame Katherine Swynford, governess of our daughters, Philippa and Elizabeth of Lancaster, for the expenses of their wardrobe and chamber for the past Easter term."[114] As is becoming clear, references to Katherine in records dating from the late 1370s and early 1380s, although sparse, suggest that she was now a permanent fixture in the duke's life and that of his daughters, and that he seized every opportunity to have her with him.

John was based at the Savoy from May to July 1380. In May the young Richard II, now thirteen, bound himself by treaty to marry Anne of Bohemia.[115] With talk of a royal marriage in the air, John now turned his attention to finding suitable spouses for his older children. On June 24, 1380, Elizabeth of Lancaster, now a spirited young woman of seventeen, was wed to John Hastings, third Earl of Pembroke, at Kenilworth;[116] from Elizabeth's point of view, this union was not entirely satisfactory, for her new husband was just eight years old. It is likely that Katherine Swynford, who played an important role in Elizabeth's life, was involved in the preparations for her wedding and was present. Afterward, Elizabeth had her own household as Countess of Pembroke, and no longer needed Katherine's care.

Elizabeth had grown into a headstrong and extroverted girl, very different from her serious older sister. Her tomb effigy in Burford Church, Shropshire, shows a tall, slender woman with long fair hair and markedly Plantagenet features; evidently she favored her father in looks. While she was intelligent and literate, dancing and singing were her great talents, and she so excelled at the former that she would one day be awarded a prize for being the best dancer at Richard II's court. Richard thought well of her, and in 1383 pardoned a murderer at her instigation.[117] But although Katherine instilled in Elizabeth her own love of learning and literature, and a sense of piety that would become more evident as she grew older,[118] time was to prove that she had not been entirely successful in her role as governess, because the example she had set in her own conduct with Elizabeth's father proved the most unsuitable role model for an impressionable girl who was driven by her own youthful passions, which marriage to a child nine years her junior could not satisfy.

It seems odd that the duke should marry off his second daughter before his first, Philippa, who at twenty was quite old to remain unwed, but John possibly hoped to use her as a diplomatic pawn in his bid for the Castilian throne. Marrying her to one of his allies could secure invaluable political support.

With Philippa, Katherine seems to have been more successful as a mentor. John's eldest daughter had grown into an amiable, literate, and pious young woman who liked to read psalms and edifying devotional texts, yet she also had the skills that befit her to grace any European court, and was an avid participator in courtly games of love. Before 1386 the poet Eustace Deschamps composed a *ballade* entitled *Des Deux Ordres de la Feuille at de la Fleur* (Of the Two Orders of the Leaf and the Flower), in which he describes a popular May Day intellectual pastime in which courtiers declared themselves partisans of one or the other, the two symbols being regarded as either male or female. The finer details of this play have been lost in time, but Philippa, Deschamps tells us, was the chief patroness of the Order of the Flower.[119] Unlike her sister, though, her life would never be tainted with scandal.

Philippa's tomb effigy depicts a lady with small, delicate features—did she take after her mother?—and a long, graceful neck. The sixteenth-century Portuguese genealogy in the British Library, in which Queen Constance's image (already discussed) appears, shows Philippa with reddish hair and a fuller face, although this may be a fanciful representation.

By 1380, John's hopes of winning Castile were improving. In 1379, Enrique of Trastamara died and was succeeded by his son, the melancholic and irresolute Juan I, another Francophile. In July 1380, John achieved notable diplomatic success when Ferdinand I, King of Portugal, agreed to renew an alliance he had made with the duke in 1372. With Ferdinand's friendship secured, John's ambitions appeared more realistic.[120]

The duke now sought for a bride for his heir, Henry of Derby, who was thirteen, the same age as the King. Following Edward III's policy of marrying his sons to English heiresses and thus extending their landholdings, affinities, and influence, John set his sights on Mary de Bohun, younger daughter and co-heiress of his late friend, Humphrey de Bohun, Earl of Hereford, Essex, and Northampton. Her mother, Joan FitzAlan, was the duke's cousin and much liked by him. Mary was thus very well connected, being related to the House of Lancaster through her mother, but she was also very young, only eleven or thereabouts. Eleanor, her elder sister and co-heiress, was married to Thomas of Woodstock, Earl of Buckingham, John's youngest brother, and Mary was living with them at Pleshy in Essex.[121]

Not being content with his share of the Bohun inheritance, Thomas was determined to lay his hands on the rest, which comprised the earldoms of Hereford and Northampton, and he put relentless pressure on young Mary to give it all up and take the habit of a Poor Clare nun. But in July 1380, with the connivance of her mother and John of Gaunt, Mary's aunt, Elizabeth de Bohun, Countess of Arundel, kidnapped her from Pleshy while Thomas was away campaigning in France, and took her to Arundel Castle in Sussex. On July 28, on payment of 5,000 marks (£475,947), John of Gaunt secured from Richard II a grant of Mary's marriage to himself, thwarting his brother's ambitions, for the grant was in part payment of large sums owed to the duke for military expenses.[122] A furious Thomas, says Froissart, "never after loved the duke as he had hitherto done," although his wrath eventually abated and the two remained outwardly friendly.[123] Soon afterward—certainly before March 1381—Mary was married with great ceremony and rejoicings to Henry of Derby at twelfth-century Rochford Hall in Essex, her mother's home.[124] As Philippa and Elizabeth of Lancaster were present, it is probable that Katherine Swynford was too; there is later evidence to suggest that Mary de Bohun was fond of her, and Katherine would one day become a member of her household. After the wedding ceremony, Mary remained with her mother, with the duke paying for her maintenance; because of her youth, he and the countess had agreed that the consummation of the marriage should be delayed until Mary was fourteen.

◆　　◆　　◆

On December 2, 1380, while attending Parliament at Northampton,[125] John of Gaunt ordered the payment of £50 (£19,384) to Katherine for Philippa of Lancaster's wardrobe and chamber expenses, and commanded that in future she be assigned £100 (£38,768) per annum for the same in equal portions at Easter and Michaelmas.[126] Since Philippa was now twenty, it is likely that Katherine was expected to be more of a companion and chaperone to her, rather than a governess.

Kettlethorpe was not far from Northampton; with Katherine perhaps heavily pregnant at this time, John may well have ridden over to visit her. In her condition, it is hardly likely that she was present at Leicester at Christmas, when the King, Princess Joan, and the rest of the royal family were John's honored guests.[127] However, Philippa Chaucer was there, probably in attendance on Duchess Constance, and at New Year the duke presented her with yet another silver-gilt hanap, worth £5.2s.1d (£1,979).[128]

On January 20, 1381, at Leicester Castle, John granted Katherine the wardship of the lands and heir of the late Elys de Thoresby, a member of his retinue who lived about twelve miles west of Kettlethorpe; in return she was to perform all the services "due and accustomed." But the next day a second grant of this wardship was issued, with the clause about the services omitted.[129] Might we assume that Katherine herself had persuaded the duke to leave it out, or that he amended it himself? The latter is more likely, for Katherine was probably not at Leicester at this time, and John probably had very good reasons for not wishing her to be burdened with feudal services. For this grant may well mark the birth of their third son and fourth child, Thomas Beaufort, who had perhaps been conceived at Kenilworth the previous April and was born probably at Kettlethorpe in January 1381. It has often been asserted that Thomas was born in 1377, since he was described as a "young gentleman" in February 1397,[130] but this probably refers purely to his rank and distinguishes him from his eldest brother, who was a knight.

Like his Beaufort brothers, Thomas was given a favoured Lancastrian name, probably in honor of Thomas, Earl of Lancaster, John's great-uncle, who had been executed in 1322 for opposing the inept Edward II, and was now popularly—but quite unjustifiably—reputed a saint. Thomas could also have been named for John's brother, Thomas of Woodstock, perhaps to mollify him for the loss of Mary de Bohun's inheritance.

Historians have long speculated that there were perhaps other Beaufort children who did not survive infancy. Duchess Blanche had borne seven children in nine years of marriage, and Katherine's record in the same time span, when she was deeply involved with John and still mostly in her twenties, is only four. Possibly she suffered one or more miscarriages, stillbirths, or neonatal deaths in the four years that probably lay between the births of Joan and Thomas. Such occurrences were common at all levels of medieval society—four of Blanche's children had died young—and it was rare for all one's offspring to survive infancy in that age of high infant mortality.

In March 1381, John again increased Constance's chamber allowance, another gesture that might have been prompted by his conscience. Gifts given by him to Katherine around this time may mark a joyful reunion and his gratitude for the birth of their son: There were two tablets of silver and enamel costing 7 marks (£877), a belt of silver costing 40s.9d (£765), and a silver *chaufour*, or chafing pan, bought for 33s.4d (£626). The latter, which had three legs and a handle, and could be stood over a candle flame, was used to keep food warm at table. John had purchased and perhaps commissioned it from "Herman, goldsmith of London," whom he often patronized.[131] *John of Gaunt's Register* also lists other gifts "to be delivered into my own hands and paid for the same day," which by their very nature must have been purchased for Katherine Swynford. These included "a gold brooch in the form of a heart set with a diamond," again supplied by Herman the goldsmith, and "a gold brooch set with a ruby and fashioned in the form of two hands."[132]

It was probably while he was at Leicester—and certainly before March 31—that the duke gave Blanche, his bastard daughter by Marie de St. Hilaire, in marriage to Sir Thomas Morieux of Thorpe Morieux, Suffolk, who had been a knight in his retinue since 1372 and previously served as Sheriff of Norfolk and Suffolk.[133] In 1381, Sir Thomas, who was renowned for his military exploits, was appointed Constable of the Tower of London, and in 1383 he would become Master of the Horse to Richard II.[134] Froissart says he was popular in the ducal household because of his sardonic wit. John had done well by Blanche in marrying her to such a distinguished man, and in time he would make even more impressive provision for his Beaufort bastards.

After the nuptials, John rode south to London and the Savoy, where on April 3 he hosted a magnificent feast for Cardinal Pileo de Prata and the envoys from Bohemia, who were in England to conclude the King's marriage treaty.[135]

This was the last time the Savoy would serve as a setting for a state occasion, for trouble was brewing in the political cauldron, which would soon boil over and engulf the lives of John and Katherine. Back in 1379, in order to meet the heavy costs of the war with France, the government, under the duke's auspices, had imposed a poll tax—a tax on the head of every subject. At first, payment was assessed on a graduated scale, according to the means of the taxpayer—and as John of Gaunt was richer by far than anybody else, he had to have a category all of his own. But the Commons disliked this system, and in the winter of 1380–81, a new poll tax was levied, this time at a flat rate of one shilling (£19) per head, which was unjust and unfair, for while the rich could easily afford it, many of the poor faced ruin. Already there was widespread discontent at the dismal way the war was going. The people wanted victories, but instead were required to shoulder the burden of reverse after reverse. There was much anger against the government, most of it directed at John of Gaunt, who was held responsible for England's poor prowess in the war and the crippling poll tax. Tax collectors were attacked and even beheaded, there was widespread evasion, and the protests became ever more vociferous. Yet on March 13, 1381, to the outrage of many, the council ruled that the poll tax must be enforced.

John of Gaunt had other preoccupations. A truce with the Scots was about to expire, and on May 1 he received a new commission to treat with them.[136] Three days later, in the midst of his preparations for his journey north, he sent Godfrey, his barber, to Katherine with a receipt for £50 (£18,783) for some pearls he sold to her and his daughter Philippa, which had been delivered to them by William Oke, the clerk of his Great Wardrobe.[137] He also purchased some devotional books, and on May 12 paid the handsome sum of £51.8s.2d (£19,312) for various gifts and expenses attendant upon the recent admission of "Elizabeth Chaucy" to the prestigious Barking Abbey.[138] This nun was probably the "Elizabeth Chausier" who had entered St. Helen's Priory in 1377, and thus almost certainly the daughter of Geoffrey and Philippa Chaucer; there was no uniformity in spelling in the fourteenth century, and the involvement of the duke further supports this identification. John's generous gesture—he had probably used his influence with the King to secure the necessary royal nomination, for without it, the daughter of a mere civil servant would never have gained entry to the aristocratic community at Barking—was perhaps made at the instigation of Katherine Swynford or Philippa Chaucer, or both, so that Elizabeth could join her cousin Margaret Swynford. The large sum involved suggests that the duke paid Elizabeth's dowry too, which was perhaps included with the gifts.

On May 12, John left the Savoy; he could have had no idea that he would never see his beautiful palace again. Katherine probably rode northward with him via Hertford, Bedford, and Northampton, and when she said farewell to him, either at Northampton or possibly at Leicester around May 20, she cannot have suspected that this was to be the end of nine illicit but happy years together, years during which she must have come to believe that she was an accepted and permanent part of his life, the love of his heart, and the sole focus of his desire.

SEVEN

Turning Away the Wrath of God

At the beginning of June 1381, as John of Gaunt lay at Knaresborough, an army of yeomen and peasants was amassing in Kent and Essex, bent on the overthrow of a government that had imposed the cruelly oppressive poll tax and forced restrictive wage and price controls on laboring men whose services were in high demand after the depredations of the Black Death. The rebels had chosen for their leader—their "idol," it was said—a man named Wat Tyler, and for their spokesmen Jack Straw and John Ball, an excommunicate priest, who was going about the country preaching inflammatory and subversive sermons calling for the abolition of serfdom[1] and posing the question:

> When Adam delved and Eve span,
> Who was then the gentleman?

On June 10 the insurgents occupied Canterbury, then began their march on London, new recruits swelling their forces along the way, until they were at least fifty thousand strong.[2] It was as well that the chief object of their venom, the Duke of Lancaster, was by then nearing Berwick, because it was he, above all, whom they were determined to destroy—for was he not the most powerful man in the realm, and therefore the man responsible for all the woes that had befallen it? As soon as they reached the eastern approaches of the City of London and set up their camp at Blackheath on June 12, the rebel leaders sent a petition to Richard II demanding the heads of men they deemed traitors. John of Gaunt's name was at the top of the list.

We do not know where Katherine was during this Peasants Revolt. If she had indeed traveled north with John, parted from him at Leicester around May 20, and then ridden home to Kettlethorpe, she would surely have heard of the march, because there were associated risings in other parts of the country, including East Anglia. Katherine was no fool: She would have realized that her notorious relationship with the duke made her especially vulnerable, and that her very life might be in danger—a fear that was to prove justified in the coming days. So, the author of the *Anonimalle Chronicle* tells us, she "went into hiding where no one knew where to find her for a long time," no doubt taking her children with her; given that she had a new baby, she probably felt especially vulnerable.[3] Philippa of Lancaster may have gone with them, for there is no record of Philippa's whereabouts during the coming crisis, and Katherine was responsible for her.[4]

It is unlikely that Katherine went to Kettlethorpe or Lincoln, for she was too well-known in those places and could easily be found. Nor would it have been wise to go to any of the duke's properties in the threatened areas, and she was almost certainly not at the Savoy. It is possible, but not probable, that she sought refuge at Wesenham Place, a house in King's Lynn that the duke gave her at some unspecified date,[5] for John Spanye, a cobbler of King's Lynn, was ranting round the area, inciting the people to slaughter the unpopular Flemish weavers who had for decades been settled in East Anglia.[6] Of course, Katherine was a Hainaulter, not a Fleming, but an ignorant mob would not have made such a fine distinction; to them she was a foreigner, the mistress of the most detested man in the land, and thus an object of hatred. It is feasible, of course, that Katherine sought refuge in a convent, the traditional place of safety for women, but—as will be seen—there is reason to believe that she hid herself away in Pontefract Castle, that great Lancastrian stronghold in Yorkshire, and sent word to the duke of her whereabouts.

Meanwhile, as the "savage hordes approached the city like waves of sea,"[7] the young king's councillors panicked and took refuge with him in the

Tower. When, on Thursday, June 13, Richard II failed to respond to their demands, the rebels lost patience and "with cruel eagerness for the slaughter" surged across London Bridge into the city, reinforced by hundreds of sympathetic Londoners and hot-headed apprentices, to embark on a frenzy of destruction and bloodletting. "Burn! Kill!" was their chilling cry.[8]

They opened the prisons, torched houses and brothels, and broke into Lambeth Palace, which they burned, and the Temple, where they destroyed valuable documents. Flooding into the Strand in the afternoon, they saw before them the great edifice of the Savoy, white and beautiful against the summer sky. In that moment the wondrous palace was doomed, for to the insurgents it represented all that was hateful to them: the power of the despised Duke of Lancaster, the authority of feudal lordship, and the wealth of the landed classes.

Into the Savoy surged the mob, thirty thousand strong, their righteous purpose to destroy rather than loot. "They made proclamation that none, on pain to lose his head, should convert to his own use anything that there was, but that they should break such as was found." They killed the guards at the gates, then poured into the cellars, where they smashed the great casks of fine wines, and watched in glee as the gold and ruby liquid spilled over the flagstones. "We are not thieves and robbers, we are true commons, zealots for truth and justice!" the people cried. Then they raced upstairs to the duke's treasury, dragged out a wealth of gold and silver plate that they battered with axes, before hauling the lot out to the terrace and hurling it into the Thames. The jewels and precious stones they ground in mortars or underfoot, and their residue also went into the river.

Some raided the ducal wardrobe, pulling out elegant garments of cloth of gold, and armor; an expensive quilted jack (a protective garment worn under a breastplate) belonging to John of Gaunt was set up as a target for arrows, in the absence of its owner, then hacked to pieces. "We will have no king named John!" trumpeted "the yokel band." Others were ripping tapestries, cushions, napery, rich silk hangings, and illuminated manuscripts, or chopping up fine furniture. All were carried to the great hall and heaped in a pile, which was then set alight. Soon the blaze had taken hold and the palace was engulfed in flames. The conflagration was complete when three barrels of gunpowder stored in the cellars—and thought by the rebels to contain gold and silver—were hurled into the fire and exploded. One fool was cast alive into the inferno by his furious companions "because he minded to have reserved one piece of plate for himself," and in the cellars below, thirty-two of his fellows, drunk and carousing on the duke's wine, were trapped when the roof caved in, and slowly perished; their "cries and lamentations" could be heard by curious citizens "for seven days afterward."[9] In the end, all that was left of the great Savoy was a pile of charred masonry, lead, and ashes. Everything had been utterly destroyed.[10]

Meanwhile, north of London, a yeoman band was ransacking Hertford Castle, elsewhere in the Lancastrian domains there were attacks on John of Gaunt's servants and property,[11] and in Essex one of his unfortunate squires was beheaded. At Leicester the terrified keeper of the wardrobe loaded the duke's clothes and treasures onto five carts and demanded that the Abbot of Leicester take them into safekeeping, but the abbot, also "in great fear," flatly refused, so the keeper was obliged to store his hoard in the churchyard of St. Mary's Church in the Newarke.[12] Men who wore Lancastrian livery badges prudently tore them off and made themselves scarce. There can be no doubt that had the duke himself fallen into the hands of the insurgents, he would have met with a violent end.

In the midst of the chaos, and with the sky red with the glow from the burning Savoy, the fourteen-year-old king's courage shone clear. He would meet with the rebels, Richard said, and parley with them. On June 14 he rode forth to Mile End and fearlessly faced Wat Tyler, who petitioned the King for the abolition of serfdom and the right to deal with traitors—there was no mistaking whom he meant. Richard agreed to all his demands, but as this meeting was taking place, the mob was still running riot in London. This time their target was the Flemish merchant community, resented as aliens and for the commercial privileges they enjoyed and the wealth they had amassed. The rebels brutally dragged thirty-five of these unfortunate wretches out of St. Martin's Church in Vintry and systematically beheaded them in the street;[13] over a hundred more were hunted down and lynched, which surely would have been the fate of Katherine Swynford had the malcontents found her in London, as she also was a foreigner hailing from the Low Countries, and the rebels had far more cause to butcher her: If the head of John of Gaunt was among the foremost of their demands, that of his mistress would have been forfeit too.

Chaucer clearly perceived the danger that threatened his wife and her sister.[14] Not only were they aliens, but they both were also closely connected with the duke. Chaucer does not make many political references in his poems, but in "The Nun's Priest's Tale," written perhaps a decade later, he reveals how personally affected he was by the Peasants Revolt:

> *So hideous was the noise, a benedicite [bless us]!*
> *Certes he, Jack Straw, and all his meinie [retinue],*
> *Ne made never shouts half so shrill*
> *When that they would any Fleming kill.*

It sounds as if Chaucer had heard those chilling yells himself.

The mob also breached the Tower's defenses and ransacked the armory. Some burst into Princess Joan's chamber, where—as they tore her bed hangings apart—one man made so bold as to snatch a kiss from her. The shock (whether of the attack or the kiss is uncertain) was so great that she fainted. Fourteen-year-old Henry of Derby, John of Gaunt's heir, was smuggled out of the Tower in the nick of time,[15] but old Simon Sudbury, the Archbishop of Canterbury, was not so lucky: He was seized while at prayer in St. John's Chapel in the White Tower, dragged outside to Tower Hill, and there horrifically decapitated, with the rebels needing eight blows to sever his head. Sir Robert Hales, the Lord Treasurer, and John of Gaunt's physician, Brother William Appleton, suffered a similar fate.[16]

The next day, June 15, Richard II again met with the rebels, this time at Smithfield, and again—"saving only the legality of his crown"—agreed to all their demands, including one for a new version of Magna Carta. But while he was speaking with Wat Tyler, Sir William Walworth, the hard-line Lord Mayor of London, appalled at the familiarity with which the peasant leader was treating the King—calling him "brother" and staying in the saddle drinking ale when he should have been kneeling—tried to arrest Tyler. The rebel leader retaliated by drawing his dagger, whereupon Walworth fatally stabbed him. Seeing their leader cut down, Tyler's followers were ready to erupt in outrage, but the young king—with great presence of mind—stayed them, raising his hand and declaring, "I will be your leader! You shall have no captain but me!" Promising them all parchments confirming that they would be made free men, he persuaded the rebels to disperse peacefully, which they did, believing that all they asked for had been granted.

How wrong they were. Walworth immediately rode off to raise an army. Members of the council, scared out of their wits at the demonstrations that had just taken place, were determined to crush any moves to change the old order. There were to be no parchments, just summary justice and bloody reprisals—two hundred were hanged. "Serfs ye are, and serfs ye will remain," the young king now said, forgetting his promises. By the end of June the "great mischief," as Froissart called it, had been decisively crushed. The only good thing to come out of it, as far as John of Gaunt was concerned, was a degree of public sympathy and outrage ignited by the wanton destruction of his property.

By June 19 news of the Peasants Revolt and the destruction of the Savoy had reached John of Gaunt at Berwick. We can only imagine its immediate impact on him, although "he heard the tidings with a cheerful countenance, as though he were unmoved by them, and kept them to himself."[17] But his actions during the days to come strongly suggest that he was profoundly shocked and viewed his devastating losses, the violent hostility toward him, and the danger in which he still stood not just as the appalling consequences of national unrest, but also as clear proof of divine displeasure with his immoral ways. He considered, says Knighton, "on every side the past events of his life, and everything that he had done, to see whether he had offended, either privately or publicly, the King or the realm, in such wise that he might deserve the fate that had fallen upon him. And weighing all justly in his mind, he fastened his mind upon God." One thing above all "turned in his mind . . . He frequently had heard, both from churchmen [who no doubt included his Carmelite confessor, Walter Dysse] and from members of his own household, that his reputation was greatly tarnished in all parts of the realm. He had paid no attention to what was said to him, because he was blinded by desire, fearing neither God nor shame amongst men." The object of that blind desire had, of course, been Katherine Swynford. Now, "considering these things, and inspired by the grace of God, he turned about and, committing himself wholly to the divine mercy, and promising that he would reform his life, he vowed to God that he would, as soon as he was able, remove that lady from his household, so that there could be no further offense."

Walsingham says that, in making private confession of his sins, John "blamed himself for the deaths of [those] who had been laid low by impious violence" during the Peasants Revolt, and "reproached himself for his liaison with Katherine Swynford, or rather renounced it."

Practical considerations came first. Immediately, the duke, displaying great presence of mind and no sign of fear, ordered the garrisoning of all his castles.[18] That same day, June 19, he agreed with the sympathetic Scots to a renewal of the truce until February 1383.[19] Then he left Berwick and rode south, but when he sought a lodging with his former ally, Henry Percy, Percy snubbed him. Fearing no doubt to be associated with the unpopular John of Gaunt, Percy told him he would not be welcome at any of his castles until he had been assured by the King that the duke could be trusted. Bitterly insulted, a despairing John decided to retreat to Edinburgh.[20]

The shock and the strain he suffered had a profound effect on him. When dismissing his servants, who were not to be obliged to share his exile, he broke down and made an astonishing public announcement, declaring "with tears and expressions of grief" that "he observed that God wished to chastise him for his misdeeds and the evil life that he had for long led, namely in the sin of lechery, in which he had particularly associated with Dame Katherine de Swynford, a she-devil and enchantress, and with many others in his wife's household, against the will of God and the laws of Holy Church." Accordingly, he had decided to renounce Katherine (and presumably the others), and he assured those around him that he had promised the complete "amendment of his way of life to God."[21] "By these devices, so he believed, he placated the Lord's anger," observed Walsingham.

The chroniclers were unanimous in applauding the duke's belated realization of his folly, and in their version of events, it is Katherine—the woman, the temptress—who emerges as the villain of the piece. Knighton felt the duke had been lucky to be spared a worse fate, and imputed his being in the North when "those wicked wretches" struck to the work of divine Providence. Walsingham, who was convinced that John's renunciation of Katherine "turned away the wrath of God," was to write more kindly of him in the future. In fact, all the chroniclers viewed that renunciation as a crucial turning point in the duke's life, and they are hardly likely to have continued to do so had they not been convinced that it was genuine. Moreover, they clearly believed that he saw it as a turning point too.

Was it John who used the words "she-devil and enchantress," or was the description that of the anonymous chronicler of York? The passage reads as if the writer was reporting the duke's actual speech, although he could not of course have been there to hear it in person. Perhaps he heard a garbled version of it, repeated by travelers. But these particular words could well be a monastic interpolation, born of moral outrage and the belief that women employed the snares of the Devil to entice men to sin; we do not, from other sources, get a sense of the duke feeling—as did many medieval men—that in some way he had been the victim of a woman's wiles, or lured by witchcraft to fall from grace. On the contrary, he made it repeatedly clear that he himself bore the responsibility for his sins: He did not try to blame Katherine. In this respect, Walsingham's hasty qualification in his account of John's renunciation of her is most revealing: The duke, he says, "abhorred, *or rather abjured*, the fellowship of that concubine of his" [author's italics].

In Edinburgh, John was made most welcome. Lodged at Holyrood Abbey, he gave further evidence of repenting his former sinful existence, again declaring his intention of expelling Katherine from his household.[22] On June 23, again in keeping with his new resolve to change his mode of life, he summoned Duchess Constance to come north to him at once, and directed his receiver in Lancashire to entrust her with urgently needed funds.[23] Six days later, having heard that Constance was at Knaresborough, and not knowing if she was safe, he made plans for a rescue attempt, summoning a force to meet him at Berwick on July 13.[24]

John stayed in Edinburgh until July 10, awaiting Richard II's assurance that it would be safe for him to return to London and—more to the point—that the King would welcome him there. When this was forthcoming,[25] he rode speedily south via Berwick—where he was joined by his military escort—Bamburgh, Newcastle, Durham, and Northallerton, which he reached on July 19.[26] Here he met his wife, who had left Knaresborough and was traveling north in response to his summons.

Constance had suffered a nightmare journey. Terrified of becoming a target of the rebels, she had fled north from Hertford and sought refuge in Pontefract Castle, only to find the gates barred to her by its fainthearted—or perhaps overcautious—constable, who said he did not dare to admit her. Hearing this, many of her frightened servants deserted her, so, "smitten in her heart with great fear,"[27] and with only a small escort, she rode by lantern light through the night and the forest, braving footpads and outlaws, to Knaresborough Castle, where, to her relief, the castellan afforded her a sympathetic welcome.[28] This experience left her thoroughly frightened and vulnerable, and she now looked "to find safety under the wing of her lord."

Seeing the duke approaching, and with her retinue drawn up behind her, Constance went to meet him. There, on the road, she prostrated herself three times before him, as if *she* were the one in need of forgiveness—John may not have been the only one whom recent events had shocked into a fit of conscience. Quickly, he dismounted, raised her up, took her by the hand and kissed her, then listened compassionately to her woeful tale, while she in turn expressed sorrow at the perils and misfortunes that had befallen him. At length John asked her pardon for "his misdeeds to her," and "she forgave him willingly." That evening, they repaired to the Bishop of Durham's strongly fortified and moated palace, a favorite stopping place of royalty that stood two hundred yards west of All Saints' Church, Northallerton, "and there was great joy and celebration between them, and with their companions that day and night."[29]

We can only imagine with what reluctance John of Gaunt returned to his wife. Severing his emotional and physical connections with Katherine must have been deeply painful, however strong his moral convictions. There can be little doubt that he genuinely felt he had to make amends for his sins, but there was probably more to it than that. Never a man to concern himself overly with public opinion, he must yet have been aware of the need to defuse the threatening situation in which he now found himself, and to make it clear that he was abandoning a way of life that had conceivably brought down divine vengeance upon him, and indeed upon the kingdom. To have persisted in it would have been to court further disaster.

His concern was not only for himself. Perry makes the pertinent point that the duke's property had been destroyed, his physician and several officers murdered, and his wife thoroughly frightened, while the mob had violently targeted the Flemings and demanded his own head. Only by disassociating himself from Katherine, therefore, could he hope to protect her and their children.

There were political considerations too. John now had much more realistic hopes of winning the throne of Castile, and would have realized that he stood a greater chance of success—with Parliament and the Castilians, as well as the Almighty—if he presented a united front with Constance. A convincing reconciliation was therefore imperative. In this, the duke and duchess would willingly collaborate, brought together by their shared ambitions and by his increasing reliance on her knowledge of her kingdom, her judgment, and her advice.[30]

Only compelling reasons such as these could have persuaded him that he must give up Katherine Swynford. Was he sincere? Did he truly mean to sever all illicit connections with her? At the time, almost certainly he did. There is no doubt that the Peasants Revolt had been cataclysmic for him.

It might also be argued that, after nine years together and four children, John had tired of Katherine anyway, but the facts do not bear this out. The two of them were to keep in touch, mutually supportive of each other, for many years to come, while John proved a good father to their children, continued to extend his patronage to Katherine's family, and eventually risked public censure by marrying her, while she clearly continued to play an important role in his life. All those things argue a deep-seated and long-cherished love between them—in which case John's public renunciation of Katherine and all that they meant to each other must have cost him dearly and occasioned him deep private suffering. It is surely no coincidence that, on July 23, just days after he announced his intention of separating from her, he granted land for the foundation of a chapel dedicated to her name saint and the Virgin Mary—for whom he himself had a special devotion—at Roecliffe in Yorkshire;[31] nor would it be too far-fetched to imagine that he was founding this chapel in the hope that the grateful saints would guard and watch over Katherine in the difficult days ahead. On the other hand, there is no evidence that the chapel was ever built, so perhaps the duke came to a belated awareness that openly associating himself with a foundation dedicated to his repudiated mistress's name saint was not the wisest of gestures.

Knighton, often well-informed, says that as soon as John returned to his estates in England, he "at once took occasion to send [Katherine] away, that she should no longer dwell with him." The wording of this passage suggests that she was already with him when he returned—which we know was not the case—or waiting for them to be reunited at a prearranged location. As to returning to his estates, John was at Pontefract Castle from July 20 to 21, before meeting up with Constance, and at Leicester from July 28 to

August 4. Constance's presence apart, the Mayor of Leicester had called out the militia at the height of the Peasants Revolt, anticipating an attack on the castle, so it is hardly likely that Katherine sought refuge there. But she might have been at Pontefract: the twelfth-century castle was strongly fortified and garrisoned, some good way north, and easily accessible from Lincolnshire— just the kind of place where the duke would have sent his lady for safety, for he had ordered his household to go there when he went to Edinburgh, and arranged for firewood and barrels of the best wine to be delivered to them.[32] It was also the center of the Lancastrian administration and one of the fa- vored northern residences of the duke, who had expended a fortune on lav- ish improvements there, a fitting residence for Philippa of Lancaster, who—as has been noted—may have been with Katherine. And Katherine's presence there might have been one of the reasons why Duchess Constance was refused admittance. Considering that the duke's household was already lodging there, there were no grounds for the constable to bar the door to his duchess.

Knighton implies that John imparted his fateful decision to Katherine in person before sending her away. We can only imagine that excruciatingly painful interview and the devastating impact his renunciation would have had on her. Not only had she lost her royal lover, but she was also to lose her position in the Lancastrian household. There was no question now about remaining as governess or companion to Philippa of Lancaster—her name was too synonymous with scandal[33]—and in February 1382 an entry in *John of Gaunt's Register* referring to her as "recently governess of our daughters" confirms that she had ceased to occupy that office.[34] We may assume that her duties came to an end at the same time as her affair with the duke, when she delivered Philippa into his care.

What *is* likely is that, at the same time as he informed Katherine that their sexual relations must cease, John assured her that she would always have his friendship and that he would continue to look after the interests of their children—his actions in the years to come bear this out. The fact that their relations remained amicable—at the very least—confirms that he made the break as kindly as possible. Of course, they would have a legitimate reason—and need—for keeping in touch with each other: the young Beau- forts.

Shocked and desolate as she must have been, Katherine may yet have shared John's qualms of conscience and fear of divine retribution—such was the medieval mind-set. She may have been shocked to hear that he had other women during the course of their nine-year relationship. But she was also, clearly, a survivor. Initially, she probably returned to Kettlethorpe, trying to recover her equilibrium and decide what she should do. Certainly she would never be in want: The duke's generous provision for her had seen to that, while she had been a careful preserver of her son's inheritance. And there was to be further proof of John's care for her: On September 7, 1381, he substantially increased her annuity to 200 marks (£24,831) for life, in consideration of "her good service to his daughters"—and possibly to reward Katherine for sheltering Philippa during the Peasants Revolt. This grant has been seen as a payoff,[35] and it probably does mark the formal termination of Katherine's service as governess. Ten days later the duke ordered that moneys owed to her "from the issues of land and tenements" that belonged to her ward, Eustacia de Savenby, be paid; and if the tenants did not pay their dues, the lieutenant of Tickhill was to "distrain the lands and tenements of all goods and chattels."[36]

It was probably later in 1381 that Katherine (perhaps using her new funds) took a lease on the Chancery, a fine house in Minster Yard (the cathedral close)[37] in Lincoln, which was to remain her town residence until at least 1393. The fact that she kept this house for at least twelve years argues that though it might have at first been a refuge for her, a place that had no connections with the duke, in time she came to feel at home in it. The cathedral close must have held some happy memories for her: At least one of her children had been baptized (and perhaps born) there, and she was apparently well thought of by the clergy who resided in the neighboring houses. Maybe she was grateful for their support, and for the chance to withdraw into this closed and protective community, a world dominated by the regular pealing of the cathedral bells.

At the Chancery, as at Kettlethorpe, Katherine lived in some state. This important house had been the official residence of the cathedral chancellors since 1321, but was some years older than that, having been built before 1260, when it was leased by Canon Thomas Ashby; at that time, it probably occupied the site of the brick range that now fronts Pottergate, the street that lies east of the cathedral; the vanished church of St. Margaret, where Thomas Swynford was baptized, stood opposite on what is today a green situated beside by the Greestone Stairs to the city, while the Bishop's Palace lay a few yards to the west. When Chancellor Anthony Bek (later Bishop of Norwich) acquired the house in 1321, needing adequate space for study and recreation, he built a wing stretching north at right angles to the existing building, added a stately timber hall, and extended the garden, creating a grand residence. For this, he was paying an annual rent of 10s. (£172)—a pittance for such a fine house. Fourteen new windows were inserted in the property by carpenters in 1343, at which time the Chancery boasted at least one stone privy.

The chancellor was the senior clergyman responsible for overseeing the diocesan grammar schools and the cathedral library. The close, which was surrounded by a strong high wall, two turrets of which still stand in the garden of the Chancery, contained the Deanery and other spacious houses for the cathedral canons, some of which survive at least in part today. For much of the second half of the fourteenth century, thanks to the Black Death and poor endowments, chancellors were in short supply, and consequently the Chancery—the oldest of the clergy houses, and known by this name before Katherine's time—was sublet and rented out to various persons in succession, including a number of canons, the "Lady of Withornwick" (who came from a knightly family in Holderness) in 1379–81, and after her, Katherine Swynford.

By the end of the 1380–81 financial year, the Lady of Withornwick had vacated the house, then from 1381 to 1386 an unnamed female tenant paid the very reasonable annual rent of 40s. (£751), plus 10s. (£188) toward the cathedral's fabric fund. This must have been Katherine, because in 1386–87 we find "the Lady Katherine, renter of the house" doing repairs there. In 1391–92, she is again referred to in the Chapter accounts, when the new chancellor, John Huntman (who had been appointed in 1390) received a remittance from the Chapter on account of the Chancery, because it was then occupied by her by "an old grant of the Chapter" (which no longer exists), and he was obliged to ask for another house in which to live. Katherine therefore appears to have taken out a long lease on the Chancery, for at least twelve—and possibly fifteen—years, because of which poor John Huntman was unable to take possession of his official residence until after 1396. It was in 1390–92 that John of Gaunt secured a settlement highly favorable to the close in a long-running dispute with the Bail, so the Chapter are hardly likely to have put pressure on Katherine to vacate the Chancery at that time.

In moving into this almost exclusively ecclesiastical male enclave, which was inhabited by nearly 130 men in holy orders in 1377, Katherine was isolating herself from the citizens of Lincoln—with whom she was clearly not popular, as will be seen—and surrounding herself with people who had shown themselves friendly, such as the canons who had served as sponsors at the font for her son, who were now among her neighbors.[38] However, their willingness to accept such a notorious woman into their community may have stemmed not so much from their past esteem of her as from a desire to ensure that John of Gaunt continued to show favor to the close, especially in its endemic conflicts with the Bail; as a member of its confraternity, he had a great spiritual affinity with the cathedral, which must have predisposed him to partiality toward the close. The cathedral's sub-dean, John of Belvoir, seems to have been instrumental in obtaining the tenancy for Katherine. In so doing, he and his brethren were acknowledging the continuing friendship that was perceived to be between her and the duke after the ending of their love affair.

It may be too that, knowing Katherine as they had since before she became the duke's mistress, the canons realized that she was a woman of greater integrity than most people gave her credit for—and, of course, she was now no longer living in sin. One canon, John Dalton, left her a silver cup when he died in 1402; another made provision for prayers to be said for her soul and that of the duke in the Chapel of Spital in Lincolnshire. Evidently she was held in some regard by her new neighbors.

The Chancery is still lived in by the chancellor today, and a substantial amount of it survives from Katherine's time. Although the redbrick front facade with its gatehouse and great chamber dates only from the early Tudor period,[39] the north gable of the street range, and the stone-and-timber wing projecting northward at right angles from the street, which incorporates Katherine's solar and chapel and the screens passage from her great hall, are of the thirteenth and early fourteenth century, respectively. The great hall itself does not survive, but once extended across what is now the garden, lying parallel with the gatehouse; in Katherine's day it had courtyards on either side, and the central hearth was possibly on the site of the present ornamental pond. We know the hall was timber-framed because the parliamentary surveyors who inspected the property for Oliver Cromwell in 1649 mistook the derelict structure for a "large shed open to the roof"; this last detail probably refers to a medieval louver that allowed the smoke from the fire to escape. Fortunately, the commissioners recorded the measurements of this building: at 40 by 28 feet, this was no shed, but a medieval hall of imposing proportions, with entrance doors on either side. Unfortunately for posterity, it was demolished in 1714.

The dais where Katherine would have presided at table over her household, and sometimes entertained John of Gaunt, has long disappeared, but the surviving screens passage boasts three fine doorways, each adorned with corbel heads of a king and a bishop. The left one led to the buttery, which still has a fourteenth-century window, and the right gave access to the pantry and the kitchen beyond (which also had a louver), while the middle door opened on to a straight flight of stairs leading up to the chapel, where Katherine would have worshipped and heard mass. The small chapel has a fourteenth-century triple-lancet window, an aumbry for the Blessed Sacrament, and a piscina with a delicately sculpted ogee arch. The windows and floor date mainly from the late fifteenth century.

Katherine's solar, a private first-floor apartment built around 1300 and located between the Tudor frontage and the chapel anteroom, is unrecognizable today, having been divided into bedrooms and corridors. Like the adjacent chapel, it was open to the roof beams in her day. The solar was the chamber in which she had her bed (the most expensive item of furniture she would have owned), received visitors informally, sought refuge from the world, and perhaps bathed in a wooden tub lined with white cloth and filled with scented water.

The small anteroom to the chapel has a fourteenth-century squint, permitting the observation of mass in private. Such squints were sometimes used to enable people excluded from services, such as lepers, to be present without infecting others, but they were also used to facilitate the sight of one altar from another, ensuring coordination in the administering of communion, so it could be that the chapel was too small to accommodate all Katherine's household at mass, and that some people were obliged to worship in the anteroom. An alternative theory is that the anteroom, which was adjacent to her solar, may have served as Katherine's private oratory; we know that she had twice before received permission to have portable altars, so evidently she had a penchant for solitary devotion. Possibly she preferred to participate in services apart from her household.

Katherine's great chamber, the "lord's chamber" of 1343, where she—and perhaps the duke on occasion—formally received visitors, was long ago demolished to make way for the Tudor wing fronting the street. Above the pantry and kitchen to the north of the property, according to the 1649 survey, were six lodging chambers with garrets above, now also long gone. Possibly these chambers had once provided accommodation for Katherine's children and guests, with the servants upstairs in the attics.

Below the fourteenth-century wing and the gatehouse were cellars for storage. We cannot be sure that the brew house and wood house that adjoined the kitchen in 1649 and had servants' quarters above were there in Katherine's time. The parliamentary survey also records a stableyard with stone stables incorporating three bays, a hayloft above, and a tiled roof, but given Katherine's status and the likely size of her household, her stables were probably larger, for in 1391 we will find her keeping twelve horses in John of Gaunt's stable block. In 1649 the three gardens (or "courts") belonging to the Chancery contained fruit trees.[40]

To assert, as Lucraft does, that there is "much evidence" that John of Gaunt and Katherine Swynford were "very much still together" in the 1380s (a decade in which he was in fact abroad for over three years) is perhaps to overstate the case. In order to determine the nature of their relationship in the period from 1381 to 1396, we have to look for clues in just two dozen or so references to Katherine in records of this period (some of which have nothing to do with John of Gaunt). It is important to remember that these official records give us no more comprehensive a picture of relations between John and Katherine than do those that are extant for the period during which they are known to have been lovers. For these records are not complete—less so than before, in fact, for *John of Gaunt's Register* survives only up to 1383. Circumstantial evidence suggests that the duke had less frequent dealings with Katherine than he had prior to 1381.

There can be no question, though, that Katherine continued to play a part—possibly an important one—in his life, nor that other people were aware of this. John continued to provide generously for her and their children, and sent her gifts as before; moreover, it is clear that he was seen to be her protector. They obviously remained on good terms and mutually supportive, she lending him money when he needed it, and he showing marked favor to her family. Both the Dean and Chapter at Lincoln on the one part, in 1381, and Richard II on the other—in 1383, 1384, 1387, 1388, and

1389—recognized that if they wanted to please the duke and retain his powerful support, they should show favor to Katherine Swynford. And Katherine herself continued to be a woman of influence and standing, which must be attributed to her connection with John of Gaunt.

Of course, this could all have stemmed from the fact that she was the mother of the duke's children. Yet few royal mistresses had ever achieved such status, and the fact that Katherine did is surely evidence of his continuing esteem and love for her—as, of course, is the fact that he later married her, in an age when it was virtually unheard of for princes to wed the mothers of their bastards. But love can be expressed in many different ways, and it looks very much as if, until 1389 at least, John kept his word and refrained from her bed.

The soundest argument in favor of their relationship remaining platonic, at least for the present, is that Katherine is not known to have borne any more children. She was only in her thirties, and had conceived fairly frequently during her years with John and her marriage to Hugh; nor was there any effective contraception that might have facilitated the secret continuance of sexual relations.

Then there is the fact that no chronicler—and Walsingham in particular was quick to censure the duke—even so much as hinted that the affair was still going on after the public renunciation; given its notoriety beforehand, we might expect people to have been on the lookout for signs that the erstwhile lovers had fallen from grace. But there was no further scandal. No, the picture we have, at least for the 1380s—as will become clear—is one of affection and mutual support, driven and cemented by the common bond of the couple's children.

From 1381 to 1386, John of Gaunt remained at the forefront of the English political scene. He dominated the council and Parliament, and played a leading role in diplomacy. At the same time, he was pursuing his quest for the Castilian crown, vigorously promoting "the way of Spain" as England's best chance of defeating the French. Knighton says that, after the perils he had endured, the honor in which he was now held was a great consolation to him; and he seems to have achieved some peace of mind and conscience too, for at length "joy came to the duke, and to those who were dear to him." "He drew such strength from his virtue that he sought no revenge, but patiently forgave the offenses of anyone who sought forgiveness."[41] Only two men were brought to trial for having assisted in the destruction of the Savoy.

It was John who met the new queen, Anne of Bohemia—"so good, so fair, so debonair," according to Chaucer—as she disembarked at Dover, and John who escorted her through the streets of London prior to her wedding to Richard II in January 1382 at Westminster. (It was Anne who introduced the horned headdress, or "moonytire," into England, a fashion that Katherine Swynford may well have worn.) At the end of that month, John asked Parliament for a loan to finance an expedition to Castile, but the response was generally unenthusiastic.[42]

John of Gaunt never rebuilt the Savoy. Instead, he left the blackened ruin as it was, a stark reminder of the violence done to his property;[43] the site would remain derelict until Henry VII built the Hospital of the Savoy on it over a century later. The duke concentrated instead on making Kenilworth the Lancastrian showpiece, and when he was needed in London, he resided at Hertford Castle—its roof was restored in 1383 with lead from the Savoy[44]—or in the Bishop of London's palace at Fulham, or at La Neyte (also known as the Neate), the country residence of the Abbot of Westminster, located by the River Tyburn in the area that is now Bayswater and Hyde Park.[45]

Historians have long debated the implications of the quitclaim that John of Gaunt issued to Katherine Swynford on February 14, 1382, in London. Its text is as follows:

> John, by the grace of God, King of Castile, etc., greetings.
>
> Let it be known that we have remised [a legal term meaning relinquished or surrendered], released and entirely from ourselves and our heirs quitclaimed the Lady Katherine de Swynford, recently governess of our daughters, Philippa and Elizabeth of Lancaster, and all manner of actions concerning her that we have, have had, and could possibly have in the future, reckoned by an agreement of debt, transaction, or whatever other means from the beginning of this world up to the day of the completion of these presents. And so that neither ourselves, our heirs, nor our executors, nor anyone else through us, or in our name, may in

the future by reason of some premise or other, demand or be able to vindicate any claim or right concerning the aforementioned Lady Katherine, her heirs or her executors; but from all actions let us be totally excluded by the witness of these presents. In testimony of which we affix our private seal to this, with the sign of our ring on the reverse.

Confusion has long reigned as to the purpose of this document: Was it drawn up to protect John's interests or Katherine's? The answer lies in understanding what a quitclaim deed actually was. Since medieval times it has been a document in which the granter relinquishes all rights and interests in a property to the grantee. The granter is the person who has sold or transferred a piece of property, or an interest in it, and the grantee is the person who has received it. Thus, in issuing a quitclaim, the granter "quits" any claims to the property referenced in the deed. To quote a simplistic example, in the fourteenth-century poem *Sir Gawain and the Green Knight*, the knight, referring to a weapon, says: "I quit claim to it. He shall keep it as his own."

And that was exactly what John of Gaunt was doing when—on behalf of himself and his heirs—he quit all claims to the property and other assets he had granted Katherine Swynford. Which is a very far cry from asserting— as many writers have—that he intended that neither she nor her children were ever again to have any claim on himself and his heirs. On the contrary, it was a most generous and loving gesture intended to protect the interests of Katherine and the Beauforts and ensure that they were handsomely provided for.[46]

It is significant that this document was issued on St. Valentine's Day.* In the late fourteenth century it was believed that birds paired up and mated on that day; the custom of choosing a "Valentine" did not emerge until the fifteenth century, but the connection of lovers with St. Valentine may go as far back as the emergence of the cults of two Roman martyrs of that name, and the tradition probably became popular with the development of the medieval concept of courtly love. Thus, there was a clear association between love and St. Valentine's Day in 1382, when John of Gaunt issued the quitclaim deed, and the choice of this date—surely no accident—was perhaps to reassure Katherine that the duke still secretly cherished deep feelings for her, even if they could not be lovers as before.

---

* I am indebted to Joan Potton for pointing this out.

Other evidence shows that he was still very protective of her welfare and determined to be a good lord to her family. On February 20, 1382, he sent Katherine a gift of two tuns of Gascon wine, one from Bristol, the other from Rothwell.[47] *John of Gaunt's Register* shows that by 1382 young Thomas Swynford was already a member of the duke's retinue, serving as a soldier and shield bearer, which suggests that John had taken him into his service as soon as he was old enough to be useful, and promoted him quickly; Silva-Vigier credibly suggests that he willingly assumed a fatherly role in the boy's life. Now, in 1382, he placed Thomas, aged fifteen, in the retinue of Henry of Derby, a youth of his own age, to whom Thomas seems to have acquired a lifelong attachment.

That same year, Katherine and her daughter, Joan Beaufort, who was five, were briefly in attendance on Henry of Derby's young wife, Mary de Bohun, who was still living in the household of her mother, the Countess of Hereford, at Rochford Hall in Essex. As has been noted, Joan Beaufort may have been born under the countess's roof and named after her; the countess, if she had been her sponsor at the font, would have taken a special interest in her.

On February 1, 1382, John had paid the countess money for the maintenance of his daughter-in-law, Mary de Bohun, up till her fourteenth birthday,[48] which fell on February 15 that year. Officially, Mary and Henry of Derby were not supposed to start cohabiting until then, but they had breached this rule at least seven months earlier, and Mary was now pregnant. She bore a son, Edward, on April 24, at Rochford Hall, but he only lived four days. A week later the disappointed young father—who had raced to be with his wife and hastily appointed a nurse and governor for his son—was taking part in the May Day jousts at Hereford (jousting was his newly discovered passion, delightedly encouraged by his father), perhaps chafing under the duke's prohibition of any resumption of marital relations with Mary for the time being: She would not bear another child for five years.

Katherine's arrival in the countess's household may have been timed to coincide with the birth of Mary's baby. Katherine had long experience of looking after infants, and she was good with children and young people. Her association with Mary de Bohun was to endure until death severed it, suggesting that Mary regarded her as a friend and mentor. There is evidence too to show that Henry of Derby thought highly of Katherine—his regard and affection for her would become clearly evident in the years to come. Several writers[49] have asserted that Katherine became at this time a permanent fixture in Mary's chamber, and that this provided a cover for her continuing intimacy with the duke, but there is no evidence for this, and it would be three years before a household was set up for the young Earl and Countess of Derby. The lack of any further references to Katherine being in attendance on Mary in the ensuing months and years suggests that she was with her for only a short time in 1382, hardly evidence of a permanent position.

If John of Gaunt visited his son's wife when Katherine was at Rochford Hall in 1382 (and there is no evidence that he did), he could have done so without incurring any scandal, for the Countess of Hereford, their mutual friend, was there to act as chaperone. We can only imagine how difficult John and Katherine found the first meetings after their parting, how long it was before they grew used to the fact that there could be no more between them than friendship, and how long before the pain ceased to be raw. Given that they probably resumed their affair some years on, we might surmise that their feelings for each other were never fully stifled, and that desire remained lively and had constantly to be suppressed.

On May 6, 1382, back in London, the duke paid for gifts for his daughters, Mary de Bohun, and Philippa Chaucer, who received another hanap.[50] With Katherine busily dividing her time between Kettlethorpe, Lincoln, and the Derby household—and her affair with the duke officially ended— Philippa Chaucer may have felt more comfortable about resuming her duties in the duchess's household, although she remained based in Lincolnshire, probably residing with her sister, until at least 1383, and most likely till 1386. John's favor was still extended also to Geoffrey Chaucer, who—thanks no doubt to John's influence—was appointed Controller of the Petty Customs of London on May 8, 1382.

That July, John and Henry of Derby visited Lincoln[51] to witness the public recanting of a Lollard heretic, the hermit William Swinderby—whom John himself had once maintained—before Bishop Buckingham in the Chapter House of the cathedral.[52] This was another example of John's new orthodoxy, but he did successfully intervene to save Swinderby from "the bitterness of death" at the stake.[53] With Katherine's house hard by— supposing she was in Lincoln at that time—it is hard to believe that John passed up the opportunity to visit her and their children there. By the end of July he had moved on to Leicester.[54]

✦ ✦ ✦

R ichard II was to figure large in Katherine's life. While John of Gaunt
was in Lincoln, the young king, now fifteen, began exercising a degree
of personal authority over the government. Despite his youth, and a slight
stammer, he was already able to influence government policy and personally
exercise patronage. Unfortunately, he chose to extend it to a favored clique of
unworthy but flattering courtiers, among whom the arrogant and incompe-
tent Robert de Vere (son of the Earl of Oxford) was the foremost.[55] The
early 1380s would witness the gradual emergence of this court faction, its
struggle with the conservative John of Gaunt and the great nobles for supremacy, and the deterioration of John's relations with Richard II. The same
period also saw public enmity and resentment shifted from John of Gaunt,
who was now beginning to be seen as a force for good in politics, to the profligate de Vere and his satellites.

Drip-fed vitriol by his favorites, the precocious and temperamental adolescent king came not only to resent his uncle's dominance, wealth, and
power, but also to chafe increasingly at being in tutelage to him. John had an
inbred veneration for kingship, and was inclined to lecture his nephew on
his duties and obligations, and to censure him for his profligate abuse of patronage.[56] Naturally, this led to tension between them, with the teenage
Richard attempting to throw off the restraints with which the wiser and
vastly more experienced duke tried to control him, and John attempting to
instill in his truculent and changeable nephew the principles of good government. Ignoring the ties of kinship and precedence, the King actively encouraged his favorites in their opposition to his uncle. They feared him,
wrote a now-admiring Walsingham of the reformed John of Gaunt, "because of his great power, his admirable judgment, and his brilliant mind." It
was fortunate for Richard that his uncle had an unshakeable loyalty to the
Crown.

Richard II grew up to be a true sybarite and aesthete, "extravagantly
splendid in his entertainments and dress, and too much devoted to luxury."[57]
He loved good food—he was the first English king to employ French chefs,
and the first to have a cookery book (*The Form of Cury*) dedicated to him—
and his hospitality was legendary. Tall (his skeleton, found in 1871, measured six feet), fair, and handsome in a rather feminine way,[58] he adorned

himself in fine, elegant clothing, furs and jewels, on which he was to lavish a fortune, and is said to have invented the handkerchief. Artistically inclined, Richard was to commission two portraits of himself, the first surviving painted portraits of an English king. The most famous is the *Wilton Diptych* (now in the National Gallery, London), in which the young king, sumptuously gowned in cloth of gold, and with his patron saints standing protectively behind him, kneels before the Virgin and Child; on the reverse is a white hart, Richard's personal emblem. The other portrait is a full-length of the King enthroned in majesty against a gold background, which now hangs in Westminster Abbey. That these are true portraits and not just iconic representations of a king is proved by their facial similarities, which bear close comparison with the effigy on Richard's tomb.

The Monk of Evesham accuses Richard II of "remaining sometimes till midnight and sometimes till morning in drinking and other excesses that are not to be named." This could mean anything, but it may be that the writer did not wish to be too explicit. Walsingham charged Richard with being homosexual, but the King seems to have been attracted to both sexes: His devotion to his queen, Anne of Bohemia, is dramatically well-attested, and even Walsingham admitted that the royal favorite, Robert de Vere, was a notorious womanizer, a "Knight of Venus, more valiant in the bedchamber than on the field"; de Vere's torrid affair with Agnes Launcekron, one of the Queen's ladies, caused great scandal. But Richard's marriage produced no children, and he certainly was in thrall to and influenced by de Vere, who had proved himself assiduous in sycophantically cultivating his royal master. Their relationship, according to Walsingham, was "not without signs" that "obscene familiarity" was taking place, to which the disapproving chronicler attributed de Vere's rapid and undeserved promotion. It may be significant that in 1392, after de Vere had died abroad and was brought home for burial, Richard had his coffin opened so he could look upon his face one last time and stroke his hands.[59] Another contemporary chronicler, Adam of Usk, tells us that a charge of sodomy was later brought against Richard by his enemies, although this might have been mere politically desirable character assassination. It is possible that the effete Richard did indeed have latent homosexual tendencies, and that the charismatic and highly sexed de Vere was aware of this, exploited the King's devotion to the full, and was perhaps bisexual himself.

Richard's court—which Katherine would one day frequent—was to become one of the most celebrated in English history, for its chivalry, its art and culture, its literature, its strict protocol and elaborate ceremony, and its unprecedented splendor. In every respect, it reflected the majesty of its monarch, a connoisseur and showman who set a new standard of luxury in his palaces, from the bathrooms with multicolored floor tiles to the many beautiful objets d'art he acquired. It was Richard who employed Henry Yevele to modernize Westminster Hall by adding the magnificent hammer-beam roof that survives today. With his all-encompassing interests and discerning patronage, Richard II foreshadowed the multitalented princes of the Renaissance, for whom magnificence and courtesy were sacred maxims.

Froissart asserts that no English king before Richard had spent so much money on his court and household, and naturally there was much criticism of his extravagance. But female influence may account in part for that, for there is some evidence that there were far more women at court than in previous reigns—the closeness of the King's and Queen's households, the emphasis on love and chivalry, the number of women admitted to the Fraternity of the Garter, and the proportion of ladies featuring in courtly scenes—and Katherine Swynford would come in time to be a part of that female community.

There was a dark side to Richard, though. He emerged from his experiences during the Peasants Revolt with an unshakable conviction in his own heroism and superiority, and an aversion to taking advice. He was emotional, insecure, suspicious, devious, and untrustworthy. His violent outbursts of temper were legendary, and he could be ruthless and vindictive when provoked. To Katherine Swynford and her children—whom he clearly liked—he would, however, prove a good friend.[60]

W idespread conjecture that John of Gaunt's invasion of Castile was imminent was well founded, for in October 1382 a French invasion of England seemed likely, prompting calls for an Anglo-Portuguese military expedition to crush France's ally, Juan I of Castile. This was to be a veritable crusade, supported by the Church, with the Pope himself promising pardons for the sins of all those who assisted and accompanied the duke. That November, John began making preparations for the campaign he hoped would at last win him a crown,[61] but by March 1383 a shortsighted Parliament had made it clear that it would not vote the necessary funds to support what many believed were the duke's personal ambitions. Instead, Bishop Despenser of Norwich was to lead a force to France.[62]

By 1383, John of Gaunt had granted Thomas Swynford the very handsome annuity of £40 (£16,288)—further evidence of his continuing patronage of Katherine's family. And the duke was to be more generous still—in March, despite his major political preoccupations, he yet found time to grant Thomas a second annuity of 100 marks (£13,573) on his marriage to Jane Crophill of Nottingham.[63] Jane may have been related to the Crophills who were members of the Trinity Guild of St. Mary in that city, to which John of Gaunt, Duchess Constance, and Katherine Swynford also belonged;[64] this important and wealthy guild had its chapel and altar in the north transept of St. Mary's Church in High Pavement—the present church dates from ca. 1376, and the eighteenth-century Shire Hall now occupies the site of the House of the Trinity Guild, or Trinity House, as it later became known. Katherine's membership in this guild, like her properties in Boston and Grantham (see below), is perhaps indicative of the extent of her financial interests, or possibly of the willingness of corporate bodies to please John of Gaunt by showing favor to her. Apparently no one questioned the incongruity and dubious moral value of extending membership of the guild to his wife and his former mistress.

The parentage of Thomas's bride is unknown, but there are clues. The name Crophill occurs several times in the fourteenth century in Nottinghamshire, Lincolnshire, and Leicestershire. The family probably originated at Cropwell Bishop and Cropwell Butler, villages a mile apart, to the east of Nottingham, which in Domesday Book were both known as Crophill or Crophell. In the fourteenth century three Crophills became mayors of Nottingham and were kinsmen of the royal house.[65] Given her links with Nottingham, Katherine Swynford must have known the family, and it was probably she who arranged her son's marriage. Considering the Crophills' royal connections, and their status too, Katherine had done well for her son.

Jane must have been very young at the time of her marriage, or perhaps she failed to conceive for a long time or suffered a series of miscarriages and stillbirths, because the couple's only known son—named Thomas after his father—was not born until about 1406. There was probably a daughter too, the Katherine Swynford who married Sir William Drury of Rougham, Suffolk, before 1428. The estimated date of their nuptials, and the fact that this Katherine died in 1478, suggests that she too was born late in the marriage, and that the elder Katherine Swynford never knew these grand-children.

After his wedding Thomas appears to have remained with Henry of Derby; he would be knighted before February 1386.

In April 1383, John of Gaunt acquiesced in the council's decision to resolve the differences between England and Castile by peaceful means, and again put his plans on hold, deferring his invasion until the following spring. Still suspicious of his motives, the council secretly instructed the English envoys in Bayonne to prolong matters as long as possible, in order to delay the duke's departure. As it happened, Juan I refused to abandon his alliance with France, so negotiations broke down.

John spent much of April at Kenilworth.[66] Constance was with him at first, but left for Tutbury before he departed for the St. George's festivities at Windsor: She evidently still preferred to hold herself aloof from the English court and to remain in seclusion with her ladies. But the duke had maintained great state while she was with him at Kenilworth, and his daily expenditure decreased significantly after she left. Clearly he was still treating her with great respect and deference, deliberately emphasizing her status as the Queen of Castile.

John's diplomatic powers were again called into play when he was sent north that summer to negotiate a renewal of the truce with the Scots. On August 1, as he rode back south, his natural daughter, Blanche Morieux, was successfully petitioning the King for the pardon of a murderer.[67] This is the last mention of her in the historical record, and sadly we must conclude that she died not long afterward.

That August, Bishop Despenser's crusade ended in ignominious failure and an appalling loss of life—for which the bishop would be impeached and stripped of his temporalities. The council now belatedly recognized that John of Gaunt was the only man with the resources and prestige to deal with the French, and accordingly he was appointed King's Lieutenant in France and asked to prepare for a foray across the Channel to negotiate a truce with the enemy and salvage something of England's honor.

Katherine Swynford, meanwhile, had herself been petitioning the King, for on October 20, 1383, Richard granted a royal license empowering her to enclose and empark three hundred acres of land and woods within the manor of Kettlethorpe.[68] Again, the influence—direct or indirect—of John of Gaunt may be perceived, for the duke was the man of the moment, deferred to by the majority, and the King, although increasingly jealous and resentful of him, could hardly gainsay such a request. Nevertheless, the patronage Richard extended to Katherine and her kinsfolk suggests he continued to think highly of her. The enclosing of a deer park usually meant the dispossession of tenant farmers, and often led to ill feeling. To Katherine, however, it meant a further improvement to the manor and her son's inheritance. As with her failure to drain her stretch of the Fossdyke, self-interest came before the consideration of others. It was an attitude typical of many medieval landowners.

The duke moved a crucial step closer to his Spanish goal in November 1383 when, following the death of the pro-Castilian King Ferdinand, which plunged Portugal into dynastic war, the Anglophile João I—brother of the late monarch—was elected by a rebel faction to its contested throne. João, needing English help to enforce his sovereignty against the claims of Juan I of Castile (who was married to Ferdinand's daughter, a lady of doubtful legitimacy), was only too willing to offer his support for John of Gaunt's claim to Castile.

John returned from a mission to Scotland at the end of April 1384, and arrived at Salisbury for what turned out to be a tumultuous session of Parliament, for Richard FitzAlan, Earl of Arundel, launched a fierce and entirely justified attack on the King and his favorites, provoking Richard publicly to insult him. John of Gaunt tried to pacify both of them, putting Arundel's concerns in more measured terms to the King, yet angering both Richard and the court party—never before had Richard's hostility to his uncle been so evident.

At this juncture a plot was hatched against the duke, obviously with the intention of eliminating him entirely from the political scene. The plot came to light when, in de Vere's chamber, a Carmelite friar, John Latimer, was said to have privately warned the King that John of Gaunt had organized a widespread conspiracy and was planning to have him assassinated. With suspicious alacrity, Richard accepted this at face value. He confronted his uncle, lost his temper, accused him of plotting treason, and was ready to have him summarily executed without any investigation of the matter. The duke, with dignified conviction, protested his innocence and accused the King himself of working against his own life. Richard responded with an astonishing about-face, ordering that the friar be put to death summarily, but the Lords in Parliament persuaded him to have the man questioned before proceeding further. It never happened: A band of knights led by the King's half brother, the hot-headed Sir John Holland, seized Latimer as he was being hauled off to prison and had him tortured to death. Someone, clearly, didn't want the wretch betraying the origins of the plot.[69]

Parliament erupted in fury, so the King hastened to dissolve it. He then had to deal with his youngest uncle, Thomas of Woodstock, who, brandishing his sword, furiously threatened to kill anyone, Richard included, who dared to accuse his brother Lancaster of treason.[70] Deprived of the only witness, the case against John collapsed.

It looks very much as if the King and his favorites, especially Robert de Vere, were behind this attempt to overthrow John of Gaunt. Vere bitterly resented the duke's influence and had been playing on the King's jealousy of his uncle's dominance, urging him to shake it off and rule autonomously. At bottom, of course, Richard needed his uncle. Good relations were soon restored, at least on the surface and for the time being, and in June, John was again made King's Lieutenant in France and sent there to negotiate a renewal of the truce.

Katherine Swynford, like most people, would soon have learned what had happened at Salisbury, and the knowledge that her erstwhile lover and generous patron, the father of her children, had come so close to an ignoble death must have distressed her greatly. But this was not the only unpleasant event to affect Katherine in 1384. On August 17, at Reading, a commission of oyer and terminer was issued following a complaint by her against no less a person than Robert de Saltby, the Mayor of Lincoln, and other named men of that city, including its bailiffs, John Prentyss and John Shipman, for breaking into her close there, taking her goods, and assaulting her servants. On September 20, this time at Westminster, a similar commission was issued after an attack on her close in Grantham by the same men and others.[71]

Given the status of the attackers, this was no common assault by pettyminded people on a notorious woman of whose morals they disapproved; it was far more serious than that. And considering that Katherine had been living apart from John of Gaunt for more than three years now, it is highly unlikely that it was an expression of public outrage at her private life. No, these crimes were more likely to have been born out of angry resentment at Katherine's siding with the clergy in the ongoing conflict between the Bail and the cathedral close over the close's demand to be placed beyond the jurisdiction of the town authorities, a dispute that had simmered in Lincoln for some years and would not be resolved until John of Gaunt ruled in 1390 and 1392 that the close was to enjoy immunity from the jurisdiction and demands of the mayor and citizens—for which the jubilant canons gave him a gold image of his patron saint, John the Baptist, from the cathedral treasury.[72] Katherine's strong links with the close would have placed her firmly on that side of the divide. The citizens were also resentful of the duke's perceived encroachment, as constable of the castle, upon their liberties.[73] And Katherine's failure to clear her stretch of the Fossdyke would have ruffled feathers among the burghers of the town; that same year of 1384, John of Gaunt presided over a commission that failed to address the problem effectively. Moreover, the duke was known to be Katherine's patron still: The canons might have rented the Chancery to Katherine in a bid to win his support, and there were perhaps fears in the Bail that she influenced him unfairly in favor of the close and in respect of the Fossdyke. So these attacks, cunningly timed while he was abroad, were probably intended as a warning to Katherine not to involve herself—or try to prejudice her powerful protector—in the city's quarrels. Even so, they were an outrageous attack on her property, and a highly provocative intrusion in the cathedral close that did not help the cause of the citizens in the long run.

We do not know if Katherine was in Lincoln when the Chancery was raided; the presence of her servants might suggest that she was, but she may have left a skeleton staff there in her absence. There or not, the assaults must have shaken her to the core, for if the mayor himself was involved, what support could she look for in Lincoln outside the precincts of the close? It cannot have been pleasant realizing she was so hated. There is no record, however, of what happened to the perpetrators, nor of any further assaults on her property.

The second commission relating to these offenses contains the only known reference to Katherine having property in Grantham. A close then meant an enclosed piece of land, usually beside a cathedral or other important building, and containing staff housing or offices, such as the Chancery in Lincoln. Thus, her close was probably near St. Wulfram's, the most important church in the town, and the hub around which it had grown; its soaring 282-foot spire was a landmark for miles around. The house she owned here was almost certainly one of several ancient mansions that once stood in this area, and may have been of equal status to Grantham House in Castlegate, which survives today. Grantham House was originally a stone hall house built around 1380 in what was then a rural area near the church; it still stands in twenty-seven acres of gardens on the banks of the River Witham. Its medieval core is now hidden beneath sixteenth- and eighteenth-century additions and alterations. From the late fifteenth to the early seventeenth century, this house was known as Hall Place, after the wealthy family of merchants that lived there; prior to that, it was apparently owned by the Fitzwilliams. Both Margaret Tudor, Queen of Scots, and Cardinal Wolsey stayed there in the sixteenth century. The original Grantham House appears to have been of a similar type to the properties that Katherine Swynford leased in Lincoln, and probably exemplifies the kind of house she had in Grantham.[74]

These were perilous times. In February 1385, Robert de Vere—with the connivance of the King[75]—made a second attempt to bring down John of Gaunt, hatching yet another court plot to kill him at a tournament. On February 24 an outraged John, accompanied by an armed escort and wearing a breastplate, confronted Richard II at Sheen, lecturing him "with some harshness and severity" on the folly of relying on bad counsel. Early the next month, Princess Joan intervened to bring about a public reconciliation, while John's former adversary, William Courtenay, now Archbishop of Canterbury, censured the King for the way in which he had behaved toward the duke, and condemned his evil advisers—at which Richard had to be restrained from running the archbishop through with his sword and transforming him into a second Thomas à Becket.[76] Both John of Gaunt and Courtenay had voiced the increasingly widespread concern about the King's favorites, and Richard's reaction shows how unwilling he was to listen to measured criticism. His resentment of his uncle had now reached the boiling point. Yet these days John's priorities were focused not on maintaining political supremacy in England, but on Castile, as the prospect of a crown there became daily more viable. In April an English force was finally dispatched overseas to the aid of João I, who that month—after prolonged resistance to the forces of Castile—was once more defiantly proclaimed King of Portugal.

John spent the summer accompanying Richard II on a lackluster invasion of Scotland, having first lavishly entertained the King and Queen at Leicester Castle.[77] During this campaign, John's brothers, Edmund and Thomas, were created Duke of York and Duke of Gloucester, respectively. While they were all up north, tidings came of the death of Princess Joan on August 8 at Wallingford. Her end was perhaps hastened by the news that her son the King intended to proceed against his half brother, Sir John Holland, for the murder of the heir of the Earl of Stafford,[78] but Walsingham tells us that the princess, who had spent a life "devoted to pleasure," was "so fat from eating that she could scarcely walk"; it may be that her obesity, as well as stress, had predisposed her to a heart attack. Joan was buried beside her first husband, Sir Thomas Holland, in the church of the Grey Friars at Stamford, some five months after her passing, in the presence of the King; Chaucer was a mourner, having received black cloth for the occasion from the royal wardrobe,[79] while John of Gaunt must have sincerely mourned the loss of this dear sister-in-law who had been such a stalwart friend to him.

At the end of August 1385, as he returned to his estates in the Midlands, John received the most exciting and encouraging news: King João, his army boosted by English troops, had won a magnificent victory over his enemies at Aljubarrotta on August 14 and was now the unchallenged sovereign of Portugal. The duke was jubilant,[80] for the way was at last clear for João to offer him the support he needed for his Castilian venture. Late in November 1385, John appealed to Parliament to vote the necessary funds for an invasion of Castile by means of "the way of Portugal," and Parliament—in which his son Henry was sitting for the first time—at last responded favorably.

There is evidence that John of Gaunt was in contact with Katherine Swynford at this time, the first on record since he had sent her wine in 1382. During the November Parliament, the duke petitioned for the removal of Sir John Stanley from the manors of Lathom and Knowsley in Lancashire. Sir John had recently married Isabel, the daughter of Sir Thomas Lathom;

upon Lathom's death in 1370, those manors had passed to his heir, another Sir Thomas, who died underage in 1383. Because Thomas had been a minor, John of Gaunt, as his feudal lord, took him and his manors into wardship, and although Isabel was her brother's heiress, her husband had taken possession of Lathom and Knowsley on Thomas's death without first establishing his right to do so in the duke's palatine chancery. There was, of course, more to this than met the eye: Sir John Stanley, who became Robert de Vere's deputy in Ireland the following year, appears to have been a client of the favorite, and almost certainly de Vere was behind this slight to the duke and upheld Stanley's possession of the manors in Parliament.

But the law was on the duke's side. After John of Gaunt complained that Stanley had been in "grave contempt" of his ducal rights, Parliament decreed that Stanley's entry into the manors had been illegal and ordered him to vacate them and to lodge his claim in the palatine chancery. In the end John of Gaunt was just. He had vindicated his right to the manors, but he was aware that they should pass to Stanley in right of his wife. So he granted them to Katherine Swynford, who in turn, at his behest, sold them to Stanley. The duke even returned to Stanley a substantial part of the price.[81] Thus we have evidence that John and Katherine were in contact—indeed, in collaboration—at this time, and that she was willing to support him in such matters.

The King, eager to get rid of his troublesome uncle, now loaned him money for his Castilian venture,[82] and from January 1386, preparations for the great invasion went ahead.

EIGHT

The Lady of Kettlethorpe

Nearly five years after the end of their affair, Katherine could perhaps view the prospect of John leaving England for a long period with equanimity. After all, it would not be forever—there is some evidence to suggest that he never intended to take up permanent residence in Castile, but anticipated that England would remain his chief base.[1] Thus, their children would not be permanently deprived of a father, nor Katherine of the occasional contact with him.

Inwardly, she might have worried about John, for he was no longer young. Ferñao Lopes, whose description of him as he appeared in Portugal in 1386–87 may derive from the reminiscences of Philippa of Lancaster and other contemporaries, says he was still tall, lean, and upright, but estimated him to be "about sixty years old, with fewer white hairs than is normal for one of his age"—unsurprisingly, as he was still only forty-six. It does appear, though, that a lifetime of care and campaigning had prematurely aged him, and his experiences in Spain would doubtless leave their mark as well.

The duke spent the months prior to his departure putting his affairs in order, and his provision extended to Katherine's family. He took Thomas

Chaucer into his service.[2] He betrothed nine-year-old Joan Beaufort to Sir Robert Ferrers of Willisham, heir through his mother to the Boteler estates in Wem.[3] And on February 19, the day after the standard of the Cross was raised in St. Paul's Cathedral and his Castilian venture was preached as a crusade, he was in Lincoln.

John was there to attend an impressive ceremony in the chapter house of Lincoln Cathedral, in which, in the presence of nine canons, "the Lord Henry, Earl of Derby, son of the Lord John, the most high Prince, King of Castile and Duke of Lancaster" was to be admitted by Bishop Buckingham to the cathedral's confraternity, just as John himself had been admitted at the age of three. Alongside Henry, John Beaufort, now about thirteen and already knighted; Sir Thomas Swynford; Philippa Chaucer; and Sir Robert Ferrers were also made members.[4] Sir Thomas Swynford, in company with another Lincolnshire knight, Sir William Hauley, was officially in attendance on the duke that day.[5] The inclusion of Katherine's sons, her sister, and her future son-in-law in this important Lancastrian ceremony demonstrates how highly regarded, and how important, she and her family were within the duke's closest circle.

Admission to the cathedral's "order of the brotherhood"—which it claimed had been founded "when the Bible was written,"[6] but which in fact dated from ca. 1185[7]—was a socially prestigious privilege that enabled members of the laity to benefit from the prayers of the clergy in perpetuity and to be buried in the cathedral; in return, it was piously hoped, they would be generous benefactors and patrons.[8] The duke no doubt felt that he and those dear to him needed such intercessions at this crucial time. His visit to Lincoln Cathedral would have afforded him the opportunity to pray at the three altars where his name saints were worshipped, and to the Holy Virgin, to whom the church was dedicated.[9]

After the ceremony, wine and comfits were served, then the company repaired to the castle for a feast hosted by the duke.[10] Professor Goodman is probably correct in suggesting that John made this auspicious day the occasion for a farewell gathering prior to his departure. And with the focus on two of her sons, her sister, her former charge, and her patron, there can be little doubt that Katherine Swynford, whose house was nearby, was also present with her other children. Nor that her long association with the cathedral, and the omission of her name from the list of new members of its confraternity, suggest that she herself already belonged to it, and perhaps had for some years, for Sir Hugh Swynford may also have been a member.[11]

Philippa Chaucer's admission suggests that she was still resident in Lincolnshire at this time and living apart from her husband. She was probably preparing to go to Castile in the train of Duchess Constance: After all, her son Thomas was going with the duke, and with her daughter in a convent and her husband living apart from her, there was little to keep her in England.

John of Gaunt returned to London immediately after the ceremony; his duchess was then away on a pilgrimage to various shrines, praying for the success of her husband's great enterprise. She can hardly be blamed for not attending the ceremony in Lincoln, at which the Swynford connections were so prominent.[12] Instead, she was received into the confraternity of St. Albans Abbey, home of the chronicler Walsingham,[13] a place where she was much admired for her piety, which might account in part for Walsingham's past hostility toward the duke.

On March 8, Richard II formally recognized John of Gaunt as King of Castile, placing him next to himself at the council table.[14] At Easter the Pope again proclaimed the enterprise a crusade, and sent John a holy banner.[15] By then the duke had begun assembling his fleet, and there was a ceremony of farewell at court, with the King and Queen solemnly placing golden diadems on the heads of John and Constance. After that, John departed on his own pilgrimage to various shrines in the West Country.[16] On April 8, as King of Castile, he agreed to a treaty of perpetual friendship with Richard II, and on April 20 the King ordered the impressing of every ship in the realm for John's fleet.

By June 14 the duke had arrived in Plymouth; four days later his fleet was finally assembled. Preoccupied as he was with the myriad aspects of his venture, he yet had to find time to deal with the unseemly conduct of his strong-willed[17] daughter, Elizabeth of Lancaster. Bored with her child husband, who was still only fourteen to her twenty-three years, Elizabeth had willingly allowed herself to be seduced by the King's half brother, Sir John Holland,[18] a volatile schemer who in 1384 had been involved in the plot hatched against John of Gaunt at the Salisbury Parliament; it was he who in 1385 had caused outrage—and grief to his mother, Princess Joan—by killing Stafford's son, as a result of which he had been forced to flee to sanctuary until the King's wrath abated. Holland was licentious too, and around 1380 reputedly enjoyed a torrid affair with the flirtatious Isabella of Castile, Constance's sister and the wife of Edmund of Langley.[19] Now, Higden says, he had been "struck down passionately" by his love for Elizabeth of Lancaster, "so that day and night he sought her out."

When John of Gaunt learned that Elizabeth was pregnant by Holland, he arranged for her unconsummated marriage to Pembroke to be annulled; that unfortunate boy was to remarry, but he would die horribly, pierced through his genitals, in a jousting accident at Christmas 1389.[20] On June 24, 1386, Elizabeth and Holland were hastily wed[21] in or near Plymouth, narrowly averting a scandal and effecting his complete rehabilitation. The duke was to show great favor to this son-in-law, so obviously the scoundrel had charm and ability. The couple's daughter Constance was born the following year, and four other children—the eldest named John, after the duke—would follow.

Clearly the headstrong Elizabeth had inherited her father's sensual nature; it may have seemed to her that there was no harm in following the example set by her former governess, Katherine Swynford, in giving herself outside marriage to the man she loved. But Katherine was not a princess of the blood—Elizabeth was, and the corruption of her virtue was a more serious matter. It seems that Katherine had failed, by precedent or precept, to impress upon Elizabeth the need for a girl in her position to conduct herself virtuously. Fortunately, her father had dealt with her leniently and advantageously, and her marriage turned out to be successful.

In July 1386 the duke's retinues began to embark. Having appointed his son Henry to serve as Warden of the Palatinate of Lancaster during his absence, John entertained him at a farewell dinner on board his flagship on July 8. The following day a fair wind sprang up; father and son bade each other a hasty farewell, and the fleet set sail on its glorious venture.[22] With it went the duke's three daughters; his sons-in-law John Holland, who had been appointed constable of his army, and Sir Thomas Morieux, serving as marshal; Thomas Chaucer, and probably his mother Philippa; and Duchess Constance, now in high hopes of occupying her father's throne and continuing his dynasty.

Constance was possibly pregnant at this time, with a child doubtless conceived primarily for dynastic purposes. The arrival of a male heir on

Castilian soil would signify divine approval of her cause and inspire the loyalty of her subjects. It would also serve to proclaim that she and her husband were fully reconciled, and go some way toward obliterating the scandal of his former life. Alas, the child—if there was a child at all—was not of the desired sex: The contemporary chronicler Monk of St. Denis says that the duchess was delivered of a daughter soon after she and the duke disembarked at Corunna on July 25.[23] No further mention is made of the infant, so either she did not live or the monk's information was inaccurate and she never existed.

Katherine Swynford was probably living quietly in Lincolnshire when John went away—she was still renting the Chancery in 1386–87, for at that time she was having repairs done to the house.[24] Perhaps she went to the cathedral and offered up prayers for the success of the duke's enterprise, as Bishop Buckingham requested of his flock on July 28.[25] There is later evidence to suggest that she and John were in touch while he was abroad, so probably at some stage she and her Beaufort children received word of his arrival in Compostela and his decision to winter in Galicia before attempting to take Castile. In his absence, she busied herself with domestic matters and continued to administer her son's lands. In 1386, Henry de Fenton granted Katherine tenements in Kettlethorpe, further improving the Swynford inheritance.[26]

Katherine cannot have seen much of her brother-in-law, Geoffrey Chaucer, these days; maybe, with Philippa possibly gone overseas, they now had little to say to each other. Chaucer did not fare well after the duke's departure. In 1386 he was a man of substance and status, and in the summer of that year he was nominated to sit in Parliament as Knight of the Shire for Kent, taking his seat in October. But toward the end of the year, he either resigned from or was deprived of his lucrative controllerships, and he gave up—or was evicted from—his house in Aldgate. He possibly took lodgings in Greenwich or Deptford,[27] but his only income now was his royal pension, which he continued to collect himself twice a year from the Exchequer.

The loss of his house and offices coming only months after John of Gaunt's departure argues that they had indeed been granted to him through the duke's influence. But the absent John was now persona non grata in England, for the King was relieved to be rid of his too powerful and intimidating uncle, and his favorite, Robert de Vere, now reigned triumphant at court. This might explain why Chaucer—whose wife was sister to the duke's former mistress—had lost his offices and would not regain favor until Richard realized just how much he needed John of Gaunt's support.

Meanwhile, the duke had met up with his ally, João I of Portugal, and both were trying to enforce John's claims through diplomacy before resorting to war. To cement their friendship, Philippa of Lancaster was given in marriage to King João in February 1387 in Oporto Cathedral.

Philippa was to prove a model—and much-loved—queen consort. She was devoted and obedient to her husband, bore him eight children (two were named after her parents; another was the great explorer prince, Henry the Navigator), had them well-educated, and set a deeply pious and charitable example.[28] In every way she was a credit to her father, and also to Katherine Swynford, who had been in overall charge of her from the time Philippa was thirteen, and who evidently succeeded with her where she had failed with her sister. And it was perhaps Philippa's fondness for Katherine and the Beauforts that led her to treat her husband's bastard children with kindness and tolerance.[29]

It was probably before his departure that Katherine loaned John a substantial sum of money. The Pope had promised special remission of sins to those who helped finance the duke's "crusade," so Katherine, mindful of her former life, was perhaps laying up treasure in Heaven. The fact that she had such funds to lend is further testimony to her financial acumen—it will be remembered that John himself had entrusted her with large sums of money for the maintenance of his daughters, and we know she was careful with her income, and prudent in providing for the future. But when the duke was in need, she did not hesitate to assist him liberally, showing herself selflessly sympathetic to his cause, even though it took him away from her. John did not forget her generosity, and on February 16, 1387,[30] he sent instructions to his receiver in Yorkshire to repay £100 (£33,471) in part repayment of the 500 marks (£41,058) she had loaned him "in his great necessity."[31] We might infer from this that he and Katherine were maintaining some kind of contact while he was abroad: The interests of their children alone would surely have necessitated it.

In the spring of 1387, diplomatic solutions having failed, the duke took

Galicia, and at the end of March he and King João invaded León, a kingdom ruled by Juan I of Castile. But things did not go well—there were complaints that the duke's womenfolk slowed down the march; his son-in-law, Sir Thomas Morieux, died, worn out by fighting;[32] and the Castilians had laid waste to the land, so that countless men and horses died of starvation, dysentery, and heat exhaustion. "These are the fortunes of war," observed Froissart. "The duke was at his wits' end, and weighed down by anxiety. He saw his men exhausted and ill and taking to their beds, while he himself felt so weary that he lay in his bed without moving." John nearly died too, but forced himself to get up and look cheerful, for the sake of maintaining morale among his men. Nevertheless, there was much muttering about his leadership of the campaign,[33] even though the Count of Foix thought John had "conducted himself valiantly and wisely in this war," and soon King João began urging him to abandon the fighting in favor of a return to diplomacy.[34] But the duke refused.

On March 26–27, 1387, Richard II and Anne of Bohemia visited Lincoln, to be admitted to the confraternity of the cathedral. It is hard to conceive that Katherine, probably a member herself, was not among the congregation that witnessed this ceremony. Richard II thought highly of her, and may well have singled her out on that day, because the following month he appointed "Lady Katherine de Swynford" a Lady of the Garter (or, more correctly, a "Lady of the Fraternity of St. George and of the Society of the Garter"),[35] the highest English honor to which a woman might aspire. Her formal robes of scarlet wool embroidered with blue taffeta garters in gold, with the motto *Honi soit qui mal y pense* in blue silk, and a matching hood, were paid for by the King the following August.[36]

In 1387, Katherine would have gone to the glittering court at Windsor, donned her robes, participated in the Garter ceremonies with the other ten ladies of the order, and attended the great feast hosted by the King on St. George's Day. Doubtless, she met up with many people she had known during her glory days with the duke, but Katherine could now hold her head up at court in the knowledge that she was there in an honorable and legitimate capacity. Even so, her admission to the most prestigious order of knighthood in Europe was probably a tacit acknowledgment by the King of her special relationship with John of Gaunt, and of her influence with him. It might also indicate that the scandal surrounding their affair had died down and that people knew they were no longer lovers.

Edward III had begun the practice of appointing "Dames of the Fraternity" with Queen Philippa and his eldest daughter Isabella, but since the beginning of his reign, Richard II was assiduous in admitting ladies to the order, notably his mother, Joan of Kent; Duchess Constance; her sister Isabella; and Philippa and Elizabeth of Lancaster in 1378–79; and Queen Anne, Catalina of Lancaster, Eleanor de Bohun, and Lady Mohun in 1384. So Katherine Swynford was in august company. But there was an ulterior motive for her advancement. By 1387, Richard was engaged in a bitter struggle with those lords who resented his reliance on worthless favorites like Robert de Vere and his former tutor, Sir Simon Burley, and were demanding a new push to win the war with France: Richard had never yet led an army into the field—an abrogation of his duty, in the eyes of his martially minded magnates—and was essentially inclined to peace. That summer Parliament itself was to demand that he remove his offensive counselors. Richard had therefore come to a belated realization of how loyally John of Gaunt had supported him; he knew how much John cared for Katherine, and making her a Lady of the Garter was one way in which he could show favor to his uncle and solicit his support; this would not be the first time he promoted ladies to the order to forge useful alliances with his nobles.[37] It is probably no coincidence too that Chaucer's fortunes now began to improve: In July he was sent to Calais on the King's service, and in August he was acting as a justice of the peace at Dartford in Kent[38]—more sops to the duke perhaps.

But John had far more pressing matters on his mind. His campaign in León ended cruelly in dysentery, mass desertions, and disaster, he had failed to rally sufficient Iberian backing for his cause, and he now saw that there was no prospect of him ever taking Castile.[39] His army, encamped on an open plain in the burning sun, was decimated by the bloody flux. "You must believe that the Duke of Lancaster was not without trouble night or day, for he was sorely ill, and his valiant knights dead. He sorrowed for them and cried (if one can say so) every day, and took everything to heart."[40] To make matters worse, King João fell seriously ill and nearly died, as a result of which his distraught bride, Philippa of Lancaster, suffered a miscarriage. Their recovery was seen as little more than a miracle.[41]

One of those who perished of dysentery in Léon may have been Philippa Chaucer. On June 18, 1387, Geoffrey collected her annuity as usual from the

Exchequer, but on November 7, when the next installment was due, he fetched only his own pension. Nor did he ever pick up any more payments to Philippa.[42] Since the usual reason for disappearing from these records was death, it must be assumed that she died between June 18 and November 17, 1387.[43]

It has been suggested that a stone effigy of a medieval lady that was discovered in the nineteenth century beneath the floor of the church of St. Mary the Virgin at Old Worldham in Hampshire is that of Philippa Chaucer. This claim is based on the evidence of a brooch, or "fermail," on the breast of the figure, which is said to display a Roët wheel. However, the design bears very little resemblance to that emblem, and in fact is common to such brooches. The costume, moreover, is that of the first half of the thirteenth century (when the church was built), not the last quarter of the fourteenth.[44]

Of course, Philippa could have died in Lincolnshire and been buried there, perhaps at Kettlethorpe—that is the traditional version—or even in Lincoln Cathedral, to which she was entitled as a member of its confraternity. It has also been suggested that she returned to Hainault and spent the rest of her life there, having inherited property in that region.[45] But the most credible theory is that she accompanied Constance to Spain and died there, which would account for there being no record of her death in England and no known tomb. If she did succumb to dysentery in the heat of León, she was probably buried in a pit with other victims, with scant ceremony and no memorial.

Wherever Philippa died, Katherine had lost her sister, and she must have mourned her sincerely: They had evidently been close in recent years, living often in the same household. There is no record of their mutual bereavement bringing Chaucer and Katherine closer together: Their lives seem hardly to have coincided for a long time afterward. Geoffrey, who never made any reference to his wife's death in his verse, must have felt regret, but his loss did not diminish his cynicism regarding marriage—far from it, as his later poems show. Nor would he "fall in the trap of wedding" again.

It was now painfully obvious that John of Gaunt's long-cherished dream of winning the throne of Castile was never going to come to fruition. Finally accepting this, he agreed to terms with King Juan I, and at Trancoso, in

July 1387, a settlement was proposed whereby, in return for a cash payment of £100,000 (£33,470,817) and an annual pension of £6,666 (£2,231,165), John and Constance would relinquish their Castilian claims to their fifteen-year-old daughter Catalina and enter into negotiations for her marriage to Juan's son Enrique.[46]

Just before John of Gaunt concluded the peace with Juan I, he made an emotional promise to the Virgin Mary to amend his way of life, and was seen weeping in repentance for his sins.[47] This echoed the public avowal he had made in 1381, and begs the question whether he had lapsed into his old promiscuous ways. But given how ill and weak he was at this time, that is unlikely. Was he referring to Katherine Swynford? Although abroad for over a year, he was perhaps still carrying the proverbial torch for her, and might have maintained contact between them, thereby affronting his wife. If so, that contact can only have been intermittent: That summer there were alarming rumors in England, but they were just that, for even Walsingham had no idea what was actually happening in Spain; it was known that the duke's army had suffered terrible losses, but some were claiming that the hot weather had "induced deadly plague."[48] We can only imagine what Katherine and her children would have felt if they heard that.

That same month, a Castilian assassin's attempt to murder John and Constance by poison left them shaken and demoralized; the man confessed and was burned to death, apparently on the duke's orders.[49] In August, John was well enough to accompany King João to Portugal;[50] at Oporto, the next month, after confirming a treaty of friendship with Portugal that still holds good today, and is England's most ancient alliance, John took leave of his daughter and son-in-law and sailed with Constance to Bayonne.[51] He would never again set eyes on Philippa, and parting from her must have been a wrench, for she had married at the unusually late age of twenty-seven, having remained in her father's care far longer than most daughters of her caste, and there was obviously a close bond between them.[52]

On May 26, 1388, Richard II appointed John King's Lieutenant in Aquitaine,[53] and for the next eighteen months the duke would remain in the south of France, ruling the duchy. At Bayonne, in 1389, he received Thomas Chaucer into his retinue, retaining him for life at an annual fee of £10 (£5,102),[54] and appointed him Constable of Knaresborough Castle.[55] From now on, Thomas Chaucer's fortunes would be closely linked to those of the House of Lancaster.

On July 8, 1388, John of Gaunt and Juan I concluded the Treaty of Bayonne, which confirmed the proposals made at Trancoso, and in September, Catalina—now sixteen, tall, fair, and very beautiful[56]—was married to the Infante Enrique, the nine-year-old heir to Castile, at Fuentarrabia; she became Queen of Castile when he succeeded as Enrique III in October 1390.[57] One of the witnesses to the treaty, unusually, was the duke's long-serving physician, Lewis Recouchez, whose presence has led several historians to wonder if John was still unwell as a result of the rigors of the campaign.[58]

After the wedding, with the crown of Castile irrevocably beyond their reach, and their only child royally married, John and Constance no longer needed each other, and appear to have abandoned all pretense of marital unity. From now on they would effectively live apart. She was of no further political importance to him, and accordingly, there are few further references to her in the chronicles. The duke continued to provide generously for her, but there was to be no more pretense of marital felicity.

For Constance, the abandonment of her cherished hopes must have been hard to bear. In October she went to visit her daughter and new son-in-law in Castile, where she had her father's remains exhumed from the field of Montiel and honorably reburied with his ancestors. She tried to persuade King Juan to use his influence to end the Great Schism, which had left one Pope in Avignon and another in Rome, and also worked to foster good relations between her husband the duke and the House of Trastamara.[59]

Constance would not return to England until the following year, and then would live mainly at Tutbury, dissociating herself once more from the Lancastrian household and the court, and surrounding herself with her Castilian ladies and gentlemen.[60] Her withdrawal would leave the way clear for the relationship between the duke and Katherine Swynford to flourish once more.

Meanwhile, England had descended into political turmoil. Those magnates who opposed the rule of Richard II—who styled themselves the "Lords Appellant"—had finally had their way and purged the royal household of his favorites, reminding the King that he was still a minor and forcing him to accept councillors of their own choosing. Richard retaliated by having Parliament declare their actions unlawful and treasonable, but he was no match for the might of the lords. In November 1387, three of the appellants—Thomas of Woodstock, Duke of Gloucester, and the Earls of Arundel and Warwick—angrily accused Robert de Vere and the King's other favorites of treason, and on December 20, Henry of Derby, who with Thomas Mowbray had lately joined the appellants, defeated de Vere in a skirmish at Radcot Bridge and was hailed as a hero. Afterward, de Vere fled into exile, never to return. (In 1392 he was fatally savaged by a boar while hunting at Louvain.) By this point matters had reached such a crisis that for a few days in late December, Richard II, now a captive in the Tower, was effectively deposed.

It was against this background—and possibly as a result of the duke and duchess going their separate ways in the autumn—that at Christmas 1387, Katherine Swynford and her daughter Joan Beaufort were invited to stay in Mary de Bohun's household. Mary and her husband had finally been assigned their own establishment and begun cohabiting in November 1385, and in August or September 1387, at Monmouth Castle (which John of Gaunt had placed at their disposal), Mary had given birth to their first surviving son, named Henry, after his father. Again Katherine was invited to attend Mary after the birth of a child, which suggests that Mary and her husband placed much confidence in the older woman's capabilities; it might also be that the young Derbys were acquiescing to a request made by the duke that Katherine come to her, or they might have invited her to please him. Even so, she would not have been admitted to their household unless Henry of Derby regarded her as fit company for his wife;[61] he seems to have long cherished an affection and regard for Katherine, and perhaps felt that her exceptional qualities more than outweighed her tarnished reputation; and there is evidence that he liked her children too. Henry may have shared with his father a sentimental appreciation of Katherine's links with Blanche of Lancaster;[62] she had probably been more of a stepmother to him than Constance ever had, and in later years, as will be seen, he was to refer to her as his mother.[63]

Henry of Derby was now twenty, a squat and powerfully built young man, always richly and elegantly garbed, and handsome,[64] with russet-red hair and beard, as were seen when his tomb was opened in 1831. People were impressed by his courtesy, chivalry, and affability.[65] Fearless and brave, he was conventional in outlook, staunch and orthodox in his religious views, and had wide-based interests embracing jousting, crusading, literature, poetry, and music. Ambitious and restless, he had a thirst for adventure, but he could be a devious and calculating opportunist, who was also indecisive and thick-skinned. On the positive side, he was careful, cautious, serious, even-tempered, and generous. The duke was exceptionally proud of his son, delighted in his military prowess, and demonstrated great affection toward him. Obviously there was a strong bond between them.

Although they had the use of Monmouth Castle and a London house in Bishopsgate, the young couple may have been staying at this time at Kenilworth, which John of Gaunt had also made available to them. By Christmas, Mary had prevailed on Katherine and Joan to join her household, and during the festival she presented them both with gowns of silk in her livery colors of red and white, edged with miniver.[66] Again it may be that Mary was acting on John of Gaunt's instructions; she must have known that he would approve of her receiving Katherine into her chamber.

Thus, Katherine came to occupy a place of honor in another royal household. Her duties, as with Blanche of Lancaster, probably involved attending upon the young countess and helping to look after her rapidly growing family, starting with the infant Henry of Monmouth; yet, given her experience in running a large establishment, she may have enjoyed a more managerial role. Ten-year-old Joan would probably have helped with the Derbys' children, and benefited intellectually and socially from being placed in a lordly household; she grew up literate, cultivated, and pious, and must therefore have received a good education that befit her to move with confidence in courtly circles. It is clear, though, that Katherine—like her sister Philippa and other *damoiselles* in royal households—divided her time between waiting on her young mistress and her personal and family commitments in Lincolnshire, where she continued to rent the Chancery and look after the Swynford holdings.

Katherine and Joan's presence in Mary de Bohun's household testifies to their continuing inclusion in the Lancastrian inner circle. When Mary was appointed a Lady of the Garter in April 1388, Katherine was again provided with Garter robes and once more traveled to Windsor for the St. George's Day solemnities and feasting. Mary was then pregnant again, and in September 1388 she bore a second son, Thomas, who was speedily followed by a third, John, in June 1389—Henry of Derby did not spare his young wife. However, their marriage appears to have been happy, with the couple sharing a love of chess, dogs, parrots, and music (Mary, who came from a cultivated family, played the harp and cithar, Henry the recorder), and he was conspicuously faithful[67] and assiduous in sending gifts of food to satisfy his wife's cravings during pregnancy.[68] Theirs must have been a happy and lively household, and Katherine is again recorded in it at Christmas 1388,[69] further evidence of her enduring association with the Derbys.

I n February 1388, in what became known as the "Merciless Parliament," the Lords Appellant had five of the King's remaining favorites tried and convicted, and his beloved Simon Burley executed. For more than a year afterward Richard endured in humiliating tutelage to the appellants, until in May 1389, now twenty-two, he belatedly declared himself of full age, dismissed them, and asserted his regal authority. In September, Henry of Derby—ostensibly forgiven—was restored to the council: Richard knew he needed the support of John of Gaunt, who had remained in Aquitaine to conclude a new truce with the French. That year, 1389, Richard had again issued Katherine Swynford with Garter robes; he also created the duke's son-in-law, John Holland, Earl of Huntingdon, and appointed him Chamberlain of England, Admiral of the Western Fleet, and a privy councillor. Richard now wanted—needed—his powerful uncle in England. After more than three years abroad, John of Gaunt had begun making plans for his return home,[70] but on October 30 the impatient king—who had already sent funds for his voyage[71]—formally summoned him back.[72]

The ship carrying the duke docked at Plymouth on November 19, 1389.[73] He came home far wealthier than before, "with an immense sum of gold treasure,"[74] but prematurely aged—a French councillor referred to him at this time as "an old black boar"—and probably in poorer health. From Devon he journeyed eastward, obeying the royal summons, and in December, paying his uncle a great honor, the King rode out two miles from Reading to greet him and gave him the kiss of peace with enthusiastic warmth. He even removed John's Lancastrian livery collar of linked S's and placed it about his own neck, symbolizing his intention to be a good lord to the duke and "the good love heartfully felt between them."[75] In return, John would have the King's white hart badge incorporated into his SS collars.[76]

With past differences forgotten, an atmosphere of conciliation pervaded the council meeting the duke attended at Reading on December 10;[77] two days later he was at Westminster, where he received an unexpectedly warm welcome from the Mayor and Corporation of London, before attending services of thanksgiving for his return in Westminster Abbey and St. Paul's Cathedral,[78] where he no doubt paid his respects at Blanche's tomb. By Christmas he was back at Hertford Castle.[79]

On January 21, 1390, John of Gaunt and Thomas of Woodstock were finally appointed to the council.[80] John's return to the political scene in England ushered in an era of greater political stability and order. The King was now happy to place great trust and confidence in him, and anxious to work with him to promote peace with France. He promised his uncle he would listen to good counsel and bestow his patronage more wisely than in the past. For his part, the duke proved moderate and staunchly loyal, acting as a peace broker between the King and the former appellants, and as a buttress to the throne he so honored, slipping effortlessly into the role of elder statesman, "the most sufficient person in the realm."[81] No longer was he so hated by the people, for time had proved their fears of his ambitions groundless. Even Walsingham had nothing but praise for him.

Richard II's desire to retain his uncle's goodwill is evident in the honors he bestowed on him soon after his return: On February 16, 1390, he entailed palatinate powers with the Duchy of Lancaster on John and his heirs in perpetuity,[82] whereas Edward III had granted these powers for life only. And in March, in the face of heated opposition to the duchy being alienated from the Crown, he created John Duke of Aquitaine (or Guienne) for life,[83] the King and Queen themselves ceremonially bestowing the ducal circlets on John and Constance. From now on John would be known as "Monseigneur de Guienne."

With his return to political prominence in England, the duke now sought a London residence of his own. The ruins of the Savoy still lay blackened and stark on the Strand, a reminder to all of what he had lost, and he had no plans to rebuild it. But by 1391, thanks no doubt to the good offices of his friend John Fordham, Bishop of Ely since 1388,[84] he leased Ely Place in the fashionable suburb of Holborn, a property that Katherine Swynford would come to know well, for it was to remain John's London house for the rest of his life.

Since 1286, Ely Place—or the Bishop of Ely's Inn,[85] as it was known—had been the London residence of the Bishops of Ely. It occupied the area between Leather Lane, Charterhouse Street, and what is now Holborn Circus, and thus traversed modern Hatton Garden; it was therefore very conveniently situated for Westminster and the City of London. There had been a building on the site since the sixth century, and parts of the walls that survive today date from the 1100s, being eight feet thick. To the north of the palace site is Bleeding Heart Yard, the name of which has nothing to do with John of Gaunt but commemorates a murder in 1626; and to the west is Ely Court, where lies the Mitre Tavern, founded in 1546. In 1327, John of Gaunt's mother, Philippa of Hainault, had lodged at Ely Place upon her arrival in England.

Rebuilt by Bishop Thomas Arundel between 1373 and 1388 above the remains of the older house, the property leased by John of Gaunt was a large and imposing palace with "commodious rooms"; it was set in extensive gardens that were famous in the fourteenth and fifteenth centuries for their roses and strawberries, the latter mentioned in Shakespeare's *Richard III*; there was also a vineyard. A massive stone gatehouse adorned with the bishop's arms fronted the street.

Within the palace complex (and now adjoining Bleeding Heart Yard) was the bishops' magnificent private chapel, dedicated to the Saxon St. Etheldreda, founded in 1251 and completed around 1300; a Catholic church since the 1870s, it was extensively rebuilt both before and after suffering severe bomb damage during the Second World War, but the crypt, with its massive walls and pillars, stone floor, and original twelfth-century black-beamed ceiling, survives from John of Gaunt's time, as do the east and west thirteenth-century windows, although their glass is modern; it was here that the duke and his household—and Katherine, in time—worshipped. This is all that is left of the great palace.[86]

Opposite Ely Place, in Chancery Lane, was the town house of John Buckingham, Bishop of Lincoln, who knew John of Gaunt and Katherine Swynford well. In 1391 the signatures of the duke and the bishop headed a petition by local residents demanding that Parliament put a stop to the slaughtering of animals and the dumping of offal near their houses.[87] John's brothers, the Dukes of York and Gloucester, visited him at Ely Place in October 1392, when all three received gifts of money from the citizens of London.[88]

Katherine herself is absent from the records dating from the period immediately following John's return to England. She was still renting the Chancery in 1391–92, and remained responsible for Kettlethorpe and

Coleby, so we must presume that she was mainly resident in Lincolnshire at this time. But there is plenty of evidence that the duke was now busying himself with planning the futures of their children, and it would not be surprising if he were in contact with Katherine in this respect at least.

Although John always treated the Beauforts as cherished members of his family circle, he was concerned to ensure that his provision for them did not conflict with the interests of his legitimate heirs and would not make inroads into the Lancastrian inheritance. Instead of creating a land base for his bastards, he was to find other forms of income and preferment for them through careful marriages and the Church, and in this way avoided all cause for jealousy between his various offspring. Indeed, there is much evidence to show that the Beauforts were held in great affection and esteem by their half siblings, and by Henry of Derby in particular. And not only by them, for the King himself—anxious to cement his ties with John of Gaunt, and also, it seems, moved by affection—was to show much favor to his Beaufort cousins.

In January 1390 and January 1391, young Henry Beaufort, who was probably no more than fifteen years old, but was already destined for the Church—a traditional way of providing for bastard sons—was given the respective wealthy prebends of Thame and Sutton in the diocese of Lincoln; in August 1390 he was also assigned the prebend of Riccall in the diocese of York. It was not unheard of for one so young to be granted church offices, and these benefices would have provided for Henry's maintenance and education. "His father the duke sent him to Oxford" to study civil and canon law,[89] and in the academic year 1390–91 he was a scholar at Queen's College, Oxford, having already undertaken some studies at Peterhouse, Cambridge, in 1388–89, when he was only about thirteen. As his later career would prove, he was a precocious child of above average ability and intelligence. The duke took a keen interest in his education, and must have visited him more than once at Queen's College, as a payment in the college accounts of 30s. (£415) "for wine for the Duke of Lancaster" testifies; he also had wine sent to "Master Henry Beaufort" at Oxford.[90] It may have been after his year at Oxford that Henry Beaufort was sent to Aachen in Germany, where he is said to have studied civil and canon law in his youth.[91]

In the spring of 1390, seventeen-year-old John Beaufort—"a great favorite with his father"[92]—was among the thirty English knights who distinguished themselves tilting against the champions of France at the famous international jousts of St. Inglevert near Calais; his father had put his name forward for this the previous November. His half brother Thomas Swynford also took part, and the duke may have nominated him too. They were in company with that passionate jouster Henry of Derby, John Holland, and Henry Percy's heir and namesake, who bore the nickname Hotspur. The English contingent, lauded as "the bravest of all the foreigners," returned home in early May,[93] but only days later Henry of Derby and Thomas Swynford departed for Calais, hell-bent on going to fight the Turks in Tunisia in what was known as the Barbary Crusade. John of Gaunt was in Calais to see them off,[94] but refused safe conduct through France, they decided instead to respond to a call for aid from the Teutonic Knights, who were fighting their own crusade against the heathen of Eastern Europe, and raced back to England to take up what they plainly regarded as a worthier cause.

Katherine, like many medieval mothers, quickly had to accustom herself to her sons going off to fight in foreign parts, for John Beaufort, meanwhile— partly financed by his father[95]—*had* been permitted to travel through France with four knights toward Genoa to join the Barbary Crusade, in which he was to serve under the French Duke of Bourbon; in designating Beaufort leader of the English contingent, Bourbon tacitly acknowledged his high status.[96] In December, after the Christian forces failed to take Al-Mahdiya, near Tunis, young John returned to England to be reunited with his family.

With John of Gaunt in such favor, the fortunes of Geoffrey Chaucer too were in the ascendant. In July 1389, when Richard was urging the duke to return to England, Chaucer had been appointed Clerk of the King's Works, an important post that gave him overall responsibility for improvements to royal property and the building of new royal residences. By 1390 he was supervising a large workforce employed on the restoration of the royal chapel at Windsor Castle; probably in that year his precocious son Lewis was sent up to Oxford, where he may have kept company with his cousin, Henry Beaufort.

By September 1391, Chaucer had been replaced—for reasons we don't know—as Clerk of the King's Works, for at that time we find him serving as deputy forester in the royal park at North Petherton in Somerset (where in 1394–95 his son Thomas was joint petitioner in a lawsuit with his new wife, Maud Burghersh), and probably writing his most famous work, *The Canterbury Tales*, which was almost certainly inspired by the *Decameron* of Boccaccio (from which some of the tales were lifted) and a pilgrimage Chaucer had made to St Thomas à Becket's shrine at Canterbury in 1388. Evidently, he had been in financial difficulties for some time, but in 1394 the King granted him a life pension of £20 (£8,750), which eased matters a little, although he was to apply for advances on his income several times until 1399, which suggests that he continued to struggle to make ends meet. Chaucer remained in his post at North Petherton until at least 1398, and living so far away, it is hardly likely that he had much contact with Katherine Swynford, but in the years to come, John of Gaunt and Henry of Derby were to show favor to him and his son, which may have owed more than a little to her influence.

John of Gaunt accompanied Henry of Derby and Thomas Swynford back to England and said his farewells to them at Hertford Castle. With Mary de Bohun—again pregnant—Henry and his companions rode north to Lincolnshire, where they made offerings in Lincoln Cathedral for the success of their holy venture. It would be surprising if they had not visited, or even lodged with, Katherine Swynford while in Lincoln. Around July 19, 1390, hugely backed by the duke to the tune of £4,000 (£1,607,802), Henry, with Thomas Swynford and a large company of knights, esquires, and servants, took ship from Boston for Prussia and Lithuania.[97] Some weeks later Mary de Bohun gave birth to her fourth son, Humphrey, naming him after her father.

As his son sailed away, John of Gaunt was lavishly entertaining King Richard and Queen Anne to a great hunting party at Leicester Castle, where he strove to bring about a reconciliation between the King and the former Lords Appellant. There is no mention of Katherine or the Beauforts among the many bishops, lords, and ladies described by Knighton as being present, and Christmas that year saw John at Eltham Palace, where the King returned his hospitality.[98]

The following year, however, evidence suggests that Katherine and John had rekindled their relationship. The duke's household check rolls for the year 1391–92 fortunately survive,[99] and they show that all four Beauforts were now intermittently in attendance on him and based in his household; John Beaufort was stabling six horses there. The rolls also reveal that Katherine Swynford was stabling twelve horses at the ducal residences at this time, which not only proves that she and John had renewed their ac-

quaintance, but also strongly suggests that she was again occupying a substantially important place in his life. It shows too that she was well-attended
whenever she came to visit the duke, as became a lady of high standing. The
sum of 12d (£13.82) per day was allocated to her while she was lodging in
his household, compared with 6d (£6.91) each for the Beauforts and 4d
(£4.61) for Henry of Derby. It is unlikely this was for their own keep, but
rather, for that of their horses.

Not that Katherine was residing with John permanently at this time. She
rented the Chancery until at least 1393,[100] and her intermittent presence in
his establishment must have been in part due to her desire to see her children. She would have recognized that it was greatly to their benefit to live in
the household of so great a lord. She had clearly brought them up well, and
perhaps it was decided long before that the Beauforts would come to their
father on his return from his Castilian venture.

Considering that John and Constance were now living apart, that he was
aged beyond his years though not sufficiently to dampen the old Adam in
him, and that they would marry in due course, it is logical to conclude that
he and Katherine had grown close again. Constance's withdrawal left them
free to rekindle their relationship, and it is possible that they had become
lovers once more, although if this was the case, they must have been very discreet about it, for Katherine was openly visiting the duke, attended by an entourage, without attracting adverse comment. Although there is no hint of
scandal in the chronicles, it is clear from what Froissart—an eyewitness at
the court of Richard II—states, that in 1396 people at court were saying
that the duke had married the woman who had been his concubine for
a long time, "inside and outside his marriage," which must mean after it
ended in 1394, since we have established that their liaison began after John
married Constance. Elsewhere, Froissart says that John loved and maintained Katherine after Constance's death. This all strongly suggests that a
sexual relationship between them was regarded as an established fact, and
not only in the distant past. Katherine was now about forty-one, young
enough to bear children but old enough to have passed menopause, so pregnancy might not have been a risk.

Of course, this may be putting too modern an interpretation on their relationship: John had twice publicly repented of his former life, and promised
to God the complete amendment of his ways; and Katherine had not only
accepted his renunciation of their love, but had perhaps bought herself a

papal indulgence by donating funds to his "crusade." This suggests a sincere degree of repentance on both sides. Each of them may have been reluctant to prejudice the state of grace they had reached by backsliding into immorality, and they might well have considered the effect that discovery of a sexual affair might have on their maturing children and their wider families. On the other hand, aristocratic society took a lenient view of extramarital affairs, so any evidence that the duke and Katherine Swynford were once again lovers would probably have been accepted with tolerance in courtly circles. And privately, within the family—and even by the King, whose treatment of Katherine proves he was aware that she was more than the average royal mistress—it may have been known that if the opportunity ever arose, John intended to marry Katherine.

It may also be that the horror John had clearly felt in the aftermath of the Peasants Revolt was now a distant memory. He and Katherine were both heart-free and no longer young. Maybe they decided to seize the chance of happiness while they could. And, so long as discretion was maintained, who could have blamed them?

I n the spring of 1391 the duke was probably at Lincoln—he dated a letter there on March 5, omitting the year, to the ruler of Lithuania, asking him to release two of Henry's knights,[101] so the letter almost certainly belongs to 1391. That same month, he arranged for Gascon wine to be sent to Katherine in Lincoln by cart from London.[102] Perhaps he had visited her at the Chancery and wished to reward her hospitality; perhaps there was more to it than that. He was back at Westminster when Henry of Derby and Thomas Swynford returned from their crusading adventure (and a winter spent enjoying the hospitality of the Teutonic Knights) around April 30; John Beaufort was there to greet them when they disembarked at Hull.[103] It was probably after their return that the duke invited Thomas Swynford to serve him as one of his chamber knights; Thomas's presence in the duke's household is attested to by the surviving check rolls.[104] On May 12, 1393, as a signal mark of royal favor, Richard II would grant an annuity of 100 marks (£15,179) to Thomas and his wife Jane.[105]

As we have seen, John of Gaunt was well aware of the pressing need to make suitable provision for his bastard children, and in December 1390 the King licensed him, along with Sir Thomas Percy and the Lancastrian receiver in Northamptonshire, to grant the manors of Overstone, Maxey, Eydon, and a half share in Brampton Parva[106]—together worth £88 (£35,372) a year—to John Beaufort, with reversion to Thomas and Joan Beaufort. Henry Beaufort's name is missing from the reversions because he was already earmarked for a career in the Church.[107]

John of Gaunt spent the Christmas of 1391 at Hertford, bringing his minstrels with him.[108] Katherine and their daughter Joan were among the guests, as were Henry of Derby and his family; and at New Year, Henry gave gifts to Katherine and Joan. Katherine received a gold ring set with a diamond, and Joan "a pair of paternosters" (rosary beads) of coral and gold.[109] Joan was soon to marry Sir Robert Ferrers, who at nineteen was about four years her senior; the date of their wedding is not known, but it certainly took place by September 30, 1394, and is likely to have been celebrated in 1392, because their daughter Elizabeth is described as being eighteen years old and more in 1411: She had thus been born in 1393 at the latest. Joan also had another daughter, Mary,[110] probably named in honor of Mary de Bohun, whose patronage Joan had long enjoyed. After their wedding, Joan and her husband remained in John of Gaunt's household.[111]

In the spring of 1392, John of Gaunt was at Amiens negotiating with the French king, Charles VI,[112] who hailed him as the most revered knight in Christendom.[113] The duke "took the view that the war had lasted long enough and that a good peace would benefit the whole of Christendom,"[114] but all he could secure was a year's truce. While he was away, Mary de Bohun bore a daughter, Blanche, at Henry of Derby's manor house at Peterborough, a residence she seems to have favored.[115] The duke returned to England in April, and before June, thanks to his influence, John Beaufort was appointed one of the King's household knights, with an income of 100 marks (£13,903) per annum—an acknowledgment of the younger John's proven military expertise.[116] Soon afterward, Henry of Derby departed on another crusade, to Prussia this time,[117] and Henry Beaufort returned to Queen's College, Oxford, where he would complete a degree in theology in the summer of 1393.[118] On November 23, 1392, Constance's pleasure-loving sister, Isabella, Duchess of York, died;[119] she was "buried by the King's command at his manor of Langley, in the friars' church,"[120] where Richard II himself would one day be temporarily laid to rest.

Katherine's lease on the Chancery is known to have run until at least 1393, and she may not have vacated the property until 1396.[121] There is no evidence of her role in the duke's busy life at this time, nor that she was a guest in the Lancastrian household at Christmas 1392. References to her children are rare, but all were comfortably settled by 1393: John in the royal household, Henry at university, Joan married, and Thomas with his father. Further evidence of family solidarity emerged in December of that year, when Henry of Derby—just back from his crusade and a long pilgrimage to the Holy Land—ordered new suits of armor to be sent to Hertford Castle for the use of himself and Thomas Beaufort in the jousts he planned to hold there. The duke joined his family at Hertford for the Christmas festivities of 1393, and this time Katherine Swynford *was* among the company. Henry presented his wife and "Dame Katherine Swynford" with four lengths of luxurious white damask silk, at 78s.4d (£1,778) each.[122] That she was given the same gift—and costly material—as the countess strongly suggests that Katherine was now a very prominent member of the duke's circle.

In January 1394, Henry hastened to London to take part in yet another tournament; in the midst of the excitement, he remembered to send a hamper of fish delicacies to Hertford for Mary,[123] who was pregnant for the seventh time. Katherine also said farewell to John Beaufort, who departed early in 1394 on another crusade in Lithuania and Hungary, during which he is thought to have fought with the Teutonic Knights at the Battle of Lettow. Katherine was living in Lincoln or at Kettlethorpe for at least part of 1394: On February 27, in order to lay claim to his inheritance, Thomas Swynford was required to present proof of age at Lincoln, and Katherine was ordered to be present; she was there one Friday when he and his many witnesses turned up with their evidence, which was sometime between June 22, 1394, and June 22, 1395.[124] After this, Sir Thomas apparently took possession of his manors and established himself at Kettlethorpe; his mother Katherine would nevertheless remain in control there, for Thomas was often absent in the service of the House of Lancaster.

In the Hilary Parliament of 1394, John of Gaunt found himself the object of vitriolic criticism by the abrasive Earl of Arundel, who was jealous of his influence with the King. It was contrary to the King's honor for him to be often seen walking arm in arm with the duke, Arundel complained, and to wear the Lancastrian livery collar; furthermore, he said, the duke had so intimidated the lords with "rough and bitter words" that they were now afraid to speak up in council or Parliament; and the King should not have alienated Aquitaine from his uncle nor given him money to invade Castile. Arundel had hoped to play on the King's vanity by implying that the monarch was the duke's client, but a "grieved and displeased" Richard spoke up vigorously for his uncle and forced Arundel to apologize publicly to him—after which Parliament declared the duke free from any cause for blame, and Arundel, who had received no support from the other nobles, retired to sulk in private.[125] Afterward, John of Gaunt, clearly fearing that his integrity and loyalty had been impugned, wrote to the King: "I dare to call God to witness, and all loyal men, that never have I imagined, or tried to do, anything against your most honorable estate."[126]

Following his sons' departure, John also left England that spring: In March 1394 he went to France, where, on March 27, he concluded a four-year truce with the French.[127] He was therefore out of the country when Duchess Constance died on March 24 at Leicester Castle,[128] leaving him a free man.

NINE

My Dearest Lady Katherine

I t is unlikely that John of Gaunt had gone to France earlier in the month knowing that his wife was dying. There is no indication that Constance suffered a long illness—she was at a hunting party and festive gathering at Much Hadham in July 1393[1]—and in those days even a virus could prove fatal.[2] Moreover, her funeral was delayed until July so the duke could attend it; after signing a peace treaty at Leulighen on March 24,[3] the day of her death, he was obliged to remain in France until late June.

The year 1394 was to witness the tragic deaths of three royal ladies in quick succession, although "the grief of all these deaths by no means equaled that of the King," for on June 7, at Sheen, Queen Anne died of the plague, plunging Richard II—who had loved her "even to madness"[4]—into such all-consuming grief that he was to order that the wing of the palace in which she had breathed her last be razed to the ground.[5] Then, on July 4,[6] just ten days after John of Gaunt's return to England, and a month after she had borne her seventh child—a daughter called Philippa—Mary de Bohun passed away at Peterborough, at only twenty-six, possibly a victim of puerperal fever. Katherine Swynford may have been in attendance on her during her last weeks, and the loss of her young patroness must have caused her considerable grief.

Meanwhile, John of Gaunt had traveled north to Leicester to attend Constance's burial before the high altar in the collegiate church of St. Mary in the Newarke at Leicester, and a hasty decision was made to have Mary interred there the next day in the choir,[7] while all the mourners were gathered; these obsequies took place with great ceremony, and at staggering expense, totaling £584.5s.9d (£255,621),[8] on July 5 and 6, just days after Mary had died.[9]

It has been suggested that Constance was buried at Leicester because the duke neither wanted her to lie beside him for eternity nor considered that she merited a great state funeral; yet he did not choose to be buried with his beloved Katherine Swynford either, while the cost of Constance's obsequies and her interment in the established mausoleum of the House of Lancaster strongly suggests that John wanted every honor paid to the memory of the woman who—whatever tensions had lain between them—had been his duchess for twenty-two years.

Having received two salutary reminders of the frailty of human life, John of Gaunt soon afterward ordered alabaster effigies of himself and Blanche of Lancaster for their tomb in St. Paul's Cathedral, and he was to raise "a tomb of marble with an image of brass like a queen on it" for his "dear companion, Dame Constance."[10] He also, in his will of 1399, arranged for an obit to be celebrated every year on the anniversary of her death in perpetuity, for the safety of her soul.[11] In 1413, Henry V commissioned an effigy of his mother, Mary de Bohun, from a London coppersmith, which would lie on her marble tomb.[12]

The third royal funeral was somewhat more dramatic. At the end of July, when Queen Anne was buried with great pomp in Westminster Abbey, the Earl of Arundel, still smarting after his forced apology to John of Gaunt, had the insolence to turn up late, provoking an outraged Richard II to strike him in the face and draw blood, thereby desecrating the sanctity of the church, which had to be reconsecrated before the funeral could continue. Arundel was committed to the Tower for several weeks, then made to swear an oath guaranteeing his future loyalty *and* pay the King a large indemnity.[13]

John of Gaunt prudently went north; on August 24 he was with his grieving family at Pontefract, and the following day, having heard to his dismay that there were people at court questioning his own loyalty to the

King—and mindful that Richard's temper was on a short fuse—he wrote him a letter protesting his loyalty.[14] This evidently paid off, for in September the King confirmed him as Duke of Aquitaine, which meant that John would have to go there without delay, in order to enforce the royal authority and look after his interests in the duchy. Immediately he began assembling his retinue at Leicester, prior to sailing from Plymouth early in October.

John Beaufort was going with him[15]—it is possible that, around this time, the duke planned to create a new fief for the young man in Aquitaine, although this was not to remain a viable prospect for long[16]—and Katherine was no doubt bracing herself for another prolonged parting from John, and from their son. Silva-Vigier suggests that she actually accompanied the duke to Aquitaine on this occasion, but there is no evidence or comment in the chronicles or official records to support this theory, which there surely would have been had she gone. The fact that the Chancery was not leased to the new chancellor until after 1396, and that alternative accommodation had to be found in 1391–92, strongly suggests that Katherine was still living there during the duke's absence in 1394–95.

By the time he left for Aquitaine, John had probably made up his mind to marry Katherine Swynford. The text of a letter from Pope Boniface IX dated September 1, 1396, makes it clear that "when Constance, of blessed memory, had come to the end of her life, Duke John and Katherine, desiring to marry," had applied for a dispensation, which was necessary because of the compaternity created by John long ago acting as godfather to Katherine's daughter.[17] This reads as if the approach to the Pope had been made as soon after the death of the duchess as was decent, and also suggests that John had already resolved to marry Katherine as soon as he was free to do so; this would in part explain the esteem in which she had been held by his family and the King, and may also have been why Katherine had never remarried. Armitage-Smith thought that the duke may have inquired even before Constance died if there were impediments to his marrying Katherine, although that is unlikely, as Constance's death seems to have been rather sudden. Any inquiries were probably made after her demise.

According to Pope Boniface, the couple, "being not unaware that John had lifted from the font a daughter of the same Katherine, begotten by another man, and that later the same Duke John adulterously knew the same Katherine, she being free of wedlock, but with marriage still existing between the same Duke John and the aforesaid Constance, and begot offspring of her; and believing that marriage between them was now allowable because, the impediment of the aforesaid compaternity not being notorious but rather occult," sent a petitioner (whose name is unknown) to the Holy See to obtain the necessary dispensation. The Pope obligingly delivered to this petitioner a brief, "signed by our own hand, and containing therein a declaration of our having given our consent in this matter by word of mouth."[18] Because the impediment was not notorious, Boniface had felt it necessary to give only an oral dispensation. The "credential brief" in which it was enshrined does not survive, and there is no record of the date when it was issued. Given the time it would have taken for the petitioner to travel from England to Rome, where the legitimist Papacy was now based, the delays that may have been encountered in obtaining the brief (although the Pope would not have wished to inconvenience his staunch supporter, the Duke of Lancaster, too greatly), and the fact that the marriage did not take place until January 1396, the dispensation might not have been applied for until a year had elapsed since Constance's death, and the marriage been further delayed by John setting his affairs in order in Aquitaine: he did not return to England until December 1395. This is not to say that marrying Katherine was not a priority with John, just that before he could proceed he had to wait for a decent interval to pass after Constance's death, for the Pope to act, and to meet his own obligations.

It was virtually unheard of at that time for a royal duke to marry his mistress, especially one who was the daughter of a humble foreign knight, and John could have been in no doubt that the union would prove highly controversial. Twice he had entered into wedlock for political reasons: once successfully, the other time far less so. Even now, at fifty-five, and old by contemporary standards, he was an eligible prize in the European marriage market, and could easily have made a political alliance that favored his cherished peace process with France, or an advantageous union with an heiress that would have handsomely augmented the Lancastrian domains. That he did not pursue such alliances speaks volumes. Instead, he was resolved to make the unusual, highly unconventional, and indeed brave choice of marrying for love. There can be little doubt that his feelings for Katherine played a large part in his decision—Froissart says he "had always loved and maintained this Lady Katherine," and the settlements that he was to make on her during their marriage are ample evidence of his feelings for her.

But there was more to it than that. "From affection to [their] children, the duke married their mother," Froissart adds, making it seem as if Katherine did not come into the equation, although the chronicler may have drawn this conclusion himself, unable, along with many other people, to comprehend that the mighty Duke of Lancaster had so far forgotten himself as to marry for love. Yet love for Katherine aside, John's desire to see the Beauforts legitimized was surely a powerful enough motive for marrying her, and perhaps just as important to the duke. They were now growing up and proving themselves able and gifted, and he must have wanted them to enjoy the high offices of Church and state for which their royal blood befit them and he'd had them educated; and he perhaps also had a view to forging advantageous noble alliances through them. Also, in the wake of that series of tragic deaths, he may have felt the hand of time upon him; fifty-four and—as we have seen—aged beyond his years, although he must have been reasonably fit because he was contemplating going crusading against the Turks in distant lands. Nevertheless, he perhaps felt an impulsion to seize whatever happiness he could while he could still enjoy life, *and* secure his children's future before he died. These things, Katherine and the children, were clearly so important to him that he was prepared to brave public opinion to have his desire.

No doubt with this aim in mind, John made provision for his eldest son by Katherine, and for the Chaucers, probably before he went abroad. It was possibly in 1394, and certainly before September 28, 1397, that John Beaufort was married to Margaret Holland, daughter of Thomas Holland, Earl of Kent, the son of the late Princess Joan by her first husband; Margaret was therefore a niece of the King, and she had been born about 1381–85. By 1395, in order to provide for the young couple, the duke had purchased for John Beaufort the reversion of the manors of Curry Rivel, Langport, and Martock in Somerset.[19]

Around the same time, John made a gift of 20 marks (£2,917) to Thomas Chaucer, doubled his pension to £20 (£8,750), and paid £100 (£43,749) to secure his marriage to a wealthy heiress, Maud, the daughter of Sir John Burghersh of Ewelme; she came from a respected baronial family and brought him large estates in Surrey and Oxfordshire.[20] Such lavish generosity toward Katherine's nephew indicates not only a desire to please her, but also a genuine appreciation of Thomas Chaucer's worth. Nor was Thomas's father Geoffrey, still ensconced in the wilds of Somerset, forgotten, for it was during this year of 1394–95 that Henry of Derby sent him a grant of money and a fur-lined scarlet robe.

Summoned by the King, who wanted the duke's support for the French marriage alliance that Thomas of Woodstock was so hotly opposing, John of Gaunt,[21] armed with the Pope's brief, returned to England in December 1395. He was no longer feeling in the best of health, and the crossing from Calais to Kent must have been disagreeable for him, even painful: for when, late in November, he had visited Brittany and opened ultimately unsuccessful negotiations for a marriage between his grandson, Henry of Monmouth, and Duke John de Montfort's daughter, he declined an invitation to attend the wedding, as "it will be very hard-going and very uncomfortable to him to sail."[22] This suggests he was suffering some bodily infirmity at this time, possibly the recurrent malady to which he was to refer in 1398, which may be one reason why he made a short pilgrimage to the shrine of St. Thomas à Becket at Canterbury upon returning to England, no doubt to give thanks for his safe return home, pray for relief for his complaint, and ask the saint's blessing on his coming marriage.

John was still in Canterbury at the beginning of January 1396; his son Henry sent him nineteen ells of velvet there as a New Year gift.[23] He left soon afterward for Langley, Hertfordshire, to pay his respects to Richard II and seek his permission to marry Katherine Swynford. More than twenty years later, Walsingham claimed that the marriage came as a surprise to the King, but as his foremost subject, it is hardly likely that John of Gaunt, that great traditionalist and pillar of the monarchy, would have omitted his feudal obligation to obtain royal sanction for the marriage to go ahead. It is also doubtful that the duke's request came as a surprise to Richard, who apparently readily gave his consent.[24] His manner toward his uncle, however, although cordial, was noticeably cool and, some said, "without love."[25] He wanted John's backing, it was true, but he did not want him dominating political affairs as before. This change in Richard marked the beginning of the end of John's political influence, which would now slowly but steadily decline; his health, of course, could also have been a factor. Nevertheless, John was to maintain a constant presence at court in the coming years, and would witness every royal charter up till July 1398.[26]

Katherine herself must have been in Lincolnshire at this time, probably living at the Chancery, although she was still exercising authority as the Lady of Kettlethorpe—on December 4 she presented a new rector to the parish church there. This was none other than John Huntman, Chancellor of Lincoln Cathedral, who had to seek alternative accommodation in 1391–92 because Katherine was in possession of his official residence, the Chancery. In appointing him Rector of Kettlethorpe, was Katherine attempting to compensate in some way for the inconvenience she had caused?

John did not delay long at court. Having obtained the King's permission to depart, he set off north to Lincolnshire, to Katherine, to make her his wife without further delay. They "publicly contracted marriage"[27] very soon after the Octave of the Epiphany,[28] which fell on January 13, 1396—possibly their wedding took place the next day,[29] or even as late as February,[30] though this is far less likely. The ceremony in Lincoln Cathedral was probably conducted before the splendid chancel screen by the aging Bishop Buckingham, who is known to have been in Lincoln later that month.[31] Evidently, John's health had improved, for, as he and Katherine later confided to the Pope, their marriage was consummated "by carnal copulation."[32] There can be no doubt that they were lovers once more.

Katherine was now the Duchess of Lancaster, and in the absence of a queen, the first lady in the land—a position she could not expect to enjoy for long, because the coming spring would see the signing of a new peace with France that was to be cemented by the marriage of Richard II to Charles VI's six-year-old daughter, Isabella.

Katherine's feelings at this time may only be imagined. They must have encompassed love and gratitude with regard to the man who was now her husband, and perhaps a sense of relief that the long years of self-denial, steadfastness, waiting, and uncertainty were over—not to mention triumph and elation at having come to a safe harbor at last, and at making such a spectacular marriage in the process, something no other royal mistress of that age—and only a privileged few in other periods—would ever achieve. She was set up for life, and would never again have to worry about financial security.[33] There was also the comforting knowledge that the way was now clear for her Beaufort children to be formally legitimized, and that their futures were secure—as indeed were those of Thomas Swynford and Katherine's Chaucer relatives.

But Katherine must also have been aware that society at large might not view her as the most suitable wife for the duke. Notoriety and a tarnished reputation had never been desirable qualities in royal wives; moreover, John was a prince of the highest rank and renown, and could have advantageously made a grand marriage for profit or policy; that he should stoop to marry a woman of far lower degree, however highly regarded she was by his family, was unthinkable. But he had defied convention and done so, and now here she was, exalted above all other women in the realm.

In order to emphasize her royal status, and perhaps at the same time hopefully to obliterate memories of her immoral past, Katherine assumed as her coat of arms the three gold wheels of St. Katherine, her patron saint, who was strongly associated with royalty, virtue, and erudition in the popular imagination. These wheels were blazoned on a red shield, and they would have been prominently displayed on hangings, trappings, furnishings, clothing, and livery badges. They appeared in profusion on the vestments she was to give to Lincoln Cathedral, and also adorned her tomb there,[34] while the image of St. Katherine appears in the *Beaufort Hours*, a manuscript commissioned after 1401 by John Beaufort, who clearly wanted to honor his mother and associate her memory with the saint.[35] The conversion of the silver Roët wheels into gold Katherine wheels suggests both a deep devotion to her name saint and a conscious effort on the part of the new duchess to construct a far more respectable public image for herself.[36]

It is highly likely that the duke was also involved in this medieval version of "spin doctoring," or was even the inspiration behind it. After all, he had a vested interest in the heraldic emblems of the Lancastrian inheritance and in the way people regarded his wife, whose character and demeanor reflected on his own nobility and honor; at the very least, Katherine would have had to consult him on this matter and seek his approval—married women in the Middle Ages enjoyed little autonomy, even if they had become used to making their own decisions during a long widowhood, as Katherine clearly had. One may infer from the sources quoted in this chapter, however, that John was a loving husband eager to make his lady happy. It may be that it was he who, after their marriage, arranged for the reburial of her father in St. Paul's Cathedral, or for the erection of a memorial tablet on Sir Paon de Roët's existing grave there.

It was to Katherine's advantage that "she had a perfect knowledge of court etiquette, because she had been brought up in princely courts continually since her youth"; this made her eminently well-qualified for her new rank,[37] and it would have given her confidence as she came to grips with the realities of her new status.

The newly wedded duke and duchess made a short trip up north together before facing the court; possibly John wished to test the water by taking Katherine on a tour of his domains. By January 23 they were lodging at Pontefract, a place that might have held bitter but long-exorcised memories for them, but clearly became a favored retreat during their marriage. High on its escarpment, the castle enjoyed commanding views of the River Aire; the royal lodgings were in the turreted trefoil-shaped donjon, which the duke had heightened twenty years earlier so it dwarfed all the other towers. Here, he and Katherine would have resided in great comfort and luxury, for he had lavished huge sums of money on the place.[38]

By March 10 they had moved northwestward to Rothwell Castle, a thirteenth-century royal hunting lodge owned by the duke, which lay hard by his manor of Leeds. They stayed there until March 31,[39] before traveling south.

It may have been at this time—it was certainly in 1396—that they broke their journey at Coventry, where they were admitted as members of the prosperous Guild of the Holy Trinity, St. Mary, St. John the Baptist, and St. Katherine. The ceremony either took place in St. Mary's Guild Hall (constructed between 1340 and 1460) in the heart of the town, or at the guild's chapel in the collegiate church dedicated to St. John the Baptist, which had been founded by John's grandmother, Queen Isabella, the widow of Edward II; in 1344, she gave land in Coventry to the Guild of St. John for the founding of the chapel. This Guild had later amalgamated with those of St. Katherine and Holy Trinity. Since their patron saints were both represented, John and Katherine would have felt a special affinity with this guild.[40]

The new duchess made her debut at court sometime in April, probably at the St. George's Day celebrations, for she was issued with Garter robes that year. Her appearance, and the announcement of her marriage to the duke, gave rise to stunned shock and widespread disapproval, for most people regarded it as a disastrous misalliance:[41] "the wedding caused many a man's wondering for, as it was said, he had held her long before."[42]

"Everyone was amazed at the miracle of this event," wrote Walsingham with some irony, "since the fortune of such a woman in no way matched a magnate of such exalted rank." Froissart says the marriage "caused much astonishment," in France as well as in England, "for she was of humble birth, far unmeet to match with his Highness, and nothing comparable in honor to his two former wives, the Duchess Blanche and Duchess Constance," while he was the richest, most powerful, and most eligible catch in the land. In the fifteenth century the chronicler John Capgrave recalled how the duke had married Katherine "against the opinion of many men." Even in our own time such a marriage would cause comment. "Men of title and privilege simply do not marry their mistresses," observed the late Queen Mother, so we may imagine how much greater an outcry the union of John and Katherine provoked in 1396.

"When the news of this marriage reached the great ladies of England, such as the Duchess of Gloucester, the Countess of Derby [sic; Mary de Bohun had, of course, died in 1394], the Countess of Arundel [a Mortimer, and a descendant of Edward III] and other ladies with royal blood in their veins, they were surprised and shocked, considering it scandalous, and thought the duke much to blame. They said that he had sadly disgraced himself by marrying his concubine, a woman of light character"—for such they apparently still perceived Katherine to be. Many thought John of Gaunt a fool, including perhaps Chaucer, who was the same age: Around this time, in a poem dedicated to his friend Henry Scogan, he wrote that he was beginning to see himself as beyond the age for love and marriage. What, then, did he think of the duke?

What rankled most with the great ladies was that the new Duchess of Lancaster would take precedence before them. "Since she has got so far," they sniffed, "it will mean that she will rank as the second lady in England, and the young queen will be dishonorably accompanied by her." But they were plotting their revenge. "For their parts, they would leave her to do the honors of the court by herself," they declared, "for they would never enter any place where she was. They themselves might be disgraced if they permitted a woman of so base a birth, and concubine to the duke for a very long time, inside and outside his marriage with the Princess Constance, to have place before them. Their hearts would burst with vexation, and rightly so!"[43]

The two people who were the most incensed and "outrageous" about the marriage were Thomas of Woodstock, Duke of Gloucester, "a man of an high mind and a stout stomach" who "misliked his brother matching so meanly" and considered him "a doting fool," and Thomas's wife, Eleanor de Bohun. "They considered that the Duke of Lancaster had overstepped all bounds when he took his concubine to wife, and said they would never recognize her marriage, or call her lady or sister." However, John's other brother, Edmund of Langley, "soon got over it, for he was most often in the company of the King"—who, we may infer, supported the marriage—"and his brother of Lancaster. The Duke of Gloucester was of different stuff, for he respected no one's opinions."[44]

To make matters worse, by means that are not recorded, the existence of an impediment to the marriage—that of compaternity—somehow became "publicly known," and because John and Katherine could produce "no apostolic letters authorizing its dispensation"—they had been given only an oral brief, not a full dispensation—they became "apprehensive" that their marriage could "very likely be impugned, and an annulment follow, and grave scandals arise therefrom." They therefore "made humble supplication" once more to Pope Boniface, "that we deign of our apostolic benignity to provide for them concerning the aforesaid" and pronounce on the legitimacy of their children.[45] They must then have spent many anxious months awaiting his reply, and hoping that no English bishop would see fit in the meantime to inquire into the validity of their union.

Richard II, however, was welcoming to Katherine; it was he who had issued her with Garter robes so she could participate in the St. George's Day ceremonies. After those were completed, the duke and duchess moved to London, where they probably took up residence at Ely Place. There, on May 16, John assigned Katherine the generous sum of £600 (£243,620) per annum, to be paid by his Receiver-General, for the expenses of her wardrobe,[46] obviously anticipating that his new duchess would dress herself and furnish her apartments as lavishly as her rank merited. Like John's previous wives, Katherine had her own separate wardrobe and household; we know nothing of its composition, however, or the names of her officers and ladies.[47]

In June the King granted his uncle a charter of liberties for the Duchy of Lancaster, and proposed that his future queen's sister, Michelle of Valois, be married to John's grandson, Henry of Monmouth.[48] Richard also supported

John in forbidding Henry of Derby to brave the dangers of a campaign in Friesland with the Duke of Gueldres.[49]

John's worsening health may account for his fears for the safety of his heir, who had been on perilous expeditions in the past, some financed by his father;[50] yet his anxiety did not apparently extend to his younger son, John Beaufort, who went crusading against the Turks in Hungary and Bulgaria in 1396, and in September was present at the siege of Nicopolis, a campaign that ended in the mass capture and slaughter of the Christian army and left Bulgaria under Muslim domination for five centuries. John Beaufort, fortunately, came home to tell the tale.

Before long the storm that followed upon her marriage abated and Katherine became accepted at court and within the royal family. This probably had a lot to do with Richard II's support and his improving relations with John of Gaunt, but it was undoubtedly due in no small part to Katherine's own personal qualities, her discretion and dignity, and her well-bred understanding of how to conduct herself as a duchess. "The lady herself was a woman of such bringing up and honorable demeanor that envy could not but in the end give place to well-deserving."[51] Above all, "she loved the Duke of Lancaster and the children she had with him, and she showed it."[52] None could have impugned her sincerity.

In July 1396, with the conclusion of the new treaties between England and France, preparations were set in train at last for the King's marriage to Isabella of Valois. Early in August, John apparently went to Calais with the King for a meeting with the Duke of Burgundy, returning to England by July 23.[53] Sometime before Michaelmas, perhaps at Katherine's request, the duke arranged for two pipes of wine to be conveyed from London to Barking Abbey and given to her daughter, Margaret Swynford;[54] and before September 15 he took Katherine to St. Albans Abbey to visit Abbot Thomas de la Mare, who was dying after ten years of chronic ill health brought on by an attack of the plague.[55] The abbot had been a friend of the Black Prince and the exiled King John II of France, and would have shared many memories with John of Gaunt.[56] The purpose of the visit was no doubt to ask for his blessing and say a sad farewell. Later that month the duke and duchess were at Hertford Castle, where they had probably been lodging for most of the month.

Meanwhile, on September 1, in Rome, Boniface IX had pronounced their marriage valid:

> We therefore, who freely seek the peace and tranquillity and health of mind of all Christ's faithful, especially of those who are illustrious because of sublime dignity, desiring to avoid such scandals to the extent that we can under God, and wishing salubriously to provide otherwise for the abovementioned circumstances, being inclined to such supplications, we ratify, approve and confirm by apostolic authority the aforesaid marriage contracted between John and Katherine, and we reinforce it by the protection of the present document.

He then proceeded to pronounce on the legitimacy of their children:

> And so that the same John and Katherine may freely and licitly remain in the said marriage contracted between them, the impediment and other matters described above completely notwithstanding, we dispense them through the same authority by the tenor of the present letters, declaring legitimate offspring received and to be received from this marriage.

This clearly refers to the Beauforts and to any other children that might be born to the couple—obviously the Pope had no idea that Katherine was about forty-six and highly unlikely to become pregnant again. But he had provided for that contingency anyway, and he concluded his letter with the warning that anyone presuming to question the validity of the marriage would incur the "indignation of Almighty God."[57] That, of course, was sufficient to silence any critics, and John and Katherine would doubtless have been relieved to receive this dispensation. It may have arrived in England before they left for France, which was shortly after October 7.

The King having already crossed the Channel, Henry of Derby and Joan Beaufort accompanied their father and Katherine when they traveled to Calais in October. On October 27, at a lavish ceremony near the town attended by much pomp and pageantry (the wedding celebrations were rumored to have cost Richard £200,000, more than £81 million in today's values), the two kings met; Charles VI had already experienced attacks of the madness that was to blight his life and reign, but he was enjoying a lucid interval on this occasion, and cordial pleasantries were exchanged.

On October 28, with John and Katherine and a host of other lords and ladies looking on, little Isabella was carried to her father's pavilion and formally handed over by Charles VI to her bridegroom, who thanked him "for so gracious and honorable a gift" and kissed the little girl. He then "commended her to the Duchesses of Lancaster and Gloucester"—the senior royal ladies—"and the Countesses of Huntingdon and Stafford and other ladies," including Joan Beaufort, who all received her with great joy before escorting her to Calais in twelve packed chariots.[58] Evidently the Duchess of Gloucester had abandoned her resolve to have nothing to do with Katherine, while the latter's prominent role in the ceremonies demonstrates how quickly she was accepted by the establishment and how respectable she had become.

The little queen had already been assigned a French *gouvernante*, Lady de Coucy,[59] who took charge of her and was her sole companion in her richly appointed chariot on that ride to Calais. Of course, Katherine was one of the chief ladies in attendance on Isabella and would have joined the other noble ladies in assisting the bride in her wedding preparations. But her association with Isabella was not limited to that, for Froissart, well-informed about events at Richard II's court at this time, later stated that she "had been sometime the companion of the young Queen of England," and that she remained so until the late summer of 1397. She evidently took on this role at the time of Isabella's marriage, and her influence would have been invaluable during the period immediately following it, when the court was traveling back to England and Isabella was being initiated into her new position. Who better to act as her companion and mentor than the Duchess of Lancaster, the second lady in the land, with her experience of looking after royal princesses and who was clearly good with children?

Katherine, along with her daughter Joan Beaufort, the Duchess of Gloucester, and the Countess of Huntingdon, was given a gold livery collar to wear at the royal wedding.[60] A heavy chain denoting rank, worn to proclaim the wearer's affiliation to some king or great lord, it might have been adorned with the Lancastrian SS links, but more likely was bestowed by the King and incorporated his white hart emblem and perhaps fleurs-de-lis in honor of the bride.

On November 4, in the church of St. Nicholas at Calais, Isabella was married to Richard II by Thomas Arundel, the new Archbishop of Canterbury; she was then not quite seven years old, and not a little precocious—

"it was pretty to see her, young as she was, practicing how to act the queen."[61] The ceremony was followed by sumptuous feasting.

The King and Queen (her dolls packed away with her trousseau) and all their party, including John and Katherine, crossed back to Dover in November, the voyage taking just three hours. They dined and slept at Dover Castle the first night, then made their way toward London via Canterbury, Rochester, Dartford, and Eltham, where the duke and duchess and the other lords and ladies presented costly gifts to Isabella before taking their leave of the royal couple and hastening ahead to make ready for the young queen's state entry into London.

On November 13, Isabella made her way in triumph to the Tower, and on the following day was ceremoniously conducted to the King at Westminster; such were the crowds in the capital that nine people were crushed to death.[62] It appears she was never crowned—a summons to her coronation on Epiphany Sunday 1397 survives,[63] and an unreliable London chronicle states she was crowned on January 8,[64] but there is no other evidence for such a momentous event. John and Katherine entertained her at their London "hostel"—Ely Place—probably late in 1396 or early in 1397, the duke presenting her with a massive gold cup and basin, while Katherine gave her a much smaller cup, more suitable for a child to use.[65] Isabella spent most of what was to prove a short married life in the care of Lady de Coucy at Windsor Castle or Eltham Palace, indulgently treated by her husband, of whom she became inordinately fond.

Papal confirmation of the marriage of John and Katherine not only ended all the nasty rumors and backbiting, but also had an enormously beneficial impact on the lives of the Beauforts. Joan Beaufort had recently been widowed—her husband, Robert Ferrers, died sometime between May 1395 and November 1396—and she was evidently now viewed as a highly desirable bride, for in November 1396, probably as soon as her parents returned to England, the powerful northern baron, Ralph Neville, sixth Baron of Raby, married her as his second wife. John of Gaunt, clearly pleased to have the thirty-two-year-old Neville as a son-in-law and ally, settled a handsome annuity of £206.13s.4d (£89,914) on the couple for life.[66] Neville's estates were in Durham and Yorkshire, and Joan was to make her home there. His first wife, Margaret Stafford, who had died in June of that year, bore him twelve children, so Joan, at just nineteen, became stepmother to a sizable family on her marriage; yet those children, as will be seen, would have little cause to love her in the future.

It was probably at the request of John of Gaunt that in January 1397 the Pope issued a bull appointing Henry Beaufort the Dean of Wells Cathedral in Somerset, launching the twenty-year-old cleric on what was to prove a spectacular and meteoric career in the Church. John also pressed the King, with whom he was now on the best of terms, and who was desirous of his continuing support against the war lobby, to regularize the position of the Beauforts, and on February 6, "yielding to the prayers of your father," Richard issued Letters Patent formally legitimizing them in law:

> To our most dear cousins, the noble men, John the knight, Henry the clerk, Thomas the young gentleman, and to our beloved damsel the noble Joan Beaufort, the most dear relatives of our uncle, the noble John, Duke of Lancaster, born our lieges, greeting, and the favour of our royal majesty. Whilst internally considering how incessantly and with what honours we are graced by the very useful and sincere affection of our aforesaid uncle, and by the wisdom of his counsel, we think it proper and fit that, for the sake of his merits, and in contemplation of his favours, we should enrich you (who are endowed by Nature with great probity and honesty of life and behaviour, and are begotten of royal blood, and by the divine gift are adorned with many virtues) with the strength of our royal prerogative of favour and grace.[67]

It was a gesture calculated to ensure the duke's continuing friendship and loyalty, for the Pope's brief legitimizing the Beauforts, although morally satisfactory, carried no weight under the laws of inheritance in England: It was purely a spiritual expunging of the stain of bastardy, and could not lift the legal bar to them inheriting lands or titles. What was required was an Act of Parliament confirming their legitimacy in common law, and this Richard secured.[68]

The King's Letters Patent were read out on February 6, 1397, in Parliament by Thomas Arundel, Archbishop of Canterbury;[69] then, on February, it appears that a "mantle ceremony" was performed in the Parliament chamber, with the duke and duchess and their four offspring standing together beneath a mantle known as a "care cloth"; normally, when the single parents of bastards married, they and their children stood under the care cloth during the wedding ceremony. Even so, only the Church recognized them as legitimate; feudal inheritances were strictly safeguarded from bastard interlopers, and under English common law, until 1920, "mantle" children could not inherit property. In the case of the Beauforts, the care cloth was used symbolically,[70] while an act—unique in English history—was passed confirming their legitimization and declaring them fully capable in law of inheriting "whatsoever dignities, honors, preeminences, status, ranks and offices, public and private, perpetual and temporal, feudal and noble, there may be, as fully, freely, and lawfully as if you were born in lawful wedlock."[71]

Being formally declared legitimate facilitated the full acceptance of the Beauforts into the royal house, removed all barriers to their preferment in the peerage and the Church, and further improved their prospects—literally overnight in the case of the chivalrous John Beaufort: On February 10 the King created him Earl of Somerset, girding him with the sword and placing on his shoulders a cloak of velvet, "a garment of honour."[72] That April, John Beaufort would be made a Knight of the Garter. Formerly, he had borne a shield of blue and white (the Lancastrian livery colors, and now his own too) differenced by the red bend sinister of bastardy charged with the arms of Lancaster; now he took for his arms the quartered leopards and lilies of England with a segmented border in blue and white. It was probably at this time too that he adopted the famous portcullis badge that would later feature so prominently in Tudor heraldry.[73] Katherine, the herald's daughter, must have felt wonderfully gratified to see her children legitimized and her son a belted earl. The wits of Richard II's court, however, derisively referred to the Beauforts as "Fairborn," an interpretation of their name that was still being used ironically a century later,[74] proof that the taint of bastardy still clung to the family. Notwithstanding this, the legitimization of the Beauforts was to have massive implications for the future of the monarchy, and indeed for the history of England itself.

The next day, February 11, the King licensed John of Gaunt to settle a jointure on Katherine, namely the estates he had received from the Crown in 1372 in exchange for the earldom of Richmond. These lay mainly in Yorkshire, Norfolk, and Sussex, and comprised the honors, castles, and manors of Knaresborough and Tickhill, and the wapentake (hundred) of Staincliffe, all in Yorkshire; the hundreds of North Greenhoe, North and South Erpingham and Smithdon, in Norfolk; 200 marks (£23,601) annual rent from

St. Mary's Abbey, York; the castle, manor, and free chase of the High Peak in Derbyshire; the manors of Gringley and Wheatley in Nottinghamshire, of which Katherine was already in possession; the manors of Willingdon and Maresfield in Sussex, Wighton, Aylsham, Fakenham, and Snettisham in Norfolk, and those of Glatton and Holme in Cambridgeshire; Pevensey Castle and adjoining land in Sussex; Ashdown free chase and the bailiwick of Endlewick in Sussex; the advowsons of St. Robert of Knaresborough and Tickhill; the free chapels of Castleton (High Peak), Maresfield, and Pevensey Castle; and the priories of Wilmington and Withyam, both in Sussex.[75]

Katherine was to hold all these properties for the term of her life, to ensure that she was securely provided for in the event of her being left a widow. On her death they would revert to the heirs of the duke's body, and not therefore to the Beauforts, thus preserving the Lancastrian inheritance intact.

Furthermore, during this year of 1397, John also arranged for some of that great inheritance to be held jointly by him and Katherine during their lives, a gesture that can only be viewed as a mark of his love and respect for her, and proof that their marriage was more than just a means of legitimizing their children.[76]

With her jointure settled, the duchess left court with the duke and traveled north to Pontefract once more. They were there on March 17, 1397, but had returned to London by April 15,[77] after perhaps having been present when Henry Beaufort was ordained as a deacon around April 3 -7.[78] That month, Henry achieved the accolade of being appointed Chancellor of Oxford University.[79]

The fortunes of Thomas Beaufort were also advanced at this time. On July 6, 1397, he was retained for life by the King with an annuity of 100 marks (£11,801),[80] and by November of that year he had married Margaret, daughter of Sir Thomas Neville of Hornby and niece of Joan Beaufort's husband, Ralph Neville. She was then living in Katherine's household with a governess, and considered too young as yet to cohabit with her husband.[81]

Some writers assert that Katherine's daughter, Margaret Swynford, the nun at Barking, had died by 1397, for she is not listed among the sisters who took vows of obedience that year to the new abbess in the presence of the Bishop of London, but she was still very much alive, for in 1419 she herself was elected Abbess of Barking, and in fact she survived until 1433, dying around the ripe age of seventy. Carvings of the names of Henry and Thomas Beaufort (with the date 1430) on surviving fragments of masonry from Barking Abbey, recorded in 1720, and a bequest of vestments by Thomas Beaufort in his will proved in 1427, are perhaps further evidence that Margaret, then abbess, was their half sister.[82] Her cousin, Elizabeth Chaucer, did swear allegiance to the new abbess in 1397, along with fourteen other well-born nuns,[83] but that is the last surviving reference to her; her date of death is not recorded.

There is barely a mention of Katherine in the sources covering the remaining years of her marriage to John of Gaunt. We can only assume that she was living the traditional life of a royal duchess, concerning herself with household matters, charitable enterprises, and pious works; overseeing the Swynford interests, involving herself in the lives of her children, and being a "dearly beloved companion" to her husband. As the mistress of many Lancastrian castles and manors, she would have moved about the country more frequently than in the years of her widowhood, and lived in far greater luxury than ever before. How could she not have made comparisons with how things had been when she was John's mistress, or in the years of their separation? Now, having achieved the highest position to which she could ever have aspired, and won her man in the process, it seems she was content to keep a low profile and remain a background figure in his life, much as she had done in the past, as his mistress.

For most of the first eighteen months of her marriage, Katherine was often at court, where she enjoyed a prominent position, but political events were thereafter to overshadow her life with John, leading to tragedies that would deeply affect them both, and put their very lives in danger. Therefore, it is necessary to digress and recount them here, even though Katherine was not directly involved.

John of Gaunt might have been high in favor with the King, who confirmed him as Duke of Aquitaine for life on July 6, 1397,[84] but Richard, in whom resentment had simmered for a decade, was now determined to force a reckoning with the former Lords Appellant. He told John and Edmund of Langley that he had received intelligence from Thomas Mowbray, himself a former appellant, that their brother of Gloucester and the Earls of Arundel and Warwick were plotting to depose and imprison him. Plaintively, he asked for their advice. "Their plan is to separate my queen from me and shut her up in some place of confinement," he told them, looking as if he were suffering great anguish of heart and sounding very convincing. His uncles did their best to calm him down, saying they would never suffer their brother to harm either him or the Queen, and as Richard had hoped, they consented to the arrests of the plotters.

In fact, both dukes were reluctant to take sides: Quite simply, "they did not wish to be involved."[85] John's overriding concern would have been for his son, who had collaborated with Gloucester, Arundel, and Warwick back in 1387–88, and thus laid himself forever open to accusations of treason; and he would naturally have been anxious to safeguard the future of the Lancastrian dynasty. Thus, in order to avoid becoming further embroiled in the gathering storm, John and Edmund, with their families, immediately "retired to their own castles, the Duke of Lancaster taking with him his duchess, who had for some time been the companion of the young Queen of England."[86] Thus ended—for a time, at least—Katherine's close association with Isabella of Valois. Instead she found herself "hunting stags and deer" with her husband. However, both dukes were "bitterly" to regret their decision to leave court at this crucial time, for it deprived them of their last chance to save their brother and avert a disturbing political crisis.[87]

"Shortly after the Duke of Lancaster had gone away," continues Froissart, "the King decided upon a bold and daring move." Gloucester, Arundel, and Warwick were arrested, Richard apprehending his uncle in person. On August 15, John of Gaunt was back at court and present in the House of Lords when the three nobles were accused of committing treason in 1387–88, and later that month he and his son Henry of Derby were ordered to muster forces for the King.[88]

Gloucester had been taken to Calais after his arrest, and was almost certainly murdered there—suffocated in a feather bed—on the orders of the King, before September 15.[89] On September 9, in a bid to retain John of Gaunt's support, Richard created John Beaufort—who was willingly to assist in the prosecution of the appellants—Marquess of Somerset and Dorset. On September 21 the three arrested appellants were called upon to answer for their treason. Gloucester, of course, was not present; Arundel argued that he had been formally pardoned, but he was condemned all the same (with the Duke of Lancaster—as High Steward of England—pronouncing sentence), and beheaded the same day; Warwick, who had pleaded guilty and thrown himself on the King's mercy, escaped with forfeiture and life imprisonment. Three days later Thomas Mowbray, another former appellant, now Captain of Calais, announced in Parliament that Gloucester was dead.[90]

John of Gaunt made no public protest about his brother's murder, even though, according to Froissart (whose evidence may not be reliable), he and Edmund held the King responsible for it, and planned to meet in London to discuss what action they should take; they had "considerable support," but instead of speaking out, they made their peace with the King, having heard that he was growing suspicious of John of Gaunt too. Maybe John felt he had no choice, given that he was in fear for his son.[91] "But the common view was that they could have prevented the arrest of their brother, had they foreseen it."[92] This sinister episode effectively marks the end of John of Gaunt's active intervention in affairs of state, and indeed his political influence, and it may have coincided with—or exacerbated—the onset of failing health.

"So King Richard was reconciled with his uncles over the death of the Duke of Gloucester, and went on to rule more harshly than before."[93] Apparently, Richard's ire did not at that time extend to Henry of Derby, who had supported the proceedings against his former colleagues. Naturally, Richard had no wish to alienate John of Gaunt, that stout bulwark of the throne. The King was Henry's guest during that September, and on September 29, in a mass preferment of peers calculated to reward those who had supported him in the recent proceedings, he created his cousin Duke of Hereford. John of Gaunt's sons-in-law, John Holland and Ralph Neville, were made Duke of Exeter and Earl of Westmorland, respectively, and John Beaufort was granted eleven of Warwick's manors;[94] on November 20 he would be appointed Constable of Wallingford Castle for life.[95]

Richard II's proceedings against the former appellants mark the beginning of his descent into tyranny. He was done with being told how to govern his kingdom, and determined from now on to rule by divine right as an absolute monarch. In the process, he became obsessed with projecting his own majesty, and introduced increasingly elaborate and rigid ceremonies and protocols at court. He would sit for hours crowned and silent on his high throne at Westminster, "more splendidly and in greater state than any previous king," and "if he looked on any man, he must kneel."[96]

"He began," says Walsingham, "to act the tyrant and oppress the people." Crippled by debt because of his extravagant lifestyle, he imposed forced loans on his subjects, irrevocably alienating them in the process. As his unpopularity increased, he became paranoid about his own security, and instituted a large bodyguard of Cheshire archers to protect his person.[97] In his own eyes, he could do no wrong. He was, he told Parliament, "absolute Emperor of his kingdom of England."[98]

But his contemporaries knew him to be arrogant, rapacious, vindictive, cunning, and vain;[99] they hated and feared this new imperious Richard. Rumors persisted that Arundel, his head and body miraculously reunited, had been restored to life, so to put paid to them, on October 1, John of Gaunt was assigned the unpleasant task of viewing Arundel's exhumed body in London;[100] he and Katherine were probably staying at Ely Place at this time. By November 1, John had gone north to Hertford with Katherine and his son, the new Duke of Hereford.[101] The duke and duchess spent Christmas at Leicester,[102] which must have afforded a welcome respite from the political turmoil at Westminster.

Henry had stayed in London. Sometime in December, while riding to Windsor, he entered into a fateful conversation with Thomas Mowbray. Out of the blue, Mowbray startlingly revealed that four of the King's most favored lords were plotting to kill Henry and his father when they came to Windsor after Parliament met in the New Year; the King would then seize the Lancastrian domains. It appeared there were also secret moves afoot to reverse the pardon granted posthumously to the duke's forebear, Thomas, Earl of Lancaster, who had been executed by Edward II in 1322; if that happened, John of Gaunt would be disinherited. Mowbray feared that he and Henry "were on the point of being undone, in revenge for what was done at Radcot Bridge," for he believed Richard would not allow their treason as former appellants to go unpunished, and that he could not be trusted to keep his oath.[103]

There is some evidence to suggest that Mowbray was not exaggerating the danger. On March 1 and 3, 1398,[104] one of Richard's most favored councillors, Sir William Bagot, MP for Warwickshire, entered into two sinister-sounding recognizances, the first for £1,000, to be forfeit from him should he "in time to come make suit for disherision [disinheriting] of John, Duke of Lancaster, his wife, or any of his children"; the second stated that "if John, Duke of Guienne and Lancaster, his wife, or any of his children shall in time to come be by him [Bagot] slain, upon proof thereof he shall be put to death without other judgment or process." This looks like evidence of a plot to disinherit and murder not only John of Gaunt, but Katherine and their children, and it appears that Bagot was to be the scapegoat for whoever was behind the plot, should things go wrong.[105] In 1399, under a new king, Bagot was to admit in court that he had once intrigued to assassinate the duke,[106] and there is some later evidence that Bagot, Mowbray, and Richard II himself were the conspirators.[107] It is unlikely, however, that Katherine ever discovered how close she herself had come to becoming the victim of an assassination attempt.

Henry reported this alarming exchange to John of Gaunt, who thought it best to tell the King about it. Naturally, given the nature of the conversation they had had, both Henry and Mowbray—who was outraged at his confidences being reported to Richard—wished to portray themselves in the best possible light, and each ended up accusing the other of treason before Richard. Adam of Usk claims that Mowbray himself—who had been implicated in the death of Gloucester, and perhaps believed that Henry's complaint was prompted by his father in reprisal for that, with a view to bringing Mowbray to grief[108]—began plotting to murder John of Gaunt when the duke traveled to Shrewsbury for the coming Parliament, but that the latter was warned and managed to escape the snare.

The strain told on John. At the beginning of February, after Parliament rose, he was suffering from a high fever and obliged to retire with Katherine to nearby Lilleshall Abbey for a couple of days to recuperate.[109] By this time he was, as he confided to the King in a letter, suffering from a recurrent illness that proved intermittently incapacitating, and this was probably one such attack.[110] Lilleshall Abbey, where John rested with Katherine, was a remote but imposing Norman house of red sandstone founded by Arroasian (later Augustinian) canons in 1148 and extended in the thirteenth century. Extensive ruins remain today, and the west front is especially magnificent.

Confronted with the prospect of his own mortality, John had to face the possibility that Richard II had designs on the Lancastrian inheritance, and Katherine would certainly have shared her husband's anxieties on that score, and indeed been concerned for him too. The King had already moved against three Lords Appellant, so what was there to keep him from proceeding against the other two? Even if he stopped short of indicting Henry for treason, he might yet use devious means to seize the duchy for the Crown. As soon as he was well enough, John sought from Richard an assurance that he would not use the forfeiture of Thomas, Earl of Lancaster, in 1322 as an excuse to appropriate the duchy's lands, a request Richard readily granted.[111]

So far, then, there had been no tangible evidence that the King was entertaining any sinister intentions toward the House of Lancaster. On February 5 he again showed generosity to John Beaufort, appointing him to the prestigious offices of Warden of the Cinque Ports and Constable of Dover Castle, the key defensive fortress of the realm, and on May 9, Beaufort would be named Admiral of the North and West.[112] In granting these offices, Richard was acknowledging John Beaufort to be one of the leading lords in the kingdom, a worthy son of his father.

John of Gaunt was evidently in better health by February 5, for on that day the King again commissioned him to treat for peace with the Scots, and on February 20 he was at Pontefract again, on his way north.[113] He may have left Katherine there to await his return, for it is unlikely she accompanied him to Scotland, in view of the lawlessness of the border regions.

There was much adverse comment when, on February 27, 1398, Henry Beaufort, a proud and ambitious young man of just twenty-one, was named Bishop of Lincoln by the King. He had been provided to the See by a bull of Pope Boniface IX, who was ever eager to gratify the wishes of the influential Duke of Lancaster, the duke having shamelessly canvassed for the appointment; normally thirty was the minimum age for bishops. Even for the son of the mighty John of Gaunt, this was too rapid a promotion, and a flagrant abuse of the power of the Papacy. Evidently, the aged Bishop Buckingham thought so too, because, rather than meekly submit to being translated to the less prestigious See of Coventry and Lichfield—ostensibly for the benefit of his health, but in reality to make way for his successor—he insisted on continuing with his episcopal duties in Lincoln up until July 12 that year. By then he was too infirm to carry on anywhere, and was sent to live out his days in Canterbury, where he died on March 10, 1399. On July 14, 1398, having resigned as Chancellor of Oxford and renounced most of his other offices in order to focus on his episcopate, Henry Beaufort was consecrated Bishop of Lincoln, receiving his temporalities five days later at

Tutbury.[114] He was to prove a typical career bishop, busy and competent in all his affairs, who would enjoy power within the state as well as the Church, and whose interests embraced both the secular and the sacred, yet who saw himself, before all else, as a Lancastrian prince. With his preferment, Katherine found herself the mother of a marquess, a countess, and a bishop—attainments she could never at one time have dreamed of for her bastard children.

In the middle of March 1398, near Kelso, John of Gaunt appointed deputies to serve on the northern Marches, then rode south, unaware that he had just completed his last diplomatic mission—appropriately in the interests of peace.[115] From that time on, he was to play little part in public life, a clear indication that his health was failing fast, along with the sudden cessation of his witnessing royal charters in July 1398.[116] Worry about his son must have been a contributing factor.

The quarrel between Henry and Mowbray was still unresolved, and for Richard II a godsent opportunity to press home his advantage, for he had come to see the House of Lancaster, with its enormous power and vast wealth, as a threat to himself and his throne, and was indeed resolved to neutralize it. On March 19 the two protagonists again appeared before the King at Bristol, and since honor had to be satisfied and neither party was willing to be reconciled, the case was referred to the Court of Chivalry to consider a "wager of battle." John of Gaunt, "greatly upset," according to Froissart, went to Westminster with Henry on March 25, but he and Katherine had retired to Leicester by April 14, and so John was consequently spared the ordeal of witnessing Richard II, on March 29 at Windsor, ordering that, since there were no witnesses to the fateful conversation, the issues between Henry and Mowbray be settled by judicial combat between the protagonists[117]—an outdated but still legal (until 1819) process whereby guilt was apportioned to the man left dead or disabled, or the one who ended the fight by crying "Craven!" In this case "the duel was to be a matter of life and death."[118]

Henry raced north to break the news to his father and to hone his skills for the coming fight. John of Gaunt now faced the terrible prospect of his beloved son and heir being killed and branded a traitor, but on the other hand, Henry was an expert swordsman and jouster, and his father may have been optimistic as to the outcome. For all that, the duke "was much annoyed and disturbed" by the King's actions, although he did not wish to say a word against Richard because Henry's honor was involved, as was his own.[119] A sense of disaster threatening may well have overshadowed the family's time at Pontefract, where they resided from at least June 9 until July 14 before moving to Rothwell.[120] It would appear that Richard was unaware of his uncle's increasing frailty, for at the beginning of July he renewed his commission as Lieutenant of the Marches.[121]

Early in August, Henry received word that the trial by combat would take place on September 16. Richard may have been trying to lull John of Gaunt into a false sense of security when, on September 8, he confirmed and extended his powers in the palatinate of Chester, upgraded the earldom of Chester to a principality, and appointed the duke its hereditary constable.[122] But this was to be the last public office ever granted to John, whose relinquishment of the Duchy of Aquitaine that year suggests an awareness that he was no longer able to bear the responsibilities that possession of that turbulent domain entailed. In his place, at the end of August, the ever upwardly mobile John Beaufort was appointed King's Lieutenant in Aquitaine for seven years.[123]

At last September 16 dawned, the day everyone concerned had been awaiting or dreading, and the two protagonists faced each other at Gosford Green, Coventry, with the King (who was lodging at Sir William Bagot's house), the young queen, the Duke and Duchess of Lancaster, the whole court, and vast crowds of sightseers looking on. But as the contestants sat there on their steeds, poised to charge, the King threw down his staff and forbade them to proceed. Instead, they were summoned to kneel before him, and without further preliminaries he sentenced Henry to ten years' banishment and Mowbray to exile for life. Both were commanded to leave England by October 20.[124] At a stroke, Richard had rid himself of the two remaining appellants.

"The whole court was in a state of turmoil."[125] The summary sentences—handed down without any charges being made or any form of trial—stunned everyone and provoked much criticism of the King, not the least because Henry was "extraordinarily popular" in England.[126] At last Richard had revealed his hand, showing that he had meant all along to have his revenge on every one of the former appellants. On the plea of John of Gaunt, he did immediately reduce the term of Henry's banishment to six years, but he was otherwise implacable. Banishing Henry and Mowbray was a clever move on his part, for he must have been aware by now that the duke did not have much longer to live, and with Henry abroad at the time his father died it would be far easier for the King to appropriate the vast Lancastrian estates.

For John of Gaunt and his son, however, it was a tragedy, for it meant that Henry had to leave his father, with whom he had always enjoyed a touchingly warm relationship, at a time when the latter's health was failing fast and it must have been obvious that the prospect of their meeting again in this life was remote indeed. John may have made this point, to no purpose, in his plea to the King. More than that, the future security of the Lancastrian patrimony, which for over thirty years the duke had preserved and enriched as the inheritance he would leave his son and the heirs of his dynasty, was now clearly under threat. Many historians have observed that he made no public protest; Froissart says that he "was very angry and felt that the King should not have reacted as he had . . . And the more sensible of the barons agreed with him." Nevertheless, while he "deplored the matter in private, [he] was too proud to approach Richard II, since his son's honor was involved." That is understandable, but given the King's unpredictable humor, he probably did not dare to protest for fear that it would only worsen the situation, and because so much was at stake. After all, he had pleaded with the King in private and failed to soften his resolve.

The prospect of death was undoubtedly in John's mind at this time, for on September 17, only one day after Richard pronounced his terrible judgment, the duke obtained from him a license to found a chantry for himself and Katherine in Lincoln Cathedral, where their souls could be prayed for in perpetuity by two chaplains.[127] When his time came, John would be buried in the double tomb he had built for himself and Blanche in St. Paul's, but he desired to retain a spiritual affinity in death with Katherine, who must already have decided that she would be laid to rest in Lincoln Cathedral, a place with which she had long enjoyed a close association, and where she and John were married. That she had the right to burial there is perhaps further evidence that she was a member of the cathedral's confraternity, although her long residence in the close might have qualified her for the privilege, as well as her royal status.

After their marriage John and Katherine had forged even closer links with Lincoln Cathedral. They bestowed rich gifts. In his will, John left a gold chalice graven with a crucifix and an image of Christ, a gold table, large gold chandeliers, and a stone altar he called "Domesday" that was encrusted with sapphires, diamonds, pearls, and rubies, all of which were from his own chapel, as well as new vestments of red cloth of gold adorned with gold falcons, and an altar cloth with the images of Jesus Christ, the Virgin Mary, and the twelve Apostles embroidered in gold thread.

During her marriage and widowhood, Katherine also gave beautiful vestments, some from her own chapel; these comprised "a chasuble of red baudekin [rich silk] with orphreys [ornamental bands or borders] of gold with leopards powdered [sprinkled] with black trefoils, and two tunicles and two albs of the same suite"; twenty "fair copes," each having "three wheels of silver in the hoods . . . a chasuble of red velvet with Katherine wheels of gold, with two tunicles and three albs, with all the apparel of the same suite . . . five copes of red velvet with Katherine wheels of gold, of the which three hath orphreys of black cloth of gold, and the other two hath orphreys with images of Katherine wheels and stars." There were also four other copes "in red satin figured with Katherine wheels of gold, with orphreys having images, staffs, and Katherine wheels," and "two cloths of red velvet embroidered with Katherine wheels of gold of diverse lengths and diverse breadths." All were "of the gift of the Duchess of Lancaster," and they were recorded in an inventory taken in 1536, when they were still proudly numbered among the cathedral's treasures. These descriptions give some indication of the splendor in which the duke and duchess worshipped, while the proliferation of Katherine wheels testifies to the duchess's desire to be identified with her patron saint.[128]

Immediately after obtaining his license from the King, John rode with Katherine to Leicester Castle. To show that he bore the duke no ill will for the misdeeds of his son, Richard visited them there from September 20 to 24,[129] and on the last day of his stay he granted Mowbray's lordship of Castle Acre in Norfolk to Thomas Beaufort.[130] Were these sops to lull John into believing that Richard planned no further moves against the House of Lancaster?

During his visit Richard must have seen a deterioration in John of Gaunt's health. For some time, says Froissart, John was "low spirited on account of the banishment of his son," and he was clearly not a well man. Although on October 3, Richard was apparently anticipating that his uncle might undertake another trip to Scotland in 1399, this was perhaps a ploy to make people believe he thought the duke would live to see his son return from exile, in order to deflect any suspicions that he had his eye on their lands, for on that same day he went so far as to issue letters authorizing Henry to receive his inheritance in the event of John's early demise.[131]

Katherine was probably present with John at Eltham Palace that month to witness Henry taking his leave of the King. Their own sad farewells were made soon afterward, and on March 13, Henry, riding through vast crowds of people "weeping and crying after him," left London for Dover, where he was to board a ship bound for France.[132] On his father's advice he had arranged to spend his exile in Paris, at the French court,[133] near enough to England for him to be able to speedily return if necessary.

John of Gaunt, now overtaken "by a sudden languor, both for old age and heaviness [depression],"[134] and "gravely desolated" by the absence of his son and the prospect of never seeing him again,[135] rode north with his beloved Katherine to Leicester Castle, arriving there by October 24.[136] He would not leave this long-favored residence alive.[137] As Silva-Vigier and Goodman point out, the greater part of his short married life with Katherine had been darkly overshadowed by Richard II's tyranny and then the duke's sickness—and there was to be no happy ending. In November his health deteriorated further, and at Christmas, according to Froissart, he became very ill. It may have been at this time that he took to "his chamber bed, travailed in that infirmity."[138] This was by far the worst manifestation of the illness he had suffered from intermittently for at least a year, a malady that some believed had been brought on or exacerbated by the strain of recent events.[139]

The nature of that illness cannot be determined for certain, but there are possible clues. The following "indecent tale" was deemed so disgusting by the duke's Edwardian biographer, Armitage-Smith, that he had the whole text, and his own dismissive observations, printed in Latin; later historians, such as Pearsall and Bevan, have also cast doubt on its credibility. But were they right to do so? A closer look at the evidence is required.

In the 1440s, Thomas Gascoigne, Chancellor of Oxford University, claimed in his treatise, *Loci e Libro Veritatum* (Passages from a Book of Truths), that John of Gaunt "died of putrefaction of his genitals and body, caused by the frequenting of women, for he was a great fornicator." According to Gascoigne, Richard II visited John of Gaunt as he was "lying thus diseased in bed," and the duke "showed this same putrefaction" to the King, laying bare his corrupted genitals and other parts. Gascoigne, who attributed this illness to "the exercise of carnal intercourse with women," and who says he got his information from "a faithful student of theology who knew these things and told them to me," wrote this passage to illustrate his typically clerical theory that excessive sexual intercourse had dire consequences for men; yet it seems strange that the private shame of the Duke of Lancaster, the great-grandfather of the then-reigning king and the progenitor of his dynasty, should be chosen as an exemplar and thus exposed. Surely Gascoigne would have had to be sure of his facts before writing something so injurious to the duke's posthumous reputation?[140]

Armitage-Smith observed that Gascoigne, a respected and honest preacher who was vehement in his opposition to Lollards, was biased against the duke, who had once been notorious for his support of Wycliffe. But there is some evidence that may corroborate his allegations. Richard II *was* in the Midlands in January 1399,[141] so it is possible that he did visit his uncle. One source asserts that not only did Richard visit John at this time, but that John raged at him for exiling his son, while the Scottish chronicler, Andrew Wyntoun, writing two decades later, has Richard speaking courteously to him with "pleasant words of comfort," the effect of which was promptly spoiled when he threw unpaid bills on the duke's deathbed.[142]

If Gascoigne's story is true, there were enormous implications for Katherine. First, we know that her marriage had been consummated in 1396, so there is the possibility that she herself had been infected with the venereal disease contracted by her husband. The fact that she outlived John by only four years, mostly in retirement, may be significant. Second, the worsening symptoms of John's illness would have put paid to any lovemaking between them. Third, there was the emotional impact on Katherine, who would have had to come to terms with the ghastly consequences of her husband's earlier promiscuity, a constant reminder that he had not been faithful to her in former years. Maybe, though, she had long since reconciled herself to that, and forgiven it, as it was her Christian duty to do. But watching her dearly beloved lord die in agony can only have been painful in the extreme.

Yet what of any corroborating evidence? That may perhaps be found in the great St. Cuthbert window in the south choir aisle of York Minster, which was gifted between ca. 1430 and 1445 by the duke's former clerk, favored protégé, and executor, Thomas Langley, Bishop of Durham and Dean of York, who owed his early advancement in the Church largely to John's patronage, knew him very well, was much respected by his son and grandson, and was Lord Chancellor under three Lancastrian kings. John of Gaunt had been a devotee of St. Cuthbert, and he appears in this window, kneeling at a prayer desk. On it is a book displaying the Latin text of the first line of Psalm 38: "O Lord, rebuke me not in Thy wrath, neither chasten me in Thy hot displeasure."

Of course, it might be that Langley wished purely to emphasize the devout—and conventional—contrition of his former patron for any sins he had committed, but a reading of the entire psalm may reveal Langley's inside knowledge of what the duke had really suffered. In particular, verse 3: "There is no soundness in my flesh because of Thine anger, nor is there any rest in my bones because of my sin"; verse 5, "My wounds stink and are corrupt because of my foolishness"; verse 7 "For my loins are filled with a loathsome disease: there is no soundness in my flesh"; verse 8, "I am feeble and sore broken"; and verse 10, "My heart panteth, my strength faileth me: as for the light of mine eyes, it also is gone from me"—had John indeed gone blind toward the end? The psalm also refers to his enemies laying snares for him and saying mischievous things, which could well refer to the events of 1397–98. Saddest of all, perhaps, in this context, is verse 11: "My lovers and my friends stand aloof from my sore; and my kinsmen stand afar off."[143] Does this, with its specific reference to "lovers," suggest that Katherine herself could not bear to go too near John in his extremity? Probably not, for Froissart says of Katherine, "She loved the Duke of Lancaster . . . and she showed it, in life and in death."

Langley must have known the words of this psalm well, as would many other clerics and educated people; why else would he—normally a man of discretion, and utterly loyal to the House of Lancaster—have used it, with all its references to a physical rather than spiritual malaise, unless he knew it to be especially apt? And why, if the duke had not had such a disease, did Langley choose to draw attention to this particular text?

Given that John of Gaunt may have died of a venereal disease, what could it have been? The only symptoms described or perhaps alluded to were intermittent attacks of illness in the late 1390s, putrefying genitals, and blindness. Syphilis was then unknown in Europe; it is thought to have been introduced from the Americas in the late fifteenth century. Gonorrhea, however, had been known from ancient times, as had other sexually transmitted diseases such as nonspecific urethritis and chlamydia. John is likeliest to have contracted such an illness in the years prior to 1381, when he reached forty-one, and in many cases symptoms do not appear for some years. When they do appear, men can suffer painful urination, swollen testicles, a whitish discharge from the penis, infection and reddening of its opening, genital itching, and infertility—it may be significant that the duke fathered no more children after 1385. His children need not necessarily have inherited the disease, because their mothers were probably not infected—at least not at the time they gave birth. Moreover, John seems, however, to have been a generally fit man up until his fifties, apart from nearly dying of dysentery in Spain in 1387. In later life, however, untreated venereal diseases can cause arthritis, rheumatism, prostatitis, heart problems, meningitis, paralysis, and/or blindness.

None of this is conclusive, and against it, of course, we may argue that, had John of Gaunt died of a venereal disease, it would have merited some mention by other chroniclers. Given the private nature of such a disease, however, it may be that the only people who perhaps knew the truth about the duke's illness were members of his inner circle—Langley may have been present at his deathbed,[144] and might possibly have been the "faithful student of theology" who confided in Gascoigne—and that they kept it to themselves until he had been dead for at least thirty years.

Over in Paris, an anxious Duke Henry was told by one of his knights, Sir John Dymoke, whom he had sent as a messenger to his father, that the duke's physicians had said he was suffering from such a dangerous disease that he could not live for long. This alarming report dissuaded Henry from visiting the courts of Castile and Portugal, where his sisters were established, and from going on pilgrimage to St. James of Compostela.[145] Who knew when he might enter his inheritance, or even be permitted to return to pay his last respects to his dying parent?

On New Year's Day 1399, Katherine presented John with a gold cup, her last gift to him.[146] On January 6, the Feast of the Epiphany, the duke sent to

Lincoln Cathedral the treasures he intended to bequeath to it in his will, instructing that they be exhibited on the high altar.[147] Clearly he believed he was laying up treasure in Heaven also.

At this time, Henry Beaufort was in Oxford, serving on a committee advising the Crown. Since he was to escort his mother south after his father's death, he may have hastened to Leicester to be with the duke at the end. There is no record of John's other children being present, so perhaps it was only Katherine and the young bishop who kept vigil by the sickbed.

On February 3, 1399,[148] John of Gaunt had his extremely detailed and meticulously thought-out will drawn up, the complexity of which is evidence that his mental faculties remained acute until the last. He began by commending his soul to God "and to His very sweet mother St. Mary, and to the joys of Heaven," and directing that his body be buried in St. Paul's Cathedral "next to my former dear companion Blanche." He made provision for the eternal celebration of his obit and those of "my very dear former companions, Blanche and Constance, whom God preserve," and left handsome sums to churches, religious houses, and prisons.

Then came his lavish bequests to his duchess, which are surely further evidence of his love for her. "I leave to my very dear wife and companion, Katherine, the two best *nowches* [ouches] which I own, after the *nowche* which I leave to my esteemed lord and nephew, the King." An ouche was a brooch or a setting for a precious stone; the word derives from the medieval Latin *nusca*, meaning an ornament. John also left Katherine "my largest gold chalice," which the King had given him, "together with all the gold chalices which she herself has previously given to me"—a touching insight, this, into private gifts revealing shared devotional interests. Katherine was also bequeathed "all the sacred images, buckles, rings, diamonds, rubies, and other things which are to be found in a small cypress casket which I have, and to which I myself carry the key. After my death this will be found in the purse which I carry also on my person." These must have been John's most cherished and personal possessions.

"I leave further [to Katherine] a complete vestment of cloth of gold, the bed and the furnishings, with all the copes, carpets for the chamber, cushions, pillows, embroidered cloths for the tomb, and all other pieces belonging thereto, having a red ground diapered with a black trellis and, at each intersection of the diaper, a gold rose, with the letter M[149] in black, and black leopards in alternate sections of it. And to her also, I leave my great bed of black velvet embroidered with iron compasses and garters and a turtle dove in the middle of the compasses, together with the carpets and hangings and cushions, etc., belonging to the same bed and chamber." This must have been one of the couple's nuptial beds, and its symbols further express their piety: The compass symbolized the Creator measuring out the world; the dove was a symbol of the Holy Spirit.

John also left Katherine "all the other beds made for me, called in England 'trussing beds' [portable beds with hangings], with the carpets and other appurtenances, and my best circlet with the fine ruby, and my best collar with the cluster of diamonds, and my second cover of ermine, and two of my best ermine-lined mantles, together with the suits of clothes accompanying them. And to the said most dear companion, I leave all those possessions and castles which she had before our marriage, together with the other property and jewels which I have given to her since the said marriage, and, finally, those possessions and jewels which are in the keeping of my said companion and not listed in the inventory of my possessions." Later in the will, Katherine was left £2,000 (£758,325)—by far the largest bequest made by the duke.[150]

All of this gives a very vivid impression of the luxury in which Katherine had lived as Duchess of Lancaster, but it also paints a picture of a mutually supportive married couple, a generous husband, and an esteemed and loved wife. When John was gone, Katherine would want for nothing, and she would have many reminders of him to cherish: beds they had shared, personal jewels, and rich garments.

To the King, John bequeathed, among other things, "my best covered gold chalice, which my dearest Lady Katherine gave to me on New Year's Day." There were generous bequests to his elder children: hangings, beds, armor, plate, and jewels to Henry; a circlet and a chalice for Philippa; a covered gold chalice for Catalina; a bed, carpets, and an ouche for Elizabeth. As for the Beauforts: "I leave to my very dear son, John Beaufort, Marquess of Dorset, two dozen plates and two dozen saucers, two goblets of silver for wine, a silver chalice engraved, two basins and two ewers of silver," plus £1,000 (£379,163). "To the reverend Father in God and my beloved son, the Bishop of Lincoln [who was to be a supervisor of the will], a dozen plates and a dozen saucers, two silver goblets for wine, a silver chalice engraved, with a basin and one silver ewer, and my entire vestment of velvet with the things belonging to it, and also my missal and my psalter, which belonged to my lord and brother, the Prince of Wales, whom God preserve. I leave to my very dear son, Thomas Beaufort, their brother, a dozen plates and a dozen saucers, two silver goblets for wine, and six silver cups," and 1,000 marks (£126,388). "I leave to my very dear daughter, their sister, the Countess of Westmorland and Lady Neville, a bed of silk and a covered gold chalice, also a ewer."

The will also reveals that the duke generously left "my very dear chevalier Sir Thomas Swynford" 100 marks (£12,639). He also directed that a chantry be founded at Leicester for the repose of his soul and that of "my former very dear wife Constance." In a codicil to the will, added after it had been sealed, he granted Katherine "some portion" of "diverse seigneuries, manors, lands, building, rent, services, possessions, or benefices from churches" that he had purchased "before the marriage between myself and my very dear companion, Katherine, was celebrated"; she was to hold these for life, and "some portion" of their revenues was to "remain completely hers . . . in her hands." The rest was to go to John Beaufort, for himself and his heirs, while revenues from other property held by Katherine but not part of this grant were to be paid to Thomas Beaufort.[151]

John of Gaunt died later that day, February 3, 1399, at Leicester Castle, at the age of fifty-eight.[152] The fact that he left the drawing up of his long will until what proved to be his last day on earth, and in it mentioned the possible eventuality of his dying outside London, suggests that he expected to live longer and even recover sufficiently to be able to return to that city, and that the end came after he took a sudden turn for the worse. His death ended one of the greatest and most poignant love affairs in English history. It left his son Henry—now Duke of Lancaster, Earl of Leicester, Lincoln, and Derby—in possession of a landed inheritance worth more than £43 billion in modern terms, and Katherine a widow for the second time. At forty-nine, she now donned once more the robes of widowhood, in which she is depicted on her tomb brass, robes similar to those worn by her sister-in-law, Eleanor de Bohun, on her brass in Westminster Abbey. They comprised a long flowing gown, a barbe, a wimple, and a veil. By this date it had become de rigueur for royal and noble widows from the rank of baroness upward to wear the pleated barbe above the chin, and ladies of knightly rank or lower obliged to wear it below. Katherine, as a dowager duchess, would have worn it covering her chin, with the nunlike wimple falling over her shoulders. On public occasions she may have worn a ducal coronet on top of the wimple. Noble widows such as Katherine usually wore this garb until they died or remarried.[153]

In his will, John had left instructions that, like Job, "my body should remain on the earth for forty days," uninterred.[154] This was not only an exercise in humility and penitence typical of its time, but also gave the executors time in which to arrange the obsequies. The embalmed body would have been placed in a coffin in the castle chapel, where Katherine would surely have regularly kept vigil beside it: Again we may recall Froissart saying that she showed her love for the duke in death.

Early in March the duke's corpse was brought south to London in solemn procession. Katherine, as chief mourner, was escorted by her son, Bishop Beaufort, and Robert Braybrooke, Bishop of London, an old friend of her husband. On March 12 the body was to rest overnight at St. Albans Abbey in Hertfordshire, but when the cortège arrived, the abbot refused to admit anyone, or assign lodgings to any of the mourners, because of Beaufort's presence, fearing that if the latter were allowed to officiate at the Requiem Mass, the abbey's cherished exemption from his episcopal jurisdiction might be compromised. An undignified row ensued, and was only resolved when, at Braybrooke's urging, the outraged bishop undertook to indemnify the abbey against any derogation of its immunities. Only then would the abbot admit everyone and himself insist on celebrating the Requiem Mass with the two bishops. The following day, Bishop Beaufort graciously—and diplomatically—confirmed the abbey's privileges. But it took the gift of a precious reliquary, presented on his next visitation, to mollify him.[155]

On the evening of March 13 the duke's body rested in the abbey's chapel of St. John at Barnet,[156] and the following day it was carried to London and—according to his wish—brought to the church of the Carmelites, his favored order of friars, south of Fleet Street, "to have exequies sung that same night and Requiem Mass the following morning." Today, an inn, the Old Cheshire Cheese in Wine Office Court, stands on the site of the Whitefriars' guesthouse where Katherine probably lodged, unless nearby Ely Place had been made ready for her.

On March 15 the hearse was borne to St. Paul's for a final nocturnal vigil. Then, forty days after his death, on Passion Sunday, March 16, in the presence of the King and all the nobility, and following a final Requiem Mass, John of Gaunt was laid to rest with great honors beside his once-beloved Blanche in the "incomparable sepulchre" Henry Yevele had built for them near the high altar.[157] At the committal, twenty-five large candles were grouped symbolically around the coffin: ten for the Ten Commandments, seven for the Seven Works of Charity, five for the Five Wounds of Christ, and three for the Holy Trinity.[158] The chantry chapel in which the tomb was housed was finally completed by March 1403, and the chantry formally founded on December 20, 1411.[159] The chapel was sumptuously appointed with vestments, altar cloths, and hangings left by the duke, and a silver and enameled cross "of renowned beauty" presented by Bishop Beaufort.[160]

The duke's grandson, eleven-year-old Henry of Monmouth, the future Henry V, may have represented his exiled father, Henry, Duke of Lancaster, at the funeral—he and his siblings were all issued with black mourning robes[161]—but it is just possible that Duke Henry, who had immediately put his Parisian household into mourning,[162] had covertly hastened back from Paris to attend it himself, in disguise, for three warrants issued under his privy seal were dated in London on March 17, 18, and 20.[163]

TEN

The King's Mother

With all the preparations for the duke's obsequies and the sorting out of affairs following his death, Katherine can have had little time to mourn. Now, with the funeral behind her, she faced life alone without the man she had loved for more than thirty years.

Before she could make any decisions about her future, she had to look to her financial affairs. Immediately following the duke's death, the royal escheators had wrongfully taken into custody her dower lands along with the Lancastrian estates, so Katherine had to petition Richard II to restore them to her, which he did promptly on March 9. He also confirmed an annuity of £1,000 (£379,163) charged upon the duchy lands,[1] which had been granted to her by John. But on March 18 the King did what had no doubt been in his mind for some time: Without any legal pretext, he extended Henry's exile for the term of his life, and declared the Lancastrian inheritance forfeit, annexing the duchy to the Crown and distributing its lands among his favorites.[2] It was a shocking turn of events, and one of the grossest examples of Richard's tyrannical rule.

The King had shed no tears for his late uncle, and had even communicated his passing to Charles VI "with a sort of joy."[3] Yet his affection for Katherine and her family is evident in the measures he took to mitigate the impact of the forfeiture on them. He allowed Katherine to keep the lands left to her for her dower, and when in May his escheators—whose zeal far exceeded their competence—seized lands in Lincolnshire, Leicestershire, Northamptonshire, and Norfolk that she had held before her marriage to the duke, he ordered that these lands be released to her.[4] Thereafter, she made no known protest about the forfeiture of the Lancastrian inheritance, kept very much to herself, and thus managed to remain on good terms with the King.

On March 20, Richard confirmed the annuity of 100 marks that John of Gaunt had granted in 1383 to Thomas Swynford and his wife,[5] and the same day he compensated Thomas Chaucer for the loss of the offices granted him by the late duke. John Beaufort was scheduled to go to Aquitaine at the beginning of April, but the King postponed his departure and kept him in attendance at court; on April 16 he was one of the witnesses of Richard's will.[6] Perhaps John took advantage of the respite to help his mother settle her affairs, or to be a moral support to her at this time of mourning. In April, Richard provided Garter robes for Joan Beaufort and Jane Crophill, Thomas Swynford's wife. Katherine was not among those for whom such robes were provided—she would not have been expected to attend the Garter ceremonies so early in her widowhood.

K atherine did not choose to reside at any of her dower properties. She probably visited them rarely, if at all, for there is little or no trace of her at any of them, and of course she only held them for a short time; their function was chiefly to provide her with an income from rents and feudal dues. Instead, she went back to the cathedral close in Lincoln, where she had sought refuge during that earlier parting from John, and which had evidently come to represent home to her. In absenting herself from London and the court, she removed herself from the turmoil of political life that had engulfed her last years with John, and hopefully in so doing found a kind of peace.

Having arranged for Thomas Swynford to take over the running of Kettlethorpe and Coleby, she leased one of the most desirable houses in Minster Yard, the one known today as the Priory. The exact date on which she took up residence there is not recorded, but it must have been early on in her widowhood; she was certainly renting the house in 1400–1401, and held it until she died.[7] She did not pay the rent of 46s.8d (£869) per annum, but opted instead to make repairs to the house, which may have given her something on which to focus during her widowhood.

The Priory is now a private school, and it was not known by that name until the early nineteenth century, when it housed an earlier school for young ladies, which was established by 1824; however, it will henceforth be referred to as the Priory for ease of reference. The present house is set back from the street and somewhat isolated from the other houses, standing against the fortified wall that was built around the cathedral close in the early fourteenth century, and lying to the north of the Chancery, farther along Pottergate. In Katherine's day the New Gate of the close stood outside the house, next to which was the Priory's own, smaller gatehouse, long since demolished; the cathedral's octagonal Chapter House is opposite.

As with the Chancery, a parliamentary survey, drawn up in 1649, exists for the Priory, providing us with many valuable details about the property leased by Katherine. The Priory's largely Victorian exterior conceals the core of the thirteenth-century house lived in by Katherine, which was once a canon's residence; there had been a tenement on the site since the twelfth century. The remains of the "fair hall 40 feet long and 22 feet broad"[8] with walls between two and three feet thick, which dates from the late thirteenth century, are incorporated in the present house, along with sections of its walls and two of its original entrance doorways, while at the screens end there survives between two pointed-arch doors an imposing stone buffet delicately sculpted with ball flowers and a frieze of quatrefoils, built into the stone wall. There is also a carved basin for the washing of hands. The survey records "a buttery or cellar at the lower end of the hall, and at the upper end a fair parlor wainscoted, 28 feet long and 21 feet broad, with a closet adjoining." This parlor probably occupied Katherine's original solar wing at the south end of the hall, where she would have had her private chambers. Like that in the Chancery, the hall would have been open to the roof beams in the fourteenth century, with a louver to let out smoke from the central hearth. In this wing there was also, in 1649, "one other beer cellar there with pantry and buttery," and among the rooms on the second floor, above the parlor, was a "chapel chamber," which probably dated from at least Katherine's day, for a household oratory had been licensed in 1259.

When the close wall was built, around 1316–28, a strong three-storied stone tower with its own spiral staircase, octagonal chimney shaft, and embattled parapet was built into it, linking it with the north side of the hall of the Priory, and forming part of the house. The parliamentary survey describes how the stone stairs led up to "two lodging rooms," which may have been guest chambers or accommodation for household officers. The contemporary chimney shaft, rare in such houses, suggests an unusual degree of comfort and privacy for its time, while a small extension to the east side of the tower, which has traces of medieval windows, may have housed latrines. The ground-floor room, which has mullioned windows, was probably used as a buttery and pantry. There is now no fireplace in the first-floor chamber (now the music room), but this was clearly an important room because it still boasts windows surmounted by ogee arches on both sides, which would have been there when Katherine leased the property. It may be that all trace of the original hearth has been lost. The second-floor room has one window with an ogee arch, and a fireplace with a chamfered stone lintel that was uncovered in 1966.

In those days, a long range of buildings abutted the close wall between the gatehouse and the Priory itself, but all that survives are a row of corbels. In the seventeenth century these comprised a brewhouse, stable, and hayloft; they may have served as stables in Katherine's time. The surveyors mention "an orchard and garden adjoining on the south side of the said dwelling, walled about with stone walls," which occupied about two acres, and yards of a similar size.

The Priory was largely rebuilt around 1670, when the staircase in the tower was replaced, and new windows and a porch were added in Victorian times.[9]

Its proportions and architectural features show that, in the fourteenth century, the Priory had clearly been a house of some distinction, and after Katherine filled it with the sumptuous beds, furnishings, and treasures left to her by John of Gaunt, it would have been splendid indeed, and a fitting residence for the dowager Duchess of Lancaster.

That Katherine enjoyed good relations with the Dean and Chapter of Lincoln during her widowhood is strongly suggested by her decision to live among them, the rich gifts she made to the cathedral, and the fact that one canon, John Dalton, left her a silver cup in his will.[10]

✦ ✦ ✦

There are all too few references to Katherine during the period of her widowhood. She lived out a quiet existence in Lincoln, taking no part in public life and playing no role in the cataclysmic events that were to take place later in 1399. She seems to have retained an interest in Kettlethorpe, and it may have been she who, in the absence of Thomas Swynford, provided a new rector there, William Wylingham, on July 16 of that year. Professor Goodman suggests that Kettlethorpe, with its frequently flooded meadow, may have been too damp for comfort for the middle-aged Katherine,[11] so she may not have been there often.

Her sons, however, were to become increasingly involved in the political life of the kingdom. When Richard II went campaigning in Ireland in June, Henry Beaufort was in his train, looking after his nephew, Henry of Monmouth. John Beaufort, meanwhile, was raising a force to take to Aquitaine, but he would soon be deploying it in England instead,[12] for in seizing the Lancastrian inheritance, Richard had made a fatal blunder, spurring an outraged Henry, Duke of Lancaster, to vigorous action.

With a small force of retainers, Henry left Paris and sailed for England, landing at Ravenspur on the Humber estuary on July 4, intent on recovering what was rightfully his and unseating the tyrannical king. He advanced unopposed through the Lancastrian lands in the North, took York, and rallied Joan Beaufort's husband, Ralph Neville, to his cause. John Beaufort, on the other hand, while secretly writing to Henry to declare his support,[13] publicly declared for Richard and joined the army that Edmund of Langley raised to defend the King. But Henry swept all before him, and at the end of July, Richard's forces surrendered to the conqueror.

At that point an alarmed Richard returned from Ireland, but his cause was already lost. On August 19 he was captured at Conway and taken as prisoner to the Tower. The first thing the victorious Henry of Lancaster did when he arrived in London was pay his respects at his father's tomb in St. Paul's.

Henry and Thomas Beaufort, Ralph Neville, and Thomas Swynford all hastened to declare their allegiance to Henry. On September 29, Richard was forced to abdicate, and the next day, standing before his father's seat in Westminster Hall, Henry challenged the realm of England and was proclaimed King, the first sovereign of the House of Lancaster. Technically he was a usurper, but the heir nearest in blood to the throne, Edmund Mortimer, a descendant of Lionel of Antwerp, was a child of only eight, so there was no viable alternative.

The new king was crowned on October 13 in Westminster Abbey. With his accession, the great Duchy of Lancaster became vested in the Crown (and remains so today), and almost immediately afterward Henry confirmed John of Gaunt's bequests to Katherine Swynford.[14] There had always been a deep affection between the former Henry of Derby and his stepmother; Katherine long played a maternal role in Henry's life, and is known to have referred to him as her "son,"[15] while he now began officially calling her "the King's mother"—a term he was under no obligation to use—as is evidenced in a grant he made to her on November 9 of four barrels of wine a year for life.[16]

The affection in which Henry held Katherine and her family is evident in his generosity toward them. In 1398, Geoffrey Chaucer had resigned his office of forester and returned to London; now he and his son Thomas immediately made known their loyalty to the new king. Of course, Henry and Geoffrey were old acquaintances, friends even—only five years earlier Henry had given the poet money and a scarlet gown lined with fur. He evidently thought so highly of him that on the very day of his coronation he doubled his pension—a mark of high favor perhaps prompted by Chaucer's humorous "A Complaint to his Purse," a plaintive, tongue-in-cheek plea of penury. The King also confirmed a grant made to Chaucer by Richard II in October 1398, of an annual tun of wine. On October 14, Henry IV also confirmed John of Gaunt's 1383 annuity to Sir Thomas and Lady Swynford, and on October 31 granted Thomas custody of Somerton Castle in Lincolnshire.[17]

Thomas Chaucer was appointed Constable of Wallingford Castle on 16 October, and made Sheriff of Oxfordshire in 1400. His impressive career in public life owed much to Lancastrian patronage and to the connection of his aunt, Katherine Swynford, with John of Gaunt. He served as Chief Butler to four monarchs—Richard II, Henry IV, Henry V, and Henry VI—being reappointed by Henry IV in 1402. Between 1401 and 1431 he would sit as MP for Oxfordshire in fourteen Parliaments, and he was speaker four times between 1407 and 1414. A justice of the peace, diplomat, successful vintner, landowner, and shrewd investor, he became "immensely rich" and greatly respected.

Of his brother Lewis, far less is known. He is last recorded in 1403 as serving as a member of the garrison at Carmarthen Castle with Thomas Chaucer.[18]

Late in October the former King Richard was sentenced to perpetual imprisonment, and soon afterward was taken to Pontefract Castle, spending a night en route at Katherine's castle of Knaresborough. At Pontefract, Sir Thomas Swynford, Henry IV's highly trusted former comrade-in-arms, was one of his guardians. John Holland, who had remained loyal to his half brother Richard was deprived of the dukedom of Exeter, and on November 3, John Beaufort, who had also publicly supported the former king, was deprived of the marquessate of Somerset, being relegated to the rank of earl.[19] There were calls for his execution, but Henry produced the private letters that John had sent him, expressing his fidelity, and on November 7 made him his chamberlain during his pleasure, "trusting in his loyalty and prudence," and admitted him to the royal council.[20] On November 18, Thomas Beaufort was granted three manors by the King,[21] and in 1400 he would be made a Knight of the Garter. Under Henry IV, the Beauforts—to whom the King would officially refer as his brothers and sister[22]—would rise to ever greater heights and prosper accordingly.

Joan Beaufort and her husband Ralph Neville were always on good terms with Henry. In 1400, Joan bore her first child, the Richard Neville who would grow up to be the famous Earl of Salisbury and the father of Warwick the Kingmaker, his namesake. Fourteen other children were born of the marriage, the eldest daughter named Katherine, and by 1450, through a successful series of alliances, the Nevilles—and the Beauforts too—would be linked by blood or marriage to every noble family in England.

On Christmas Eve 1399, Katherine's brother-in-law, Geoffrey Chaucer, now nearing sixty, took a fifty-three-year lease on a house within the precincts of Westminster Abbey, overlooking the garden of the Lady Chapel.[23] The length of this lease suggests he must have been in apparent good health and expected to live for some time yet to enjoy his new home, which he got rent-free, thanks to the generosity of the King. But on February 21, 1400, he was to collect his pension in person for the last time, and in

June the final payment of it was delivered to his representative. It seems he had fallen ill and was unable to go to the Exchequer himself. He died at Westminster, with only twenty-three of the planned 160 *Canterbury Tales* completed, probably on October 25, 1400, and, as a tenant of the abbey, was buried in the south transept of the church near the entrance to St. Benedict's Chapel; a leaden plate bearing his Latin epitaph was hung on a pillar nearby. The elaborate tomb erected by the poet Nicholas Brigham to Chaucer's memory near his burial place, in what was to become Poets' Corner, was not built until 1555–56.[24]

Early in 1400 the disaffected John Holland was found to have been involved in a plot to assassinate Henry IV and restore Richard II, and soon afterward was captured by the Countess of Hereford at Pleshy, Essex, and beheaded there on her orders. His widow, Elizabeth of Lancaster, had remarried by December 12; her third husband was the gallant John Cornwall, Baron Fanhope, who had dazzled her with his performance in a tournament at York that July. Rumor had it that the amorous Elizabeth had not only gone to bed with him before the wedding, but also failed to obtain the King's license for their marriage. Yet Henry IV indulgently forgave his wayward sister and thus avoided yet another public scandal; in 1404 he even allowed her a dower from Holland's forfeited estates.[25]

It is probably no coincidence that Richard II, whom Holland had sought to restore, died soon afterward, in February 1400, in Pontefract Castle— deliberately starved, it is thought, by his jailers on the orders of the King. Adam of Usk says he perished "miserably . . . as he lay in chains . . . tormented by Sir N. Swynford with starving fare," but this must be a reference to Sir Thomas Swynford, who was one of the former King's custodians.[26] Swynford, says Usk, was "the chief agent" of Richard's death. This grim insight reveals the darker side of Sir Thomas's character and how zealous he was in the service of Henry IV. Further evidence to suggest Sir Thomas's involvement in the probable murder is to be found in a payment made by the Exchequer "to a valet of Sir Thomas Swynford, coming from Pontefract to London, to certify to the King's council of certain matters which concern the King's advantage, including the hire of one horse for speed."[27] We have no means of knowing whether Katherine ever learned that her son was responsible for Richard's death, but she must have known of his role as jailer at Pontefract, and like everyone else, she would have heard the news of the former king's timely demise, so she may have speculated, or been suspicious, as to what had taken place.

Whether he was to any degree responsible for the former king's murder, Sir Thomas Swynford prospered under Henry IV: In 1401 he was made Sheriff of Lincolnshire, and by May 15 of that year he had been granted the stewardship of the Lancastrian honor of Tickhill, while in 1402, Henry IV chose him as one of his chamber knights,[28] a position that brought him into close personal contact with the King.

O n February 12, 1400, Henry IV granted Katherine the manor of Laughton-en-le-Morthen near Tickhill in Yorkshire to augment her dower.[29] He also, around this time, assigned her £200 (£74,495) a year from duchy lands in Huntingdonshire and 700 marks (£86,911) per annum from those in Lincolnshire,[30] and confirmed her allowance of £1,000 from her late husband. Katherine was now enjoying an income of at least half a million pounds in modern terms, without even taking into account the issues from the dower properties that John of Gaunt had left her. That made her a substantially wealthy woman. Yet apart from living in some state at the Priory, there is no evidence that she used her wealth to finance a lavish lifestyle, or that she traveled outside Lincoln and its environs, or that her hospitality became renowned; all these factors may suggest that she was in poor or declining health during her widowhood, or so devastated by the loss of the duke that she became reclusive and lost interest in material things. The only other reference to her during the year 1400 concerns a grant that was made to her at Kettlethorpe on October 13, so evidently she was still capable at that time of looking after her son's manors in his absence.

One of the properties that formed part of Katherine's jointure was the town of Aylsham in Norfolk, which had been granted to John of Gaunt by Edward III in 1372; John rebuilt its parish church around 1380. Like Katherine's other dower properties, Aylsham was to revert to the Crown on her death. Curiously, in the eighteenth century the antiquarian Francis Blomefield, in his monumental history of Norfolk,[31] refers to Aylsham—without citing his source—held at this time by "Katherine, wife of John Leeches [sic]," which has led some writers, notably Walter Rye in the 1920s, to conclude that during her second widowhood Katherine married a third time, to a member of the Leech family, who were prominent in local society and (according to Rye) were tenants of the Duchy of Lancaster and bore arms. This supposition cannot be correct, for had Katherine remarried, she would have had to surrender her substantial jointure, which in fact did not revert to the Crown until her death. The few references we have concerning her in the years of her widowhood all show her based in the vicinity of Lincoln.

Furthermore, the use of the style "Dame Katherine, Duchess of Lancaster" in Katherine's tomb inscription suggests that she had become a "vowess" in widowhood, that is, taken a vow of perpetual chastity before a priest or bishop.[32] Vowesses were not nuns: They remained in the world and could dispose of their property. If Katherine had taken such vows, she was following a fashionably pious trend that had emerged in the last quarter of the fourteenth century and would not die out until the Reformation. Both her daughter, Joan Beaufort (who bequeathed to her son a gold ring "with which I was sworn to God"),[33] and her famous descendant, Margaret Beaufort, the mother of Henry VII, became vowesses, Margaret while still married to her fourth husband, with his permission.

Katherine owned a number of other dower lands and properties in Norfolk, and also a house in Bishop's Lynn (now King's Lynn) called Wesenham Place, which had been granted to her by John of Gaunt at an unspecified date; he purchased it from John Wesenham, a wealthy Lynn merchant, financier and oft-elected mayor who had strong links with the court.[34] The grant is known only through an entry on the Duchy of Lancaster enrollment book for the period October 1399 to September 1405, and the reference indicates occupancy of the house by Katherine at some time, although given no other evidence for her being there, she is unlikely to have stayed there often. Unfortunately, there is no surviving evidence as to where the house stood or what it looked like.

The fact that Katherine possessed houses in Lincoln, Boston, Grantham, and King's Lynn, all flourishing ports, and is known to have had dealings with merchants from some of those towns, suggests that she had long had mercantile interests—possibly in the wool trade—that have gone unrecorded. We know she inherited from her father some property in Hainault, which was perhaps managed by stewards who assisted her in her business ventures, for Hainault was a major wool-trading center. Investing money in such enterprises may have been one way in which, prior to her marriage to John of Gaunt, she sought to expand the Swynford inheritance.

＊　　＊　　＊

It is unlikely that—with the exception of Bishop Beaufort, who was based at Lincoln Cathedral, a stone's throw from the Priory—the widowed Katherine saw much of her sons. In the summer of 1400, John and Thomas Beaufort accompanied Henry IV on a military expedition to Scotland,[35] and after the King came south in September, John Beaufort accompanied him on a tour of North Wales,[36] while Thomas was appointed Sheriff of Oxfordshire. John was granted the lands of the Welsh rebel Owen Glendower in November,[37] and he was in London in December for a council meeting and to prepare for the coming visit of the Byzantine Emperor Manuel II. At this time Katherine was again looking after affairs at Kettlethorpe: In a deed dated there on October 13, Thomas Aylemere of Kettlethorpe confirmed to her, as Duchess of Lancaster and Lady of Kettlethorpe, the grant or purchase of a small garden plot.[38]

In 1401, John Beaufort was appointed Captain of Calais, an office he would hold until his death,[39] and that same year he was chosen to escort Richard II's grieving young widow, Queen Isabella, back to France.[40] Later he was in Calais negotiating a truce with the French. On November 26, 1401, the King gave further evidence of holding John in high favor by standing godfather to his eldest son, who was named Henry in his honor, and by granting the infant a generous annuity of 1,000 marks (£121,492).[41]

It is unlikely, with all this going on, that John Beaufort had much leisure to visit his mother, and from Michaelmas 1401, Katherine was even more isolated because Henry Beaufort was at Oxford for most of the academic year.[42] Then, in May 1402, he went to court, where—thanks to his royal blood and his clever brain—he soon became one of the chief statesmen of the realm. In the month of his arrival there, he and his brother Thomas witnessed the appointment of proctors for the proposed marriages of Henry of Monmouth, now Prince of Wales, and his sister Philippa,[43] and in the autumn Bishop Beaufort was appointed to the King's council.

Henry IV remarried in 1402: His bride was Joan of Navarre, and John Beaufort was present at the proxy wedding that took place on April 3 at Eltham. In June, John was entrusted with escorting the King's daughter, Princess Blanche, to Germany for her marriage to Rupert, Duke of Bavaria and King of the Romans.[44]

That month, John Leventhorpe, the King's trusted Receiver-General of the Duchy of Lancaster, traveled to Lincoln to speak with Katherine.[45] We do not know the nature of their business, and it was not unusual for Leventhorpe to leave his office in London and travel about the duchy estates in the course of his work. It is possible that Katherine realized that her health was beginning to fail and that she wished to put some of her affairs in order.

Thomas Beaufort received his first military command as Captain of Ludlow Castle on the Welsh Marches in August 1402;[46] that year, Henry IV confirmed John of Gaunt's bequest of an annuity to him. In November, however, the King refused to accede to a parliamentary petition that John Beaufort be restored to his former rank of marquess; both Henry and indeed John Beaufort himself felt that particular title was "alien," too closely associated with Richard II and with Robert de Vere, for whom it had been created.[47] John was sent to Brittany that month to escort Queen Joan to England; their party docked at Falmouth in February 1403, and on February 7, Bishop Beaufort officiated at the royal wedding in Winchester Cathedral.[48] There is no record of Katherine attending, nor does she seem to have been present at the new queen's coronation on February 26, which suggests that her health did not permit her to travel far, for these were great state occasions for most of the nobility, and as dowager Duchess of Lancaster she would have occupied a position of honor at them.

At the end of February, Henry Beaufort was appointed to the high office of Chancellor of England, a post he would hold under three successive sovereigns. The following month John Beaufort was sent to take up his command in Calais, where he seems to have remained until June.[49] That March, work on John of Gaunt's new chantry in St. Paul's was completed—the chantry priests were established there in July—and on March 8, Henry IV granted license to his late father's executors to found the chantry for Constance, for which the late duke had made provision in his will.

The next reference to Katherine is ominous. At Eltham, on April 12, 1403, in response to a petition by her, the King granted that two of the four tuns of wine received by her each year could be sent instead to Thomas Swynford and his wife.[50] Because this petition was made so close to her death, it is more than possible that Katherine was ill and knew she would no longer need so much wine for her household, and so asked for half of it to be given to her son.

In May we find Thomas Beaufort still serving as Captain of Ludlow. Sadly, neither he nor his brother John, abroad in Calais, would ever see their mother again. She died, perhaps unexpectedly soon, probably in the solar wing of the Priory, on May 10, 1403, at the age of about fifty-three.[51]

She was buried in Lincoln Cathedral, in the Angel Choir, on the south side of the sanctuary, in the western arch of the two bays near the high altar. As Duchess of Lancaster, she was entitled to such an honorable burial place, and no doubt her son, Bishop Beaufort, saw that she got it; he probably officiated at the funeral—for which no information survives—and may well have commissioned his mother's table tomb, or carried out instructions she had left for it in her will. Harvey makes a good case for its being designed by Thomas Prentys, a master sculptor from Chollaston in Northamptonshire, for Katherine's tomb has similarities to others he is known to have designed.[52] Silva-Vigier romantically suggests that Katherine's heart was buried with John of Gaunt in St. Paul's, but that is highly unlikely, since heart burial had become virtually obsolete in England by that time.

Katherine's fine tomb chest of Purbeck marble, with its molded plinth and lid, had armorial shields encircled by garters along each side; it was surmounted by a canopied brass depicting Katherine in her widow's weeds and bearing her arms impaled with those of John of Gaunt, while above it was raised a vaulted canopy with trefoiled arches, cusped lozenges, and miniature rose bosses. The canopy and associated stonework would have been painted in bright colors. Her epitaph, recorded by Lancaster Herald, Francis Thynne, around 1600, was as follows:

> Ici gist dame Katherine Duchesse de Lancastre
> jadis feme de le tresnoble et tresgracious prince John Duk
> de Lancastre fils a tresnoble roy Edward le tierce, la quelle
> Katherine mourust le X jour de May l'an du grace MCCCC
> tiers de quelle alme dieu eyt merci et pitiee. Amen.[53]

This translates as:

> Here lies Dame Katherine, Duchess of Lancaster,
> once the wife of the very noble and very gracious Prince,
> John, Duke of Lancaster, son to the very noble King
> Edward III, the which Katherine died the 10th day of
> May in the year of grace 1403, on whose soul
> God have mercy and pity. Amen.

On June 27, 1403, annuities amounting to £1,300 (£416,705) that had been paid to Katherine out of the issues of the Duchy of Lancaster were transferred to Queen Joan.[54] The late duchess's passing had apparently occurred virtually unnoticed, for no chronicler comments on it, and there is no record of court mourning. She died as she had lived during those sad years of her widowhood, quietly and without any stir, almost as a private person. Certainly the wording of her epitaph does not reflect the grandeur of her own position, but rather emphasizes her husband's rank and lineage and her need for divine mercy; this emphasis on humility and an awareness of the innate sinfulness of human nature, as well as specific sins, was typical of the age and probably derived from the aging Katherine's own feelings about herself and her life.

Lucraft has pertinently pointed out that we would know more about the latter if Katherine's will had survived, but there is no trace of it, either in Lincoln or in the Prerogative Court of Canterbury records.[55] We know that a will was made because not long after her death the Lincoln Chapter's Clerk of the Common rode to Liddington in Wiltshire to discuss the proving of her testament with Bishop Beaufort;[56] and in her own will of 1440, Joan Beaufort bequeathed to her eldest son a psalter willed to her by "the illustrious lady and my mother, Lady Katherine, Duchess of Lancaster," which she directed should go to each of her sons in turn, clearly intending it to be an important family heirloom.[57] Of the will's other provisions, there is the likelihood that Katherine bequeathed Gisors Hall in Boston to Thomas Beaufort.

On May 19, 1403, sixteen days after Katherine died, the Priory was leased to Canon Richard of Chesterfield, but he withdrew from the agreement on June 29 "on account of fear of the Queen"; it seems that Joan of Navarre, with the King's consent, had promised the house to Elizabeth Grey, the widow of Philip, Lord Darcy, who lived in a house nearby. Katherine had probably known her, given their close proximity and the fact that Elizabeth Grey's daughter-in-law, Margaret Grey, the present Lady Darcy, later became Sir Thomas Swynford's second wife; Elizabeth Grey could well have been a friend of Katherine's; indeed, Katherine may even have asked Queen Joan to arrange for Lady Darcy to lease the Priory after her death. Be this as it may, the King did grant it to her.[58]

Plans for the foundation of the chantry chapel at Lincoln for which John of Gaunt had obtained a license in 1398 were shelved: Three times, in 1400, 1402, and 1413, the duke's executors acknowledged their failure to carry out his wishes.[59] Not until 1437 do we hear that an altar had been set up, but even then no formal foundation had apparently been made.[60]

Katherine's chief legacy to history was her Beaufort children. John Beaufort continued to serve as Captain of Calais until 1404 or 1405, when Sir Thomas Swynford was acting as his deputy. In 1407, John Beaufort asked Henry IV to clarify his status and that of his siblings, and on February 10 the King confirmed the statute of 1397 that legitimized them, but added the words *excepta dignitate regali* (excepting the royal dignity) in his Letters Patent, denying them the right of succession to the Crown,[61] an act of dubious legality that would be called into question in the years to come, for it was never approved by Parliament, and the original act had been left unamended. There has been speculation that Henry IV had always privately feared the implications of the Beauforts being legitimized, and while he himself had four strapping sons and must have known that John Beaufort's loyalty—and that of his siblings—was beyond question, he could not rely on the fealty of subsequent generations; so this clause probably reflects his determination to preempt any future threat to the senior Lancastrian line.

John Beaufort died on Palm Sunday, March 16, 1410, at only thirty-seven, in the Hospital of St Katherine-by-the-Tower, a royal charity founded in 1148 by Matilda of Boulogne, the wife of King Stephen, to offer spiritual comfort and alms to the poor; given the fact that its patrons had always been royal ladies, that John Beaufort died there, and that John of Gaunt had founded a chantry in the hospital—as well as its connection with her name saint—it is highly likely that the hospital had been under Katherine's patronage when she was Duchess of Lancaster.[62] John was buried in St. Michael's Chapel in Canterbury Cathedral, near his uncle the Black Prince and the shrine of St. Thomas à Becket, a resting place probably chosen for him by Henry IV, who was himself buried nearby in 1413.[63]

John was succeeded as Earl of Somerset by his eight-year-old son, Henry. His widow, Margaret Holland, became the wife of Henry IV's third son, Thomas, Duke of Clarence, and in due course she and her second husband were interred in the same tomb as John Beaufort, with the effigy of Margaret recumbent between those of her two spouses. The latter are similar, but John's effigy is shorter; his face, distinguished by its Plantagenet nose and heavy-lidded eyes, may well be an attempt at a likeness.

Henry Beaufort was the most dynamic of Katherine's sons. In 1404 he was translated from the See of Lincoln to that of Winchester. He stood high in the counsels of Henry IV, and his son, Henry V (who succeeded his father in 1413), was one of the mainstays of the House of Lancaster, and played a prominent role in the history of England during the first half of the fifteenth century, becoming enormously rich and influential in the process; it has been said that he was probably the greatest royal creditor of the age.[64] In 1418 he narrowly missed being elected Pope. Three years later he was nominated godfather to Henry V's only son, and when that infant became Henry VI in 1422, he was entrusted to the care of Henry and Thomas Beaufort. During the minority of Henry VI, Bishop Beaufort was a leading figure on the regency council, and in 1426 was made a cardinal, achieving one of the highest accolades the Church could bestow. In 1431 he was one of the judges who condemned Joan of Arc to be burned at the stake. He died at Wolvesey Palace, Winchester, in the spring of 1447, at seventy-two, and was buried in the chantry he had founded in Winchester Cathedral; his parents were among those for whom he had requested that perpetual prayers be said there.[65] He had one bastard child, a daughter, Joan. It has often been stated that her mother was Eleanor FitzAlan, daughter of the Earl of Arundel,[66] but there is no evidence to support that claim.[67]

There is a fine effigy of Cardinal Beaufort, wearing his red robes and wide-brimmed hat, on his tomb, and a stone head of him at Bishop's Waltham Palace, Hampshire. It has recently been suggested that a portrait of a cardinal by the celebrated Flemish artist Jan Van Eyck may also portray him. The sitter was once thought to have been Cardinal Niccolo Albergati, but his well-fleshed appearance and fur-trimmed robe does not comport with what we know of the ascetic Albergati. Henry Beaufort was in Ghent in 1432, at the time this portrait is thought to have been painted, and clearly the sitter was an important man.[68] Could this cardinal, with his closely shaven face, large nose, keen brown eyes, and pleasant, playful smile, have been the son of Katherine Swynford and John of Gaunt?

• • •

The very able Thomas Beaufort also had a distinguished career in royal service. In 1403, soon after his mother's death, he was made Admiral of the Northern Fleet,[69] and on July 21 fought under the future Henry V at the Battle of Shrewsbury. He again served as admiral in 1408–49, and in 1410 reached the pinnacle of his career when he was appointed Chancellor of England, as well as Captain of Calais. He resigned the chancellorship in 1412, the year he became Earl of Dorset and also saw military service in France; Henry V had abandoned the peace policy of his grandfather, John of Gaunt, and resurrected England's ancient claim to the French throne. Thomas was the King's Lieutenant in Aquitaine in 1413, and in 1415, with his cousin Thomas Chaucer, fought for Henry V in the French campaign that ended with the jubilant English victory at Agincourt. The town of Harfleur was also taken, and Thomas Beaufort made its captain. He was appointed Lieutenant of Normandy in 1416, and created Duke of Exeter on November 18 of that year.[70] Two years later he took an active part in Henry V's ruthless push to conquer Normandy, and was created Count of Harcourt on July 1.

Thomas was widely renowned for his highly developed sense of chivalry, his moral rectitude, his Christian piety, and his charity to the poor and to travelers. He was impervious to corruption, refusing all gifts and rewards, and he forbade swearing, tale-bearing, and lying in his household.[71] It is tempting to wonder if he had been deeply humiliated by the irregularity of his birth and his former bastardy, and if his stiff propriety was a subconscious attempt to compensate for those stigmas.

When the King's brother, Thomas, Duke of Clarence, was defeated and killed at the Battle of Beaugé in 1421, Thomas Beaufort was taken prisoner by the French; he was released the following year. Soon afterward, Henry V died, having entrusted the guardianship of his heir, the infant Henry VI, to his "dear and true Duke of Exeter, full of all worthyhood,"[72] whereupon Thomas returned to England to share responsibility for the upbringing of his nephew with his brother, Bishop Beaufort. From 1424, their cousin, Thomas Chaucer, was also a member of the regency council.

Thomas Beaufort died on December 31, 1426, and was buried in the Lady Chapel of the abbey of Bury St. Edmund's in Suffolk. He left no heir, his only son Henry having died young. In his will, he made provision for masses to be celebrated for the souls of his parents, and left a silver-gilt cup to his half brother, Sir Thomas Swynford.[73] His tomb was lost when the Lady Chapel was pulled down in 1538 during the Dissolution of the Monasteries. In 1772 a lead coffin thought to be Thomas Beaufort's was found by workmen on the supposed site of its altar. The remains it contained, well-preserved in cerecloth, were reburied in a wooden casket near the northeast crossing pier.[74]

Thomas Chaucer, who had turned down a knighthood, died on March 14, 1434, and was buried at Ewelme. His only daughter Alice married William de la Pole, Duke of Suffolk, and thus became a duchess, the highest rank to which a woman could aspire outside the royal family. Her son, John de la Pole, Duke of Suffolk, was to marry Edward IV's sister Elizabeth of York, and their son, John de la Pole, Earl of Lincoln, was acknowledged as heir to the throne by Richard III after the latter's son died in 1484. Thus, the descendants of Geoffrey Chaucer, the son of a London vintner, were raised to the highest echelons of the nobility and, but for a turn of fate, might have become kings of England—all largely due to Geoffrey's sister-in-law having become the mistress and later wife of the mighty Duke of Lancaster.

Joan Beaufort proved to be a strong-willed, formidable lady, with wide literary interests—she liked pious works, romances, and histories, and the poet Thomas Hoccleve dedicated a book to her.[75] Yet she also demonstrated a deep religious piety that embraced the mysticism of Margery Kempe, the holy woman of Lynn. In 1404, Joan's husband, Ralph Neville, Earl of Westmorland, conscious of his lady's royal connections and dynastic importance, disinherited his legitimate son by his first wife in favor of Joan's children, provoking a legal wrangle that would drag on for years, but in which the ruthlessly determined Joan would ultimately triumph.

In 1424, Joan's daughter, Cecily Neville, married Ralph Neville's ward, Richard, Duke of York. York was the grandson of Edmund of Langley, fifth son of Edward III and younger brother of John of Gaunt, and he was also descended, through Philippa of Clarence and the Mortimers, from Lionel of Antwerp, Edward III's second surviving son. He thus had a strong claim to the throne, which he would assert in 1460 during the Wars of the Roses, insisting that he had a better right to rule than Henry VI. York was killed that same year at the Battle of Wakefield, but his claim was inherited by his son,

Edward, Earl of March, the eldest of the fourteen children born of his marriage to Cecily Neville.

Ralph Neville died in 1425, and was buried in Staindrop Church, County Durham, beside his first wife. His effigy may be seen there today, lying between those of both his ladies, but although Joan founded a chantry at Staindrop for herself and her husband in 1437, she was never to be buried with him. Either she disdained to lie for eternity near his first wife, or she wanted to be with her mother: In her will, dated May 10, 1440, the thirty-seventh anniversary of Katherine's death, Joan asked if the Dean and Chapter of Lincoln would enlarge her tomb enclosure so that she could be interred "in the same altar where the body of Lady Katherine, Duchess of Lancaster, my mother, is buried."[76] On November 28, 1437, she had obtained a royal license for her second foundation, a perpetual chantry in Lincoln Cathedral for the souls of both her parents, finally fulfilling their wishes almost forty years after John of Gaunt obtained license to found such a chantry "for the good estate of himself and Katherine his wife." The foundation, which dated from July 16, 1439, was to be formally called the "Chantry of Katherine, late Duchess of Lancaster, in the cathedral church of Lincoln." Two chaplains were appointed to celebrate mass each morning at seven at the altar beside the tomb, and Joan made provision for prayers to be offered for Henry IV, Henry V, and her late husband, Ralph Neville, as well.[77]

Joan herself died on November 13, 1440, at Howden, Yorkshire, at fifty-nine, and was buried with Katherine as she had wished; their two table tombs stood side by side, and Joan's also had a memorial brass and arms encircled by garters and Lancastrian collars of SS. Her epitaph, engraved on a brass plate, was recorded by Sandford in the seventeenth century; unlike Katherine's, it depicted its subject in a heroic vein, asserting, "The whole nation mourns her death."[78] After Joan's interment, when the tomb space was enlarged, an ornamental wrought-iron grille was set up to enclose it, as she had requested.[79] As Bishop Beaufort was a supervisor of his sister's will, he may have been responsible for commissioning her tomb.[80]

There is a miniature of Joan and her daughters in the Neville Book of Hours,[81] and in it there appears a scroll on which is written the first verse of Psalm 50: "Have mercy on me, O God, according to Thy great Mercy." This echoes the sentiments in Katherine Swynford's epitaph, and expresses a similar humility, awareness of sin, and penitence. But verse 6 of the Psalm says, "For behold, I was conceived in iniquities: and in my sins did my mother conceive me." If Joan was responsible for this psalm being quoted in the miniature, which is possible, then Jackie Goodman, the wife of Professor Goodman, may be making a very valid point when she suggests that Joan's sense of her own sinfulness derived from the circumstances of her birth and her early awareness of her bastardy, and that to some extent she bore the burden of her mother's guilt, which she attempted to expunge all her life by religious observance and the study of contemplative literature, just as her brother Thomas had sought to occupy the moral high ground.* Hence her desire to share Katherine's sepulchre, honor her memory, and secure for her eternal salvation.[82]

We have seen how, by 1450, through advantageous marriages, Joan's Neville children came to be related to nearly every peer in the realm. But there was greater glory to come. In 1461 her grandson, Edward, Earl of March, deposed Henry VI and seized the throne as Edward IV, first sovereign of the House of York. Henry was briefly restored in 1470 through the machinations of the man who had once been the mainstay of Edward's throne, Warwick the Kingmaker—another of Joan's grandsons. When Henry VI was murdered in 1471, the direct line of the royal House of Lancaster, the kings descended from John of Gaunt and Blanche of Lancaster, became extinct. In 1483, Edward IV himself died, and yet another of Joan's grandsons, his brother, Richard III, ascended the throne. Thus did Katherine, the herald's daughter, become the great-grandmother of kings.

O f course, John of Gaunt had many other descendants; indeed, he could justifiably be termed the "grandfather of Europe." In the Iberian kingdoms, and among the Burgundian Habsburgs, his memory was long honored as a noble progenitor of dynasties. In 1406 his grandson— Catalina's son, Juan II—succeeded to the throne of Castile. In 1469, Juan II's daughter, Isabella, Queen of Castile, would marry Ferdinand, King of Aragon, and thus unite Spain as its joint sovereigns. Their youngest daughter, Catalina of Aragon, born in 1485, was named for her great-grandmother, Catalina of Lancaster (who had died paralyzed in 1418), and became—with her name anglicized as Katherine of Aragon—the first wife of Henry VIII of England, and by him the mother of Mary I. Thus

_____

*I am indebted to Jackie Goodman for sharing her interesting theory concerning Joan Beaufort.

the bloodline of John of Gaunt was continued in the royal families of Spain and, through intermarriage, Austria, and was carried back into the English royal family.

It flowed in Portugal, too, where Philippa of Lancaster died of plague in 1415. In 1433 her son Duarte I succeeded to the Portuguese throne, and for the next two hundred years her descendants would rule there. Her sister, the spirited Elizabeth of Lancaster, Katherine Swynford's other erstwhile charge, died in 1426 and was buried in Burford Church, Shropshire, where a fine painted effigy graces her tomb.

John and Katherine had many descendants in the Beaufort line. John Beaufort's eldest son, Henry, Earl of Somerset, died young at seventeen in 1418, when he was succeeded by his fourteen-year-old brother John. Their sister, another Joan Beaufort, married James I, King of Scots, in 1424, and thus Katherine's granddaughter became a queen. Through Queen Joan, the sovereigns of the royal House of Stewart (later Stuart) traced their descent from John of Gaunt and Katherine Swynford.

In 1443 the younger John Beaufort was created Duke of Somerset by Henry VI, the second of Katherine's descendants to achieve ducal rank. That year, his wife, Margaret Beauchamp, bore their only child, a daughter, the Lady Margaret Beaufort. John Beaufort did not long enjoy his dukedom. He died, perhaps by his own hand, on May 27, 1444, and was buried in Wimborne Minster, Dorset, leaving his daughter as his heiress. In 1450 the young Lady Margaret was the unwitting focus of a plot by William de la Pole, Duke of Suffolk (the husband of Alice Chaucer), to marry her to his son and make her Queen of England upon the murder of Henry VI—a treasonable plan that cost the duke his head. Yet it was proof enough that a Beaufort claimant to the throne was a viable prospect to some.

In October 1455, Margaret Beaufort, at the age of twelve, was married to Edmund Tudor, Earl of Richmond, the twenty-five-year-old son of Henry V's widow, Katherine of Valois, by Owen Tudor, with whom she had formed a misalliance—some say a marriage, although there is no proof of that—in the late 1420s and 1430s. Margaret's marriage did not last long, for Edmund died in November 1456, leaving his young wife pregnant. Their son, Henry Tudor, was born on January 28, 1457. After the deposition of Henry VI in 1461, Henry Tudor was deprived of the earldom of Richmond and forced to spend most of his youth in exile.

From the 1450s on, the Beauforts were prominent in public life. John

Beaufort's brother Edmund succeeded to the dukedom of Somerset and was a mainstay of Henry VI—and one of the chief rivals of Richard, Duke of York—at the onset of the Wars of the Roses, before his death in 1455 at the Battle of St. Albans. His son, Henry Beaufort, the third duke, another prominent Lancastrian, was executed in 1464, and *his* brother Edmund lost his head in 1471, after fighting for Henry VI at the Battle of Tewkesbury; another brother, John, fell in the battle. Thus, the male line of the Beauforts died out. Henry, the last duke, had never married, but he left a bastard son, Charles Somerset, born around 1460. He later became Earl of Worcester, and died in 1526, in the reign of Henry VIII. The present Duke of Beaufort, whose dukedom was created in 1682 by Charles II—in recognition of his "most notable descent from King Edward III by John de Beaufort, eldest son of John of Gaunt by Katherine Swynford"—is descended from him. There is an amusing but apocryphal story of how Henry Charles FitzRoy, eighth Duke of Beaufort, showed Queen Victoria documents containing proof that John of Gaunt had married Katherine and fathered John Beaufort before the birth of Henry IV, thus rendering spurious the claims of every English sovereign after 1399; Victoria is said to have thanked him for bringing the papers to her attention, then promptly threw them into the fire.[83]

From the outbreak of the Wars of the Roses, the possibility that the Beauforts might have a claim to the throne was taken more seriously. Henry IV had barred them from ever succeeding, but on dubious legal grounds, a matter that exercised not a few legal minds. In the 1470s the exiled Henry Tudor clearly regarded himself as Henry VI's heir and the rightful Lancastrian claimant to the throne, and when Richard III usurped the throne in 1483, after having almost certainly eliminated Edward IV's sons—the so-called Princes in the Tower—Henry Tudor vowed to marry the Princes' sister, Elizabeth of York, and take the English throne. In retaliation, Richard III publicly asserted that Henry had no true claim to it because the Beauforts had been "gotten in double adultery,"[84] an assertion that was only half true but has been accepted by many as a fact. We have seen, however, that the evidence overwhelmingly suggests that Katherine Swynford was a widow when she became the mistress of the married John of Gaunt.

In August 1485, Henry Tudor invaded England and defeated Richard III at the Battle of Bosworth, where the latter was killed. In October the victor was crowned Henry VII, first sovereign of the House of Tudor, and in January 1486 he married Elizabeth of York, thus uniting the Houses of Lancaster and York. Henry and Elizabeth were both Katherine Swynford's great-great-grandchildren. In 1485, in Henry VII's first Parliament, Richard II's statute of 1397, which removed the stigma of bastardy from the Beauforts, was reenacted.

Notwithstanding this, the Tudor sovereigns made very little of their descent from Katherine Swynford, which is perhaps understandable; her notoriety had not dimmed—witness Richard III's libel, which clearly presupposed that people would know what he was talking about and that her ancestry left something to be desired. It may be for this reason that Katherine merits barely a mention in Tudor chronicles. Much as he had glossed over scandal in an epitaph for his grandmother, Katherine of Valois, when it came to providing a new inscription for John of Gaunt's tomb in St. Paul's, Henry VII laid emphasis on Katherine's beauty rather than her virtues, as has been noted. It is unlikely that his fourth daughter, Katherine, born at the Tower a century after Katherine Swynford's death, was named after her, as some have suggested;[85] probably she was named after the Queen's sister, Katherine of York, or Katherine of Valois.

In the reign of Henry VIII, who succeeded his father in 1509, Katherine was still discreetly omitted from the royal pedigree. In a pageant given at Leadenhall in 1520 to honor the Holy Roman Emperor Charles V, an actor representing John of Gaunt sat at the foot of a tree, from which rose many branches representing all the kings and queens who could claim lineage from him. Some were sprung from Katherine too, but she was not alluded to. Again, in plans drawn up for Henry VIII's funeral by the Garter King of Arms, reference is made tantalizingly to a "banner of Lancaster with the marriage," which probably refers to the union of Henry VII and Elizabeth of York rather than that of John of Gaunt and Katherine Swynford.[86] Thus, Katherine was virtually erased from history, and the fleeting references made to her by historians over the centuries usually referred disparagingly to her immorality or made brief mention of her being the ancestress of the Tudors. Until 1954, that is, when Anya Seton's *Katherine* was published, and people began taking a more sympathetic and romantic view of its heroine.

After Katherine died, the Swynfords lived on at Kettlethorpe, and for a time her son Sir Thomas continued his career in royal service, being involved in 1404–1406 in peace negotiations with France and Flanders.[87]

From 1406 he was retained by his half brother, Thomas Beaufort, and there is no further record that he was employed by the Crown. He does not appear to have fallen from favor, though, for in 1411, when Thomas was having problems laying claim to "diverse inheritances in the county of Hainault" that had "lately descended" to him "from the most renowned lady Katherine de Roelt, deceased, late Duchess of Lancaster, his mother," Henry IV stepped in to assist "our beloved and truly trusted knight." And Thomas was in need of such help, having recently been declared an outlaw because of his debts to a London draper.[88]

We do not know who was then in possession of those lands in Hainault, which Katherine had clearly owned—it was possibly Roët relatives who entrenched themselves thinking their tenure would not be disturbed by their English kinsfolk. But whoever it was, "certain persons in those parts" were determined not to be ousted: They had expressed their doubts that Sir Thomas Swynford "was begotten in lawful matrimony," and had "not permitted the said Thomas to possess the said inheritance or to receive the farms, rents, or issues thereof." The implication was surely that Thomas was Katherine's bastard son by John of Gaunt, their affair having become notorious on the Continent as well as in England. But Henry IV was quick to set the matter straight: In October 1411 he issued a mandate under his Great Seal firmly attesting to Sir Thomas's legitimacy:

> Be it known unto you all that the aforesaid Thomas is son and heir of the aforesaid Katherine, begotten and born in lawful wedlock, and that a certain writing of the said Thomas, to these our present letters annexed, sealed with his seal of arms, is his deed; and that he and his father, and all his paternal ancestors, have in times past borne the said arms and used the like seal.[89]

We hear no more of the matter, or whether Thomas was successful in his claim. Possibly, his absence from royal service can be accounted for by his need to visit Hainault to pursue it and perhaps set his affairs there in order. In 1426–27 there is a record of him reclaiming Kettlethorpe;[90] perhaps he needed to lease or mortgage it to finance himself while living abroad.

Thomas's wife, Jane Crophill, died between 1416 and 1421. She had borne him two known children: his heir, Thomas, around 1406 (he was twenty-six when his father died in 1432),[91] who spent his youth in the service of his uncle, Thomas Beaufort;[92] and a daughter, named Katherine after her grandmother. This Katherine had married William Drury of Rougham, Suffolk, by 1428, and bore him six children before dying in 1478.[93] By 1427, Cardinal Beaufort had secured an heiress, Elizabeth, daughter of William Beauchamp of Powick, as a bride for young Thomas Swynford.[94]

Before July 1421, Sir Thomas Swynford had married a second time, to Margaret Grey, daughter of Henry, Lord Grey de Wilton, and widow of John, Baron Darcy.[95] There was one son of this marriage, William Swynford, to whom Cardinal Beaufort left £400 (£181,426) and some silver plate in his will.[96] Sir Thomas died on April 2, 1432, and was probably buried in Kettlethorpe Church, although there is no proof of that, since the church has long been rebuilt and there are no records of the medieval memorials. His widow, Margaret, survived until 1454. Having enfeoffed his estates to trustees, he died effectively landless.[97]

His son, the younger Sir Thomas, did not long outlive him: He was dead by January 8, 1440, when his heir, Thomas Swynford III, was four or five years old. In 1468 this latter Thomas conveyed Kettlethorpe and Coleby to his uncle, William Swynford, the son of the first Sir Thomas by his second wife; William passed away before 1483, having willed those properties back to his nephew.[98] When Thomas Swynford III died childless on May 3, 1498, the male line of Hugh and Katherine Swynford's descendants came to an end, and Kettlethorpe and Coleby passed to the heirs of Thomas's daughter Margaret, the wife of Thomas Pauncefote.[99]

Kettlethorpe descended in turn to the Beaumonts, the Meryngs, and others before coming into the possession of the Amcotts family in the eighteenth century. Their arms are still displayed above the front door. The brick walls that still encircle the gardens were built in the mid-seventeenth century, while the hall itself was largely remodeled in 1713, at which time the fourteenth-century gatehouse was probably reconstructed. A drawing by J. Claude Nattes of the refurbished house, then called Kettlethorpe Park, survives from 1793, and depicts a large but undistinguished residence. In the early nineteenth century the hall was allowed to fall into a decline; in 1857, Weston Cracroft-Amcotts had it demolished and built a plain red-brick Victorian house, into which was incorporated some of the medieval fabric surviving from Katherine's time.

That is the house that stands today, on seventeen acres of grounds. Traces of Katherine Swynford's deer park also survive. In 1983, Kettlethorpe was purchased by the Rt. Hon. Douglas Hogg, QC, MP, Viscount Hailsham, whose coat of arms, like that of the Swynfords who once inhabited the manor, bears three boars' heads.[100]

In the second half of the fifteenth century, during the Wars of the Roses, the tomb of John of Gaunt and Blanche of Lancaster was defaced and the original painted alabaster effigies destroyed.[101] In the late fifteenth or early sixteenth century, John and Katherine's descendant, Henry VII, had the tomb restored and a new epitaph set up to the "illustrious Prince John, named Plantagenet, King of Castile and Léon, Duke of Lancaster, Lieutenant of Aquitaine, Grand Seneschal of England." This is the epitaph that incorrectly states that it was Constance, and not Blanche, who was buried with the duke, and in which Katherine's beauty rather than her virtue was emphasized: "His third wife was Katherine, of a knightly family, and an extraordinarily beautiful and feminine woman; they had numerous offspring, and from these came the maternal family of King Henry VII."[102] The chief function of the epitaph was to publicize the duke's illustrious descendants and connections. New effigies, wearing Tudor costume and armor—the duke in a surcoat emblazoned with his arms, the duchess in an ermine-trimmed mantle—with hands clasped in prayer, were placed on the tomb, probably in the 1530s, since Blanche's headdress is of that date; an earlier headdress would have had longer lappets.

During the Reformation, the chantry founded for the souls of John and Blanche was dissolved and its endowments appropriated by the Crown.[103] It appears that little damage was done to the tomb itself, which was described in 1614 as "a most stately monument."[104] A drawing of it was made in ca. 1610;[105] Wenceslaus Hollar did an engraving,[106] as did Sir William Dugdale, Garter King of Arms,[107] then Richard Gaywood (around 1664–65) for the royal genealogist Francis Sandford.[108] These pictures show an arcaded tomb chest with trefoil motifs and a fine triple-arched canopy with a tabernacle screen, on which the duke's armorial achievements—his lance, cap of maintenance, and shield—were displayed. The canopy or tabernacle was defaced during the civil war and never repaired.

On September 4, 1666, when Old St. Paul's Cathedral was destroyed during the Great Fire of London, John of Gaunt's tomb "suffered the violence of the late conflagration" and was irrevocably lost, "burnt to ashes."[109] It is unlikely, therefore, that the corpses of John and Blanche were among those dragged from the ruins and propped up in Convocation House Yard for passersby to gawp at.[110]

Katherine's tomb, and that of her daughter Joan, standing side by side, were described by John Leland in the early sixteenth century,[111] and also engraved by Dugdale around 1640.[112] Today those tombs stand end-to-end, with Joan's, the smaller, apparently cut down at some stage, at the foot of Katherine's. There are matrices where the canopied brasses once lay, and Katherine's tomb has indents to show where armorial shields were originally displayed. The patterned vault of the heavily restored canopy, its east and west abutments, and the wrought-iron grille on its buttressed stone plinth are all that survive of the chantry chapel that once housed the tombs.[113]

The perpetual chantry set up by Countess Joan lasted until the mid-sixteenth century. It was dissolved during the reign of Edward VI, at which time it was valued at £13.6s.8d (£4,203) and contained two chalices, two silver cruets (for holding holy water and communion wine), a silver pax, and a silver sacring bell.[114]

In 1644 the tombs were defaced, the brasses ripped off and stolen, and the stonework of the chantry badly damaged during the sacking of Lincoln Cathedral by Cromwellian soldiers in the civil war;[115] a "bargeload" of spoils was floated down the River Witham to the sea, and the brasses and other tomb furniture may well have been on it.[116] By 1672 the tomb chests had been moved into their present positions and the canopy clumsily restored.[117] A nineteenth-century plan for a "Gothic" restoration of the monuments was fortunately abandoned.[118] Of the tombs of John of Gaunt's three wives, Katherine's is the only one to survive. Claims on the Internet that the tombs are empty and the remains of Katherine and Joan were despoiled by the Roundheads are unsubstantiated; there is no record of the bodies being disturbed, and they are probably still in a vault under the pavement beneath the tombs.

On May 10 each year, Katherine's name is always included in the obit prayer offered up during Evensong in Lincoln Cathedral. She is worthy of remembrance, and not only because of the famous and illustrious people who have descended from her and John of Gaunt—among them the present Queen Elizabeth II, who is also Duchess of Lancaster; the late Diana, Princess of Wales; nearly every monarch in Europe; six American presidents—George Washington, Thomas Jefferson, John Quincy Adams, Franklin Delano Roosevelt, George W. Bush, and George H.W. Bush; Sir Winston Churchill; the poet Alfred Lord Tennyson and the philosopher Bertrand Russell, "besides many other potent princes and eminent nobility of foreign parts."[119] Her memory is also honored because she is a unique figure in the annals of medieval England, a royal mistress who became a duchess and the foundress of the Tudor dynasty, and above all a lady, as Chaucer said, so "well deserving" of the fame that is still hers today.

APPENDIX:

Anya Seton's Katherine

In my efforts to discover the truth about Katherine Swynford—or as much of the truth as we can ever know or guess at—I have remained very conscious of the fact that Anya Seton's novel continues to exert a tremendous influence over many people's vision of Katherine. I can testify myself to the novel's popularity: During the course of many events at bookshops and elsewhere, I have frequently been asked what my next project is to be about, and there is invariably a frisson of excitement in the audience when I say, "Katherine Swynford." Afterward, I can guarantee that several delighted people will come over and say, "I read *Katherine* . . ." Even in the solemn stillness of Lincoln Cathedral, the notice by Katherine Swynford's tomb reads: "This is Katherine, of Anya Seton's famous historical book." The Cathedral Library holds annual study days on Katherine, and tickets are in high demand. If you enter "Katherine Swynford" on any Internet search engine, you will get thousands of responses.

Of course, there have been other fictional portrayals of her—she is the model for Bronwen Morgan in Susan Howatch's ambitious saga, *The Wheel of Fortune*, and she also appears prominently in Jean Plaidy's *Passage to Ponte-*

fract, a fictionalized life of Richard II. But nowhere is she depicted so vibrantly as in *Katherine*, which has been called one of the best historical novels ever written, "an all-time classic"[1] on a par with the works of Margaret Mitchell, Mary Renault, and Dorothy Dunnett.

Seton spent several years researching *Katherine*, and her book has been repeatedly commended for its historical accuracy. It has even been listed in the bibliographies of works of historical nonfiction, which is no mean achievement. On the debit side, this has resulted in it achieving more credibility for accuracy than it deserves: Jeannette Lucraft, in her recent academic study of Katherine Swynford, has asserted that I myself quoted details from it as facts in my book *Lancaster and York*; actually (and apologies are hopefully in order), they came from F. George Kay's *Lady of the Sun*, a biography of Alice Perrers published in 1966, and it may be that Kay, in his day, relied more heavily on *Katherine* than he should have, as Lucraft is correct in asserting that those details are not to be found in any contemporary source. It is important to note that *Katherine* is essentially a novel, and although its author made impressive and commendable efforts to get her facts right, there are three good reasons why we should not accept hers as a valid portrayal of the historical Katherine Swynford.

First, *Katherine* is essentially of its own time. Seton's John of Gaunt is derived partly from nineteenth-century perceptions of him[2] and partly from Clark Gable's portrayal of Rhett Butler in *Gone With The Wind*:[3] one Internet reviewer described John of Gaunt, as depicted in the novel, as the "sexiest hero since Rhett Butler." Then, by her own admission, Seton applies Freudian psychology in determining reasons for her characters' behavior. Above all, the morality that informs *Katherine* is essentially that of the 1950s, not the 1300s: The heroine agonizes over her illicit love in the manner of an early nineteenth-century romantic, and when it comes to sex, she is a passive partner, leaving her man to initiate it. Also, she believes that a marriage based on love is a normal aim for any woman, a concept quite foreign to the fourteenth-century mind.

Second, *Katherine* is as much about Anya Seton as it is about Katherine Swynford. Anya Seton was born Ann Seton in 1906,[4] the only child of two highly successful, eccentric, and fame-hungry writers.[5] Ernest Thompson Seton (1860–1946) was born in Durham, England, but later emigrated to Canada and the United States and wrote more than fifty celebrated books on wildlife and anthropology, while his highly independent wife, Grace Gallatin (1872–1959), published seven popular books about her own exotic travels. Both of Ann Seton's parents journeyed widely in order to research their books, and she inherited their restless spirit, wanderlust, and thirst for fame and fortune. Like her heroine, Katherine Swynford, she grew up to be stunningly beautiful, and although clever and extremely knowledgeable, was essentially a socialite and a style icon who was feted by the high society of New York and Greenwich, Connecticut. A thousand guests attended her first wedding.

By the age of seventeen Ann had abandoned her former ambitions to be a doctor or an opera singer; she now dreamed of becoming a writer. She was already keeping journals that reveal her adolescent obsession with her appearance and her early amorous adventures. In 1923, after a passionate courtship, she married a young Rhodes scholar, Hamilton Cottier, and then spent two very interesting and enjoyable years living with him in England at Oxford before moving to the duller academic world of Princeton, New Jersey, where her husband was based from 1925. By 1928 she was the mother of two children, Pamela and Seton, and feeling restless and suffocated by boredom. A highly publicized divorce in Reno, Nevada, was quickly followed by a second marriage in 1929, to an investment counselor named Hamilton Chase, by whom Ann had another daughter, Clemencie.

In the 1930s, Ann began writing in earnest, selling articles on homemaking to magazines. She published her first short story in 1938, and in 1941, her debut novel, *My Theodosia*, immediately hit the best-seller lists, bringing Anya Seton—as she was now calling herself—fame, fortune, and legions of fans. In 1946 alone her earnings from her books totaled a staggering $94,000. Nine more hugely successful novels were to follow; all were Book of the Month Club choices, and two were made into Hollywood films. In 1954 there were calls for *Katherine* to be made into a movie starring Charlton Heston and Susan Hayward, but in the moral climate of 1950s America—in which one critic branded the book as "obscene and evil"[6]—it never happened, because it would have been impossible to show two adulterous lovers living openly in sin, producing four bastard children and then enjoying a happy ending without incurring any penalties for their immorality.[7] In some ways the novel mirrors Seton's own colorful private life, which was the subject of extensive media interest. And her sympathetic portrayal of Katherine Swynford must reflect her own views on adultery and illicit sex. It is on record that she at first found the accusations of immorality amusing, then offensive, then simply tedious.

Seton became renowned for her meticulous research—she refused to compromise historical accuracy in the interests of telling a good story, and she traveled widely in search of information, feeling that she could not put her subjects in authentic settings unless she visited the places where they had lived. She spent four years researching *Katherine*, and journeyed all around England; even today, people remember her hard at work in Lincoln Cathedral Library. She hated it when her books were described as "historical romances," preferring to call them "biographical novels." She might have said "autobiographical," for she invested them with many of the moral, emotional, psychological, and cultural aspects of her own life.

Anya Seton was divorced from her second husband in 1968, and published her last book, *Smouldering Fires*, in 1975. Although her journals reveal that she remained obsessed with her "love life" well into her seventh decade, her declining years were overshadowed by an advancing illness that prevented her from writing. She died in 1990, her fame long forgotten.

The third reason we should be cautious in accepting Anya Seton's portrayal of Katherine Swynford as historically accurate is that *Katherine* is essentially a romantic novel in the classic sense. Not just an old-fashioned love story, it is an emotional assertion of the self and a vivid exploration of the individual experience of its heroine. It is progressive in that it champions the beauty of sexual freedom and in its implied condemnation of conservative morality, yet it also captures a sense of the spiritual with its theme of love and redemption. Threaded through it are the classic romantic clichés of remembered childhood, unrequited love, cruel conflict, and lonely exile. It is an intense book, a romantic novel in the widest sense: Passion and the sublime are at its core. And Katherine herself is the perfect romantic heroine: beautiful, sensuous, and loving.

Despite its substance, and Seton's own objections, *Katherine* was more often than not regarded as a lightweight "romance novel," and frequently displayed in this category in bookshops and libraries. Hence, when bodice-rippers became the fashion in the 1970s, *Katherine*, with its few discreetly erotic sex scenes, appeared outdated and fell from favor, as did Anya Seton's other novels. Yet for many readers, clearly, it remained a favorite book, and recent years have seen its reappearance in print, both in Britain and the United States, where an edition featuring the full original text (which was never printed in Britain) is now available. There can be no doubt that this book, with its lovely but flawed heroine, is held in deep affection by a large number of people. Once again, it is important to remember, however, that although— as Anya Seton herself stated—it is based on history, it is a work of fiction.

GENEALOGICAL TABLE 1:

THE ROËT FAMILY

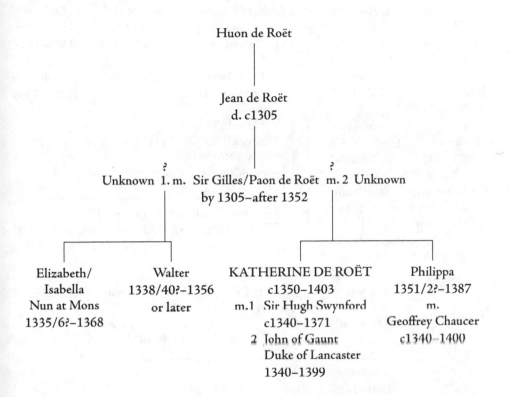

Huon de Roët

Jean de Roët
d. c1305

Unknown 1. m. Sir Gilles/Paon de Roët m. 2 Unknown
by 1305–after 1352

| Elizabeth/ Isabella Nun at Mons 1335/6?–1368 | Walter 1338/40?–1356 or later | KATHERINE DE ROËT c1350–1403 m.1 Sir Hugh Swynford c1340–1371 2 John of Gaunt Duke of Lancaster 1340–1399 | Philippa 1351/2?–1387 m. Geoffrey Chaucer c1340–1400 |

THE DESCENDANTS OF EDWARD III OF ENGLAND

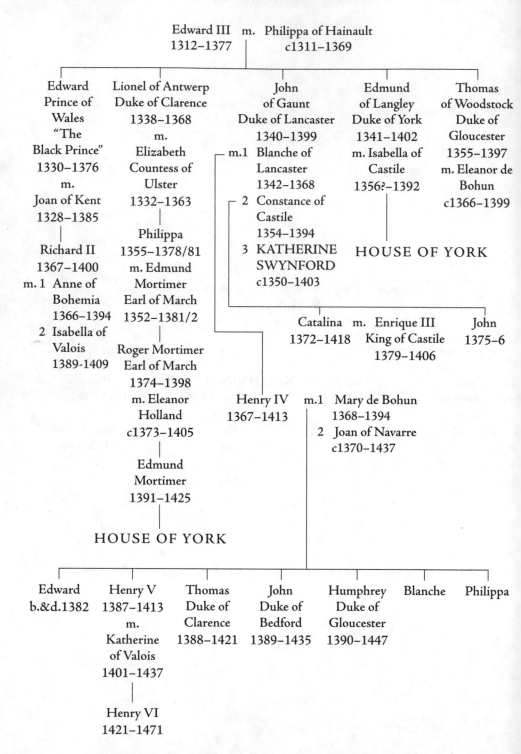

THE HOUSE OF LANCASTER

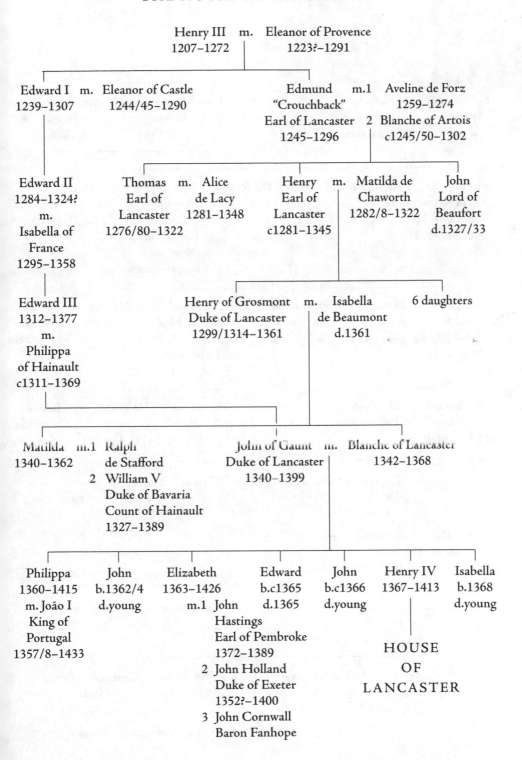

Henry III m. Eleanor of Provence
1207–1272 | 1223?–1291

Edward I m. Eleanor of Castle
1239–1307 | 1244/45–1290

Edmund m.1 Aveline de Forz
"Crouchback" | 1259–1274
Earl of Lancaster 2 Blanche of Artois
1245–1296 | c1245/50–1302

Edward II
1284–1324?
m.
Isabella of
France
1295–1358

Thomas m. Alice
Earl of de Lacy
Lancaster 1281–1348
1276/80–1322

Henry m. Matilda de
Earl of Chaworth
Lancaster 1282/8–1322
c1281–1345

John
Lord of
Beaufort
d.1327/33

Edward III
1312–1377
m.
Philippa
of Hainault
c1311–1369

Henry of Grosmont m. Isabella
Duke of Lancaster | de Beaumont
1299/1314–1361 | d.1361

6 daughters

Matilda m.1 Ralph
1340–1362 de Stafford
2 William V
Duke of Bavaria
Count of Hainault
1327–1389

John of Gaunt m. Blanche of Lancaster
Duke of Lancaster | 1342–1368
1340–1399

Philippa
1360–1415
m. João I
King of
Portugal
1357/8–1433

John
b.1362/4
d.young

Elizabeth
1363–1426
m.1 John
Hastings
Earl of Pembroke
1372–1389
2 John Holland
Duke of Exeter
1352?–1400
3 John Cornwall
Baron Fanhope

Edward
b.c1365
d.1365

John
b.c1366
d.young

Henry IV
1367–1413

Isabella
b.1368
d.young

HOUSE
OF
LANCASTER

GENEALOGICAL TABLE 4:

THE SWYNFORD FAMILY

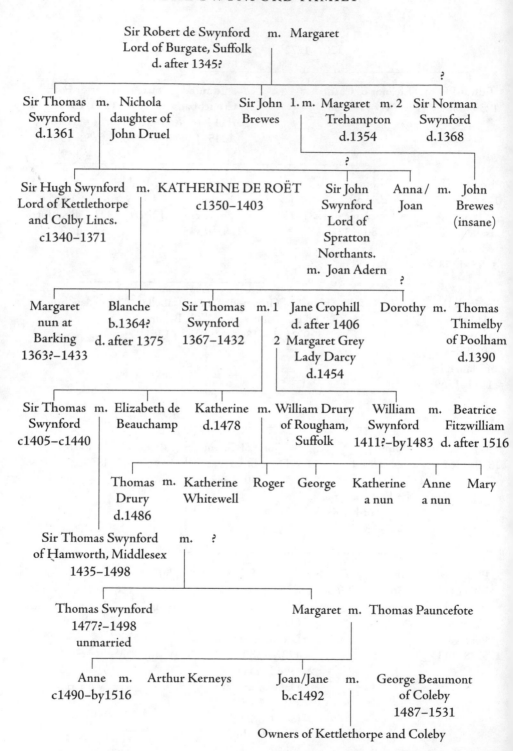

Sir Robert de Swynford   m.   Margaret
Lord of Burgate, Suffolk
d. after 1345?

Sir Thomas   m.   Nichola   Sir John   1. m.   Margaret   m. 2   Sir Norman
Swynford   daughter of   Brewes   Trehampton   Swynford
d.1361   John Druel   d.1354   d.1368

Sir Hugh Swynford   m.   KATHERINE DE ROËT   Sir John   Anna /   m.   John
Lord of Kettlethorpe   c1350–1403   Swynford   Joan   Brewes
and Colby Lincs.   Lord of   (insane)
c1340–1371   Spratton
                                                                              Northants.
                                                                              m. Joan Adern

Margaret   Blanche   Sir Thomas   m. 1   Jane Crophill   Dorothy   m.   Thomas
nun at   b.1364?   Swynford   d. after 1406   Thimelby
Barking   d. after 1375   1367–1432   2 Margaret Grey   of Poolham
1363?–1433   Lady Darcy   d.1390
                                                                      d.1454

Sir Thomas   m.   Elizabeth de   Katherine   m.   William Drury   William   m.   Beatrice
Swynford   Beauchamp   d.1478   of Rougham,   Swynford   Fitzwilliam
c1405–c1440   Suffolk   1411?–by1483   d. after 1516

                    Thomas   m.   Katherine   Roger   George   Katherine   Anne   Mary
                    Drury   Whitewell   a nun   a nun
                    d.1486

Sir Thomas Swynford   m.   ?
of Hamworth, Middlesex
1435–1498

Thomas Swynford   Margaret   m.   Thomas Pauncefote
1477?–1498
unmarried

Anne   m.   Arthur Kerneys   Joan/Jane   m.   George Beaumont
c1490–by1516   b.c1492   of Coleby
                                                                           1487–1531

Owners of Kettlethorpe and Coleby

THE CHAUCER FAMILY

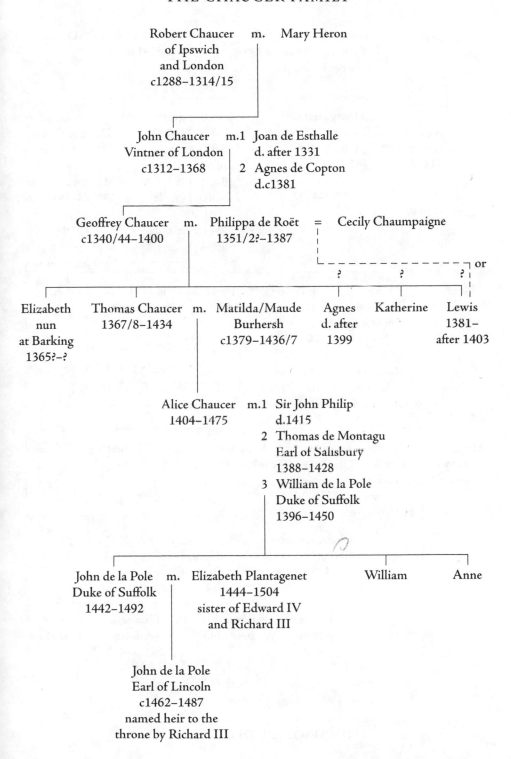

Robert Chaucer   m.   Mary Heron
of Ipswich
and London
c1288–1314/15

John Chaucer   m.1   Joan de Esthalle
Vintner of London   d. after 1331
c1312–1368   2   Agnes de Copton
d.c1381

Geoffrey Chaucer   m.   Philippa de Roët   =   Cecily Chaumpaigne
c1340/44–1400   1351/2?–1387

?   ?   ? or

Elizabeth   Thomas Chaucer   m.   Matilda/Maude   Agnes   Katherine   Lewis
nun   1367/8–1434   Burhersh   d. after   1381–
at Barking   c1379–1436/7   1399   after 1403
1365?–?

Alice Chaucer   m.1   Sir John Philip
1404–1475   d.1415
2   Thomas de Montagu
Earl of Salisbury
1388–1428
3   William de la Pole
Duke of Suffolk
1396–1450

John de la Pole   m.   Elizabeth Plantagenet   William   Anne
Duke of Suffolk   1444–1504
1442–1492   sister of Edward IV
and Richard III

John de la Pole
Earl of Lincoln
c1462–1487
named heir to the
throne by Richard III

GENEALOGICAL TABLE 6:

THE BEAUFORTS

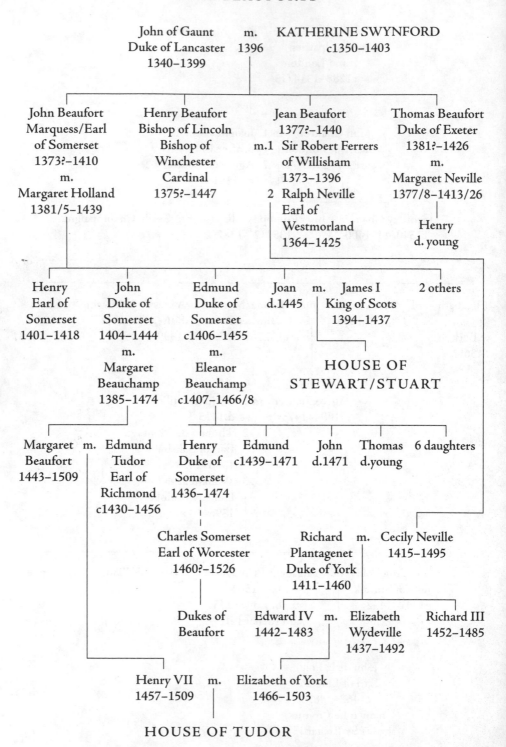

John of Gaunt
Duke of Lancaster
1340–1399

m. 1396

KATHERINE SWYNFORD
c1350–1403

John Beaufort
Marquess/Earl
of Somerset
1373?–1410
m.
Margaret Holland
1381/5–1439

Henry Beaufort
Bishop of Lincoln
Bishop of
Winchester
Cardinal
1375?–1447

Jean Beaufort
1377?–1440
m.1 Sir Robert Ferrers
of Willisham
1373–1396
2 Ralph Neville
Earl of
Westmorland
1364–1425

Thomas Beaufort
Duke of Exeter
1381?–1426
m.
Margaret Neville
1377/8–1413/26

Henry
d. young

Henry
Earl of
Somerset
1401–1418

John
Duke of
Somerset
1404–1444
m.
Margaret
Beauchamp
1385–1474

Edmund
Duke of
Somerset
c1406–1455
m.
Eleanor
Beauchamp
c1407–1466/8

Joan
d.1445

m. James I
King of Scots
1394–1437

2 others

HOUSE OF STEWART/STUART

Margaret
Beaufort
1443–1509

m. Edmund
Tudor
Earl of
Richmond
c1430–1456

Henry
Duke of
Somerset
1436–1474

Edmund
c1439–1471

John
d.1471

Thomas
d.young

6 daughters

Charles Somerset
Earl of Worcester
1460?–1526

Richard
Plantagenet
Duke of York
1411–1460

m. Cecily Neville
1415–1495

Dukes of
Beaufort

Edward IV
1442–1483

m. Elizabeth
Wydeville
1437–1492

Richard III
1452–1485

Henry VII
1457–1509

m. Elizabeth of York
1466–1503

HOUSE OF TUDOR

NOTES AND REFERENCES

1. PANETTO'S DAUGHTER

1 Wylie

2 Brooke Lejeune. See Genealogical Table 1, which is compiled from numerous sources.

3 Gilles Rigaud de Roeulx, who died in 1308, was a grandson of Eustace IV, Sire de Roeulx, and nephew of Eustace V. By his marriage to Isabeau de Ligne, Lady of Montreuil, he was the father of seven children, including Eustace VI, Fastre, and Gilles. It has been suggested that this second Gilles may have been Katherine's grandfather, who was baptized Gilles but usually bore the nickname Paon. This is unlikely, because the arms of the lords of Roeulx—and thereby Gilles's eldest son, Eustace VI de Roeulx—were "or, three lions gules," and as a younger son, Paon would have borne the same arms differenced, which he did not. Cook, "Chaucerian Papers"; Perry, "Judy Perry's Katherine Swynford Coat of Arms"; www.geocities.com; *The Wijnbergen Armorial*. Turton (*Plantagenet Ancestry*) failed to find genealogical evidence to link Paon with the lords of Roeulx.

4 His name is spelled Paon in the *Cartulaire des Comtes de Hainaut* and by Froissart. Jean Froissart, one of the greatest of medieval chroniclers, was born in Hainault and came to England in 1361, where he was "brought up in the court of the noble King Edward the Third, and of Queen Philippa his wife, and among their children." In 1362 he was appointed one of the clerks of the chamber to the Queen, his countrywoman. He left England in 1366 and accompanied the Black Prince on a campaign in Gascony. Although he remained nominally in Queen Philippa's service until 1369, he did not re-

turn to the English court until 1395, when he met Richard II. He would have known John of Gaunt, and probably also Katherine Swynford, whom he would have found interesting because she too was a Hainaulter. Froissart's chronicles are vividly written, but although they make for entertaining reading, especially in their repetition of court gossip, their accuracy cannot be relied upon, chiefly because he wrote mainly from memory, or relied on hearsay, and has been proved wrong in several instances.

5 For Paon's descent, see Brook.

6 Ibid. The lion was the heraldic lion of Hainault.

7 Speght; Rietstrap; "The Visitation of the County of Warwick"

8 "Inventories of Plate, Vestments, etc."

9 Howard

10 Galway, "Philippa Pan, Philippa Chaucer." "Paonnet" is not a diminutive form—that would be "Paoncel" or "Paonciel"—and may be just an affectionately extended nickname.

11 Notably Froissart

12 *Cartulaire des Comtes de Hainaut*

13 Perry

14 Galway, "Philippa Pan, Philippa Chaucer"

15 *Calendar of Patent Rolls*

16 Cook, "Chaucerian Papers"

17 Galway, "Philippa Pan, Philippa Chaucer"; Hardy

18 Several genealogical sites on the Internet give names for Paon's wife (a few even ludicrously calling her "Mrs. de Roët"!), but none cites any contemporary source to substantiate their claims. Some identify her as "Chenerailles Bonneuil (1315–72)," but these are names of places rather than people: There are four places called Chenerailles or Chenerilles in France, and seven places called Bonneuil. "Chenerailles" does appear as a name in French genealogies, but without specific sources being cited, it is impossible to pursue this claim further. See, for example, www.goldrush.com

19 See, for example, Turton; www.childsfamily.com; dannyreagan.com; www.rootsweb .com

20 Some Internet Web sites state that Katherine's mother was Katherine d'Avesnes, a sister of William III, Count of Hainault (ca. 1286–1337), father of Queen Philippa, and therefore a daughter of John II d'Avesnes, Count of Hainault (1247–1304) by Philippine, daughter of Henry II, Count of Luxembourg. There are two problems with this claim: First, Katherine is nowhere listed with William III's known sisters, Margaret, Alice, Isabella, Jeanne, Marie, and Matilda; and second, if she was born at the latest by 1304, the year her father died, she is hardly likely to have borne a child, Katherine, around 1350. Others assert that Katherine d'Avesnes was the daughter, not the sister, of Count William III. That would make her Queen Philippa's sister, and Katherine Swynford the Queen's niece, something disapproving chroniclers would surely have commented on, because such a relationship would have placed Katherine and John of Gaunt—Philippa's son—firmly within the forbidden degrees of consanguinity—as would also have been the case if Katherine's mother was the Queen's aunt. When applying for a dispensation to marry Katherine, John of Gaunt did not cite such an impediment. Furthermore, William III is recorded as having had six or seven daughters—Sybilla, Margaret, Philippa, Joan, Agnes, Isabella, and perhaps

Elizabeth, who in 1375 died a nun at St. Leonard's Abbey, Bromley, Middlesex (see Manly, *Some New Light on Chaucer*).

21 It has recently been suggested that Paon married Jeanne de Lens. There is a record of Simon Lalaing, Lord of Quievrain and Hordaing, and Bailiff of Hainault, 1358–60, marrying the daughter of Gilles de Roeulx, Lord of Écaussines by Jeanne de Lens, who was possibly a relative of the Lord of Ligne. In 1414, Jacqueline, daughter of a lord of Lalaing, was made a prebendary of the Abbey of St. Waudru in Mons, like Paon's own daughter Elizabeth more than half a century earlier. There is nothing conclusive here. The arms of Simon Lalaing do not incorporate those of Rouelx or Roët, and there were at this time several members of the Roeulx family called Gilles; genealogical records are incomplete, and any one of them could have married a Jeanne de Lens; Gilles Rigaud de Roeulx married Alice de Ligne, and his son married Isabeau de Ligne. Nor is Paon anywhere referred to, especially by the knowledgeable Froissart, as the Lord of Écaussines. The St. Waudru "connection" is probably purely coincidental: One would expect to find daughters of these local lords and gentlefolk entering this prestigious abbey. See Perry, "Katherine Swynford" (katherineswynford.blogspot.com).

22 Galway, "Walter Roët and Philippa Chaucer"

23 Froissart

24 Weever. A king of arms was a herald with expert knowledge of the laws of arms and aristocratic pedigrees, whose chief responsibility was to ensure that coats of arms were correctly awarded and borne. His was an increasingly important function in a world in which kings and lords were obsessively preoccupied with chivalry and heraldry. A king of arms also played a diverse ceremonial role, officiating and umpiring at tournaments or serving as an envoy in time of war.

25 His appointment would appear to be borne out by a grant of ca. 1334 from the "King of Arms of the Duchy of Guienne, Sergeant of Arms" to two brothers surnamed Andrew, which bears a drawing of a seal bearing three plain silver wheels, the arms of Paon de Roët. Thomas Speght, who in 1598 published the works of Chaucer with biographical details, states that he had it on the authority of a sixteenth-century herald, Robert Glover, that Paon was Guienne King of Arms; doubtless Glover too had seen the tomb inscription. Apart from the latter, the grant of ca. 1334 is the only fourteenth-century source to identify Paon as Guienne King of Arms, although there is some disputed evidence that the post existed sporadically from the late thirteenth to the late fifteenth century; during the latter period, its holder was apparently little more than a glorified herald. Doubt has been cast, however, on the authenticity of documents dating the office from the reign of Edward I, and if they are indeed forgeries, then there is no historical evidence beyond the grant and inscription cited above for the existence of a Guienne King of Arms before the reign of Henry VI (1422–61). It is on record, however, that during the fourteenth century several new kings of arms were appointed, among them Windsor, Norroy, Surroy, and Clarencieux, so it is not beyond the bounds of probability that Guienne was at that time a new creation. "The Visitation of the County of Warwick"; Crow and Olsen; Goodman, *Katherine Swynford*; Ruud; McKisack; Brewer; Howard.

26 Froissart

27 Ibid.

28 Ibid.

29 McKisack

30 Cited by Lettenhove, introduction to Froissart

31 A prebend was a member of the chapter of a monastery or convent. This prebend had become vacant due to the death of one Beatrix de Wallaincourt.

32 Galway, "Philippa Pan, Philippa Chaucer"

33 Newton

34 The Vatican suppressed St. Katherine's feast day in 1969.

35 Weever incorrectly calls her Anne.

36 Weever

37 Lucraft, *Katherine Swynford*, believes that when Thomas Speght, the Elizabethan editor of the works of Geoffrey Chaucer (whom Philippa was to marry), referred to her as *altera filiarum*, he meant "second daughter," but Speght was perhaps using the alternative meaning of *altera* and referring to Philippa as the "other" sister, who was less famous than Katherine; had he described her as the second daughter of Paon, that would have made Philippa the elder of the two, as they had an older sister, Elizabeth, although Speght may not have known that, in which case he may indeed have meant that she was younger than Katherine.

38 In a royal writ of deliverance of cloth and furs for Queen Philippa's ladies, dated March 10, 1369, both Philippa Chaucer (who was almost certainly Paon's married daughter) and Philippa Picard are listed; the former was then a *damoiselle* (lady-in-waiting) of the Queen, the latter a *veilleresse* (night watcher) of the Queen's Chamber. Philippa Picard may have been the daughter of Henry Picard, a rich London vintner, who was Mayor of London in 1356 and a fellow guildsman of Chaucer's father.

39 *Cartulaire des Comtes de Hainaut*; Leese

40 *Cartulaire des Comtes de Hainaut*

41 Galway, "Philippa Pan, Philippa Chaucer"; *Foedera*; *Complete Peerage*. Paon is mentioned again in the *Cartulaire* on May 1 and August 4, these entries referring to his routine expenses.

42 Perry

43 It is intriguing to discover that a shield bearing what appears to be Paon's coat of arms, impaling the arms of the See of London (which feature crossed swords), was painted on the ceiling of Old St. Paul's. It was one of a number of painted shields placed there that have been dated no later than 1525, and which were recorded in the reign of Charles II by Thomas Dingley. Similar arms were also recorded in 1575 by the Elizabethan antiquary William Lambourne in a window in the Divinity School of Oxford, "in one place contiguous to the shield of the See of London," implying a connection with the painted arms in St. Paul's. In northern Europe it was—and still is—the practice for bishops to marshal their personal arms with those of their diocese; however, since the Roët arms were not borne by any bishop of London, it has been suggested that those on the ceiling belonged to a member of the Roët family who was perhaps appointed Dean of St. Paul's. There has been speculation that this could have been a son of Walter de Roët, but unfortunately, no Roët features on the roll of deans of St. Paul's, which is complete from 1322 to the Reformation, so the likelihood is that these arms were in fact those of a late medieval bishop of London and were misrepresented by Dingley. Perry; Dingley; Lambarde.

44 Cited by McKisack

45 Froissart

46 Power; Labarge

47 For a description of Blanche of Lancaster and a discussion of her birth date, see Chapter 2.

48 See Chapter 2.

49 Walsingham; Waleys Cartulary. Thomas Walsingham (d. 1422) was a Benedictine monk of St. Albans Abbey, one of a number of notable chroniclers of St. Albans. He wrote several works, including a continuation of Matthew Paris's *Chronica Majora*, up to 1422, and a chronicle of England (*Historia Anglicana*) covering the period 911 to 1419. His chronicles are especially valuable for the period 1377 to 1422. However, Walsingham's approach to the writing of history was partisan and credulous. He was sternly moralistic and bordered at times on the histrionic. For him, events like the Peasants Revolt of 1381 were the judgment of God on a wicked people. He considered the reformer John Wycliffe to be the "mouthpiece of the Devil," and for many years he was John of Gaunt's most vehement and vitriolic critic, largely on account of John's perceived anticlericalism. His condemnation of John's affair with Katherine Swynford is to be found in his brief *Chronicon Angliae*, which for very good reasons is known to historians as the "Scandalous Chronicle"; it covers the period to 1388. Walsingham's lacerative and damning disparagement of John of Gaunt in this chronicle ensured that it would be many centuries before historians came to take a more considered and objective view of him, despite the fact that, in his later works, written under the Lancastrian kings, Walsingham himself revised his opinions and wrote of John in a more sympathetic tone, effectively rehabilitating his memory.

50 Murimuth

51 Walsingham

52 Froissart

53 Jean le Bel

54 *Register of Edward, the Black Prince*

55 Froissart

56 Walsingham

57 Henry Knighton (d. ca. 1396) was an Augustinian canon and chronicler of the abbey of St. Mary-in-the-Meadows, Leicester. His chronicle covers the period from the tenth century to 1395. He was particularly well-informed, thanks to his links with John of Gaunt and his household, John being a generous patron of the abbey and personally known to Knighton. Consequently, Knighton displays a sympathetic Lancastrian bias in his writing—he consistently (and uniquely among the chroniclers) takes a favorable view of John and often refers to him as "the good Duke" or "the pious Duke."

58 *Register of Edward, the Black Prince*

59 There has been speculation that Walter had a daughter named Isabel or Elizabeth (possibly after his sister, whose name is also given in both variants). In the parish church of Beddington in Surrey there is the memorial brass of one of the local lords of the manor, Sir Nicholas Carew, son of Edward III's Keeper of the Privy Seal, who died in 1432. Beside him is depicted his first wife, Elizabeth or Isabel Delamere (or de la Mare), who is usually described (although not in contemporary sources) as the daughter and heiress of Stephen Delamere, lord of the manor of Delamers, Hertfordshire, by his wife Alice. Nicholas married Elizabeth around 1374, and she died before 1398,

when he married his second wife, Mercy Hayme. Historians have long speculated that Elizabeth was not a Delamere at all, but a Roët, for the arms on the brass are those of Carew impaling not the arms of the Delamers (of which there are many versions), but what looks like the arms of Paon de Roët; furthermore, it has been suggested that, if she was a Roët, then she was perhaps the daughter of Walter de Roët. There is one major problem with this theory. Elizabeth had two sons by Nicholas Carew, one of whom eventually inherited his father's lands. Had Elizabeth been Walter de Roët's daughter and heiress, she would have inherited the lands he himself had inherited from his father, and they would have passed eventually to her son, and to his descendants. Therefore, there could have been no lands in Hainault in 1411 for Sir Thomas Swynford, Katherine's son, to claim, since Katherine could not have inherited any from her father or brother. Then there is the matter of the arms, which clearly show three Katherine wheels, and not the three plain wheels borne by Paon de Roët; these arms once appeared in stained glass in Beddington Church, and were described in 1611 in an armorial manuscript (now in the British Library) by Nicholas Charles, Lancaster Herald, as Carew impaling three silver Katherine wheels on a field of red; the Beddington arms also have downward-facing projections on the wheels, which Paon's lack. They can be identified, therefore, with the arms of the Street family, who were to be found in Hertfordshire, Kent, and Somerset up to the late sixteenth century; the Street arms are virtually the same as those depicted in Beddington Church and described by Lancaster Herald; thus Elizabeth Carew could have been a Delamere after all, and she was certainly not a descendant of Sir Paon de Roët or a daughter of Walter de Roët. The likelihood is that Walter de Roët died without heirs between 1356 and 1403, and that his patrimony was divided between his surviving sisters as co-heiresses. Haines; Perry; *Victoria County History of Berkshire*; Fairbairn.

60 Crow and Olsen
61 Galway, "Philippa Pan, Philippa Chaucer"; Braddy; Crow and Olsen; Ackroyd
62 Gardner; Manly: *Some New Light on Chaucer*; Galway, "Philippa Pan, Philippa Chaucer"; Selby et al. It has also been suggested that Pan. is short for Pantolf, the Pantolfs being a Shropshire family of gentry, who were lords of Wem. The countess's accounts record Philippa Pan being escorted from "Pullesdone" to Hatfield in 1357; there is no such name as "Pullesdone" listed in modern Ordnance Survey atlases of Britain, but spellings of place names tend to change over time, and it has been postulated that this place was either Pudleston near Hereford, Pilsdon in Dorset, or Puleston, which lies northeast of Newport, Shropshire, not that far from Wem(70). Pullesdon has sometimes been identified with Puleston, therefore, and some historians have claimed that Philippa Pan was a member of the Pantolf family. The problem with this theory is that the Pantolfs of Wem had died out in the thirteenth century, their lands inherited by the Botelers through marriage to the Pantolf heiress. A younger branch of the Pantolf family, the lords of Great Dawley, had also died out, by 1240, when their holdings were divided between four co-heiresses. Had there been any other male relatives, *they* would surely have inherited any Pantolf lands rather than those lands descending to heiresses. Thus it is very unlikely that Philippa Pan belonged to the Pantolf family. Manly, *Some New Light on Chaucer*; Crow and Olsen; Galway, "Pullesdon"; *Victoria County History of Shropshire*; *Complete Peerage*.

63 Manly, *Some New Light on Chaucer*; Gardner; Howard; Stow, *London*; www.British

History.ac. Soper Lane and the Church of St. Pancras no longer exist. The site was near Bucklersbury.

64 Gardner; Ackroyd
65 *Calendar of Close Rolls; Foedera*
66 Galway, "Philippa Pan, Philippa Chaucer"
67 Gardner

2. THE MAGNIFICENT LORD

1 Froissart
2 Goodman, *John of Gaunt*
3 Knighton
4 Fowler, *The King's Lieutenant; Foedera*
5 Blanche's date of birth has been much debated. Froissart, who is not always reliable, says she was born in 1347, and this date would appear to be supported by a statement in the *Calendar of Close Rolls* that she was fourteen on July 16, 1361, the date her father's lands were apportioned. If Blanche's birth year was 1347, then she must have been born before May 3, as it was on that date that she was betrothed to John de Segrave, heir to an ancient baronial family. But according to *John of Gaunt's Register*, Blanche was born in 1344; this is unlikely, as her parents were then living in Gascony, and being born abroad would have rendered her ineligible to succeed to an inheritance in England, which she in fact did without her claim being contested. However, in two of the twenty-six Inquisitions Postmortem for her father drawn up in 1361, her birth date is given as the Feast of the Annunciation (March 25) 1342; in the rest, and in the eleven Inquisitions Postmortem for her sister, her age is usually given as "twenty-one and more." This suggests that proof of her age was not furnished to all the escheators who conducted the Inquisitions, but that in two counties people did know when Blanche had been born, which is credible for March 25 was Lady Day, one of the important feasts of the Church and a popular day for collecting rents. So while it is not conclusive, the overwhelming impression this evidence conveys is that people viewed Blanche as an adult in 1361, not as a young girl of twelve. The inference must be that she was born on March 25, 1342. For Blanche's date of birth, see Anderson; Fowler, *The King's Lieutenant; Calendar of Close Rolls; Complete Peerage; Verity; Calendar of Inquisitions Post Mortem.* Blanche never did marry John de Segrave, for he died in 1349.
6 Walsingham; *Calendar of Entries in the Papal Registers*
7 Chaucer, *The Book of the Duchess*. I have used mainly the vivid translation by Brian Stone in *Love Visions* (London, 1983).
8 Kittredge; Chaucer, *The Book of the Duchess*; Howard; Chute
9 Only the ruined cloisters and baptistry of the abbey remain. Most of the fabric was destroyed in 1540 on the orders of the Emperor Charles V.
10 Goodman, *John of Gaunt*
11 *Calendar of Patent Rolls*; Goodman, *John of Gaunt*
12 Goodman, *John of Gaunt*; Crow and Olsen
13 Froissart
14 Ibid.
15 Cited by McKisack and Rose

16　She may have been the daughter of a Jean "Vilain" de St. Hilaire. Froissart; *Calendar of Close Rolls*; Crow and Olsen; Lettenhove, Froissart, editorial notes.

17　Froissart; Armitage-Smith

18　*Rotuli Parliamentorum*

19　Ibid. On April 7, 1399, Richard II confirmed the grant of this annuity, which was presumably paid until Marie died.

20　Additional mss. The countess's accounts record New Year's gifts to John's cook and clerk of the kitchen.

21　On December 20 one of her father's servants was paid for bringing letters from Blanche to Countess Elizabeth, and these letters might have been about Blanche's forthcoming visit or travel arrangements.

22　Only meager ruins survive of this once great and prosperous abbey, the burial place of its founder, Henry I.

23　Exchequer Records: E. 403

24　Capgrave

25　The King paid £58 (£19,560) for jewels alone for the occasion and gave the young couple jewelery and plate costing £389.11s.6d (£131,378). Exchequer Records: E. 101, E. 403; *Calendar of Close Rolls*.

26　Anderson

27　Yardley; Emery

28　*Calendar of Entries in the Papal Registers*

29　*Calendar of Patent Rolls*

30　Jambeck

31　Howard. "An ABC" was a translation of a French poem, "Le Pèlerinage de La Vie Humaine," by Guillaume Deguilevilles, which evoked the Virgin Mary as the object of courtly love in its most spiritual sense, and Chaucer almost certainly wrote it in the 1360s. Its title is not contemporary, but was added in the next century by the poet John Lydgate.

32　Lane

33　Special Collections, S.C. 1; Goodman, *John of Gaunt*

34　Exchequer Records, E. 403

35　*John of Gaunt's Register*; Goodman, *John of Gaunt*. John of Gaunt's *Registers*, containing details of ducal warrants, grants, and payments, survive in full for the periods 1372–76 and 1379–83, and are stored in the National Archives at Kew. These registers are an invaluable source of information about Katherine Swynford, who is referred to in no fewer than thirty-two documents, while Kettlethorpe, where she lived after her marriage, is referred to in eleven.

36　Bishop Buckingham's Register

37　Knighton

38　Ellis; Goodman, *John of Gaunt*; Fox and Russell

39　Most of Leicester Castle was in ruins by the seventeenth century. The arcaded great hall survives, although much altered, and now houses the crown court. Its red-brick frontage was added in ca. 1690. Parts of the castle walls survive, as does the church of St. Mary de Castro. The inner bailey is now Castle Yard. The castle mound itself has been leveled to accommodate a bowling green. Henry VIII did not suppress the collegiate foundation in the Newarke, because it contained the tombs of his Lancastrian ancestors, but it was dissolved in 1547 under his son, Edward VI, and St. Mary's Church and the college buildings were demolished soon afterward. Trinity Hospital, which was restored in 1776 and 1902, is now an old people's home, and stands in the Newarke, opposite the modern Leicester College of Art and Technology, in the basement of which are some medieval archways. The aisled hall and the chapel at the eastern end of the hospital are the only surviving parts of the original fourteenth-century building. The ruined turreted gateway leading to the Newarke dates from the fifteenth century. The Newarke itself is now a busy road.

40   Leland, *Itinerary*; Leland visited the Newarke in the early sixteenth century.

41   Goodman, *John of Gaunt*; Somerville; Fowler, *The King's Lieutenant*; *Victoria County History: Leicestershire*; Webster

42   *Calendar of Patent Rolls*

43   *John of Gaunt's Register*, Duchy of Lancaster Records: DL. 28; Goodman, *John of Gaunt*. Hardly anything survives at Hertford Castle from John of Gaunt's time. The castle was in ruins by 1609, when it passed into private ownership. The buildings that still stand, including the remains of the fifteenth-century gatehouse, are mostly of a later date, and house the civic offices.

44   Goodman, *John of Gaunt*; *Early Lincoln Wills*; *John of Gaunt's Register*; *Calendar of Patent Rolls*; Duchy of Lancaster Records, DL. 28; *Calendar of Entries in the Papal Registers*

45   *Calendar of Inquisitions Post Mortem*

46   Cited by Silva-Vigier

47   *Calendar of Close Rolls*; *Calendar of Patent Rolls*

48   *Foedera*

49   *Calendar of Patent Rolls*; Somerville

50   Joan, "the fair maid of Kent," was the daughter of the King's uncle, Edmund of Woodstock, Earl of Kent (who had been unjustly executed for treason in 1330), and therefore a cousin of the Black Prince. Born in 1328, she was brought up in the Queen's household. At the tender age of twelve she apparently fell in love with one-eyed Sir Thomas Holland (or Holand), and secretly precontracted herself to him. After exchanging vows before witnesses—which were as binding as a marriage in the eyes of the Church—the young couple consummated their union, but then Sir Thomas went away on a crusade in Prussia. It may be that he was thought to have died, for around 1341–42 arrangements were made for Joan to marry young William de Montagu, Earl of Salisbury, and they lived together as man and wife until 1347. But in 1349, after Holland returned, very much alive, and reclaimed Joan, the Pope ruled that his union with her was valid, that her marriage to Montagu was null and void, and that Joan was to return to Holland and live with him as his lawful wife. This she willingly did, despite Montagu's protests, and the marriage was blessed with five children (one of whom was later to marry the daughter of John and Blanche) before Sir Thomas Holland died in 1360. Froissart; *Foedera*; Hicks; Goodman, *John of Gaunt*.

51   McKisack; *Dictionary of National Biography*; Silva-Vigier

52   *Calendar of Inquisitions Post Mortem*; Froissart

53   Ormrod

54   Knighton; *Records of the Borough of Leicester*; Ramsay

55   *Complete Peerage*

56   *Rotuli Parliamentorum*

57 Silva-Vigier

58 Walker. A wealthy nobleman might normally have at best sixty men in his retinue.

59 Cited by Hicks

60 Knighton

61 McKisack; *John of Gaunt's Register*; Armitage-Smith

62 He is described as the eldest son of John and Blanche in both the Harleian and Sloane mss. In the sixteenth century Leland visited St. Mary's Church in the Newarke at Leicester, and saw the tombs of "two men children under the arch" next to the head of the effigy of Henry, Earl of Lancaster, who was buried on the north side of the high altar. These were almost certainly two of the infant sons of John of Gaunt.

63 Exchequer Records: E. 403

64 *John of Gaunt's Register*

65 Ibid.

66 Froissart

67 Knighton

68 Ibid.

69 Knighton; Walsingham

70 *John of Gaunt's Register*

71 *Anonimalle Chronicle*. The *Chronicle* is fiercely anti-Lancastrian and critical of John of Gaunt.

72 Froissart; John of Gaunt's Will, in *Testamenta Eboracensia*

73 Knighton

74 *John of Gaunt's Register*

75 Stow, *London*

76 For the Savoy Palace, see *John of Gaunt's Register*; Palmer, A. and P.; Webster; Dalzell; Stow: *London*; Rose; Beaumont-Jones; Powrie; Green, V.H.H.; Duchy of Lancaster Records, DL. 28, DL. 42; Silva-Vigier; Dunn; Goodman, *John of Gaunt*; Armitage-Smith; Fowler, *The King's Lieutenant*; Delachenal. The remains of John of Gaunt's palace were razed by Henry VII, who founded the Hospital of the Savoy on the site. In 1553 the hospital was suppressed by Edward VI during the Reformation, although the chapel served as a parish church until at least 1598. By the seventeenth century the hospital buildings were dilapidated and crumbling, and had become the haunt of thieves and vagrants. In the eighteenth century part of the complex was used as a military prison housing, among others, deserters who had been sentenced to die by firing squad in Hyde Park. By 1820 the old hospital was largely derelict, and in 1864 fire destroyed all that was left of it except the walls, which were cleared to make way for the approaches to the new Waterloo Bridge. The site remained empty until 1880, when Richard D'Oyly Carte purchased it in order to build the Savoy Theatre. All that is left of the Savoy today are parts of the stone walls of Henry VII's chapel. Nothing survives from John of Gaunt's time.

77 Fortescue; Armitage-Smith; Goodman, *John of Gaunt*; Barnes

78 Goodman, *John of Gaunt*

79 *The London Spy*, Ned Ward (1699), cited by Hahn

80 Goodman, *John of Gaunt*

81 Cited by Armitage-Smith

82 Binski; Shaw

83 Dugdale, *History of St. Paul's*; Sandford

84 The duke's privy seal, bearing his arms and helm only, is in the British Library; his great seal as King of Castile and León is in the collection of the Society of Antiquaries of London.

85 Cotton ms. Nero Dvii f 7r.; Goodman, *John of Gaunt*

86 Goodman, *John of Gaunt*; Baker; Hutchinson

87 *John of Gaunt's Register*. A late fourteenth-century stained-glass window in the parish church of St. Mary at Long Sutton in Lincolnshire has a figure of St. George killing the dragon, for which John of Gaunt has traditionally been thought to be the model. John was lord of this manor, then one of the most prosperous communities in the area, and it is indeed possible that he donated the glass, as he probably did at Old Bolingbroke, also in Lincolnshire, where the east window of the chancel bore his arms. But in the absence of other evidence, apart from the Long Sutton glass being of a quality commensurate with John's status and wealth, we cannot be certain if the oral tradition relating to the glass has any basis in fact. Perry; Hebgin-Barnes; Knightly.

88 Lopes

89 Walsingham; Armitage-Smith

90 Froissart

91 *Rotuli Parliamentorum*

92 *John of Gaunt's Register*

93 Chaucer, *The Book of the Duchess*

94 Froissart; Jones, *Ducal Brittany*

95 Walsingham

96 Cited by Hicks

97 *Westminster Chronicle*

98 Goodman, *John of Gaunt*; Panton; *Extracts from the Account Rolls of the Abbey of Durham*

99 *John of Gaunt's Register*

100 Cotton ms. Nero

101 Cox; Shaw; Fox and Russell; *John of Gaunt's Register*; *Calendar of Patent Rolls*; Legge

102 *John of Gaunt's Register*; Duchy of Lancaster Records, DL. 28

103 Chaucer, *The Book of the Duchess*

104 Pearsall; *The Kalendarium of Nicholas of Lynn*

105 *Calendar of Entries in the Papal Registers*; *Rotuli Parliamentorum*

106 *John of Gaunt's Register*; *Calendar of Patent Rolls*

107 Chaucer, *The Book of the Duchess*

108 Goodman, *Honourable Lady*; *John of Gaunt*; Wathey; Froissart; *The Kalendarium of Nicholas of Lynn*; McFarlane

109 Goodman, *John of Gaunt*; Cowling

110 *Political Poems and Songs*

3. THE TRAP OF WEDDING

1 The drawing is in Dugdale's *Book of Monuments* in the British Library.

2 Dudley

3 Claims have also been made that four carved heads on the gateway of Butley Priory near Woodbridge, Suffolk, represent Katherine Swynford, John of Gaunt, Henry IV,

and Henry Beaufort. The gatehouse, however, dates from 1311–32—it is all that remains today of the original twelfth-century priory, while the royal arms on the gateway predate 1340, when Edward III had them quartered with the ancient lilies of France in pursuance of his claim to the French throne. The heads most probably survive from this earlier period, and there is, moreover, no written evidence in the records of Butley Priory to connect John of Gaunt or Katherine Swynford with it; Suffolk was one of only two English counties where John did not hold any manors or other property. Butley Priory is now a hotel. Wood; Armitage-Smith.

4 ms. 61, fol. lv. Corpus Christi College, Cambridge

5 Ackroyd

6 Williams

7 Loomis

8 Goodman, *Honourable Lady*

9 For Katherine's appearance and character generally, see Lucraft, "Missing from History"; Silva-Vigier; Given-Wilson; Goodman, *Honourable Lady*; Bruce; Tilbury

10 The correct medieval form of his name was Hugh de Swynford, but in order to comply with popular usage I have chosen to omit the *de* throughout the text.

11 Silva-Vigier

12 For the Swynford family, see chiefly Perry; *Excerpta Historica*; Nicolas; Cole.

13 It has been claimed that Sir Thomas Swynford was possibly a younger son, or more likely a grandson, of Sir Thomas de Swynford of Knaith in Lincolnshire, who died in 1312, but that is less likely. Sir Thomas was certainly related to John de Swynford, who was Lord of Burgate in 1311, but seems not to have been Sir Robert's father—and to Sir John de Swynford, who was MP for Huntingdonshire and died in 1332; their shields all bore three gold boars' heads on a field of silver. Another reason for believing that Sir Thomas was Robert's son is that, in the fifteenth century, Thomas's great-granddaughter, another Katherine Swynford, was to marry into the Drury family, whose seat was at Rougham, Suffolk, and whose favored place of burial was Burgate parish church; this suggests a longstanding connection with Burgate. Farrer; *Excerpta Historica*; Cole; Campling; Perry.

14 The name is given variously as Copledike, Cobledike, or Cubbledykes. This family had acquired Coleby in 1315.

15 *Calendar of Inquisitions Post Mortem*; Goodman, *Katherine Swynford*; *John of Gaunt's Register*; Chancery Records, C. 143

16 *Calendar of Patent Rolls*; Cole. Although it is often stated that Nichola's father was Sir Robert de Arderne of Drayton, Oxfordshire, she was probably the daughter and heiress of John Druel, who in 1311 was lord of the manor of Newton Blossomville, Bedfordshire; his wife was named Amice. The Druel family had been at Newton Blossomville since at least the thirteenth century, and two of its members were rectors of the parish church of St. Nicholas. Nichola must have been John Druel's daughter or heiress, because she inherited Newton Blossomville. When she married Sir Thomas Swynford, he became lord of this manor in her right, and apparently settled there until 1357, when he and Nicola conveyed Newton Blossomville to Sir Ralph Basset of Drayton. *Complete Peerage*; Cole; *Calendar of Close Rolls*; *Victoria County History: Buckinghamshire*; Lipscombe.

17 *Calendar of Patent Rolls*; *Calendar of Close Rolls*; Cole; Exchequer Records, E. 358

18 *Victoria County History: Bedfordshire*

19 Feet of Fines, 30 Edward III, no. 8, cited by Cole

20 Cole; *Calendar of Close Rolls*

21 Ibid.

22 *John of Gaunt's Register*

23 This was something of a family tradition, for Hugh's uncle, Sir Norman Swynford, had served Duke Henry in four military and diplomatic enterprises; see Fowler; Duchy of Lancaster Records, DL. 27.

24 *Calendar of Inquisitions Post Mortem*

25 *Calendar of Patent Rolls*

26 Galway, "Philippa Pan, Philippa Chaucer"

27 Bishop Buckingham's Register

28 There is no historical evidence for them being married at St. Clement Danes Church in the Strand, as several Internet sites—following Anya Seton—assert.

29 *Excerpta Historica*; Perry; Birch

30 Williams; Krauss; Gardner

31 *Calendar of Inquisitions Post Mortem*—IPM for Sir Thomas Swynford, 1361; Perry

32 *Calendar of Inquisitions Post Mortem*

33 Thorold

34 *Calendar of Inquisitions Post Mortem*. Nothing remains of the fourteenth-century church today; it was mostly rebuilt in the nineteenth century, and the only medieval survival is the fifteenth-century battlemented tower.

35 For Kettlethorpe generally, see www.kettlethorpe.com; Perry; Cole; Mee; Leese; Goodman, *Katherine Swynford*; *John of Gaunt*; Tilbury; *Calendar of Inquisitions Post Mortem*; "Kettlethorpe," Strutt and Parker Sale Brochure, 1981 (Lincoln Reference Library).

36 *Calendar of Inquisitions Post Mortem*

37 For Coleby generally, see *Calendar of Inquisitions Post Mortem*; Perry; Richardson; *Coleby Village: Home of Koli*; Tempest. Today, Coleby is a small rural hamlet with picturesque stone buildings.

38 *Calendar of Patent Rolls*

39 Crow and Olsen; Goodman, *Katherine Swynford*

40 Wickenden; Knighton; Goodman, *John of Gaunt*; Mee

41 Hill, *Mediaeval Lincoln*

42 Silva-Vigier

43 Camden

44 Additional mss.

45 *Archaeological Journal*, XXI, 1864

46 For "John of Gaunt's Palace" see chiefly Hill, *Mediaeval Lincoln*; Green, *Forgotten Lincoln*; *The History of Lincoln*; Mee. By the eighteenth century the "palace"—now known as "Broxholme's great house"—had been divided into three tenements; John of Gaunt's arms were in place until at least 1737, but in 1783 much of the house was pulled down. In 1849 what was left was auctioned off and soon afterward demolished. A beautiful Decorated triple-lighted oriel window boasting ogee canopies, finials, quatrefoils, and carved figures and foliage, was removed in its entirety from the south end of the condemned building and set in the castle gatehouse, where it may be seen today. A fragment of the medieval house survives, and a fifteenth-century window. Opposite the

"palace" stood "another ancient building known as 'John of Gaunt's stables,' " but according to William Camden, this was "more likely to have been his palace than the other," which suggests that the "stables" were in a better state of repair than the "palace" in the late sixteenth century. In 1784 the skeptical Grimm referred to "the old house pretended by some to have been the stables of John of Gaunt, by some a religious house, and by others the old town hall and a prison." In fact, the building was St. Mary's Guildhall, erected around 1150–60; today only parts of two walls remain from that time, the rest having been demolished in 1737. Additional mss. For Lincoln generally, see Hill, *Mediaeval Lincoln*; Duffy, *Calendar of Patent Rolls*; Goodman, *Katherine Swynford*; *Honourable Lady*; *John of Gaunt*; Silva-Vigier; Crow and Olsen; Beaumont-Jones; Hamilton Thompson; Powrie. Lincoln Castle now houses the Georgian gaol and the Assize Courts.

47 *Calendar of Patent Rolls*

48 For Katherine's daughters, see Perry; Loftus and Chettle; Sturman; *John of Gaunt's Register*.

49 Stapleton; Cole

50 Farmer; Attwater

51 William de Belesby, Sheriff of Lincolnshire in 1382 and 1388, was married to one Elizabeth Swynford, the daughter and heiress of William de Swynford of the Huntingdonshire branch of the family, who also held lands in Lincolnshire; it is also possible that Gilbert de Beseby, the chamberlain at Kettlethorpe, was a member of this family, as spellings of surnames often vary. Andrew Luttrell, who died in 1390 and whose father had commissioned the famous *Luttrell Psalter*, probably married another Swynford girl, for the Swynford arms were once visible on his brass in Irnham Church. Lansdowne mss.; Perry.

52 Speculation that there was another daughter of Katherine and Hugh is probably unfounded. A Katherine Swynford appears on a list of nuns at Stixwould Priory, a Cistercian house twelve miles east of Lincoln, in 1377. Since Margaret Swynford was old enough to enter a London convent in 1377, it is just possible she had a sister old enough to enter Stixwould that year, and as noted, it was not unheard of for girls to enter nunneries when they were still in childhood. It is also possible that one of Katherine's daughters by Hugh was given her mother's name. But there is nothing else to suggest that this Katherine Swynford was the daughter of Hugh and Katherine. There were many branches of the Swynford family, and little evidence to show how they were interrelated, therefore this nun could have belonged to any of them. Furthermore, Stixwould was a poor house compared to those in which Margaret Swynford and her cousins Elizabeth and Agnes Chaucer were placed in 1377 and 1381. Founded in the twelfth century, it now housed just twenty-eight nuns; back in the late thirteenth century it was one of only five nunneries able to export at least fifteen sacks of wool, but after the Black Death there was clearly a decline, for by the late fourteenth century Stixwould's assets were modest, and in 1419 the nuns were excused payment of a subsidy on account of their poverty. More to the point, by the mid-1370s, Katherine Swynford was sufficiently wealthy to have found a far better foundation for one of her daughters. Therefore, it is highly unlikely that the nun at Stixwould was her child. McHardy, *Clerical Poll Taxes*; Nichols; Knowles and Hadcock; Graves; *Victoria County History: Lincolnshire*; Joy; Perry.

53 *Calendar of Entries in the Papal Registers.* The full text of the petition, and a translation into English, is given by Kelly.

54 Perry

55 Kelly

56 *John of Gaunt's Register*

57 Perry; Goodman, *Katherine Swynford*; Crow and Olsen

58 *Calendar of Patent Rolls; John of Gaunt's Register;* Crow and Olsen

59 Exchequer Records, E. 403

60 He was buried with his brother and namesake in St. Mary's Church in the Newarke (Lane).

61 Bishop Buckingham's Register

62 *John of Gaunt's Register*

63 Ackroyd; Ayala; Honoré-Duvergé

64 *Calendar of Patent Rolls;* Crow and Olsen

65 Chancery Records, C. 81. It was Robert Glover, Somerset Herald, who, between 1571 and 1588, first identified Philippa Chaucer with Philippa de Roët. The Elizabethan antiquary, John Stow, also stated that Geoffrey Chaucer "had to wife the daughter of Paon Roët." That this identification is correct is almost conclusively proved by the appearance of the Roët arms on the tomb of Philippa's son, Thomas Chaucer. Crow and Olsen; Speght; Krauss: *Three Chaucer Studies.*

66 Ibid.

67 *Calendar of Patent Rolls*

68 *Dictionary of National Biography;* Chute

69 McKisack

70 Gardner

71 Howard

72 Pearsall

73 Gardner

74 Gardner; Lounsbury

75 Given-Wilson; Gardner; Lounsbury

76 Emerson; Armitage-Smith; Hardy; Bryant; Johnson; Packe; Norwich. For Pedro's deposition, see Chandos Herald; Froissart; *Foedera;* Russell; Gardner; *Calendar of Patent Rolls.* Regarding Chandos Herald, in ca. 1385 an anonymous herald of Sir John Chandos wrote a laudatory poem about the exploits of Edward, Prince of Wales in 1366–67. His fulsome praise for John of Gaunt, and the likely date of the poem, led John Palmer to suggest that it may be the work of a Lancastrian propagandist who supported John's claim to the kingdom of Castile.

77 *Excerpta Historica; Foedera*

78 Bolingbroke Castle remains to this day the property of the Duchy of Lancaster; it was maintained as a royal castle until the sixteenth century, but thereafter fell into decay. The walls and towers were largely destroyed by the Parliamentarians in 1643, and the gateway collapsed in 1815. The remaining walls and mounds have recently undergone excavation, which revealed some buried stonework, and partial restoration. These ruins are located off an unclassified road in the village of Old Bolingbroke.

79 *Calendar of Inquisitions Post Mortem; Calendar of Close Rolls*

80 *Calendar of Inquisitions Post Mortem; John of Gaunt's Register*

81 *Calendar of Inquisitions Post Mortem*

82 Jones, Major, Varley and Johnson; Jones, Stocker and Vince; also the works on Lincoln listed under note 46.

83 Cole

84 Froissart

85 Chandos Herald; Froissart

86 Some historians place Henry's birth in the spring of 1366, but that was when his brother John was born; and on June 1, 1367, we find Edward III rewarding one Ingelram Falconer for delivering letters from Duchess Blanche in which she announced Henry's arrival, while on July 14 the King also rewarded Blanche, widow of Sir Robert Bertram, for bringing him news of the birth. Goodman, *John of Gaunt*; Exchequer Records, E. 43, E. 403.

87 It was worn by Henry V at Agincourt in 1415, and is now one of the most precious gems in the Imperial State Crown.

88 Froissart; Russell; *Foedera*; Exchequer Records, E. 403; Chancery Records, C. 53

89 He would appear to have reached the age of twenty-one by July 8, 1389 (Pearsall).

90 Williams; Krauss, *Three Chaucer Studies*; Delany; Howard

91 *John of Gaunt's Register*; Williams; Gardner

92 Perry; Loftus and Chettle

93 Manly; Kelly

94 Kelly; Perry; Christopherson

95 Crow and Olsen. It is sometimes claimed that Geoffrey Chaucer never even bore arms; they were not generally granted to merchants until the mid-fifteenth century, and the arms sometimes attributed to his father, John Chaucer, are probably spurious. But a seal used by Thomas Chaucer at Ewelme in 1409, which bears the legend [G]HOFRAI CHAVCIER, has a shield displaying a bend entire, an unbroken diagonal stripe across a field. These are not the arms customarily used by Thomas Chaucer, whose shield sported a bend countercharged in red and silver, with the disposition of colors in each half of the field and at each end of the bend itself, reversed on the other. It is this latter shield that appears on later portraits of Geoffrey, including those at Harvard University and in the National Portrait Gallery, and on his sixteenth-century tomb in Westminster Abbey. There can be little doubt, therefore, that these were his arms, that the chargings on the seal are an early version, somewhat worn and obliterated, and that Thomas, who used the same arms, was Geoffrey's son. This is borne out by Thomas once signing himself "son of Geoffrey Chaucer," and being described as such by the fifteenth-century Oxford theologian Thomas Gascoigne, who was personally acquainted with him.

 There are also several instances in this period of men choosing to display their mother's arms rather than their father's, if the mother was of higher rank. The arms of Maud Burghersh were more prestigious than any Chaucer could have borne, for she came from a prominent baronial family. And of course Geoffrey Chaucer must have been only one among many male relatives whose arms do not appear on the tomb. As Martin Ruud says, Thomas Chaucer was a snob, not a bastard.

 It has also been pointed out that there is no record of Thomas Chaucer ever claiming the property in Hainault he inherited from his mother, as Thomas Swynford did in 1411; this too has been seen as evidence of bastardy. But it is worth mentioning that we similarly lack any record of Walter de Roët or his sisters inheriting those lands, or of the date of death of Paon de Roët, who left them to his children. We only know of the existence of such an inheritance through Thomas Swynford's claim, and only because it was contested. A reasonable conclusion is that the records relating to this inheritance, which cannot have been substantial, have simply been lost, so perhaps Thomas Chaucer did get his share. See, for example, Thomas's seal in Cotton ms. Julius, BL. Cvii, f.153; Exchequer records, E. 164; Leese; Howard; Ruud.

96 *John of Gaunt's Register*; Leese; Pearsall

4. MISTRESS OF THE DUKE

1 *Cartulaire des Comtes de Hainaut*
2 *Register of Thomas Appleby*; Palmer, "Historical Context . . ."
3 *John of Gaunt's Register*
4 Sloane ms. 82, f. 5; Harleian mss.; Lane
5 Goodman, *John of Gaunt*; *Register of Thomas Appleby*. I am indebted to Professor Goodman for sending me the latter reference.
6 Froissart, *Le Joli Buisson de Jonece*
7 *Register of Thomas Appleby*. There is other evidence that Blanche died in 1368. Dr. J.J.N. Palmer cites a letter John of Gaunt wrote in France on August 17, 1369, in which the duke asks that his cousin, Blanche Mowbray, Lady Poynings, be invited to attend the obit to mark the first anniversary of the duchess's death; there is also a letter of December 1368 from Louis de Male, Count of Flanders, to Queen Philippa, rejecting a proposal that John of Gaunt marry his daughter Margaret, so Blanche was dead by then, which is why there is no record that she was issued with the customary new robes at Christmas 1368, nor with mourning garments for Queen Philippa the following year. Palmer, "Historical Context . . ."; *John of Gaunt's Register*; Brewer. Stow also gives Blanche's date of death as 1368.
8 Walsingham, *Gesta Abbatum . . .* ; Silva-Vigier. Later, John of Gaunt would donate two pieces of expensive gold cloth to the abbey "for the soul of Blanche his wife, whose body lay here one night."
9 Dugdale, *History of St. Paul's Cathedral*
10 Stow, *London*; Webster
11 She was the niece of Henry, Duke of Lancaster, being the daughter of his sister Eleanor, who married Richard FitzAlan, Earl of Arundel.
12 *John of Gaunt's Register*
13 Ibid.
14 Brewer; Pearsall; Perry; Galway
15 Brewer
16 Stone, introduction to Chaucer, *Love Visions*
17 Pearsall
18 Goodman, *John of Gaunt*; Silva-Vigier; Palmer, "Historical Context . . ."
19 Brewer
20 Froissart
21 Exchequer Records, E. 403
22 On November 28, 1368, Philippa had been listed as one of thirteen *damoiselles* of the

Queen who were to be given new robes for Christmas; as a member of the King's household, Geoffrey Chaucer also received such robes. Pearsall.

23 Froissart

24 Froissart, *Le Joli Buisson de Jonece*

25 Brewer; Pearsall; Perry; Galway; Exchequer Records, E. 101

26 *Testamenta Eboracensia*

27 *John of Gaunt's Register*; Duchy of Lancaster Records, DL. 28. Over the years, there are numerous references to the annual obits in *John of Gaunt's Register* and the Receiver-General's accounts for the Duchy of Lancaster, further proof of John's enduring devotion to Blanche's memory.

28 Bruce

29 Cole

30 Froissart

31 *John of Gaunt's Register*; Exchequer Records, E. 101

32 Froissart

33 *John of Gaunt's Register*

34 Froissart

35 The palace was damaged by fires in 1597 and 1704, and completely demolished in 1800.

36 Froissart; Gardner

37 Froissart

38 Ibid.

39 Armitage-Smith

40 Additional ms. 12531, fol. 10, detached leaf

41 Froissart also says that the marriage took place at St. André-de-Cubzac, just north of Bordeaux, while Sandford, writing in the late seventeenth century, claims they were married in the Abbey of St. Andrew in Bordeaux.

42 *John of Gaunt's Register*

43 *Testamenta Eboracensis*

44 Goodman, *John of Gaunt*

45 *John of Gaunt's Register*

46 Ibid.; Froissart

47 *John of Gaunt's Register*; Exeter Cathedral Archives

48 *John of Gaunt's Register*; Goodman, *John of Gaunt*

49 Froissart

50 *John of Gaunt's Register*

51 *Calendar of Inquisitions Post Mortem*; *Calendar of Close Rolls*; Richardson

52 It has been erroneously claimed that he was buried in Spratton Church, Northamptonshire, but the fine effigy of a knight that lies there in fact graces the tomb of another retainer of John of Gaunt, Hugh's kinsman Sir John Swynford, Lord of Spratton, who died in 1372. Displayed on this effigy is the earliest-known representation of a collar with the famous Lancastrian SS links. Goodman, *John of Gaunt*; Gardner; *Victoria County History: Northamptonshire*.

53 Norris

54 Brewer; *John of Gaunt's Register*

55 Brewer

56 Walsingham

57 See Holmes, *The Good Parliament*, for example.

58 Gardner

59 Emerson

60 *Anonimalle Chronicle*

61 *John of Gaunt's Register*

62 Ibid. Philippa and Elizabeth were given gold filets set with balas rubies to wear on their heads, and their robes were lavishly embroidered with pearls and trimmed with furs.

63 Ibid.

64 Ibid.

65 Ibid.

66 *Calendar of Patent Rolls; Complete Peerage*

67 Goodman, *Wars of the Roses*

68 *Calendar of Entries in the Papal Registers*

69 The Monk of Evesham corroborates the theory that the affair began only after John had married Constance.

70 Walsingham; Percy ms.; Armitage-Smith. The late fifteenth-/early sixteenth-century Percy ms. 78 at Alnwick Castle claims that John of Gaunt begot John Beaufort "in the days of the Lady Blanche, his first wife."

71 Lord Berners, in his sixteenth-century translation of Froissart, says that Katherine "was concubine to the Duke in his other wives' days."

72 *Original Letters; English Historical Documents, vol. IV*

73 Froissart

74 *John of Gaunt's Register*

75 Lopes

76 Froissart

77 *John of Gaunt's Register*

78 See, for example, Roger Joy.

79 *Calendar of Close Rolls*

80 *John of Gaunt's Register*

81 Ibid.

82 *Calendar of Inquisitions Post Mortem; Calendar of Patent Rolls*

83 Ibid.

84 *Calendar of Patent Rolls*

85 *John of Gaunt's Register*

86 Duchy of Lancaster Records, DL. 29

87 *John of Gaunt's Register*

88 Ibid.

89 Exchequer Records, E. 403

90 *John of Gaunt's Register*

91 *John of Gaunt's Register;* Goodman, *John of Gaunt*

92 Knighton

93 Packe. According to Froissart, Constance's sister Isabella was "young and beautiful," but there the similarity to Constance ended, for Isabella was a lively, flighty girl, worldly rather than devout, with loose morals. In years to come her name would become a by-word for scandal at court, for her extramarital affairs were notorious. Nevertheless, the

legitimacy of the three children she bore her husband was never called into question. Armitage-Smith; Goodman, *John of Gaunt*; Howard; Silva-Vigier.

94 *John of Gaunt's Register*
95 Both Armitage-Smith and Lucraft place his birth date in 1373.
96 Froissart
97 Ibid.
98 Walsingham, *Ypodigma Neustriae*. Since 1689, Beaufort has been called Monmorency-sur-Aube.
99 Duchy of Lancaster Records, DL. 27; Froissart
100 Goodman, *Katherine Swynford*; Jones and Underwood
101 By Sandford, for example
102 Armitage-Smith; Jones and Underwood. Professor Goodman has an interesting theory that the Beauforts were in fact surnamed in honor of Roger de Beaufort, brother of the last Avignon Pope, Gregory XI (Pierre Roger de Beaufort). Roger came from a prominent Provençal family and had been a prisoner of John of Gaunt, held in honorable custody at Kenilworth Castle, since 1370. In 1377 he stood godfather there to the son of his custodian, Sir John Deyncourt. Beaufort was a chivalrous knight, and he and his brother the Pope were highly regarded by the duke, which has prompted Professor Goodman to suggest that John may have wished to compliment Beaufort by naming his children by Katherine after him, and that this may also have been an attempt to hide their paternity. Of course, Beaufort could have been complicit in this matter, but it was hardly complimentary of John to name his bastards after the Pope's brother, and—even more insultingly—thereby imply that Beaufort had fathered them. Goodman, *Katherine Swynford*.

5. BLINDED BY DESIRE

1 Howard
2 Knighton
3 *Troilus and Criseyde*
4 *Anonimalle Chronicle*
5 Thynne
6 See Chapter 8.
7 For late medieval attitudes to sex and morality, see, for example, Given-Wilson and Curteis; Goodman, *Honourable Lady*; Gardner; Silva-Vigier.
8 *John of Gaunt's Register*
9 Ibid.
10 Ibid.; Brewer
11 *John of Gaunt's Register*
12 *Letters of Mediaeval Women*
13 *John of Gaunt's Register*. Lady Wake had been born Alice FitzAlan, daughter of the Earl of Arundel, and she was a niece of Henry, Duke of Lancaster, a cousin to Duchess Blanche, and married to Thomas Holland, eldest son of Princess Joan. Thus, she was eminently suited, through her connections alone, to look after the Lancastrian children.
14 Ibid.

15 Ibid.; Bruce

16 *John of Gaunt's Register*

17 Ibid; Goodman, *John of Gaunt.* Tutbury Castle is now an extensive ruin, having been largely slighted by Cromwell's troops in the civil war. Three towers remain, as does John of Gaunt's gateway, but most of the other buildings are fifteenth century or later.

18 Chute

19 Goodman, *Honourable Lady.* For the governess's role, see Goodman, *Honourable Lady, John of Gaunt*; Lucraft, "Missing from History"; Chute; Lewis, *Cult of St. Katherine*; Tilbury.

20 *John of Gaunt's Register*

21 Ibid.

22 Ibid.

23 Ibid.

24 Ibid.

25 Ibid.

26 Pearsall

27 *John of Gaunt's Register; Rotuli Parliamentorum*

28 For the *chevauchée* of 1373, see, for example, Goodman, *John of Gaunt*; Froissart; Armitage-Smith; Delachenal; Holmes; Sherborne.

29 Froissart

30 For a reassessment of the campaign, see Palmer; *Les Grandes Chroniques France.*

31 Walsingham; *Eulogium*; Russell; Froissart

32 *Calendar of Entries in the Papal Registers*

33 *John of Gaunt's Register.* On June 18, while still at the Savoy, John ordered six cartloads of alabaster from the quarry at Tutbury for two effigies to be placed on the tomb being built to the memory of "the Lady Blanche, formerly our consort," in St. Paul's; already he had decided that he wished to spend eternity by the side of his first wife. Another mention of the tomb appears on December 4 of that year in the accounts for Blanche's obit, and in January 1375 the duke paid Henry Yevele, the foremost master mason of the day, for his work on it, yet to be completed; Yevele was also working at the Savoy at this time. In 1376–77, Yevele was contracted to supply a tomb chest of Purbeck marble to accommodate the bodies of Blanche and, in time, her husband, and was paid £108 (£29,036) in part payment for it. The alabaster effigies were later painted, and an iron screen placed about the chantry. Given the expertise, time, and money—in total £486 (£205,139)—that were lavished on the tomb, it must have been magnificent indeed. It was, wrote the chronicler Monk of St. Denis, "an incomparable sepulchre." *John of Gaunt's Register*; Harvey, *Henry Yevele*; Duchy of Lancaster Records, DL. 28.

34 Lettenhove, introduction to Froissart

35 Armitage-Smith; Goodman, *John of Gaunt*; Rose; *John of Gaunt's Register*

36 Perroy; Holmes; Goodman, *John of Gaunt*

37 *John of Gaunt's Register*; Duchy of Lancaster Records, DL. 42

38 Crow and Olsen; Pearsall

39 Coleman

40 *John of Gaunt's Register*

41 For this obit, see Lewis, "The Anniversary Service"; Webster

42 *John of Gaunt's Register*; Silva-Vigier

43 Silva-Vigier

44 *John of Gaunt's Register*

45 Roger Joy

46 *John of Gaunt's Register*

47 Ibid.

48 Ibid.

49 Ibid.; Kirby. She was paid 100 marks (£11,944) per annum to house him and his attendants.

50 *John of Gaunt's Register*

51 Ibid.

52 Ibid.

53 Ibid.

54 Ibid. There is no evidence to support the recent theory identifying Blanche Swynford with John of Gaunt's bastard daughter Blanche, who married Sir Thomas Morieux in 1381 (see Chapter 6). Froissart states that Marie de St. Hilaire was Blanche Morieux's mother, and as he was in Queen Philippa's household in the early 1360s, he was in a position to know that, for Marie was one of her *damoiselles* and his countrywoman. Had Blanche Swynford lived, she would probably have married Robert Deyncourt, but there is no record of that marriage actually taking place.

55 Ibid.

56 Ibid.

57 *Foedera*; Armitage-Smith

58 *John of Gaunt's Register*

59 Ibid.

60 Ibid.

61 Ibid.

62 Ibid.

63 For Katherine Swynford's connections with Boston, see principally Thompson; Cook, *Boston.*

64 Calendar of Escheat Rolls

65 Ibid.

66 Jones and Underwood

67 In medieval times there was no rule about the use of such marks for younger sons: It was only around 1500 that John Writhe, Garter King of Arms, invented a cadency system to indicate a son's place in the family, whereby a crescent signified a second son. That rule cannot be applied to fourteenth-century heraldry, but Sandford was clearly following a well-established tradition that Henry was the second male Beaufort.

68 *John of Gaunt's Register*

69 *Records of the Borough of Leicester*

70 Ibid.; Goodman, *Katherine Swynford*

71 For Kenilworth, see Ashley; Palmer; Renn; Goodman, *John of Gaunt*; Silva-Vigier; Joy. Kenilworth passed to Henry IV in 1399 and remained in royal hands until 1563, when Elizabeth I granted it to her favorite, Robert Dudley, Earl of Leicester, who built his own palatial lodgings there. In 1575 the castle was the scene of the famous and spectacular revels that were staged when the Queen visited. By the seventeenth century it

had suffered a decline, and in 1649 it was wrecked and partially dismantled by Cromwell's soldiers. The Mere was drained at this time.

72 *John of Gaunt's Register*
73 Ibid.
74 Hill, *Mediaeval Lincoln*
75 *Calendar of Patent Rolls*; Special Collections, S.C. 1
76 Hill, *Mediaeval Lincoln*; *Calendar of Patent Rolls*
77 *John of Gaunt's Register*
78 Ibid.
79 Ibid.; *Foedera*
80 Froissart
81 Ibid.; *Foedera*
82 Walsingham; *Anonimalle Chronicle*; Rose

6. HIS UNSPEAKABLE CONCUBINE

1 *Anonimalle Chronicle*. For the Good Parliament, see chiefly *Rotuli Parliamentorum*; Walsingham; *Anonimalle Chronicle*
2 Walsingham
3 Goodman, *Honourable Lady*
4 Cited by Lindsay
5 Chandos Herald
6 Walsingham
7 Ibid.
8 *Collection of All the Wills . . .* , ed. Nichols
9 McFarlane; Saul
10 Walsingham
11 *John of Gaunt's Register*
12 Ibid. It seems, however, that Katherine's dues from the Sauneby holdings were not paid, for years later, the duke wrote to his seneschal at Tickhill Castle to say that he was "fully informed that our very dear and beloved Dame Katherine de Swynford has certain sums due to her from these lands and tenements," and commanded him to recompense her in full.
13 Walsingham
14 *Collection of All the Wills . . .*
15 *Foedera*
16 Pearsall
17 Walsingham. He was the son of Henry, Baron Percy, by Mary of Lancaster, a sister of Duke Henry. Henry Percy was created Earl of Northumberland in 1377.
18 Goodman, *John of Gaunt*
19 Froissart
20 *Anonimalle Chronicle*
21 Ibid.; Duchy of Lancaster, DL. 28
22 Froissart
23 *Calendar of Entries in the Papal Registers*

24 Armitage-Smith suggests that it was Thomas who was born in 1377.
25 *Foedera*
26 *John of Gaunt's Register*
27 Goodman, "Redoubtable Countess." I am indebted to Professor Goodman for so generously sending me a copy of the text of this fascinating lecture.
28 *Calendar of Patent Rolls*
29 *Foedera*
30 *John of Gaunt's Register*; Foljambe of Osberton mss.
31 *Foedera*
32 *Catalogue of Seals*; Joy
33 See www.trytel.com; www.rootsweb.com
34 Special Collections, S.C. 1
35 McKisack; *Rotuli Parliamentorum*; Wedgwood; Walsingham; Holmes
36 Hardy
37 Walsingham; Froissart; *Anonimalle Chronicle*
38 For Wycliffe's trial, see Walsingham; Murimuth; Tout; Holmes.
39 Stow; Walsingham
40 *Anonimalle Chronicle*; Walsingham
41 The others were the earldom of Chester, once held by the Black Prince but now in the hands of the Crown, and the bishopric of Durham.
42 *Calendar of Patent Rolls*; Goodman, *John of Gaunt*
43 Walsingham
44 *Anonimalle Chronicle*
45 *John of Gaunt's Register*
46 Walsingham, for example
47 Walsingham. The wooden effigy of Edward III may be seen in the Undercroft Museum at Westminster Abbey.
48 Ibid.
49 *Anonimalle Chronicle*; *Calendar of Close Rolls*
50 Froissart
51 *Calendar of Close Rolls*
52 For Richard II's coronation, see Walsingham; Wickham Legg.
53 Duchy of Lancaster Records, DL. 28
54 McKisack; Walsingham
55 *Calendar of Patent Rolls*
56 *John of Gaunt's Register*
57 *Calendar of Patent Rolls*; Chancery Records, C. 81
58 Barking Abbey was dissolved in 1539, and its buildings demolished. Some of its ancient fabric was incorporated into the parish church of St. Margaret, which originally stood within the abbey precincts.
59 Loftus and Chettle
60 *Calendar of Patent Rolls*
61 Walsingham
62 *Calendar of Patent Rolls*; *John of Gaunt's Register*
63 Godwin; Silva-Vigier
64 *Rotuli Parliamentorum*

65 Ibid. Soon afterward, Alice married Sir William de Windsor. She died in obscurity in 1400.
66 Goodman, *Honourable Lady*
67 Ibid.; *John of Gaunt's Register*
68 Knighton
69 *John of Gaunt's Register*
70 Walsingham; Goodman, *Katherine Swynford; Honourable Lady*; Kelly, *Divine Providence*
71 Silva-Vigier
72 Costain
73 Knighton
74 Probably Long Stretton, a village near Leicester
75 *Records of the Borough of Leicester*
76 Kelly, *Divine Providence*
77 Lucraft, "Missing from History"
78 Exchequer Records, E. 403
79 Duchy of Lancaster Records, PL. 3; *Foedera*
80 Armitage-Smith
81 Exchequer Records, E. 403; *Foedera; John of Gaunt's Register*; Duchy of Lancaster Records, PL. 3
82 Walsingham
83 Cited by Tuchman
84 Armitage-Smith
85 Exchequer Records, E. 101, E. 401, E. 403; *John of Gaunt's Register*
86 *John of Gaunt's Register*
87 Crow and Olsen
88 Ackroyd
89 Ibid.
90 Crow and Olsen
91 Waleys Cartulary
92 Cowling
93 Ackroyd
94 *John of Gaunt's Register*
95 Goodman, *Katherine Swynford*
96 Knighton
97 Ibid.
98 Duchy of Lancaster Records, PL. 3
99 He paid the expenses incurred in respect of the obit on November 7 (*John of Gaunt's Register*).
100 Duchy of Lancaster Records, DL. 28; *John of Gaunt's Register*
101 *John of Gaunt's Register*
102 Richardson; Cole; *Archaeological Journal*, XXI
103 *John of Gaunt's Register*
104 Ibid.
105 Ibid.
106 Ibid.
107 Ibid.

108 Ibid.

109 I am indebted to Joan Potton for this suggestion. The seventeenth-century antiquary, William Dugdale, stated that Abbess Matilda herself was a daughter of Hugh and Katherine Swynford, but he was probably confusing her with Margaret Swynford. Matilda de Montagu was in fact the daughter of Edward, first Baron Montagu, and related to the earls of Salisbury. Dugdale, *Monasticon.*

110 *John of Gaunt's Register*

111 Froissart; *John of Gaunt's Register*

112 *John of Gaunt's Register.* Lady Mohun's daughter Philippa later married Edward, Duke of York, the eldest son of Edmund of Langley.

113 *John of Gaunt's Register*

114 Ibid.

115 Ibid.

116 Ibid.

117 *Calendar of Patent Rolls*

118 Lucraft, "Missing from History"

119 Deschamps; McDonald; Chute; Goodman, *Honourable Lady*

120 Saul; Russell

121 Froissart

122 *Calendar of Patent Rolls*

123 *John of Gaunt's Register*; Waleys Cartulary

124 Froissart; Holmes; *John of Gaunt's Register*; Duchy of Lancaster Records, DL. 29

125 Walsingham; *Rotuli Parliamentorum*

126 *John of Gaunt's Register*

127 Ibid.

128 Ibid. These gifts were all paid for on March 6, 1381.

129 Ibid.

130 *Rotuli Parliamentorum*

131 *John of Gaunt's Register.* Although these gifts were paid for on March 6 at the same time as payment was made for the duke's New Year gifts and his wedding gift to Mary de Bohun, the wording of the entry in the *Register* makes it clear that they had not yet been given to their intended recipient, for they were purchased "for us to give to Dame Katherine Swynford."

132 Ibid.

133 Ibid. Sir Thomas's name is sometimes given as Morrieux, Murrieux, or Morreaux. Among John's wedding gifts to Blanche were twelve silver spoons, twelve silver saucers, two basins with ewers, and a basket with a silver lid. On June 1, 1381, John granted Thomas and Blanche Morrieux a generous annuity of £100 (£37,566), the same amount he had settled on his legitimate daughter Elizabeth the previous year. Further grants and gifts to the couple, "for their good services," would follow in the years to come.

134 For Sir Thomas Morieux, see Nicolas, *Controversy*; Armitage-Smith; Walker.

135 Perroy, *Hundred Years War*; Goodman, *John of Gaunt*

136 *Foedera*

137 *John of Gaunt's Register*

138 Ibid.

7. TURNING AWAY THE WRATH OF GOD

1 Froissart

2 Froissart was probably exaggerating when he put the figure at 100,000. For the Peasants Revolt, see chiefly Walsingham; *Anonimalle Chronicle*; Knighton.

3 Goodman, "Redoubtable Countess"

4 Goodman, *Honourable Lady*

5 Duchy of Lancaster Records, DL. 42, DL. 29; Somerville. There is no record of the date on which John of Gaunt granted Wesenham Place to Katherine Swynford, so she may not have owned it at this time. No trace remains of the house today. I am indebted to Roger Joy for his sadly abortive searches in the Norfolk County Record Office and elsewhere in respect of Wesenham Place, and to Sean Cunningham at the National Archives, who tracked down the references to this grant in the duchy records.

6 Goodman, *Honourable Lady*

7 Gower

8 Ibid.

9 Knighton

10 Many records of the Duchy of Lancaster were lost in the blaze (*Calendar of Patent Rolls*). For the sacking of the Savoy, see Stow, *London*; *Westminster Chronicle*; Knighton; *Anonimalle Chronicle*; *Calendar of Patent Rolls*.

11 *John of Gaunt's Register*

12 Knighton

13 *Anonimalle Chronicle*

14 Goodman, *Honourable Lady*; Gardner; Brewer

15 Exchequer Records, E. 37

16 Knighton; Froissart; *John of Gaunt's Register*

17 Knighton

18 *John of Gaunt's Register*

19 *Foedera*

20 Knighton; *Anonimalle Chronicle*; Walsingham; Froissart; Wyntoun. Percy was later to apologize to the duke for his conduct (*Anonimalle Chronicle*).

21 Knighton; *Anonimalle Chronicle*; Walsingham

22 Knighton

23 *John of Gaunt's Register*

24 Ibid.

25 Ibid.

26 Froissart; Knighton; Walsingham; *John of Gaunt's Register*; Duchy of Lancaster Records, PL. 3

27 Knighton

28 Ibid.; *Anonimalle Chronicle*

29 *Anonimalle Chronicle*; Goodman, *Honourable Lady*; Leland, *Itinerary*. Nothing remains of the palace, which was a ruin by 1658. The site is now occupied by a cemetery.

30 Froissart

31 *John of Gaunt's Register*. The present church of St. Mary in Roecliffe was not built until 1843.

32 Ibid.

33 Walsingham

34 *John of Gaunt's Register*

35 Goodman, *Honourable Lady*; Lucraft, "Missing from History"

36 For these grants and the termination of the wardship, see *John of Gaunt's Register*. Katherine had to relinquish this wardship on June 17, 1383, because Eustacia, now married to John de Boys, had reached "full age, that is to say fourteen years or more," and John of Gaunt agreed to "turn over to her the lands and tenements formerly in our hands."

37 The Chancery is now number 11, Minster Yard.

38 Much of this information about Katherine Swynford's clerical neighbors in the cathedral close comes from notes taken by the author at the excellent and informative lecture on Minster Yard given by Cathedral Librarian Dr. Nicholas Bennett on Katherine Swynford Study Day, June 2006. Regrettably, I have not had access to the full text. Dr. Bennett's research will be a valuable addition to our knowledge of Katherine's life at the Chancery, and hopefully it will be published in the near future—too late, sadly, for this book.

39 This is the earliest brick frontage in Lincoln, and dates from ca. 1485.

40 For the Chancery, see Hill, *Mediaeval Lincoln*; Goodman, *Katherine Swynford*; Jones, Major, Varley and Johnson; Major; Pevsner and Harris; "A Visit to the Chancery," pamphlet prepared for the annual Katherine Swynford Study Day, Lincoln Cathedral Library; Mee; Jones, *Four Minster Houses*; *Registrum Antiquissimum*.

41 Knighton

42 McKisack; *Rotuli Parliamentorum*

43 Walsingham; *Anonimalle Chronicle*; Knighton

44 *John of Gaunt's Register*

45 *Westminster Chronicle*

46 I am indebted to Abigail Bennett and other experts in medieval Latin at the University of York for translating the quitclaim deed. Roger Joy, who has made an extensive study of the subject, also believes that this quitclaim was intended to preserve the security of Katherine's tenure of her property, but I have reached my own conclusions independently.

47 *John of Gaunt's Register*. A similar gift was sent on that day to Amy de Melbourne.

48 Ibid.

49 See, for example, Perry; Lucraft, "Missing From History."

50 *John of Gaunt's Register*

51 Ibid.

52 Bishop Buckingham's Register; McFarlane; Knighton

53 Knighton

54 *John of Gaunt's Register*

55 Hicks

56 Walsingham

57 Monk of Evesham; cf. Walsingham; Adam of Usk

58 Monk of Evesham

59 Walsingham

60 For Richard II, see, for example, Walsingham; Adam of Usk; Black; Schama; McHardy; Mosley; Hicks; Stow, *Annals*; Armitage-Smith; McDonald.

61 *John of Gaunt's Register*

62 *Rotuli Parliamentorum*

63 Calendar of Patent Rolls

64 Harriss; Perry

65 Jane may have been the daughter of—or related to—Nicholas de Crophill, who was mayor in 1348–49 and 1360–61. Her more exalted connections are revealed in a petition of 1349 in the *Calendar of Entries in the Papal Registers*, in which an Alan de Crophill is referred to as the kinsman of Edward III; David II of Scotland (who had married King Edward's sister Joan); Henry, Duke of Lancaster; and Ralph, Baron de Stafford, among other notable persons. This kinship has exercised several genealogists. Alan de Crophill was the son of Sir Ralph de Crophill, who died around 1332, by his wife Matilda, who married, as her second husband, John, Baron Verdun. Matilda, whose maiden name is not recorded, appears in the *Calendar of Entries in the Papal Registers* as one of three persons to whom a plenary indult (an indulgence bestowed by the Pope) was granted in 1345; the others were Sir James de Pipe (or Pype) and Sir Richard de Stafford (flourished 1337–69), the brother of Ralph, first Earl of Stafford. Given that there must have been some association between these persons, it has been suggested that Matilda was Earl Ralph's sister, but she is nowhere listed among his seven known siblings. A Matilda de Stafford is listed among Sir Richard's children, but she could not have been born until after 1337, and as there are no other Matildas in the Stafford family tree, we can safely assume that Matilda de Crophill was not born a Stafford. Sir James Pipe, however, was certainly Ralph's half brother, being the son of Sir Thomas de Pipe by the earl's mother, Margaret Basset, widow of Sir Edmund de Stafford.

The Crophills did have a proven royal connection by marriage, but later than 1345. Sir Ralph de Crophill's grandson (probably by a former wife), Sir John de Crophill of Sutton Bonington, Nottinghamshire, who died in 1383, married in 1371 Margery, daughter of Theobald, Baron Verdun, whose second wife had been Elizabeth de Clare, a granddaughter of Edward I and a cousin of Edward III. Thus, although the familial relationship referred to in the petition of 1349 cannot be established, by the time Thomas Swynford married Jane Crophill in 1383, the Crophills could again claim kinship, albeit distantly, with the King. It is interesting to note that John, Baron Darcy of Knaith, is listed in the 1349 petition as another of the men to whom Alan de Crophill was kinsman. Years later Sir Thomas Swynford was to marry, as his second wife, Margaret Grey, the widow of Baron Darcy's grandson. Clearly there were enduring social links between the Darcys, the Crophills, and the Swynfords. See www.rootsweb.com; Erdeswick; *Complete Peerage*; Weir, English Aristocratic Pedigrees; *Calendar of Entries in the Papal Registers*.

66 *John of Gaunt's Register*

67 *Calendar of Patent Rolls*; *Rotuli Parliamentorum*; Armitage-Smith; Perry

68 *Calendar of Patent Rolls*

69 Higden; Monk of Evesham; Walsingham; Goodman, *John of Gaunt*; Armitage-Smith; *Westminster Chronicle*; Tuck

70 Walsingham; McKisack

71 *Calendar of Patent Rolls*; Hill, *Mediaeval Lincoln*

72 McHardy; Hill, *Mediaeval Lincoln*

73 Hill, *Mediaeval Lincoln*; Goodman, *Katherine Swynford*; Lincoln Cathedral, Dean and Chapter Muniments, Bj12/8

74 Street; *Grantham House*
75 *Westminster Chronicle*; Walsingham
76 King; *Westminster Chronicle*; Higden; Walsingham
77 Knighton
78 Hicks; Knighton; Walsingham
79 Ackroyd
80 Froissart; *Westminster Chronicle*
81 *Complete Peerage*; *Dictionary of National Biography*; Goodman, *John of Gaunt*; *Rotuli Parliamentorum*
82 *Rotuli Parliamentorum*; *Westminster Chronicle*; Froissart; *Foedera*

8. THE LADY OF KETTLETHORPE

1 For this evidence in detail, see Armitage-Smith.
2 Leese
3 *Complete Peerage*; *Oxford Dictionary of National Biography*; Weir, English Aristocratic Pedigrees. The Oxford DNB appears to have confused him with his father, another Robert Ferrers of Willisham, who was John of Gaunt's retainer from 1378 and died in 1381. It was his son, Robert Ferrers, born around 1372–73, who married Joan Beaufort. The younger Robert's mother was Elizabeth, Baroness Boteler.
4 Crow and Olsen; Lincoln Cathedral Dean and Chapter Muniments: Chapter Acts 1384–94, a.2.27.f.13r
5 Walker
6 Quoted from a twelfth-century Bible in Lincoln Cathedral Library (Silva-Vigier).
7 Crow and Olsen
8 Goodman, *John of Gaunt*; Howard; Pearsall
9 Goodman, *Honourable Lady*
10 Silva-Vigier
11 Ibid.
12 Goodman, *Honourable Lady*
13 "Liber Benefactorum"
14 *Westminster Chronicle*
15 Walsingham
16 Knighton; Higden; *Westminster Chronicle*; "Liber Benefactorum"
17 Higden calls her *viropotens*, which means, literally, "mighty."
18 Higden. Armitage-Smith judged this story too scandalous to bear repetition in English, so he quoted it in Latin.
19 Wells
20 *Complete Peerage*; Special Collections, S.C. 8; Walsingham. He had taken, as his second wife, Philippa Mortimer, Elizabeth's cousin.
21 Higden
22 Knighton; *Eulogium*; Froissart
23 *Chronique du Religieux de Saint-Denys*; Goodman, *John of Gaunt*
24 Jones, Major, Varley and Johnson
25 Bishop Buckingham's Register
26 Amcotts mss. (VI/A/22/2)

27 Ackroyd

28 Lopes; Russell; Goodman, *John of Gaunt; Honourable Lady; Dictionary of National Biography*

29 Bevan

30 The year is sometimes—probably incorrectly—given as 1386, but this does not take account of the medieval calendar. In England, until 1752, the New Year officially started on Lady Day, March 25—thus February 16, 1386 should probably read February 16, 1387. To confuse matters, the Roman year began on January 1, which was celebrated in England as New Year's Day. Effectively there were two new years in England, January 1 and March 25.

31 Foljambe of Osberton mss. (Osberton Deeds, IX, I, 787)

32 Nicolas, *Controversy*

33 Froissart

34 Fernão Lopes wrote a Portuguese chronicle that was commissioned by Duarte I, John of Gaunt's grandson. Lopes wrote discreetly and admiringly of John, basing his account on the recollections of people who had known him, and his work reflects the respect in which the House of Lancaster was held in Portugal.

35 Gillespie; Begent; McDonald

36 Beltz; Silva-Vigier

37 McDonald; McHardy

38 *Calendar of Patent Rolls*

39 Walsingham; Lopes; Froissart

40 Froissart

41 Lopes

42 Exchequer Records, E. 403; Honoré-Duvergé

43 Pearsall; Crow and Olsen; Brewer

44 Sometimes the dress in tomb sculptures is old-fashioned for its period, but Philippa was married to a prominent man with links to the court, and she was an honored servant of the Duchess of Lancaster: Hers would have been no rustic burial, and if any effigy were made for her, it would surely have sported the mode of its own period. Some Internet Web sites (see, for example, www.johnowensmith.co.uk) claim that Thomas Chaucer, Philippa's son, was lord of the manor of East Worldham from 1418 to 1434, but that is incorrect. This manor was granted to the Crown in 1374, and nearly a century later was still in the hands of Edward IV when Thomas's daughter, Alice Chaucer, petitioned him for the restoration of lands there that she claimed had been granted to her by Henry VI. There is no evidence that the Chaucers had any earlier interests there. It is far more likely that the effigy represents a lady of the Venuz family, who held the manor of East Worldham from the eleventh to the fourteenth century. See www.british-history.ac.uk; www.astoft.co.uk; Hampshire Record Office, Accession No. 52M70; Norris; *Victoria County History: Hampshire*

45 Jones, *Four Minster Houses*

46 Lopes

47 Goodman, *Honourable Lady*; Walsingham

48 *Westminster Chronicle*

49 Lopes

50 *Foedera*

51 Ibid.; Lopes; *John of Gaunt's Register*

52 Goodman, *John of Gaunt*

53 *Foedera*

54 Crow and Olsen

55 Hicks

56 Froissart; Guzmán; Armitage-Smith; Goodman, *John of Gaunt*

57 *Foedera*; Russell; Palmer and Powell; Goodman, *John of Gaunt*; Ayala; *Westminster Chronicle*; Perroy

58 Goodman, *John of Gaunt*. Lewis Recouchez was later Master of St. James's Hospital, Westminster, the leper hospital that originally stood on the site of St. James's Palace.

59 Ayala; Froissart; Armitage-Smith; Russell

60 Armitage-Smith; *Oxford Dictionary of National Biography*

61 Goodman, *Honourable Lady*

62 Ibid.

63 *Calendar of Patent Rolls*

64 Froissart; Hardyng

65 Froissart

66 Goodman, *Honourable Lady*; Given-Wilson and Curteis; Wylie; Duchy of Lancaster Records, DL. 28

67 Given-Wilson and Curteis. His only known bastard son, Edmund Labourde (who died young), was born probably in 1401, when Henry had been a widower for seven years.

68 Goodman, *Honourable Lady*; *John of Gaunt*; McFarlane; Wylie; Bevan; Duchy of Lancaster Records, DL. 28

69 Goodman, "Redoubtable Countess"

70 *Foedera*

71 Exchequer Records, E. 403; Nicolas, *Controversy*

72 *Foedera*

73 Higden; *Rotuli Parliamentorum*

74 Knighton

75 Goodman, *John of Gaunt*

76 Ibid.; *Calendar of Patent Rolls*; *Westminster Chronicle*; Walsingham; *Rotuli Parliamentorum*; Saul

77 Higden

78 *Westminster Chronicle*; Chancery Records, C. 53

79 Walsingham; Duchy of Lancaster Records, DL. 29; Lewis, "Indentures of retinue"

80 *Rotuli Parliamentorum*

81 Ibid.

82 Ibid.; *Westminster Chronicle*

83 *Foedera*

84 Goodman, *John of Gaunt*

85 Stow, *London*

86 For Ely Place, see, for example, Ashley; Dalzell; Stow, *London*; Goodman, *John of Gaunt*; McHardy; Sharman. After Elizabeth I had forced the Bishop of Ely to surrender Ely Place to the Crown in the late sixteenth century, Sir Christopher Hatton acquired the freehold—hence the name Hatton Garden. The old palace was demolished in 1772,

when the present Ely Place—a gated cul-de-sac of Georgian houses, incorporating the Church of St. Etheldreda—was built; it still remains a sanctuary.

87 *Calendar of Close Rolls*; McHardy. The London Silver Vaults now partially occupy the site of the bishops' house.

88 Barron; Legge

89 Froissart

90 Armitage-Smith; Emden; Harriss; Goodman, *John of Gaunt*; Silva-Vigier; Le Neve

91 *Dictionary of National Biography*; Saul; Silva-Vigier

92 Leese

93 Boucicaut; *Chronique du Religieux de Saint-Denys*; Froissart; Kirby

94 Additional mss.

95 Duchy of Lancaster Records, DL. 28

96 Froissart; Jones and Underwood

97 Froissart; Kirby; Duchy of Lancaster Records, DL. 28; *Westminster Chronicle*

98 Exchequer Records, E. 403

99 Waleys Cartulary, rolls A1, A2, A4, A9, B9; Goodman, *Katherine Swynford*; Rosenthal, in which are to be found the printed checkroll lists; Wylie

100 Jones, Major, Varley, and Johnson

101 Goodman, *John of Gaunt*; Edinburgh University Library ms.183, f.135v

102 Duchy of Lancaster Records, DL. 28

103 Kyngeston

104 Waleys Cartulary

105 *Calendar of Patent Rolls*; Goodman, *Katherine Swynford*

106 One of two adjoining Northamptonshire hamlets now known as Chapel Brampton and Church Brampton.

107 *Calendar of Patent Rolls*; *Complete Peerage*; Chancery Records, C. 137; Duchy of Lancaster Records, DL. 28. The present Overstone Manor is a hotel dating from the 1930s and has nothing to do with the original manor house, which has long since disappeared; nor does anything remain of the medieval village, which was rebuilt in the eighteenth century.

108 Duchy of Lancaster Records, DL. 28

109 Goodman, *Honourable Lady*; Wylie; Duchy of Lancaster Records, DL. 28

110 Goodman, "Redoubtable Countess"; Tuck; Harriss

111 Waleys Cartulary

112 *Foedera*; Froissart (for example); Additional mss.

113 Knighton

114 Froissart

115 Bruce

116 *Calendar of Patent Rolls*; Duchy of Lancaster Records, DL. 28

117 Duchy of Lancaster Records, DL. 28; Kyngeston

118 *Victoria County History: Oxfordshire*; Jacob

119 Higden

120 Walsingham

121 Jones, Major, Varley, and Johnson

122 Goodman, *Honourable Lady*; Duchy of Lancaster Records, DL. 28

123 *Calendar of Patent Rolls*; Duchy of Lancaster Records, DL. 28

124 *Calendar of Inquisitions Post Mortem*

125 *Rotuli Parliamentorum*; Armitage-Smith

126 Galbraith; Bruce

127 *Westminster Chronicle*; Walsingham; Palmer, *England, France and Christendom*

128 The date of her obit is given in John of Gaunt's will as March 24. Higden, Knighton, and Walsingham all give the date incorrectly as March 25.

9. MY DEAREST LADY KATHERINE

1 St. Paul's Cathedral mss., B, Box 95

2 Goodman, *John of Gaunt*

3 *Foedera*

4 Walsingham

5 Adam of Usk; Stow: *Annals*; Froissart

6 The date is sometimes incorrectly given as June 4, the day of Philippa's birth, but in 1406, Mary's obit was celebrated on July 4, which must have been the anniversary of her death.

7 Leland

8 Duchy of Lancaster Records, DL. 28

9 Walsingham; *Westminster Chronicle*; Knighton (who gives the dates). After St. Mary's College was suppressed in 1548, and the collegiate church demolished, Mary de Bohun's remains were moved to the chapel of Trinity Hospital, Leicester. Tradition has long had it that a chest tomb bearing a poorly preserved alabaster effigy of a woman, which dates from the late fourteenth century, is hers, but that is unlikely because the figure is wearing widow's weeds, and we know that Henry V commissioned a copper effigy of his mother. The effigy is possibly that of Dame Mary Hervey, an early benefactress of the hospital.

10 Leland. Constance's tomb was destroyed when St. Mary's Church was demolished during the Reformation.

11 *Testamenta Eboracensia*

12 Leland; Duffy

13 McKisack; *Calendar of Close Rolls*

14 Legge

15 Chancery Records, C. 61

16 Tuck; Harriss; Jones and Underwood

17 *Calendar of Entries in the Papal Registers*

18 Ibid.

19 Jones and Underwood; Harriss

20 Duchy of Lancaster Records, DL. 28

21 Froissart

22 Jones, *Ducal Brittany*

23 Goodman, *John of Gaunt*; Duchy of Lancaster Records, DL. 28; Walsingham

24 Harriss

25 Walsingham

26 Chancery Records, C. 53; Armitage-Smith; Harriss

27 *Calendar of Entries in the Papal Registers*

28 Walsingham; *Complete Peerage*; Monk of Evesham; Froissart

29 Goodman, *Katherine Swynford*

30 According to Harriss, who gives no evidence to support this date

31 McHardy; Bishop Buckingham's Register

32 *Calendar of Entries in the Papal Registers*

33 Joy

34 Engraved by Dugdale and Gervase Holles in the seventeenth century. See Sanderson.

35 Dugdale, "Book of Monuments"; Holles

36 Lewis, *Cult of St. Katherine*; Lucraft, *Katherine Swynford*. "The Beaufort Hours" is B.L. Royal ms. 2. AXVIII.

37 Froissart

38 For Pontefract, see Goodman, *John of Gaunt*; Armitage-Smith. The castle was dismantled by the Parliamentarians in 1648 after a year-long siege, and only ruins remain today.

39 *Calendar of Patent Rolls*; Duchy of Lancaster Records, PL. 3; Goodman, *John of Gaunt*. All that remains today of Rothwell Castle is a pillar of rubble that once formed part of a rectangular building, and the buried foundations of a range of lodgings. The castle was largely dismantled before 1497, when a timber-framed house was built on the site. This was demolished in 1977.

40 *Register of the Guild of the Holy Trinity*

41 Trokelowe; Walsingham

42 *An English Chronicle*

43 Froissart

44 Ibid.

45 *Calendar of Entries in the Papal Registers*

46 Duchy of Lancaster Records, DL. 28. I am indebted to Professor Goodman for sending me this reference.

47 *John of Gaunt's Register*

48 Perroy, *Diplomatic Correspondence*

49 Froissart

50 Goodman, *John of Gaunt*

51 Froissart

52 Ibid.

53 Goodman, *John of Gaunt*

54 Duchy of Lancaster Records, DL. 28. Again, I am grateful to Professor Goodman for this reference.

55 Walsingham

56 Goodman, *John of Gaunt*; *Dictionary of National Biography*

57 *Calendar of Entries in the Papal Registers*

58 Walsingham; Capgrave

59 Some writers incorrectly identify her as Philippa de Coucy, granddaughter of Edward III and widow of Robert de Vere, Duke of Ireland, but Froissart says that of all the French ladies there, only Lady de Coucy accompanied Isabella, for there were many of the principal ladies of England present, including the Duchess of Ireland, i.e., Robert de Vere's widow.

60 Scarisbrick
61 Froissart
62 Stow, *London*
63 *Foedera*
64 *Chronicles of London*
65 Goodman, *Katherine Swynford*; Monstrelet
66 *Calendar of Close Rolls*
67 Froissart
68 Jones and Underwood
69 *Rotuli Parliamentorum*; Armitage-Smith
70 Strictly speaking, the Beauforts were not "mantle children," for they had not been born to single parents who subsequently married, but were the fruits of an adulterous relationship.
71 *Rotuli Parliamentorum*; Given-Wilson; Lindsay; *Calendar of Patent Rolls*; Jones and Underwood; *Foedera*; Walsingham
72 *Rotuli Parliamentorum*
73 Lindsay; Brooke-Little; Scott-Giles. A plate showing John Beaufort's arms before and after his legitimation is in Given-Wilson. The Beaufort yale badge was not introduced until 1435.
74 Jones and Underwood; *Dictionary of National Biography*; Percy ms. 78, cited by Armitage-Smith
75 *Calendar of Close Rolls*; *Calendar of Patent Rolls*; Somerville; Harriss; *Sussex Feet of Fines*
76 *Calendar of Patent Rolls*; Goodman, *John of Gaunt*
77 Duchy of Lancaster Records, PL. 3
78 *Oxford Dictionary of National Biography*; Harriss
79 Emden
80 *Calendar of Patent Rolls*
81 Leeds Central Library ms. GC DL/3 f.14v; Armitage-Smith
82 Loftus and Chettle; Perry; Dugdale, *Monasticon*
83 Rickert
84 Chancery Records, C. 61
85 Froissart
86 Ibid.
87 Ibid.
88 *Calendar of Patent Rolls*
89 Froissart
90 For Richard II's proceedings against the former appellants, see, for example, *Eulogium*; Monk of Evesham; Walsingham; McKisack; Lindsay; King; Froissart; Schama; Armitage-Smith; Williams; Palmer: *England, France and Christendom*; Tuck; *Foedera*; *Chronicque de la Traïson et Mort de Richart Deux*.
91 Goodman, *John of Gaunt*
92 Froissart
93 Ibid.
94 *Rotuli Parliamentorum*; Walsingham; Adam of Usk; *Calendar of Patent Rolls*; *Calendar of Close Rolls*
95 *Complete Peerage*

96 *Eulogium; An English Chronicle*
97 Goodman, *John of Gaunt*
98 *Rotuli Parliamentorum*
99 Walsingham
100 Rose; Walsingham; *Calendar of Patent Rolls.* On October 14, by way of reward, Richard granted John some of Arundel's forfeited property. *Calendar of Patent Rolls.*
101 Ibid.
102 Norfolk Record Office, Norwich, ms. 15171
103 *Rotuli Parliamentorum; Oxford Dictionary of National Biography; Chronicles of the Revolution*
104 The date is usually given as 1399, but that cannot be correct, for by then John of Gaunt was dying. Circumstantial evidence strongly suggests that these documents date to 1398.
105 *Calendar of Close Rolls;* Tuck
106 Walsingham
107 *Chronicles of London;* Saul
108 Goodman, *John of Gaunt*
109 Ibid.
110 B. L. Harley ms. 3988, ff.39r-40d
111 *Calendar of Patent Rolls*
112 *Rotuli Parliamentorum; Calendar of Patent Rolls*
113 Duchy of Lancaster Records, PL. 3
114 Walsingham; Armitage-Smith; *Calendar of Entries in the Papal Registers;* Harriss; Emden; McHardy; B. L. Arundel ms. 68, f.19v; Lambeth Palace Library ms. 20, f.171v; *Handbook of British Chronology;* Perry and Overton
115 *Foedera;* Armitage-Smith; *Calendar of Documents Relating to Scotland; Rotuli Scotiae*
116 Chancery Records, C. 53
117 *Rotuli Parliamentorum; Calendar of Patent Rolls; Chronicque de la Traïson et Mort de Richart Deux;* Goodman, *John of Gaunt*
118 Froissart
119 Ibid.
120 *Calendar of Patent Rolls*
121 *Rotuli Scotiae*
122 Armitage-Smith
123 Chancery Records, C. 61; *Calendar of Patent Rolls*
124 Armitage-Smith; *Chronicque de la Traïson et Mort de Richart Deux;* Walsingham; *Eulogium;* Froissart; *Rotuli Parliamentorum;* Monk of Evesham; *Chronique du Religieux de Saint-Denys*
125 Froissart
126 Ibid.
127 *Calendar of Patent Rolls;* Harvey, "Catherine Swynford's Chantry"; Froissart
128 "Inventories of Plate"; Wickenden; Lincoln Cathedral Dean and Chapter Muniments ms. Bj/2/10, f.12r
129 *Calendar of Patent Rolls*
130 Ibid.; *Complete Peerage*
131 *Calendar of Patent Rolls*
132 Froissart. Mowbray went on a pilgrimage to Jerusalem and died of plague at Venice, on his way home.

133 Ibid.

134 Wyntoun

135 Bevan

136 *Calendar of Patent Rolls*

137 There persists to this day a false tradition that John of Gaunt died at Ely Place in London. This derives from Leland, *Collectanea* (although in his *Itinerary*, Leland states that John died at Leicester), and of course Shakespeare. See Lane; Norwich.

138 Wyntoun

139 "The Kirkstall Chronicle"; *Eulogium*

140 Gascoigne; the original ms. of his treatise is in Lincoln College, Oxford; Goodman, *John of Gaunt.*

141 *Calendar of Patent Rolls*

142 *Plantagenet Encyclopaedia*

143 Goodman, *Honourable Lady; John of Gaunt;* Fowler, "On the St. Cuthbert Window"; Sharman

144 Sharman

145 Froissart; Vale; Kirby; Goodman, *John of Gaunt*

146 *Testamenta Eboracensia*

147 Lincoln Cathedral Dean and Chapter Muniments; Wickenden; "Inventories of Plate"

148 John of Gaunt's will is dated February 3, 1398, but in view of the medieval legal calendar, which ended on March 25, the year should read 1399. The best text of the will is preserved at York; see *Testamenta Eboracensia.* A contemporary copy is in Bishop Buckingham's Register at Lincoln, but this bears the incorrect date of 1397, an error that has often been copied. The will was published by Nichols (*A Collection of All the Wills . . .*) in 1780. The Latin text is reproduced by Armitage-Smith, and an English translation is given by Silva-Vigier. See Post, for the dating of the will.

149 For Margaret Marshal, Duchess of Norfolk, his cousin, from whom he had purchased these items

150 Goodman, *Honourable Lady*

151 *Calendar of Patent Rolls;* Norwich Public Library ms. NRS 11061

152 The date is given by Walsingham as February 3, the date of the will, and the date on which the duke's obit was celebrated at St. Paul's (Dugdale). Duchy of Lancaster Records, DL. 28; Post.

153 Norris

154 *Testamenta Eboracensia.* The less reliable Lincoln text says "unembalmed."

155 Walsingham; Armitage-Smith; Harriss; Lucraft: *Katherine Swynford; Calendar of Patent Rolls;* Froissart; Radford; Cook, "Chaucerian Papers"

156 This stood on the site of the Church of St. John the Baptist, first built ca. 1400.

157 Cited by Duffy; Post; *Testamenta Eboracensia;* Walsingham; Adam of Usk

158 *Testamenta Eboracensia*

159 *Calendar of Close Rolls; Calendar of Patent Rolls;* St. Paul's Cathedral mss.

160 Duffy

161 Duchy of Lancaster Records, DL. 28

162 Froissart

163 Duchy of Lancaster Records, DL. 28; Post

10. THE KING'S MOTHER

1 *Complete Peerage*; Chancery Records, C. 81; Special Collections, S.C. 8

2 *Rotuli Parliamentorum*; Somerville; McKisack

3 Froissart; Rose; Goodman, *John of Gaunt*

4 *Calendar of Close Rolls*. I have found no other record of the lands Katherine held in Leicester, Northamptonshire, and Norfolk prior to her marriage to John of Gaunt.

5 *Calendar of Patent Rolls*

6 *A Collection of All the Wills* . . .

7 Now number 2 Minster Yard. Lincoln Cathedral Dean and Chapter Muniments, Dean and Chapter Acts, Liber VI (i), ff.2, 3; Major; Jones, Major, Varley, and Johnson.

8 These measurements cannot have been taken very accurately, as the remains of the medieval hall measure 44 by 26 feet.

9 For the Priory, see Jones, Major, Varley, and Johnson; Major; Silva-Vigier; Pevsner and Harris; Jones, *Four Minster Houses*; *Calendar of Patent Rolls*.

10 *Early Lincoln Wills*. His name is also given as Peter Dalton.

11 Goodman, *Katherine Swynford*

12 Special Collections, S.C. 8; Exchequer Records, E. 403; *Calendar of Patent Rolls*

13 *Chronicque de la Traïson et Mort de Richart Deux*

14 Trokelowe

15 Goodman, *Katherine Swynford*

16 *Calendar of Patent Rolls*; Chute; Lucraft, *Katherine Swynford*

17 *Calendar of Patent Rolls*

18 Crow and Olsen

19 He was also required to surrender the Warwick lands to the King. *Rotuli Parliamentorum*.

20 *Calendar of Patent Rolls*; Exchequer Records, E. 28

21 *Calendar of Patent Rolls*

22 Lucraft, *Katherine Swynford*

23 The site is now occupied by the Henry VII Chapel.

24 The date usually given for Chaucer's death, October 25, 1400, was inscribed on the Tudor tomb, and may well have been copied from the original epitaph plate that was displayed in the abbey. Chaucer's bones were uncovered in 1889 when Robert Browning was buried in Poet's Corner, and the coroner then estimated that he had been about five feet six inches tall. There are no grounds for accepting recent assertions that he was murdered on the orders of Henry IV (Jones, *Who Murdered Chaucer*).

25 Goodman, *Honourable Lady*; *Calendar of Patent Rolls*; Exchequer Records, E. 28

26 Goodman, *Katherine Swynford*. Perry suggests that the reference was to Sir Norman Swynford, but this is unlikely in view of evidence from the Exchequer Records that will shortly be cited in the text.

27 Bruce; Wylie; Beltz

28 *Calendar of Patent Rolls*; Given-Wilson, *Royal Household*

29 Duchy of Lancaster Records, DL. 42

30 Duchy of Lancaster Records, DL. 29

31 Blomefield and Parkin; Lucraft, *Katherine Swynford*; Perry

32 Norris

33 Goodman, "Redoubtable Countess Joan"; *Historiae Dunelmensis Scriptores Tres*

34 Duchy of Lancaster Records, DL. 42, DL. 49

35 Exchequer Records, E. 101; *Calendar of Close Rolls*

36 *Calendar of Patent Rolls; Calendar of Close Rolls*

37 Ibid.

38 *Archaeological Journal*, XXXI, London, 1874

39 *Foedera*

40 In 1406, Isabella married Charles of Valois, Duke of Orléans. She died in childbirth in 1409.

41 *Calendar of Patent Rolls*

42 Harriss; McGrath

43 *Calendar of Close Rolls*

44 Walsingham

45 Duchy of Lancaster Records, DL. 28

46 *Calendar of Patent Rolls*; Harriss

47 *Rotuli Parliamentorum*; Trokelowe; Walsingham

48 Exchequer Records, E. 404, E. 101; Goodman, *Marriage of Henry IV*

49 *Calendar of Patent Rolls*

50 Ibid.; *Calendar of Close Rolls*

51 *Complete Peerage; Desiderata Curiosa*; Lincoln Cathedral Dean and Chapter Muniments, Chapter Acts A. ii.29, ff. 2, 3

52 Harvey, "Catherine Swynford's Chantry"

53 Duffy

54 Duchy of Lancaster Records, DL. 29, DL. 42

55 Lucraft, "Missing From History"; *Katherine Swynford*; Goodman, *Katherine Swynford*. The Prerogative Court of Canterbury records are in the National Archives.

56 Lincoln Cathedral Dean and Chapter Muniments, Bj.2.10

57 Goodman, "Redoubtable Countess Joan"; *Historiae Dunelmensis Scriptores Tres*

58 Lincoln Cathedral Dean and Chapter Muniments; Jones, Major, Varley, and Johnson; Weir: English Aristocratic Pedigrees

59 Wickenden

60 *Calendar of Patent Rolls*; Goodman, *Katherine Swynford*

61 *Calendar of Patent Rolls; Excerpta Historica*

62 Lucraft, "Missing From History"; *Katherine Swynford; A Collection of All the Wills . . .* ; Jamieson. The hospital was demolished in 1825.

63 Leese; Lambeth Palace ms. 20, f.173v; *A Collection of All the Wills . . .*

64 Hicks

65 Duffy; *A Collection of All the Wills . . .*

66 Harriss, for example

67 *Calendar of Entries in the Papal Registers; Cartae et Munimenta de Glamorgan*; www.rootsweb.com; Verity, "A Non-Affair to Remember." Joan married Sir Edward Stradling of St. Donat's, Glamorganshire (1389–1453), by whom she had a son, Henry.

68 Vale. The portrait is in the Kunsthistorisches Museum, Vienna.

69 *Calendar of Patent Rolls; Calendar of Close Rolls*

70 *Calendar of Patent Rolls*

71 Worcestre

72 *Dictionary of National Biography*

73 Goodman, "Redoubtable Countess Joan"; Perry

74 *Chronicles and Memorials of St. Edmund's Abbey*; Leese; *Antiquarian Repertory*

75 Lucraft, *Katherine Swynford*; Armitage-Smith; *Oxford Dictionary of National Biography*; Goodman, "Redoubtable Countess Joan." The book that Thomas Hoccleve dedicated to Joan is Cosin ms. V.iii.9 at Durham University.

76 *Historiae Dunelmensis Scriptores Tres*

77 *Calendar of Patent Rolls*; Harvey, "Catherine Swynford's Chantry"; "Inventories of Plate"; Goodman, "Redoubtable Countess Joan"; Given-Wilson; *Collections Relative to . . . the Diocese of York*

78 Harvey, "Catherine Swynford's Chantry"; Goodman, "Redoubtable Countess Joan"

79 Goodman, "Redoubtable Countess Joan"

80 Duffy; Sandford; Harvey, "Catherine Swynford's Chantry"; *A Collection of All the Wills . . .* ; Goodman, *Katherine Swynford*. Her arms were noted around 1600 by Francis Thynne, Lancaster Herald.

81 The Neville Book of Hours is in the Bibliothèque Nationale, Paris.

82 Goodman, "Redoubtable Countess Joan"

83 www.english.upenn

84 *English Historical Documents*

85 Griffiths and Thomas

86 Perry; Goodall

87 *Foedera*

88 Perry

89 *Calendar of Patent Rolls*; Manly, *Some New Light on Chaucer*; *Excerpta Historica*

90 Hunter

91 *Calendar of Inquisitions Post Mortem*

92 Cole. Thomas Beaufort left him 50 marks (£7,076) in his will.

93 Campling

94 Elder

95 *Calendar of Patent Rolls*

96 *Excerpta Historica*

97 *Calendar of Inquisitions Post Mortem*

98 Cole

99 Ibid.

100 For Kettlethorpe, see www.kettlethorpe.com; Leese; Perry; Goodman, *John of Gaunt*; *Katherine Swynford*; Cole

101 Silva-Vigier; Lucraft, "Missing From History"

102 The epitaph was recorded by Weever. The Latin inscription was recorded by Anthony Munday in 1618, in his extended edition of Stow's *Survey of London*.

103 Exchequer Records, E. 301; Dugdale, *History of St. Paul's*

104 Holland

105 B. L. Lansdowne ms. 874, f.115

106 Benham

107 Dugdale, *History of St. Paul's*

108 Sandford

109 Ibid.; Duffy

110 Arnold

111 Leland, *Itinerary*

112 Dugdale, "Book of Monuments"

113 Harvey, "Catherine Swynford's Chantry"; Duffy; Goodman, *Katherine Swynford*

114 Duchy of Lancaster Records, DL. 43

115 John Evelyn, the seventeenth-century diarist, noted that "the soldiers had lately knocked off most of the brasses from the gravestones."

116 Kendrick, *Cathedral Church of Lincoln*

117 Dugdale, *Monasticon*. A drawing of the repositioned tombs was made in 1809 by John Buckler (B.L. Additional ms. 36369, f.87), which is reproduced in Harvey, "Catherine Swynford's Chantry."

118 Lincoln Cathedral Dean and Chapter Muniments, AIV 15; Jones, Major, Varley, and Johnson

119 Payn Roët's epitaph in St. Paul's Cathedral, cited by Silva-Vigier

APPENDIX: ANYA SETON'S *KATHERINE*

1 *The Austin Chronicle*

2 Goodman, *John of Gaunt*

3 Cantor

4 The date is sometimes incorrectly given as 1904 or 1916.

5 Anya Seton's personal papers are held in the archives of the Historical Society of the Town of Greenwich, and biographical details of her appear on many Internet sites; of these, I am indebted chiefly to "The Setons: The Setons at Home," by Lucinda H. MacKethan of North Carolina State University (www.nhc.rtp.nc.us:8080).

6 BBC: *The Big Read*

7 "National Review Online," www.nationalreview.com

SELECT BIBLIOGRAPHY

PRIMARY SOURCES

Adam of Usk. *Chronicon Adae de Usk, A.D. 1377–1404* (ed. E. Maunde Thompson). Oxford/London, 1876/1904). *The Chronicle of Adam Usk, 1377–1421* (trans. and ed. C. Given-Wilson), Oxford, 1997.

Additional mss., British Library.

Aden-Even, Paul, and Jequier, Léon. *L'Armorial Wijnbergen*. Amsterdam, 1954.

Amcotts mss., Lincolnshire Archives Office.

"The Anglo-French Negotiations at Bruges, 1374–77" (ed. E. Perroy), *Camden Miscellany*, XIX, Camden Society, 3rd Series, LXXX, 1952.

The Anonimalle Chronicle, 1333 to 1381, (ed. V.H. Galbraith). From a ms. written at St. Mary's Abbey, York. Manchester, 1927.

Antient Kalendars and Inventories of the Treasury of His Majesty's Exchequer (ed. F. Palgrave), 1836.

The Antiquarian Repertory (4 vols., ed. F. Grose et al.). London, 1775–1784.

Arundel mss., British Library.

Ayala, Pedro López de. *Crónicas de los Reyes de Castilla* (ed. Eugenio de Llaguno Amirola). Madrid, 1779–1780; ed. J.L. Martin, Barcelona, 1991.

Bishop Beaufort's Register. Episcopal Register 13, Lincoln Records Office.

Bishop Buckingham's Register. Episcopal Register 12, Lincoln Records Office.

Boucicaut, Jean. *Livre des faits du bon messire Jean de Maigre, dit Boucicaut* (ed. J.A.C. Buchon). 1835.

Bradshaw, Henry. *Statutes of Lincoln Cathedral*, vol. II (ed. Christopher Wordsworth). Cambridge, 1897.

Brooke, Ralph. *A Catalogue and Succession of the Kings of England*. London, 1619.

Calendar of Close Rolls: Richard II (6 vols.). HMSO, London, 1914–27.

Calendar of Documents Relating to Scotland Preserved in Her Majesty's Public Record Office, vol. IV (4 vols., ed. J. Bain). Edinburgh, 1888.

Calendar of Entries in the Papal Registers Relating to Great Britain and Ireland, (5 vols., ed. W.H. Bliss, et al). London, 1893, reprinted London, 1971.

"Calendar of Escheat Rolls to 1484," Rawlinson mss., Bodleian Library, Oxford.

Calendar of Inquisitions Miscellaneous, 1399–1422. HMSO, 1968.

Calendar of Inquisitions Post Mortem (18 vols). HMSO, 1898–1955.

Calendar of Patent Rolls of the County Palatine. From the Fifth to the Eleventh Year of the Regality of Duke John, A.D. 1381–1387. Record Report XL, Appendix 4.

Calendar of Patent Rolls (54 vols.). HMSO, 1893–1916.

Calendar of the Rolls of the Chancery of the County Palatine of Lancaster. First to Twelfth Year of the Regality of Duke John (A.D. 1377–1389). Record Report XXXII, Appendix I (4).

Calendar of Signet Letters of Henry IV and Henry V (1399–1422) (ed. J.L. Kirby). London, 1978.

Camden, William. *Britannia* (ed. Richard Gough). London, 1806.

Capgrave, John. *The Chronicle of England* (ed. F.C. Hingeston). Rolls series, HMSO, 1858.

Capgrave, John. *Johannis Capgrave Liber de illustribus Henricis* (ed. F.C. Hingeston). Rolls series, HMSO, 1858.

Cartae et Munimenta de Glamorgan (6 vols., ed. G.T. Clark). Cardiff, 1910.

Cartulaire des Comtes de Hainaut (6 vols., ed. Leopold Devilliers). Brussels, 1881–96.

Catalogue of Seals in the Department of Manuscripts in the British Museum, vol. III (ed. Walter de Gray Birch). London, 1887–1900.

Chancery Records (National Archives): C. 47 Chancery Miscellanea, C. 53 Charter Rolls, C. 61 Gascon Rolls, C. 81 Chancery Warrants; C. 137–140 Inquisitions Post Mortem, Series I; C. 143 Inquisitions Ad Quod Damnum.

Chandos Herald. *Life of the Black Prince by the Herald of Sir John Chandos* (ed. M.K. Pope and E.C. Lodge), 1910.

Charters of the Duchy of Lancaster (ed. William Hardy). London, 1845.

Chaucer, Geoffrey, "The Book of the Duchess," in *Love Visions*, trans. and ed. Brian Stone, London, 1983.

Chaucer, Geoffrey. *The Canterbury Tales* (trans. Neville Coghill). London, 1986, reprinted 1992.

Chaucer, Geoffrey. *The Complete Poetry and Prose of Geoffrey Chaucer* (ed. John Fisher). New York, 1977, revised 1989.

Chaucer, Geoffrey. *The Complete Works* (ed. W.W. Skeat). Oxford, 1951.

Chaucer, Geoffrey. *Troilus and Criseyde*. Corpus Christi College Cambridge ms. 61.

Chronicles of London (ed. C.L. Kingsford). Oxford, 1905.

Chronicles and Memorials of St. Edmund's Abbey (3 vols., ed. T. Arnold). Rolls series, HMSO, 1890–96.

Chronicles of the Revolution, 1397–1400 (ed. C. Given-Wilson), 1993.

Chronique de la Traïson et Mort de Richart Deux, Roy Dengleterre (ed. Benjamin Williams). English Historical Society, IX, London, 1846.

Chronique du religieux de Saint-Denys, A.D. 1380–1422 (6 vols., ed. M.L. Bellaguet), *Collection des Documents Inédites sur l'Histoire de France*, 1839–52.

Collection of All the Wills, now known to be extant, of the Kings and Queens of England (ed. J. Nichols). London, 1780.

"Collection of John of Gaunt's Warrants, 1365–1370," Corpus Christi College Oxford ms. 495.

Collections Relative to Churches and Chapels in the Diocese of York (ed. George Lawton). London, 1840, revised edition 1842.

Cotton mss., British Library.

Creton, Jean. *Histoire de Roy d'Angleterre, Richard* (ed. J.A.C. Buchon). *Collection des chroniques, Françaises*, Paris, 1826.

Deschamps, Eustache. *Oeuvres complètes de Eustache Deschamps* (11 vols., ed. A. de Queux de Saint-Hilaire and G. Raynaud). Paris, 1878–1903.

Desiderata Curiosa (2 vols., ed. Francis Peck). London, 1732–35.

"Dodsworth ms. 7: Roll of Writs of the Duchy of Lancaster," Bodleian Library, Oxford.

"Drury Family Papers," ms. compiled by Richard Montray, 1889.

Duchy of Lancaster. Calendar of Ancient Charters or Grants, Record Report XXXV, Appendix I, and XXXVI, Appendix 2.

Duchy of Lancaster. Calendar of Royal Charters. William II–Richard II, Record Report XXXI, Appendix I.

Duchy of Lancaster Records (National Archives): DL. 27 Ancient Deeds, DL. 28 Accounts Various, DL. 29 Ministers' Accounts, DL. 37 Chancery Rolls, DL. 42 Miscellaneous Books, DL. 43 Rentals and Surveys, DL. 49 Grant and Lawsuits, PL. 3 Lancaster Palatine Warrants.

Dugdale, William, "Book of Monuments," British Library Loan mss.

Dugdale, William. *Monasticon Anglicanum* (6 vols., ed. J. Caley, H. Ellis and B. Bandine). London, 1817–30.

Dugdale, William. *The History of St. Paul's Cathedral*. London, 1658; ed. H. Ellis, London, 1818.

Early Lincoln Wills, 1280–1547 (ed. Alfred Gibbons). Lincoln, 1888.

Edinburgh University Library ms. 183

An English Chronicle of the Reigns of Richard II, Henry IV, Henry V and Henry VI, written before the year 1471 (ed. J.S. Davies). Camden Society, LXIV, London, 1856.

English Coronation Records (ed. L.G. Wickham Legge). Westminster, 1901.

English Historical Documents, vol. IV: 1327–1485 (ed. D.C. Douglas and A.R. Myers). London, 1969.

Enrolments and Documents (ed. R.E.G. Kirk). London, 1900.

Eulogium historiarum sive temporis: Chronicon ab Orbe condito usque ad Annum Domini 1366; a monacho quondam Malmesbiriensi exaratum. Continuato Eulogii A.D. 1361–1413 (3 vols., ed. F.S. Haydon). Rolls series, HMSO, 1858–63.

Excerpta Historica, or Illustrations of English History (ed. Samuel Bentley). London, 1831.

Exeter Cathedral Archives

Exchequer Records (National Archives): E. 28 Council and Privy Seal, E. 37 Local Archives, E. 43 Ancient Deeds, E. 101 King's Remembrancer, Accounts Various; E. 159 King's Remembrancer, Memoranda Rolls; E. 164 Queen's Remembrancer, Miscellaneous Books;

E. 301 Certificates of Chantries and Colleges, E. 358 Miscellaneous Accounts, E. 401 Receipt Rolls, E. 403 Issue Rolls, E. 404 Warrants for Issues.

"Expeditions to Prussia and the Holy Land made by Henry of Derby," ed. L. Toulmin-Smith, Camden Society, 1894.

Extracts from the Account Rolls of the Abbey of Durham, vols. I–III. Surtees Society Publications, 1898–1900.

Flower and the Leaf and the Assembly of Ladies, The (ed. Derek A. Pearsall). Manchester, 1980.

Foedera, Conventiones, Literae . . . et Acta Publica etc. (20 vols., ed. Thomas Rymer, London, 1727–35; ed. C.P. Cooper et al.). Records Commission, London, 1816–69.

"Foljambe of Osberton" mss., DDFJ i 796 Collection of Documents, Nottinghamshire Records Office.

Fortescue, Sir John. *On the Laws and Governance of England* (ed. Charles Plummer). Oxford, 1926; Cambridge, 1997.

Froissart, Jean. *Le Joli Buisson de Jonece* (ed. A. Fourrier). Libraire Droz, Geneva, 1975.

Froissart, Jean. *Oeuvres de Froissart* (ed. Kervyn de Lettenhove). Brussels, 1867–77. *Chronicles of England, France and Spain* (ed. John Jolliffe). London, 1967.

Gascoigne, Thomas. *Loci e libro veritatum* (ed. J.E. Thorold Rogers). Oxford, 1881.

Gower, John. *The Complete Works of John Gower* (ed. G.C. Macaulay). Oxford, 1899–1902.

Les Grandes Chroniques de France (ed. P. Paris). Paris, 1837–38.

Guildhall Library, London ms., A.2/26–27: Dean and Chapter of St. Paul's: John of Gaunt's Chantry.

Hardyng, John. *The Chronicle of John Hardyng* (ed. H. Ellis), 1812.

Harleian mss., British Library.

Higden, Ranulph. *Polychronicon Ranulphi Higden Monachi Cestrensis, with the English Translation of John Trevisa* (9 vols., ed. C. Babington and J.R. Lumby). Rolls series, HMSO, London, 1864–86; ed. John Taylor, as *The Universal Chronicle of Ranulph Higden*, Oxford, 1966, which includes John Trevisa's English translation and continuation, completed 1387.

Historiae Dunelmensis Scriptores Tres (ed. James Raine). London, 1834.

Historiae Vitae et Regni Ricardi Secundi (ed. Thomas Hearne), 1729.

Hoccleve, Thomas. *Hoccleve's Works* (ed. F.J. Furnivall). Early English Texts Society, extra series LXI, 1892.

Holland, H. *Monumenta Sepulchraria Sancti Pauli*. London, 1614.

Holles, Gervase, "Lincolnshire Church Notes, 1634–1642," Lincoln Record Society.

"Inventories of Plate, Vestments etc. belonging to the Cathedral Church of the Blessed Mary of Lincoln," ed. C. Wordsworth, *Archaeologia*, 2nd Series, LIII, 1892.

Istoire et Chroniques de Flandres (ed. Kervyn de Lettenhove). Brussels, 1879.

Jean le Beau. *Chronique de Richard II* (ed. J.A.C. Buchon), 1826.

Jean le Bel. *Vray Chroniques de Jean le Bel* (ed. M.L. Polain), Brussels, 1863; 2 vols., ed. J. Viard and E. Déprez as *Chronique de Jean le Bel*, Société de l'Histoire de France, Paris, 1904–1905.

John of Gaunt's Register, 1372–1376 (2 vols., ed. Sydney Armitage-Smith). Camden Society, 3rd Series, XX–XXI, 1911.

John of Gaunt's Register, 1379–1383 (2 vols., ed. E.C. Lodge and R. Somerville). Camden Society, 3rd Series, LVI–LVII, 1937.

Kalendarium of Nicholas of Lynn, The (ed. Sigismund Eisner, trans. Gray MacEoin and Sigmund Sisner). London, 1980.

"Kirkstall Chronicle, The," ed. M.V. Clarke and N. Denholm-Young, *Bulletin of the John Rylands Library*, XV, 1931.

Knighton, Henry. *Chronicon Henrici Knighton* (2 vols., ed. J.R. Lumby). Rolls series, HMSO, 1889–95); *Knighton's Chronicle, 1337–1396* (trans. and ed. G.H. Martin), Oxford, 1995.

Kyngeston, Richard. *Expeditions to Prussia and the Holy Land made by Henry, Earl of Derby (afterwards King Henry IV) in the years 1390–1 and 1392–3, being the Accounts kept by his Treasurer during two years* (ed. Lucy Toulmin-Smith). Camden Society, 1894; New York, 1965.

Lambeth Palace Library mss., Lambeth Palace, London.

Lansdowne mss., British Library.

Leeds Central Library: GC DL/3, Duchy of Lancaster Account.

Leland, John. *De Rebus Britannicis Collectanea* (6 vols., ed. Thomas Hearne). Reprinted London, 1974.

Leland, John. *John Leland's Itinerary in England and Wales, in or about the years 1535–43* (5 vols., ed. L. Toulmin-Smith). London, 1964.

Letters of Mediaeval Women (ed. Anne Crawford). Stroud, 2002.

Letters of the Queens of England, 1100–1547 (ed. Anne Crawford). Stroud, 1994.

"Liber Benefactorum" of St. Albans Abbey, Cotton Nero ms. D VIII, fo. 132d, British Library.

Lincoln Cathedral Dean and Chapter Muniments and Accounts (Lincolnshire Archive Office) Loan mss., British Library.

Lopes, Fernão, *Chrónica de el Rei D. João I*, Bibliotheca de Classicos Portuguezes, Lisbon, 1897; *The English in Portugal, 1367–1387: Extracts from the Chronicle of Dom Fernando and Dom João* (trans. and ed. D.W. Lomax and R.J. Oakley), Warminster, 1988.

Monk of Evesham. *Historia Vitae et Regni Ricardi II, a monacho quodam de Evesham consignata* (ed. Thomas Hearne), Oxford, 1729; ed. G.B. Stow, Philadelphia, 1977.

Monstrelet, Enguerrand de. *Chronique* (ed. L.C. Douet d'Arcq). Paris, 1857–62.

Munimenta Gildhallae Londoniensis (ed. H.T. Riley), 1859–62.

Murimuth, Adam. *Adae Murimuth, Continuatio Chronicarium* (ed. E. Maunde Thompson). Rolls series, HMSO, London, 1889.

Norfolk Record Office, Norwich, ms. 15171.

Norwich Public Library, ms. NRS 11061.

Original Letters Illustrative of English History (4 vols., ed. H. Ellis), 1824–27.

Percy ms. 78, Alnwick Castle.

Political Poems and Songs Relating to English History (ed. Thomas Wright). London, 1859.

Records of the Borough of Leicester, vol. II, Being a Series of Extracts from the Archives of the Corporation of Leicester. 1327–1509 (ed. M. Bateson). Cambridge, 1901.

Register of Edward, the Black Prince, 1346–1365 (4 vols., ed. M.C.B. Dawes). HMSO, London, 1930–33.

The Register of the Guild of the Holy Trinity of St. Mary, St. John the Baptist and St. Katherine of Coventry (ed. Mary Dormer Harris and Geoffrey Templeman). Dugdale Society, London and Oxford, 1935.

Register of Thomas Appleby, Bishop of Carlisle. Canterbury and York Society, XCVI, 2006.

Registrum Antiquissimum of the Cathedral Church of Lincoln. Lincoln Record Society, Lincoln, 1973.

Rotuli Parliamentorum (6 vols.). Records Commissioners, London, 1767–77.

Rotuli Scotiae in Turri Londonensis et Domo Capitulari Westmonasteriensi Asservati (2 vols., ed. D. McPherson). London, 1814–19.

Royal and Historical Letters During the Reign of Henry the Fourth, vol. I (ed. F.C. Hingeston). Rolls series, HMSO, 1860.

Royal mss., British Library.

St. Paul's Cathedral mss., Guildhall Library, London.

Sloane mss., British Library.

Special Collections, National Archives: S.C. 1 Ancient Correspondence, S.C. 7 Diplomatic Documents, S.C. 8 Ancient Petitions.

Speght, Thomas. *The Works of Our Ancient and Learned English Poet, Geoffrey Chaucer.* London, 1598.

Stow, John. *The Annals of England.* London, 1600.

Stow, John. *A Survey of London.* London, 1598; ed. Anthony Munday, London, 1618; Dover, 1994.

Sussex Feet of Fines (ed. L.F. Salzman). Sussex Record Society, 1916.

Testamenta Eboracensia: A Selection of Wills from the Registry of York (1330–1551). (106 vols., ed. James Raine Sr., James Raine Jr., and John W. Clay). Surtees Society Publications, Durham, 1835–1902.

Thynne, Francis. *Animadversions Upon Chaucer's Works* (ed. F.J. Furnivall). Early English Texts Society, 1965.

Trokelowe, John. *Annales Ricardi Secundi et Henrici Quarti in Johannis de Trokelowe et Henrici de Blaneforde Chronica et Annales* (ed. H.T. Riley). Rolls series, HMSO, 1865.

Valor Ecclesiasticus. Records Commissioners, 1821.

"Waleys Cartulary, The," John of Gaunt's Household Rolls, East Sussex Record Office, Lewes, MS. GLY 3469, Rolls A1, A2, A4, A7, A9, B9, B10, Glynde Palace Archives.

Walsingham, Thomas. *Annales Ricardi Secundi* (ed. H.T. Riley). Rolls series, HMSO, 1866.

Walsingham, Thomas. *Chronicon Angliae, ab anno Domini 1328 usque ad annum 1388* (ed. E.M. Thompson). Rolls series, HMSO, 1874.

Walsingham, Thomas. *Gesta Abbatum Monasterii St. Albani* (3 vols., ed. H.T. Riley). Rolls series, HMSO, 1867–69.

Walsingham, Thomas. *Historia Anglicana* (2 vols., ed. H.T. Riley). Rolls series, HMSO, 1863–64.

Walsingham, Thomas. *Ypodigma Neustriae* (ed. H.T. Riley). Rolls series, HMSO, 1876.

Weever, John. *Ancient Funerary Monuments Within the United Monarchy*. London, 1631; Amsterdam, 1979.

The Westminster Chronicle, 1381–1394 (ed. L.C. Hector and B.F. Harvey). Oxford, 1982.

The Wijnbergen Armorial. Royal Dutch Association for Genealogy and Heraldry, The Hague.

Worcestre, William. *Itineraries* (ed. J.H. Harvey). Oxford, 1969.

Wyntoun, Andrew. *The Orygynale Cronykil of Scotland* (3 vols., ed. D. Laing). Edinburgh, 1872–79.

SECONDARY SOURCES

Ackroyd, Peter. *Chaucer*. London, 2004.

Alcock, N.W., and Buckley, R.J., "Leicester Castle," *Mediaeval Archaeology*, XXXI, 1987.

Anderson, Margaret, "Blanche, Duchess of Lancaster," *Modern Philology*, XLV, Chicago, 1947.

Armitage-Smith, Sydney. *John of Gaunt*. London, 1904.

Arnold, Catherine. *Necropolis: London and Its Dead*. London, 2006.

Ashdown, Dulcie M. *Ladies in Waiting*. London, 1976.

Ashley, Mike. *British Monarchs*. London, 1998.

Ashmole, Elias. *The History of the Most Noble Order of the Garter*. London, 1715.

Attwater, Donald. *The Penguin Dictionary of Saints*. Harmondsworth, 1965.

Austin Chronicle (periodical).

Baines, E. *History of the County Palatine and Duchy of Lancaster*, vol. I. London, 1836.

Baker, J. *English Stained Glass of the Mediaeval Period*. London, 1976.

Barber, Richard. *Edward, Prince of Wales and Aquitaine: A Biography of the Black Prince*. London, 1978.

Barber, Richard. *The Life and Campaigns of the Black Prince*. Woodbridge, 1986.

Barnes, Joshua. *The History of That Most Victorious Monarch Edward III*. Cambridge, 1688.

Barron, C., "The Tyranny of Richard II," *Bulletin of the Institute of Historical Research*, XLI, 1968.

BBC: The Big Read: Book of Books (ed. Nicky Munro). London, 2003.

Beaumont-Jones, T. *The Palaces of Mediaeval England, c. 1050–1550*. London, 1990.

Begent, P.J., "Ladies of the Garter," *Coats of Arms*, LVIII, 1989.

Beltz, George Frederick. *Memorials of the Order of the Garter*. London, 1841.

Benham, W. *Old St. Paul's Cathedral*. London, 1902.

Bennett, Carol. *Lincoln Cathedral*. Lincoln Cathedral Publications, 2001.

Bevan, Bryan. *Henry IV*. London, 1994.

Binnall, P.B.G., "Notes on the Mediaeval Altars and Chapels in Lincoln Cathedral," *Antiquaries Journal*, XLII, 1962.

Binski, Paul. *Mediaeval Craftsmen: Painters*. British Museum Press, 1994.

Birch, Walter de Gray. *Seals*. London, 1907.

Black, Maggie. *The Mediaeval Cookbook*. London, 1992.

Blomefield, Francis, and Parkin, Charles. *An Essay Towards a Topographical History of the County of Norfolk* (11 vols.). Fersfield, King's Lynn and Norwich, 1739–76.

Bodey, T. *Time Honour'd Lancaster*. London, 1926.

Braddy, Haldeen, "Chaucer's Philippa, Daughter of Panneto," *Modern Language Notes*, LXIV, 1949.

Brewer, Derek. *Chaucer and His World*. Woodbridge, 1978; Cambridge, 1992.

Brewer, Derek. *A New Introduction to Chaucer*. London, 1984, revised 1998.

Brooke-Little, J.P. *Royal Heraldry: Beasts and Badges of Britain.* Derby, 1994.

Brook, Lindsay L., "The Ancestry of Sir Paon de Ruet, Father-in-Law of Geoffrey Chaucer and of John of Gaunt," *Foundations: The Newsletter of the Foundation for Mediaeval Genealogy,* vol. I, no. I, 2003.

Bruce, Marie Louise. *The Usurper King: Henry of Bolingbroke, 1366–99.* London, 1986.

Bryant, Arthur. *The Age of Chivalry.* London, 1963.

Burke's Guide to the Royal Family. Burke's Peerage Ltd., 1973.

Campling, Arthur. *East Anglian Pedigrees.* Harleian Society, 1937.

Campling, Arthur. *The History of the Family of Drury in the Counties of Suffolk and Norfolk from the Conquest.* London, 1937.

Cannon, John, and Griffiths, Ralph. *The Oxford Illustrated History of the British Monarchy.* Oxford and New York, 1988; revised 1998.

Cantor, Norman. *The Last Knight.* New York, 2004.

Christopherson, K.E., "Lady Inger and Her Family: Norway's Exemplar of Mixed Motives in the Reformation," *Church History,* LV, American Society of Church History, March, 1986.

Chronicle of the Royal Family (ed. Derrik Mercer). London, 1991.

Chronicles of the Age of Chivalry (ed. Elizabeth Hallam). London, 1987.

Chronicles of the Wars of the Roses (ed. Elizabeth Hallam). London, 1988.

Chute, Marchette. *Geoffrey Chaucer of England.* New York, 1946; London, 1951, reprinted 1977.

Clinch, George. *St. Paul's Cathedral.* London, 1906.

Cole, Hubert. *The Black Prince.* London, 1976.

Cole, R.E.G. *The Manor and Rectory of Kettlethorpe, in the Parts of Lindsey, in the County of Lincoln. Reports and Papers read out at the Meetings of the Architectural Societies of the Counties of Lincoln and York, Archdeaconries of Northampton and Oakham, Diocese of Worcester and County of Leicester.* Lincolnshire Architectural Societies Report, W.K. Morton and Sons Ltd., 1911.

Cole, Roger. *Wellingore in Times Past.* Chorley, 1983.

Coleby Village: Home of Koli (ed. Mike McHale). Coleby, 2000.

Coleman, Janet. *Mediaeval Readers and Writers, 1350–1400.* New York, 1981.

Collins, H.E.L. *The Order of the Garter, 1348–1461.* Oxford, 2000.

Complete Peerage of England, Scotland, Ireland, Great Britain and the United Kingdom (13 vols., ed. George Edward Cokayne et al.). London, 1910–59; 6 vols., Stroud, 1982.

Cook, Albert Stanburrough, "Chaucerian Papers," *Transactions of the Connecticut Academy of Arts and Sciences,* New Haven, Connecticut, XXIII, 1919.

Cook, A.M. *Boston (Botolph's Town).* Boston, 1934.

Cook, Petronelle. *Queen Consorts of England: The Power Behind the Throne.* New York, 1993.

Costain, T.B. *The Pageant of England: The Three Edwards.* New York, 1958; London, 1973.

Coulton, George G. *Chaucer and His England.* London, 1908; reprinted Twickenham, 1998.

Cowling, G.H., "Chaucer's Complaints of Mars and of Venus," *Review of English Studies,* II, 1926.

Cox, J.C. *The Royal Forests of England.* London, 1905.

Crow, Martin; and Olsen, Clair. *Chaucer: Life Records.* Oxford, 1966.

Dalzell, W.R. *The Shell Guide to the History of London.* London, 1981.

Davies, R.G., "Richard II and the Church in the Years of the 'Tyranny,' " *Journal of Mediaeval History,* I, 1974.

Delachenal, R. *Histoire de Charles V* (5 vols.). Paris, 1909–31.

Delany, Sheila. *Writing Women*. New York, 1983.

Dell, R.F. *The Glynde Place Archives: A Catalogue*. East Sussex County Council, Lewes, 1964.

Dictionary of National Biography (22 vols., ed. Leslie Stephen and Sidney Lee). Oxford, 1885–1901, reprinted 1998.

Dingley, Thomas. *History from Marble: Compiled in the Reign of Charles II* (2 vols.). Camden Society, 1868.

Dobson, R.B. *Durham Cathedral Priory, 1400–1450*. Cambridge, 1973.

Douet d'Arcq, L. *Choix de Pièces Inédites au Règne de Charles VI*, vol. II. Paris, 1864.

Dudley, C.J., "Canterbury Cathedral: The Small Portrait Carvings of the Pulpitum, *c.* 1400," *Archaeologia Catianak*, XCVII, 1981.

Duffy, Mark. *Royal Tombs of Mediaeval England*. Stroud, 2003.

Dunn, Alastair. *The Peasants' Revolt: England's Failed Revolution of 1381*. Stroud, 2002.

Echevarria, A. *Catalina of Lancaster*. Hondarribia, 2002.

Elder, A.J., "A Study of the Beauforts and Their Estates, 1399–1450," Ph.D. thesis, Bryn Mawr, 1964.

Elliott, Malcolm. *Leicester: A Pictorial History*. Chichester, 1983.

Ellis, Collin. *History in Leicester*. Leicester, 1948, reprinted 1976.

Emden, A.B. *A Biographical Register of the University of Oxford to AD 1500* (3 vols.). Oxford, 1957–59.

Emerson, Barbara. *The Black Prince*. London, 1976.

Emery, A. *Dartington Hall*. Oxford, 1970.

England and the Low Countries in the Late Middle Ages (ed. C. Barron and Nigel Saul). Stroud, 1995.

The English Rising of 1381 (ed. R.I I. Hilton and T.H. Aston). Cambridge, 1984.

Erdeswick, Sampson. *A View of Staffordshire*. 1593; London, 1717; 4th edition, published as *A Survey of Staffordshire*, ed. T. Harwood, London, 1844.

Evelyn, John. *The Diary of John Evelyn* (2 vols., ed. William Bray). New York and London, 1901.

Fairbairn, James. *Fairbairn's Book of Crests of the Families of Great Britain and Ireland*. London, 1859; revised 1905; reprinted 1993.

Farmer, David Hugh. *The Oxford Dictionary of Saints*. Oxford, 1978, reprinted 1997.

Farrer, E., "Early Suffolk Heraldry," *Proceedings of the Suffolk Institute of Archaeology and History*, XXI (I), 1931.

Fowler, J.T., "On the St. Cuthbert Window in York Minster," *Yorkshire Archaeological Journal*, IV, 1875–76.

Fowler, Kenneth A. *The Age of Plantagenet and Valois*. London, 1969, reprinted 1980.

Fowler, Kenneth A. *The King's Lieutenant: Henry of Grosmont, First Duke of Lancaster, 1310–1361*. London and New York, 1969.

Fox, L., and Russell, P. *Leicester Forest*. Leicester, 1948.

Galbraith, V.H., "A New Life of Richard II," *History*, XXVI, 1942.

Galway, Margaret, "Philippa Pan. Philippa Chaucer," *Modern Language Review*, LV, 1960.

Galway, Margaret, "Pullesdon in the Life Records of Chaucer," *Notes and Queries*, CCII, 1957.

Galway, Margaret, "Walter Roët and Philippa Chaucer," *Notes and Queries*, New Series, February 1954.

Garbaty, T.J. "Chaucer in Spain, 1366: Soldier of Fortune or Agent of the Crown?" *Modern Language Notes*, V, 1967.

Gardiner, Arthur. *Alabaster Effigies of the Pre-Reformation Period in England*. Cambridge, 1940.

Gardner, John. *The Life and Times of Chaucer*. London, 1977.

Gerrard, David. *The Hidden Places of Lincolnshire and Nottinghamshire*. Aldermaston, 1989.

Gervase, Matthew. *The Court of Richard II*. London, 1968.

Gillespie, James, "Ladies of the Fraternity of St. George and of the Society of the Garter," *Albion*, XVII, 3, 1985.

Gipps, Richard, "The Ancient Families of Suffolk," *Proceedings of the Suffolk Institute of Archaeology and Natural History*, VIII, 1894.

Given-Wilson, C. *The Royal Household and the King's Affinity: Service, Politics and Finance in England, 1360–1413*. London, 1986.

Given-Wilson, C., "Richard II, Edward II and the Lancastrian Inheritance," *English Historical Review*, CIX, 1994.

Given-Wilson, C., and Curteis, A. *The Royal Bastards of Mediaeval England*. London, 1984.

Godwin, William. *The Life of Chaucer*. London, 1804.

Goodall, John A., "Some Aspects of Heraldry and the Role of Heralds in Relation to the Ceremonial of the Late Mediaeval and Early Tudor Court," *Antiquaries Journal*, LXXXII, (1), 2002.

Goodman, Anthony. *A History of England From Edward II to James I*. London, 1977.

Goodman, Anthony. *Honourable Lady or She-Devil?* Lincoln Cathedral Publications, 2004.

Goodman, Anthony, "John of Gaunt: England in the Fourteenth Century," in *Proceedings of the 1985 Harlaxton Symposium*, ed. W.M. Ormrod, 1985.

Goodman, Anthony. *John of Gaunt: The Exercise of Princely Power in Fourteenth Century Europe*. Harlow, 1992.

Goodman, Anthony, "John of Gaunt: Paradigm of the Late Fourteenth Century Crisis," *Transactions of the Royal Historical Society*, 5th Series, XXXVII, 1987.

Goodman, Anthony. *Katherine Swynford*. Lincoln Cathedral Publications, 1994.

Goodman, Anthony, "The Redoubtable Countess Joan," unpublished lecture given at the Katherine Swynford Study Day, Lincoln Cathedral Library, 2005.

Goodman, Anthony. *The Wars of the Roses: The Soldiers' Experience*. Stroud, 2005.

Goodman, A.W. *The Marriage of Henry IV and Joan of Navarre*. Pamphlet, Winchester, 1934.

Gransden, Antonia. *Historical Writing in England*, vol. II. London, 1982.

Grantham House. National Trust pamphlet, 1986.

Graves, Charles, "The Organisation of an English Cistercian Nunnery in Lincolnshire," *Citeaux: commentarri Cistercienses*, XXXIII, 1982.

Green, David. *The Black Prince*. Stroud, 2001.

Green, Herbert. *Forgotten Lincoln*. Wakefield, 1974.

Green, V.H.H. *The Later Plantagenets*. London, 1952, revised 1966.

Greening Lamborn, E.A., "The Arms on the Chaucer Tomb at Ewelme," *Oxoniensia*, V, 1940.

Griffiths, Ralph A., and Thomas, Roger S. *The Making of the Tudor Dynasty*. Stroud, 1985, revised 1993.

Guzmán, Fernán Pérez de. *Generaciones Semblanzas e Obras de los Reyes de España*. Valencia, 1779.

Hahn, Daniel. *The Tower Menagerie*. London, 2003.

Haines, Herbert. *A Manual of Monumental Brasses*. Oxford and London, 1861.

Halliday, F.E. *Chaucer and His World*. London, 1968.

Hamilton Thompson, A. *The History of the Hospital and the New College of the Annunciation of St. Mary in the Newarke*. Leicester Archaeological Society, 1937.

Hamilton Thompson, A. *St. Mary's Guildhall, Lincoln*. Lincoln, 1935.

Handbook of British Chronology (ed. F.M. Powicke and E.B. Fryde). Royal Historical Society, London, 1961.

Hardman, Philippa, "The Book of the Duchess as a Memorial Monument," *Chaucer Review*, XXVIII, 1994.

Hardy, B.C. *Philippa of Hainault and Her Times*. London, 1910.

Harris, Barbara J. *Edward Stafford, Third Duke of Buckingham, 1478–1521*. Stanford, California, 1986.

Harriss, G.L. *Cardinal Beaufort: A Study of Lancastrian Ascendancy and Decline*. Oxford, 1988.

Harvey, John. *The Black Prince and His Age*. London, 1976.

Harvey, John, "Catherine Swynford's Chantry," *Lincoln Minster Pamphlets*, 2nd Series, VI, 1976.

Harvey, John. *Henry Yevele, c. 1320–1400: The Life of an English Architect*. London, 1944.

Harvey, John. *The Plantagenets*. London, 1948.

Hebgin-Barnes, Penny. *The Mediaeval Stained Glass of the County of Lincolnshire*. Oxford, New York, 1996.

Hicks, Michael. *Who's Who in Late Mediaeval England*. London, 1991.

Hill, Francis. *Mediaeval Lincoln*. Cambridge, 1948; reprinted Stamford, 1990.

Hill, Francis. *Victorian Lincoln*. Cambridge, 1974.

History of Lincoln, The. Lincoln, 1816.

Holmes, G.A. *The Estates of the Higher Nobility in XIVth Century England*. Cambridge, 1957.

Holmes, G.A. *The Good Parliament of 1376*. Oxford, 1975.

Honoré-Duvergé, Suzanne, "Chaucer en Espagne? (1366)," *Receuil des travaux offert a M. Clovis Brunel, Mémoires et Documents Publiés par la Société de l'Ecole des Chartes*, II, 1955.

Howard, Donald R. *Chaucer: His Life, His Works, His World*. New York, 1987. Published as *Chaucer and the Mediaeval World*, London, 1987.

Hunter, Joseph, "Remarks Upon Two Original Deeds Relating to Sir Thomas Swynford, the son of Catherine Swynford," *Archaeologia*, XXXVI, 1855.

Hurry, Jamieson B. *The Marriage of John of Gaunt and Blanche of Lancaster at Reading Abbey*. Reading, 1914.

Hutchinson, F.E. *Mediaeval Glass at All Souls' College*. London, 1949.

Jacob, E.F. *The Fifteenth Century, 1399–1485*. Oxford, 1961.

Jambeck, Karen, "Patterns of Women's Literary Patronage: England, 1200–ca. 1475," in *The Cultural Patronage of Mediaeval Women* (ed. J. Hall McCash), Athens, Georgia, 1996.

Jamieson, Catherine. *The History of the Royal Hospital of St. Katherine by the Tower*. London and Oxford, 1952.

Johnson, Paul. *The Life and Times of Edward III*. London, 1973.

Jones, M. *Ducal Brittany 1364–1399*. Oxford, 1970.

Jones, Michael J.; Stocker, David; and Vince, Alan. *The City by the Pool*. Oxford, 2003.

Jones, Michael K., and Underwood, Malcolm G. *The King's Mother: Lady Margaret Beaufort, Countess of Richmond and Derby*. Cambridge, 1992.

Jones, Stanley R. *Four Minster Houses*. Friends of Lincoln Cathedral, 1974.

Jones, Stanley R., et al. *The Survey of Ancient Houses in Lincoln*, vol. I. Lincoln Civic Trust, 1994.

Jones, Terry. *Who Murdered Chaucer? A Mediaeval Mystery.* London, 2003.

Joy, Roger, "Kenilworth Castle," beehive.thisislincolnshire.co.uk.

Kay, F. George. *Lady of the Sun: The Life and Times of Alice Perrers.* London, 1966.

Kelly, H. Ansgar. *Divine Providence in the England of Shakespeare's Histories.* Cambridge, Massachusetts, 1970.

Kelly, H. Ansgar, "Shades of Incest and Cuckoldry: Pandarus and John of Gaunt. Studies in the Age of Chaucer," *Publications of the Chaucer Society,* XIII, Tennessee, 1991.

Kemp, Brian R. *Reading Abbey.* Reading, 1968.

Kendrick, A.F. *The Cathedral Church of Lincoln.* London, 1928.

Kendrick, Laura. *Chaucerian Play: Comedy and Control in the Canterbury Tales.* Berkeley, California, 1988.

Kern, A.A. *The Ancestry of Chaucer.* Baltimore, 1906.

Key Poets (ed. Jenny Green). London, 1995.

King, Edmund. *Mediaeval England.* London, 1998; Stroud, 2001.

Kirby, J.L. *Henry IV of England.* London, 1970.

Kirby, T.F., "The Oratory of the Holy Trinity at Barton, Isle of Wight," *Archaeologia,* LII, 1890.

Kittredge, G.L., "Chauceriana—'Boke of the Duchesse' and Guillaume de Machaut," *Modern Philology,* VII, 1910.

Kittredge, G.L., "Guillaume de Machaut and 'The Boke of the Duchesse,' " *Publications of the Modern Language Association,* XXX, 1915.

Knightly, Charles. *Guidebook to St. Mary's Church, Long Sutton, Lincs.* Lincoln, 1992.

Knowles, D., and Hadcock, R. Neville. *Mediaeval Religious Houses: England and Wales.* London, 1953.

Krauss, Russell, "Notes on Thomas, Geoffrey and Philippa Chaucer," *Modern Language Notes,* XLVII, 1932.

Krauss, Russell. *Three Chaucer Studies.* New York and Oxford, 1932.

Labargé, Margaret Wade. *Women in Mediaeval Life.* London, 1986.

Lambarde, William. *A Perambulation of Kent.* London, 1570; Bath, 1970.

Lane, Henry Murray. *The Royal Daughters of England* (2 vols.). London, 1910.

Langhans, Viktor, "Chaucers Heirat," *Anglia,* LIV, 1930.

Leese, T. Anna. *Blood Royal: Issue of the Kings and Queens of Mediaeval England, 1066–1399.* Maryland, 1996.

Left, G., "Wycliffe and his Heresy," *A History of the English Speaking Peoples,* II, 1970.

Legge, M.D. *Anglo-Norman Letters and Petitions.* Oxford, 1941.

Lejeune, T., "Recherches Historiques sur les Roeulx," *Annales du Cercle Archéologique de Mons,* XXXII, 1890.

Le Neve, John. *Fasti Ecclesiae Anglicanae, 1300–1541* (12 vols., ed. H.P.F. King, et al.). London, 1962–67.

Lewis, Katherine J. *The Cult of St. Katherine of Alexandria in Late Mediaeval England.* Woodbridge, 2000.

Lewis, N.B., "The Anniversary Service for Blanche, Duchess of Lancaster, 12th September, 1374," *Bulletin of the John Rylands Library,* XXI, Manchester, 1937.

Lewis, N.B., "Indentures of retinue with John of Gaunt, Duke of Lancaster, enrolled in

Chancery 1367–1399," *Camden Miscellany*, XXII, Camden Society, 4th Series, I, London, 1964.

Lindsay, Philip. *Kings of Merry England*. London, 1936, 1969.

Lipscombe, George. *History and Antiquities of the County of Buckinghamshire* (4 vols.). London, 1843.

Loftie, William John. *Memorials of The Savoy*. London, 1878.

Loftus, E.A., and Chettle, H.F. *History of Barking Abbey*, 1954.

Loomis, Roger. *A Mirror of Chaucer's World*. Princeton, 1965.

Lounsbury, Thomas R. *Studies in Chaucer: His Life and Writings* (3 vols.). London, 1892.

Lucraft, Jeannette. *Katherine Swynford: The History of a Mediaeval Mistress*. Stroud, 2006.

Lucraft, Jeannette, "Missing From History: Jeannette Lucraft Recovers the Identity and Reputation of the Remarkable Katherine Swynford," *History Today*, vol. LII (5), May 2002.

Major, Kathleen. *Minster Yard*. Lincoln Cathedral Publications, 1984.

Mallett, C.E. *History of the University of Oxford* (3 vols.). Oxford, 1923–27.

Manly, John Matthews. *Chaucer's Canterbury Tales*. New York, 1928.

Manly, John Matthews. *Some New Light on Chaucer*. New York, 1926; Gloucester, Massachusetts, 1959.

Mathew, Gervase. *The Court of Richard II*. London, 1968.

McDonald, Nicola F., "Chaucer's Legend of Good Women: Ladies at Court and the Female Reader," *Chaucer Review*, XXXV, I, 2000.

McDonnell, Kevin. *Mediaeval London Suburbs*. London, 1978.

McFarlane, K.B. *Lancastrian Kings and Lollard Knights*. Oxford, 1972.

McGrath, J.R. *A History of the Queen's College* (2 vols.). Oxford, 1921.

McHardy, A.K. *The Age of War and Wycliffe*. Lincoln Cathedral Publications, 2001.

McHardy, A.K. *Clerical Poll Taxes in the Diocese of Lincoln*. Lincoln Record Society, 1992.

McKisack, May. *The Fourteenth Century, 1307–1399*. Oxford, 1959.

Mediaeval Spain: Culture, Conflict and Coexistence. Studies in Honour of Angus MacKay (ed. R. Collins and Anthony Goodman). Basingstoke, 2002.

Mee, Arthur. *The King's England: Lincolnshire*. London, 1949.

Mertes, Kate. *The English Noble Household, 1250–1600*. Oxford, 1988.

Michell, Ronald. *The Carews of Beddington*. Sutton, 1981.

Moncrieff, Iain, "The Descendants of Chaucer," *The Genealogist*, IV, 1983.

Morris, David. *The Honour of Richmond*. York, 2000.

Mosley, Charles. *Blood Royal*. London, 2002.

Muskett, J.J. *Suffolk Manorial Families, being the County Visitations and Other Pedigrees, edited with extensive additions* (3 vols.), privately printed. Exeter, 1900–1914.

Netherlandische Genootschap voor Geslacht en Wapenkunde. Swiss Heraldic Archives, 1951–54.

Newton, Stella Mary. *Fashion in the Age of the Black Prince*. Woodbridge, 1980.

Nichols, J.A. "Mediaeval English Cistercian Nunneries," in *Mélanges a le mémoire du père Anselme Dimier*, Pupillin, Arbois, 1982.

Nicolas, N. Harris. *The Controversy Between Sir Richard Scrope and Sir Robert Grosvenor in the Court of Chivalry* (2 vols.). London, 1832–33.

Nicolas, N. Harris. *The Life of Chaucer*. London, 1843.

Norris, Herbert. *Costume and Fashion, Vol. II: Senlac to Bosworth, 1066–1485.* London, 1927.

Norwich, John Julius. *Shakespeare's Kings.* London, 1999.

Orme, N. *From Childhood to Chivalry.* London, 1984.

Ormrod, W.M., "Edward III and His Family," *J.B.S.,* XXVI, 1987.

Ormrod, W.M. *The Reign of Edward III.* London and Yale, 1990; revised edition Stroud, 2000.

Oxford Book of Royal Anecdotes (ed. Elizabeth Longford). Oxford and New York, 1989.

Oxford Companion to English Literature (ed. Margaret Drabble). Oxford, 1985, revised 1996.

Oxford Dictionary of National Biography. Oxford, 2004.

Packe, Michael. *King Edward III.* London, 1983.

Palmer, Alan, and Palmer, Veronica. *Royal England: A Historical Gazetteer.* London, 1983.

Palmer, J.J.N., "The Historical Context of the 'Book of the Duchess': a Revision," *Chaucer Review,* VIII, 1984.

Palmer, J.J.N. *England, France and Christendom, 1377–99,* 1972.

Palmer, John, and Powell, Brian. *The Treaty of Bayonne (1388) with Preliminary Treaties of Trancoso (1387).* Exeter, 1988.

Panton, Kenneth. *London: A Historical Companion.* London, 2003.

Pearsall, Derek. *The Life of Geoffrey Chaucer: A Critical Biography.* Cambridge, Massachusetts, and Oxford, 1992.

Perroy, Edouard. *The Diplomatic Correspondence of Richard II.* London, 1933.

Perroy, Edouard. *The Hundred Years War.* London, 1965.

Perry, George Gresley, and Overton, John Henry. *The Bishops of Lincoln.* Lincoln, 1972.

Perry, Judy, "Katherine Roët's Swynfords: A Re-Examination of Interfamily Relationships and Descent," *Foundations: The Newsletter of the Foundation for Mediaeval Genealogy.* Part 1 is in vol. I, I, 2003; Part 2 is in vol. I, III, 2004.

Petre, J.A., "The Nevilles of Brancepeth and Raby, 1425–1499," *The Ricardian,* V, 1981.

Pevsner, Nicholas, and Harris, J. *The Buildings of England: Lincolnshire.* London, 1964.

Philpotts, C.J., "John of Gaunt and English Policy Towards France, 1389–1395," *Journal of Mediaeval History,* XVI, 1990.

Pimlico Encyclopaedia of the Middle Ages (ed. Norman F. Cantor). London, 1999.

Plantagenet Encyclopaedia (ed. Elizabeth Hallam). London, 1996.

Post, J.B., "The Obsequies of John of Gaunt," *Guildhall Studies in London History,* V, 1981.

Power, Eileen M. *Mediaeval English Nunneries, c. 1275 to 1535.* Cambridge, 1922.

Powrie, Jean. *Eleanor of Castile.* Studley, 1990.

Prestwich, Michael. *The Three Edwards: War and State in England, 1272–1377.* London, 1980.

Radford, L.B. *Henry Beaufort.* London, 1908.

Ramsay, James H. *The Genesis of Lancaster* (2 vols.). Oxford, 1913.

Reed, Olwen. *An Illustrated History of Saints and Symbols.* Bourne End, 1978.

Reign of Richard II, The (ed. F.R.H. du Boulay and C.M. Barron). London, 1971.

Renn, Derek. *Kenilworth Castle.* English Heritage, 1991.

Richard II: The Art of Kingship (ed. Anthony Goodman and James L. Gillespie). Oxford, 1999.

Richardson, Geoffrey. *A Pride of Bastards.* Shipley, 2002.

Rickert, Edith, "Elizabeth Chausir, a Nun at Barking," *Times Literary Supplement,* London, May 18, 1933.

Rietstrap, J.B. *Handboek der Wapenkunde*. Leyden, 1856, reprinted 1943; published as *Armourial General*, vol. II, Baltimore, 1965.

Rose, Alexander. *Kings in the North: The House of Percy in British History*. London, 2002.

Rosenthal, J.T. *Nobles and the Noble Life, 1295–1500*. London, 1976.

Russell, P.E. *The English Intervention in Spain and Portugal in the Time of Edward III and Richard II*. Oxford, 1955.

Ruud, Martin B., "Thomas Chaucer, Son of the Poet," in *Thomas Chaucer: Studies in Language and Literature*, IX, Minneapolis, 1926; reprinted New York, 1972.

Rye, Walter, "John of Gaunt and Katherine Swynford," *Times Literary Supplement*, 17 April 1924.

Sanderson, Robert. *Lincoln Cathedral: An Exact Copy of all the Ancient Monumental Inscriptions, collected by Robert Sanderson and compared with and corrected by Sir William Dugdale's MS Survey*. London and Lincoln, 1851.

Sandford, Francis. *A Genealogical History of the Kings of England and Monarchs of Great Britain etc., from the Conquest, anno 1066, to 1677*. London, 1677.

Saul, Nigel. *A Companion to Mediaeval England*. Stroud, 1983, revised 2000.

Saul, Nigel. *The Oxford Illustrated History of Mediaeval England*. Oxford, 1997.

Saul, Nigel. *Richard II*. New Haven and London, 1997.

Saul, Nigel. *The Three Richards: Richard I, Richard II and Richard III*. London, 2005.

Scarisbrick, Diana. *Jewellery in Britain, 1066–1837*. Norwich, 1994.

Schama, Simon. *A History of Britain, 3000 BC–AD 1603*. London, 2000.

Scott-Giles, C. Wilfrid. *The Romance of Heraldry*. London, 1929.

Selby, W.D., et al. *Life Records of Chaucer* (3 vols.). London, 1875–87.

Senior, Michael. *The Life and Times of Richard II*. London, 1981.

Serraillier, Ian. *Chaucer and His World*. London, 1967.

Seton, Anya. *Katherine*. London and New York, 1954.

Sharman, Ian C. *Thomas Langley, The First Spin Doctor, c. 1363–1437*. Manchester, 1999.

Shaw, Henry. *Dress and Decoration of the Middle Ages*. Cobb, California, 1998.

Shell Guide to England (ed. John Hadfield). London, 1975.

Sheppard, L.C. *The English Carmelites*. London, 1943.

Sherborne, J., "John of Gaunt, Edward III's Retinue and the French Campaign of 1369," in *War, Politics and Culture in Fourteenth Century England* (ed. A. Tuck), London, 1994.

Silva-Vigier, Anil. *This Moste Highe Prince: John of Gaunt*. Edinburgh, 1992.

Somerville, R. *History of the Duchy of Lancaster, 1265–1603*. Duchy of Lancaster, London, 1953.

Sparrow Simpson, W. *Gleanings from Old St. Paul's*. London, 1889.

Sparrow Simpson, W. "Two Inventories of the Cathedral Church of St. Paul, London, dated 1245 and 1402," *Archaeologia*, L, 1887.

Stapleton, Thomas, "Historical Details of the Ancient Religious Community of Secular Canons in York Prior to the Conquest of England," in *Memoirs Illustrative of the History and Antiquities of York*, Archaeological Institute of Great Britain and Ireland, London, 1848.

Steel, Anthony B. *Richard II*. Cambridge, 1941.

Stow, George B., "Chronicles Versus Records: The Character of Richard II," in *Documenting the Past: Essays in Mediaeval History Presented to George Peddy Cuttino* (ed. J.S. Hamilton and Patricia J. Bradley), Woodbridge, 1989.

Street, B. *Historical Notes on Grantham, and Grantham Church*. Grantham, 1857.

Strickland, Agnes. *Lives of the Queens of England* (6 vols.). London, 1906.

Strong, Roy. *Lost Treasures of Britain*. London, 1990.

Strutt, Joseph. *A Complete View of the Dress and Habits of the People of England* (vol. II). London, 1799.

Sturman, Winifred M., "Barking Abbey—A Study in its Internal and External Administration from the Conquest to the Dissolution," Ph.D. thesis, University of London, 1961.

Tempest, E.B., "Coleby: Notes on the Manor and Church," typescript, Skipton, 1981.

Thompson, M.W. *A Short Guide to the Royal Village of Bolingbroke, Castle and Church*. Bolingbroke, 1981.

Thompson, Pishey. *The History and Antiquities of Boston*. London, 1856.

Thorold, Henry. *The Shell Guide to Lincolnshire*. London, 1968.

Tilbury, Linda, "Katherine Swynford, Lady of Kettlethorpe," lecture given at the Katherine Swynford Study Day on June 25, 2005, at Lincoln Cathedral Library.

Tout, T.F. *Chapters in the Administrative History of Mediaeval England: The Wardrobe, the Chamber and the Small Seals* (6 vols.). Manchester, 1920–33.

Trevelyan, G.M. *England in the Age of Wycliffe*. London, 1899.

Tuchman, Barbara. *A Distant Mirror: The Calamitous Fourteenth Century*. London, 1979.

Tuck, A. *Richard II and the English Nobility*. London, 1973.

Turton, W.H. *The Plantagenet Ancestry*. Baltimore, 1928, reprinted 1968.

Vale, M.G.A., "Cardinal Henry Beaufort and the Albergati Portrait," *English Historical Review*, CV, 1990.

Verity, Brad, "The First Duchess: Isabel de Beaumont, Duchess of Lancaster (c. 1318–c. 1359)," *Foundations: The Newsletter of the Foundation for Mediaeval Genealogy*, vol. I, V, 2005.

Verity, Brad, "A Non-Affair to Remember," *Foundations: The Newsletter of the Foundation for Mediaeval Genealogy*, vol. I, IV, 2004.

Victoria County Histories.

"Visitation of the County of Warwick, 1682–3, The," ed. W. Harry Rylands, Harleian Society, LXII, 1911.

Walker, Simon. *The Lancastrian Affinity, 1361–1399*. Oxford, 1990.

Wathey, Andrew. *Manuscripts of Polyphonic Music: The British Isles, 1100–1400*. Munich, 1993.

Webster, Norman W. *Blanche of Lancaster*. Driffield, 1990.

Wedgwood, C.V., "John of Gaunt and the Packing of Parliament," *English Historical Review*, XIV, 1930.

Weir, Alison. *Britain's Royal Families: The Complete Genealogy*. London, 1989, revised 2002.

Weir, Alison, "English Aristocratic Pedigrees, 1066–1603," unpublished.

Weir, Alison. *Lancaster and York: The Wars of the Roses*. London, 1995.

Wellingore: A Cliff Edge Village. Lincoln County Council Planning Department, 1971.

Wells, John Edwin. *A Manual of the Writings in Middle English, 1050–1400, plus eight supplements* (9 vols.). New Haven, 1916.

Wentersdorf, K.P., "The Clandestine Marriages of the Fair Maid of Kent," *Journal of Mediaeval History*, V, 1979.

Who's Who in British History (ed. Juliet Gardiner). London, 2000.

Wickenden, J.F., " 'Joyaulx' of John of Gaunt Bequeathed to the Cathedral Church of Lincoln," *Archaeological Journal*, XXXII, 1875.

Wickham Legg, L.G. *English Coronation Records*. London, 1901.

Williams, George. *A New View of Chaucer*. Durham, 1965.

Williamson, David. *Brewer's British Royalty*. London, 1996.

Women of the English Nobility and Gentry (trans. and ed. Jennifer Wood). Massachusetts, 2004.

Women and Literature in Britain, 1150–1500 (ed. C.M. Neale), 1993.

Wood, Margaret. *The English Mediaeval House*. London, 1965.

Woods, William. *England in the Age of Chaucer*. London, 1976.

Woolgar, C.M. *The Great Household in Late Mediaeval England*. New Haven and London, 1999.

Wordsworth, Christopher. *Notes on Mediaeval Services in England*. London, 1898.

Wylie, James Hamilton. *History of England Under Henry IV* (4 vols.). London, 1884–98.

Yardley, Edward. *Menevia Sacra* (ed. Francis Green). Cambrian Archaeological Association, London, 1927.

SELECTED INTERNET WEBSITES

"British History Online"

Douglass, Sarah, "Katherine Swynford," www.sarahdouglass.com.

"History and Antiquities of the County of Buckingham, The," met.open.ac.uk.

"John of Gaunt Connection, The," www.swynford.force9.co.uk.

Joy, Roger, "The Katherine Swynford Society," beehive.thisislincolnshire.co.uk.

"Katherine by Anya Seton," ivmoores.com.

"Katherine Swynford," www.livinghistory.co.uk.

"Katherine Swynford," www.middle-ages.org.uk.

"Katherine Swynford," en.wikipedia.org.

"Kettlethorpe, Lincolnshire, England: Home of Katherine Swynford," www.kettlethorpe.com.

"National Review Online," www.nationalreview.com.

Perry, Judy, "Judy Perry's Katherine Swynford Coat of Arms," www.geocities.com.

Perry, Judy, "Katherine Swynford," katherineswynford.blogspot.com.

Perry, Judy, "Katherine Swynford," members.cox.net.

"Setons, The," www.nhc.rtp.nc.us:8080.

INDEX

ABOUT THE AUTHOR

ALISON WEIR is the *New York Times* bestselling author of the novels *Innocent Traitor* and *The Lady Elizabeth*, and several historical biographies, including *Queen Isabella, Henry VIII, Eleanor of Aquitaine, The Life of Elizabeth I,* and *The Six Lives of Henry VIII.* She lives in Surrey, England, with her husband and two children.